Bird Watching

A Wiley Brand

Bird Watching

2nd Edition

**by Jessica Vaughan, Dawn Hewitt
and Julie Zickefoose**
FOREWORD BY Scott Weidensaul
Author of *Living on the Wind* and *A World on the Wing*

Bird Watching For Dummies®, 2nd Edition

Published by: **John Wiley & Sons, Inc.,** 111 River Street, Hoboken, NJ 07030-5774, www.wiley.com

For general information on our other products and services, please contact our Customer Care Department within the U.S. at 877-762-2974, outside the U.S. at 317-572-3993, or fax 317-572-4002. For technical support, please visit https://hub.wiley.com/community/support/dummies.

Wiley publishes in a variety of print and electronic formats and by print-on-demand. Some material included with standard print versions of this book may not be included in e-books or in print-on-demand. If this book refers to media that is not included in the version you purchased, you may download this material at http://booksupport.wiley.com. For more information about Wiley products, visit www.wiley.com.

Library of Congress Control Number is available from the publisher.

ISBN 978-1-394-29730-6 (pbk); ISBN 978-1-394-29731-3 (ebk); ISBN 978-1-394-29732-0 (ebk)

SKY10099229_030525

Contents at a Glance

Table of Contents

Foreword

The first time I read *Bird Watching For Dummies*, I thought I might die.

It was May of 1997, and I was huddled in a tent in the campground at Long Point Provincial Park in Ontario, where I'd come to see the park's epic spring songbird migration. Instead of birds, when I arrived, I noticed worrisomely dark clouds piling up to the west.

My battery-powered weather radio carried an ominous warning. The staticky voice mentioned deadly lightning, winds in excess of 75 miles per hour, and one-and-a-half-inch hail already associated with the squall line. "People in the path of these storms are advised to seek shelter inside strong buildings."

I had a tent. I pitched it quickly, securing a couple of the guy lines to the bumper of the car so I wouldn't fly off like Dorothy bound for Oz, put most of my gear in the tent for ballast, and checked to make sure my headlamp batteries were fresh, and my raincoat and pants were handy. I'd just finished when the storm hit. It was every bit as bad as advertised — perhaps the worst such storm I've ever ridden out in such flimsy cover. I crouched on a folded-up rubber air mattress, hoping that it might offer some electrical protection from a nearby lighting strike.

But after a while, every terror becomes a little boring. And so, to pass the time, I pulled out the page galleys for a new book by my friend Bill Thompson III: *Bird Watching For Dummies*. And here's the thing — it was so much fun that I was able to ignore thunder like an artillery barrage and wind like screaming demons. If anyone had been crazy enough to be outside, they may have wondered what sort of screwball was giggling to himself while the weather went mad.

BT3 was that kind of writer, the ideal guide for anyone new to birds and birding — friendly, witty, amusing, but also genuinely excited to share the world of birds with someone fresh. We lost Bill far too soon, and far too young, but his light touch and welcoming spirit lives on in this new edition, revised and updated by some of his closest friends. Pull up an air mattress, adopt a protective crouch, and enjoy.

Scott Weidensaul

Author of *Living on the Wind* and *A World on the Wing*

Introduction

Welcome to the second edition of *Bird Watching For Dummies*. As we embarked on this update, we were struck by how much has changed for bird watchers in the nearly three decades since this book was first written. It was a different world before everyone had a cell phone in their pocket, with on-demand access to an array of digital tools to help locate and identify birds. Our pastime is forever changed, and for the better, we would argue, as countless more people have joined our flock in recent years.

But one thing has stayed the same: You can read all you want about the subject of bird watching, download all the apps, and buy all the optics and gadgets, but the very best thing to do, if you want to become a bird enthusiast, is to get outside and watch some birds. This book is designed to get you started in the right direction and give you a sense of the fascination and joy that birds can bring to your life. If we've done our job well, reading this book will make you want to set it down, head outside, and look up!

About This Book

We want this book to appeal to bird watchers, or birders, at every level of interest and expertise. But the majority of the information that we include is aimed at encouraging the beginner to take up the hobby of bird watching, while encouraging the intermediate bird watcher to explore the fringes of advanced birding. Advanced birders can find something of value in here, too, even if it's only that the text produces smiles of recognition.

Think of this book as a reference. As such, it will serve you for the rest of your bird-watching days. You can come back to it time after time and search its pages for answers to your most nagging questions and for advice on getting better as a birder.

A few things about this book make it different from other books on bird watching or birding (we consider the terms interchangeable):

>> First, it's both fun and funny to read. We hope we give you a few laughs along the way.

>> Second, it's written from our personal perspectives, so you benefit from our own real-life experiences and mistakes.

>> Third, this book is designed so that each chapter can stand alone content-wise, sort of like a giant buffet table of food. You can skip whole chapters that don't interest you at present and read the juicy bits that seem appetizing. You can always come back later to sample the parts you skipped (but please remember to get a clean plate each time).

As you read through this book, you will notice the names of lots of different birds. We have chosen not to capitalize these names, except when they include a proper noun or name, such as Henslow's sparrow, as opposed to song sparrow. Although some bird folks claim that all bird names should be capitalized, we believe (and the rules of proper English language usage concur) that to "cap" all the first letters of every bird name is not only improper, it's also overkill. And too much capitalization can result in a bumpy ride for your eyeballs as you read through a sentence chock-full of bird names. We've tried to make it clear when we're writing about the species yellow warbler and a warbler that's colored yellow.

We don't mention brand names of products very often in this book. The market for bird-watching products is huge, constantly growing and ever-changing. It would be folly (not to mention impossible) to try to do justice to all the companies, products, and people who are out there trying to make a living in the bird-watching world.

Foolish Assumptions

We assume that if you are a beginning bird watcher (and we assume most readers of this book are), you have a lot of questions but may feel sheepish about asking these questions of another, more experienced bird watcher. That feeling of shyness is perfectly normal and happens to almost everyone who takes up a new avocation. Jessica remembers feeling that way when she first got serious about bird watching, always worrying about asking too many questions and annoying the more experienced birders she knew. This book removes a lot of that awkwardness for you. We're not promising that you won't ever have to ask a bird question again, but we are sure that lots of the questions you have now will be answered by the time you read a few chapters.

We also assume that, as you learn how to be a bird watcher, you will make mistakes — not knowing how to focus binoculars properly, not knowing how to find the bird in the binoculars, not knowing where to find birds! When you first venture out in search of birds to watch, you may have a frustrating experience. Don't worry! We've all been there. Bird watching is just like any other activity: the more you practice, the better you get.

What's great about birding is that the practicing part is incredibly fun, and we assume you like to have fun! The most important thing you can do to become a really good bird watcher (other than buy this book) is to relax and enjoy the birds you see. Without even trying to absorb information, you're gaining knowledge about the birds you watch simply by watching. How fun and easy is that?

When you positively identify your first bird species, all by yourself, and without lots of hints from a fellow birder, you realize the thrill of victory. It's that kind of experience that has kept us bird watching for all these years, and we hope will make you a lifelong birder, too.

Icons Used in This Book

We guide you along on this birding trip with a series of icons. Think of them as roadside signs along the bird-watching highway. They alert you to upcoming tips, valuable advice, pitfalls, and even a few of our own bird-watching tales.

TIP

We've used this icon to note things you can do to improve your birding-watching skills.

TECHNICAL STUFF

This icon flags bird-watching terminology so you can chatter along, and it also alerts you to technical or super-nerdy information.

WARNING

To draw your attention to common pitfalls, we use this icon.

REMEMBER

When we want to point out important information to keep in mind, we flag it with this icon.

Beyond the Book

This book comes with a free Cheat Sheet that gives you some quick tips on tools to take bird watching, identifying a mystery bird, using binoculars, birding etiquette, and more. To access this Cheat Sheet, simply go to www.dummies.com and enter "Bird Watching For Dummies Cheat Sheet" in the Search box.

Where to Go from Here

This book is designed to be read in pieces and parts (though if you decide to read it from cover to cover, that's fine too, and we'll be flattered). If you're a total beginner, read the initial three chapters first. If you're already a bird watcher, you may wish to read the chapters on birding that makes a difference, writing down and organizing your observations, or taking a field trip or birding tour.

We've included all kinds of information to help you become a better bird watcher, no matter where you are now, skill-wise. If you become more interested in watching birds after reading this book, we've done our job.

1

Watching Birds — A Natural Habit

IN THIS PART . . .

Find out what makes a bird a bird — and a bird watcher a bird watcher.

Get to know the parts of a bird.

Master binocular basics.

Acquaint yourself with field guides.

Take a bird taxonomy tour.

Learn how bird behavior and sounds help us identify birds.

Chapter **1**

Birds and the People Who Love Them

o you ever look up, see a bird in flight, and find yourself wondering what kind of bird it is? You stare at it — noting its color, its shape, the spread of its wings. You watch it flit from branch to branch and fly away. And you wonder. Maybe you describe the bird to a family member or friend who may know what it is. Or you hop online and search for birds in your area to see if you can find its picture. Or you wait, hoping to see it again just to appreciate the bird's beauty and song. That's bird watching. And you're already a bird watcher. Isn't that easy?

Unk! Ragnar See Bird!

Bird watching is an activity that comes naturally to us humans. Our ancestors watched birds — you can find their sightings painted on cave walls. Birds helped determine the seasons and were thought to predict the weather. And they provided meat for the evening feeding frenzy.

Today, bird watching (or birding) is a hobby enjoyed by millions and millions of (somewhat more advanced) people. Why? Because birds are fun to look at, birds are beautiful, many birds sing beautiful songs, and bird behavior is fascinating.

Besides, today when folks want meat for their evening feeding frenzies, they can shop at supermarkets and leave the birds alone.

Yet birds still foretell the changing seasons by their northward and southward migrations. And birds sometimes have feeding frenzies of their own just before or after a blast of bad weather. So, if you want to throw out your calendar and the local meteorologist, go right ahead. You won't need either in your cave — and you'll still have the birds.

Wings and feathers and flight, oh my!

Research indicates that birds are living examples of the dinosaurs that once roamed Earth. One of the earliest-known birds is *Archaeopteryx*, discovered from fossilized remains found in Bavaria in 1851 (see Figure 1-1).

FIGURE 1-1: Archaeopteryx — a prehistoric bird in full glide.

Archaeopteryx existed about 140 million years ago and had skeletal characteristics identical to those of small dinosaurs that lived during that same time. This creature also had a toothed jaw and feathers that allowed Archaeopteryx to glide from place to place (although its main mode of transport was likely running).

Because of these features, research suggests that Archaeopteryx is one link between dinosaurs and the creatures today that are considered birds. Even though this creature didn't have the specialized bones and flight muscles that true birds have, Archaeopteryx is considered by many to be one branch of the evolutionary tree from which all birds may have descended. The link between Archaeopteryx and birds is a greatly debated subject that gets evolutionary scientists very worked up. So, it's best to leave this one to the folks in the white lab coats. But one thing Archaeopteryx and birds have in common that seems to give them kinship is feathers. Because, at its most basic, a bird is a creature that has feathers (see Figure 1-2) — the only type of creature that has feathers.

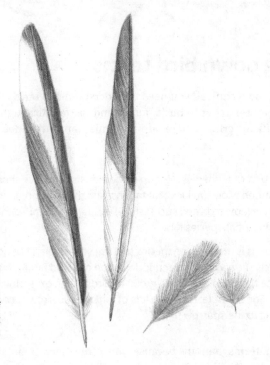

FIGURE 1-2: Feathers of a northern mockingbird — if it ain't got feathers, it's not a bird.

These feathers — along with lightweight, air-filled bones acquired through evolution — allow most birds to fly. Feathers are really highly evolved scales, like those found on reptiles such as snakes and lizards. (You can see the remnants of their reptilian ancestry on most birds' scaly legs and feet.) Besides promoting flight, feathers (also called plumage) regulate birds' temperature and provide physical protection while giving birds their shape and color.

Here's a bonus obscure fact for you: A small songbird has more than 1,000 feathers on its body. A large swan, plucked by some patient soul, was found to have more than 25,000 feathers. Figure 1-3 shows a mute swan ruffling some of its 25,000 feathers.

Breaking down bird terms

TECHNICAL STUFF

Without getting too technical, you need to understand two terms that bird watchers use a lot when referring to birds: *family* and *species.* Although an ornithology professor will likely cringe, here are Dummies-approved definitions for the two terms:

>> A *species* of bird is defined as a group of individuals that have similar appearance, similar behavior, similar vocalizations, and that interbreed freely to produce fertile (able to breed successfully) young. When you identify a bird, you determine what species it is.

>> A *family* of birds is made up of species that are very similar, but don't interbreed. You can find a more scientific definition of a bird family, but most bird watchers use this term to mean a group of birds that look, sound, and act in a similar way. For example, there are lots of different sparrow *species,* most of which belong to the sparrow *family.*

Remember both terms handily because you often hear them used when bird watchers try to identify a bird. If you see a small bird zipping through your flower garden, you may know what family it belongs to (hummingbird). Later, when you get a good look at the bird, you can identify its species (ruby-throated hummingbird).

Each species of bird has two types of names: a common name and a Latin name.

>> The common name of a bird is the one that you're most likely to know. Common names, such as American robin, are the currency of bird watching.

>> The Latin or scientific name, *Turdus migratorius* in the case of the American robin, is made up of two parts: the genus *(Turdus)* and the species *(migratorius)*. Genus and species are two parts of the scientific classification system used to name all living creatures. Think of them as you would the first and last names of a person. Latin names are used to clarify the classification of birds and to help bird watchers and ornithologists (bird scientists) avoid confusion over regional and international differences in bird names. Just because they're Latin, don't let them scare you off. You won't be getting a pop quiz! And most bird watchers you encounter won't be fluent in the Latin names of birds, so you needn't be, either.

Chapter 4 takes a closer look at the terms *species, genus,* and *family,* and how a basic understanding of bird groupings can help you become more familiar with your field guide and, ultimately, identify birds.

Bird Watching: From Guns to Binoculars

People's fascination with birds naturally made them want to get a closer look. Until late in the 19th century (that's the 1800s), the only accepted method of identifying a bird was to have it in your hand. And given the fact that very few birds hopped happily onto the palm, the quickest way to get a bird in the hand was to kill it and hold it there. From rocks to spears, and later, arrows, slingshots, and shotguns, once you had the bird in your hand, getting a good look at it was easy (but not very easy on the bird!).

Shotgun bird identification fell into deserved disfavor in 1934 when Roger Tory Peterson, generally considered the father of modern bird watching, published the first modern field guide. Combining black-and-white illustrations of all the birds found in the eastern half of North America with descriptive text for each species, Roger Tory Peterson's easy-to-use system of identifying birds was based upon a concept known as a *field mark* — a distinctive characteristic or visual clue that's a key to identifying a bird. Birds thus became identifiable by their most obvious features (the red crest of a cardinal, the long, pointed tail of the pintail duck) with the help of magnifying optics.

No longer are birds identified over the sights of a shotgun — now, the magnified view of the bird as seen through binoculars is all that's needed. Unlike the low-powered opera glasses of 60 years ago, binoculars today are so advanced that, if the conditions are right, you can see the eyelashes on an egret. (Unless you know already, you'll have to guess whether or not egrets have eyelashes.) Once separated from the shotgun, the popularity of bird watching soared, and the birds breathed a collective sigh of relief.

TAXONOMY: FROM DINOSAURS TO CHICKADEES

TECHNICAL STUFF

The method used to organize birds — that is, to decide which birds are related, which are closely related, and which are not closely related — is called *taxonomy*. Taxonomy has nothing to do with the Internal Revenue Service (though it can be a taxing exercise); rather, taxonomy is the method by which birds are placed in the evolutionary tree.

As birds evolved, they did so in many ways, just like a bush grows many branches from the ground, with each branch growing more branches, and so on. The birds that most closely resemble their ancient ancestors are considered the oldest of our birds and are found in the front of bird watchers' field guides. Those birds that kept evolving (through many more branches, then smaller branches, then twigs) are considered the newest, most recently evolved birds, and they're found near the back of field guides. Passerines (perching birds), for example, are considered fairly far advanced, and are found in the back of field guides. That group includes mostly smaller songbirds; not waterfowl, pheasants, herons, hawks, or owls, and so on. The earliest bird taxonomists used Latin to help with their classifications, and their Latin names remain the foundation of bird classification today. See Chapter 4 for more about taxonomy.

THE INFLUENCE OF SHOTGUN ORNITHOLOGY

TIP

Many bird names today still reflect the influence that shotgun ornithology held in its time. A prime example is the red-bellied woodpecker, one of North America's most common woodland birds. You'd expect a bird by that name to have a red belly. But if you go out looking for a red belly on a wild, free-flying, red-bellied woodpecker, you'll be disappointed.

Because the first bird enthusiast to catalog this species likely shot one and then examined it in the hand, we have a name that doesn't fit the bird. Although the lower belly feathers on most adult red-bellied woodpeckers are, in fact, tipped in red, these feathers are extremely hard to see when the bird's belly is pressed against some tree trunk, in typical woodpecker fashion. Ol' Mr. Trigger Happy should have named this bird the red-naped woodpecker, because that's where the red is most visible!

Taking part in the number-one spectator sport

Today in the U.S., an estimated 96.3 million people of all ages and physical abilities point their binoculars toward feathered creatures. Bird watching is second only to gardening as a favorite leisure time activity among North Americans. What's more, bird watching is considered the number-one spectator sport in North America!

Most of these 96.3 million people are watching the birds that come to their backyard feeders, but an increasing number of bird enthusiasts are venturing beyond their backyards to find more and different birds. And non-bird-watchers are noticing. The average active bird watcher is estimated to spend more than $2,000 annually in pursuit of this hobby. Some quick math tells you that $2,000 x 96.3 million bird watchers is a *lot* of moolah. We bird watchers pack a significant economic wallop!

Bird watchers of a feather . . .

Bird watchers come in many types, from casual backyard looker to rabid, globe-trotting birder, and everything in between. We're guessing that you're somewhere in between. Perhaps you already feed birds, and maybe you already own a pair of binoculars, but you don't yet consider yourself a bird watcher. Well, you've come to the right book.

Because you're reading this hypnotic prose of ours, you're already indicating an interest in the subject matter. What's great about bird watching is that you can enjoy it almost anywhere, at any time, and at any level of involvement — always at your own pace.

Most folks who get into bird watching start by seeing birds in their backyard. Or perhaps somebody tugged their arms until they took hold of the binoculars being offered and looked at — oh my gosh! — a beautiful bird! What is it? Next comes getting a bird book, borrowing a pair of binoculars, and going out on their own to see birds. Soon they find a nearby park offering a bird walk and join in. Or they join a bird club and take some local bird trips. Maybe later they decide to go on a field trip to Florida or Texas with the club. At each point, more birds are seen and more friends made. Bird watchers can evolve much as birds have evolved.

Long gone are the days when the stereotypical bird watcher was a little old lady in tennis shoes or an absent-minded professor in a pith helmet (though these folks still exist). In those happily forgotten times, bird watchers were often the object of ridicule. The nerdy Miss Jane Hathaway portrayed in *The Beverly Hillbillies* probably set bird watching back several decades as a socially acceptable activity.

If you find yourself wondering what your neighbors, coworkers, or friends will think, consider this: When you show an interest in birds, chances are, more than one of those folks will say, "I never knew you were a bird watcher! I love watching birds!"

Why watch birds?

Cheap and easy fun. That's how we like to describe bird watching. Once you've got some optics (binoculars) and a field guide to the birds, you're ready to go. Unless you want to get into a private preserve, a state park, or a national wildlife refuge that has an entrance fee, or go on a guided tour, you've spent all you need to spend to be a bird watcher. Perhaps only botanizing is cheaper — you don't need binoculars to identify plants.

Choosing Your Identity: Bird Watcher or Birder?

With bird watching's rise in popularity, a minor controversy has simmered about the proper noun or verb used to describe it: Are you birding or bird watching when you use binoculars to look at an avian creature? Do you tell your friend: "I'm a bird watcher" or "I'm a birder"? The real answer lies within your soul, or at least it's a matter of personal preference.

When the Thompson family started our bird magazine, they chose the name *Bird Watcher's Digest*, because that's what we are: watchers of birds — and we listen to them, too. We use the terms *bird watcher* and *birder* interchangeably in our editorial material.

TECHNICAL STUFF

For those who prefer exact definitions, most bird enthusiasts make these generic distinctions:

>> A *bird watcher* is someone who prefers to watch and enjoy birds. This person may be primarily interested in, but not at all limited to, their backyard for involvement with birds. *Bird watcher* is the preferred term in Great Britain, which has, per capita, the most bird watchers of any place on Earth.

>> A *birder* is perhaps more avid, more likely to travel to watch birds, and interested in seeing or listing as many birds as they can in a given outing, day, or year.

A third category for a person who studies birds is *ornithologist.* Ornithology is the scientific study of birds, and an ornithologist is a practitioner of ornithology. Much of the knowledge we have about birds has come from the work of ornithologists. But bird watchers make contributions to this science, too. See Chapter 21 for some examples.

But why get hung up on terminology? Use whichever term you prefer, or use all three, or come up with a new term! Here's a better idea: Go watch some birds!

Meeting your spark bird

For many bird watchers and birders, there's one bird that provided the catalyst, set the hook, was a spark (choose your metaphor) to begin that person's interest in birds. It varies wildly just among the authors of this book:

For Jessica, it was the pileated woodpecker that sent her running for a field guide for the first time to figure out what the heck she was looking at.

For Dawn, who was taking a college ornithology course at the time, it was the common grackles she spotted in her neighborhood.

Julie says it was a blue-winged warbler, spotted when she was eight. She heard it bathing and jungle-crawled up to watch it.

Our predecessor Bill Thompson III's spark bird was relatively nondescript, the American coot. Here's how it happened:

> *I was sprung from school on a spring Friday and was allowed to accompany the local ladies' bird-watching club, of which my mom was a member. Because I wasn't interested in the birds they sought, I ran down the dirt road in the area where we were birding to see how many rocks I could throw off the bridge into Rainbow Creek. Just as I raised the first projectile into the air, I noticed something moving below. It was some kind of bird — perhaps a duck. I knew the gals up the road had yet to see a duck that day, so I ran to tell them of the sighting. They were incredibly thrilled! Coots in spring were not that common then in southeastern Ohio. I was surprised and a little embarrassed by the profuse shower of praise from the women. Soon they had me drumming up all sorts of birds. I was proud to point out birds to them. The following month, when I got a Friday off for another bird-watching trip, I didn't throw a single rock. I was hooked on birds.*

A spark bird for you may be the scarlet tanager that your high school science teacher pointed out, or the red-tailed hawk shown to you by a scout leader. Better yet, it may be the singing male warbler you found yourself. Because you're reading this book, you may have found your spark bird already. If not, we envy you because finding your spark bird is a wonderful experience, and the start of a great adventure.

Becoming a good bird watcher

Two ingredients that a successful bird watcher has are a natural curiosity about the world and a healthy dose of enthusiasm. Both of these are invaluable. Why?

The natural curiosity leads you to do things you'd never do otherwise, such as get up at dawn on a beautiful May morning to hear the birds start singing. And the healthy dose of enthusiasm keeps you going on all those days when you've got more thumbs than there are birds to see. In that case, you make the most of the birds you *can* see.

Both of these admirable traits are great ones to pass along to friends who are beginners. It's the natural legacy and responsibility of all birders to pass the torch of curiosity and enthusiasm to those who come later.

Where the Birds Are

Birds are found almost everywhere. You'll read this statement repeatedly in this book. And here's another gem that bears repeating: Birds have wings, and they tend to use them.

TIP

What these statements mean is that anywhere you're likely to be (outdoors, of course) you'll encounter birds. Going to the Arctic Circle on New Year's Day? Keep an eye out for snowy owls and snow buntings. Going to Antarctica for the 4th of July? You'll be seeing penguins and other seabirds. Stepping out your backdoor to get some fresh air? No matter where you live, birds will be there, too. Better have your binocs handy.

The point is that you can be watching birds anytime and anywhere. Once you get the hang of it, you'll be doing exactly that.

Chapter **2**

Tools That Take You Up Close and Personal

A s a bird watcher, you need very little in the way of gear or stuff to enjoy bird watching. In fact, we recommend only two primary tools that are essential to getting the most out of this activity: *binoculars* and a *field guide* to the birds.

The only other thing that you need is a place to watch birds, and that can be almost any place. Birds are among the planet's most common and widespread creatures. (Beetles are number one.) Walk out your front door, drive to work, and look out the window — you've probably had birds accompanying you the whole trip. It's hard to be someplace where you're not a step or two away from a perky (or pesky) bird. Birds are almost everywhere.

Opting for the Optics Option

Okay. If you see birds everywhere, why do you need binoculars or other optical help?

Well, let's clarify one thing about optics: You *don't need* to have binoculars and other optics to watch birds. If you're satisfied and utterly fulfilled by looking at a bird in a tree 50 yards away and saying to yourself, "Hey, there's a bird!" you don't need optics.

But if you're like most members of our species (hard-wired to be curious about the world around us), you'll want to *identify* that bird. Is it a sparrow or a finch? Or just a blurry-yellow-thingy-with-wings? How will you know if you see it again?

Binoculars let you get a closer look. And a closer look lets you see clues to the bird's identity. With these clues (and a field guide!), you can solve the mystery of just about any bird's identity.

We don't want to show disrespect to the millions of people who are perfectly happy to see birds only at their backyard feeders. That's where most of us start out with birds. And the birds you invite for dinner can put on quite a show.

But let's face it, even birds that appear at your feeders have names, and you won't know many of them without a good look at the bird and a corresponding look at a good field guide. And beyond your backyard is a whole world of amazing birds just waiting to introduce themselves when you get them in your sights. We guarantee that if you decide to become a bird watcher, you'll be much happier looking at birds through binoculars.

TECHNICAL STUFF

Bird watchers use many different terms for their binoculars. Two of the most common are *binocs* and *bins*. Generically, binoculars and the scopes (see Chapter 10) used for birding are called *optics*, which is easier to say than *optical equipment*. (We also have heard bird watchers use some unprintable names for their binoculars, often after they missed seeing a bird because their binocs were fogged or of poor quality.)

Beg, borrow, or buy some binocs

If you're just starting out and you're unsure about investing in some optical equipment (after all, you may decide you don't *like* this bird stuff despite its obvious appeal), we suggest you beg or borrow a pair of binoculars (we frown upon stealing) from a friend, relative, scout leader, or local bird club. Many libraries and metro parks have them available to check out these days, too.

Jessica started out with a pair of heavy old bins that were her grandfather's. These old binocs were sentimental and offered a better-than-naked-eye view of birds — enough to help her get hooked on birding. Once it was clear that she was obsessed, er . . . committed, to bird watching, her family indulged her one holiday with a mid-priced binocular recommended specifically for new birders. (They are now her sentimental bins from her early birding days that she keeps stationed at her bedroom window.)

Somebody you know has some binoculars lying around that you can borrow. (Check with that neighbor who has nosebleed seats at the ball game.) Ask to use the binoculars for just a few hours. If you can borrow them for a few days or a weekend, that's better yet. You'll need a bit of time to get used to them. Take the binocs outside, weather permitting, and practice by looking at a distant stationary object. (If you do unearth some old optics, be sure to clean the lenses before using them. See Chapter 10 for more details on how to use and care for your binoculars.)

TIP

When buying binoculars, you have two rules to live by:

1. **Get the best you can afford.**

   Quality and cost are very connected in the world of bird-watching optics: The more you pay, the better quality you get. All buying decisions should be so easy.

2. **Make sure the binoculars you get are very comfortable to use.**

   They should feel good in your hands, be easy to raise and lower, and be easy to focus. They should NOT leave you with a dizzy feeling or a headache after you lower them from your eyes. (This is eye strain caused by out-of-focus or poorly aligned binoculars.)

An inexpensive pair of beginner's binoculars can cost from $50 to $100. If you buy in the upper range (near $100), chances are good that you'll have a decent optical start to your bird watching. But we guarantee that if you buy a pair of $50 binoculars (or cheaper ones), one of two things will happen:

>> You'll give up bird watching because you can't see the birds well enough (probably due to the budget optics).

>> You'll love bird watching so much that you'll want to get a better pair of binoculars at the first opportunity. We've seen this happen countless times.

The next level of quality in binoculars is the $100 to $300 range. You can get very nice binoculars in this range, especially at the upper end. If you plan to buy binoculars, check out Chapter 10, where we cover important issues that you need to consider.

Using binoculars

Using binoculars to look at birds is pretty easy once you get the hang of it. But before you try to look at a bird, you need to get focused — literally. Because not all eyes are created equal, binoculars are designed to be adjusted to accommodate your needs. We promise that reading the next section will take longer than actually adjusting your binoculars!

Keep an eye on Figure 2-1 as we walk you through how to handle your binocs.

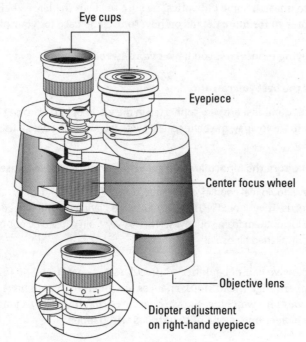

Eye cups

Eyepiece

Center focus wheel

Objective lens

Diopter adjustment on right-hand eyepiece

Setting the eye space

Some people have wide-set eyes, while others have close-set eyes. All good binoculars are made in a way that allows the two optical barrels to *pivot* —fold and open — so that the space between them can be adjusted for the user's *inter-pupillary distance* (IPD) — the space between their eyes. When using binoculars, it's key that you get the two halves of the binocs the right distance apart to get the maximum image size. This spacing should match the amount of space between your eyes.

That statement may seem overly obvious to you, but you'd be surprised how many bird watchers use binocs for years without getting the eye space aligned properly for their eyes. (If you've ever appeared in a Picasso painting and both of your eyes are on the same side of your nose, please ignore this section.)

To set the eye space of your binoculars correctly, push the two barrels together so they're at their minimum spacing. Raise the optics to your eyes and slowly expand the space between the barrels only as far as necessary to obtain the maximum amount of view or image space. If the barrels are too close together, you'll be able to see through only one barrel, or you'll only see portions of both barrels. (Not only that, but the image area you see will be circular rather than oval, and you may be able to see your hands or lots of black space.) If the barrels are too far apart, you will see two separate image circles with a black area in between.

If you've got the proper eye space for your eyes, the image area will appear to be a wide oval and you will notice the large, clear image space.

Positioning the eyecups

Surrounding each ocular lens (the one you hold toward your eyes), is a plastic ring that can be pulled or swiveled up to increase the distance between your eyeball and the lens. Conversely, it can be pushed or swiveled down to decrease the distance. Those who do not wear glasses when they use binoculars usually prefer these plastic rings (often referred to as *eyecups*) to be extended, partially or fully. (Partial extension is not possible with eyecups that fold and unfold.) Those who *do* wear glasses while using binoculars usually prefer the eyecups to be in the lowest position, since their spectacles provide sufficient distance between the ocular lens of the binocular and their eyeball.

Using the diopter: The eye equalizer

WARNING

If you are certain that you have the same vision in your right and left eyes (perhaps because you wear glasses or contact lenses or have had cataract surgery), you can skip the next paragraph.

Excluding those with corrected vision, almost everyone has one eye that is stronger than the other. Many people are near-sighted or far-sighted, but few have equal acuity. If your eyes aren't a perfectly matched 20/20, you may have a difficult time using binoculars because you can't focus clearly. We can help you with that.

The diopter adjustment on binoculars compensates for differences in visual acuity between your eyes, regardless of near-sightedness or far-sightedness. Adjusted properly, the diopter helps you to focus clearly on your target image using both eyes.

The first step is to find the diopter on your binocular. On many binoculars, the diopter adjustment is on the right eyepiece, just below the eye cup. (Refer to Figure 2-1.) Look for gradation marks, plus and minus symbols (+ and -), and possibly a texture different from the same area on the left eyepiece. If this describes your binocular, you've found the diopter!

Note that you can turn diopter adjustment rings to the left and to the right, and that the gradations have a center mark.

On some binoculars, the diopter is above or part of the central focusing knob. Gently give it a tug away from the focusing knob to unlock its position, and notice that it moves left and right, but the center is marked.

Using a diopter is an intrinsic part of focusing your binoculars. But if you are the only one using your binocular, you'll only need to set it once — unless your vision changes. For example, if you set it up without wearing glasses or contact lenses, you'll have to reset it when you use your bins with glasses on or contacts in.

Focusing

If you are certain that you have equal visual acuity in both eyes (because you wear glasses or contacts, or have had cataract surgery), you can skip steps 3 through 11. However, if you wear monovision contacts (so that you see close objects with one eye and distant objects with the other), you will need to follow all the instructions below.

To focus your binoculars properly, follow these easy steps:

1. **Make sure your binocular's barrels are optimally set for your eye space.**

   That is, pull them open wide, or push them close together — whatever is required for your eyes.

2. **Set your diopter to the central mark.**

3. **Choose a stationary object 50 or 100 feet or so away on which to focus.**

4. **Bring the binocular to your eyes and close your right eye (or cover the right objective lens — the far one — with your hand).**

5. **Turn the central focusing knob to the left or right as necessary to get that object in clear and sharp focus for your left eye.**

6. **Lower the binocular and rest your eyes for a moment, with both eyes open.**

7. **Lift the binoculars to your eyes once more and close your left eye or cover the left objective lens.**

8. **With your right eye, find the object you used to focus the left barrel.**

9. **This time, use the <u>diopter</u> to adjust the focus, turning it left or right until a clear image appears.**

   Do not touch the central focusing knob at this time!

10. **Open your left eye, so that you are looking at the object with both eyes, through both barrels.**

    That object should be crystal clear for each eye and for both eyes. If it is not, go back to step 1 and try again.

11. **If you had to "unlock" your diopter to adjust it, be sure to lock it back in place.**

From now on, the central focusing knob will adjust the focus for both of your eyes. Again, you won't have to reset your diopter unless your vision changes or you loan your bin to someone. Prove this to yourself by looking at a nearby object. Use the central focusing knob — turn it to the right until you get a sharp view of that object. It should be clear for both eyes. Now look at a distant object and turn the central focusing knob to the left to bring that object into focus. It should be sharp for both eyes. Remember where your optimal diopter setting is, so you can easily readjust it to that point if the setting is changed.

REMEMBER

Now that your bins are adjusted to accommodate your eyes, it's time to look at a bird through them. The first step is to find a bird with your naked eye. Then, remember this: *Keep your eyes on the bird and bring the binoculars up to your eyes.* If you hold your head still and keep your eyes locked on your targeted bird, finding the bird with your binoculars becomes a simple matter of raising the bins to the level of your eyes.

If your bins are properly calibrated, all you have to do when you spot a bird is turn the central focusing knob until you get a sharp image. (For additional information on using binoculars—and choosing the right bins for you—see Chapter 10.)

Take our advice: *Don't try using binoculars without a strap.* If the binocs you have are outfitted with a neck strap, by all means use it! If not, buy a good neck strap or a suspension system commonly called a binocular bra. (See Chapter 10 for recommendations.) But no matter how old or inexpensive your binoculars are, *never carry your binoculars by the strap.* Hang them around your neck, the way nature intended. Bill Thompson has a primo example of why you should heed this advice:

> In college, I was leading a bird walk for a biology class. I owned three pairs of binoculars at the time, two of which were pretty crummy, and my regular pair, which I was using. The other two I had loaned out to a couple of students to use during the walk. We were having a great spring morning of bird watching, with lots of colorful birds easily seen by all. I had asked one of the students who was using one pair of my "loaner" binocs to quit swinging them by the strap and put the strap around his neck. As we approached a high bluff overlooking a small river, I spotted a belted kingfisher. As we were *oohhing* and *ahhing* over the bird, I heard *"Oh, NO!!"* and caught a glimpse of those loaner binocs as they plummeted to their watery destiny in the river below. When the fumble-handed scholar climbed back up the bluff, huffing and puffing with the rescued optics, I put them to my eyes — out of habit, I suppose. I was pretty sure I could see tiny fish swimming in cloudy water. Inside the binoculars.

We're not sure if that student went on to become a bird watcher, but if so, we bet he always kept his binoculars around his neck using the neck strap.

Getting Up Close and Personal with Your Field Guide

The second piece of very useful equipment for bird watching is a field guide to birds. If you're a beginning bird watcher, the field guide can be a big help as you learn to identify birds.

A field guide is like a family album of birds, but even better. It contains color images of birds, maps showing where the birds can be found during certain seasons of the year, and descriptive text that covers information about the bird that can't be conveyed by either images or maps.

Remember those games you played as a kid where you matched the colors with the shapes? The purple square with the other purple square, and so on? Using a field guide to identify birds is just like that. You see a bird that you don't recognize; you make a mental note about its color, shape, and general appearance; and then you look for a matching bird image in the field guide.

REMEMBER

Bird watching is the process of seeing and identifying birds. True, you don't have to identify each bird that you see. (We can guarantee you won't, no matter how experienced you are.) You don't even have to identify *any* of the birds that you see. But we think one of the most fun things about bird watching is solving the mini mystery of each bird's identity using the clues that you're able to gather. Maybe you get a nice long look at a wading waterbird or a perched bird of prey, giving plenty of time to gather identifying clues, or *field marks.* Or you get a brief glimpse of a tiny warbler flitting through the treetops. In both cases, you can take the clues and begin your detective work using a field guide.

More information on using, choosing, and understanding a field guide is available in Chapter 11.

A matter of choice

Field guides are available in both book form and digitally in the form of apps. Most birders we know use both. Hard copies are handy for keeping track of the birds you have seen and making notes in the margins, and apps are convenient when you're not willing to lug around a lot of extra weight in your backpack. However, for new birders, we recommend starting with a hard copy, as there is something to be said for the ability to be able to compare a wide array of birds on facing or adjacent pages rather than navigating a small screen.

Depending upon where in North America you live (or where on the planet you live), you have several field guide types from which to choose:

>> Some guides cover all the birds of North America (north of Mexico) in a single book; others divide the continent up into East and West.

Bird watchers in the eastern third of the continent can get by with just an eastern guide, and those in the western third can get by with a western field guide. But those folks in the middle third of the continent need to have access to information about all the birds, east and west.

>> Specialty field guides are also available. Some cover all the birds of a given region, such as the Pacific Northwest, the Great Basin, Texas, Arizona, or Florida. Other guides are focused not upon geography but upon families of birds, such as guides to the hawks of the world, warblers of the world, or ducks, geese, and swans of the world.

>> Major, non-specialty field guides also have much variation. Some use photographs to show you the birds, while others use artwork. Some guides feature the bird image, descriptive text, and species' range maps on the same page.

Should you widen your birding to the world at large, you'll find a large array of field guides available for various countries and even regions of those countries. For instance, a country like Ecuador, with extreme topographical relief and diverse habitats, boasts some of the highest bird diversity in the world. Ecuador has so many species that it needs two regional guides, for east and west, even though it's only about the size of the state of Arizona. Similarly, Africa is almost impossibly vast, and a field guide to one African country or region might be all but useless in another.

Some guides are better for beginners; others are preferred by more experienced bird watchers. Each one has something a little different to offer, and we don't know many birders who own just one. It may seem like we're trying to get you to spend all your money but trust us: You *will* want more than just one field guide. For help in foraging through the forest of field guides, see Chapter 11.

Don't leave home without it

Even though we've been bird watching for decades, we still prefer to have a field guide handy whenever we go out to watch birds. Field guide apps make this incredibly easy, but a hard copy is good to have on hand, too. You just never know when something unfamiliar will turn up, or when the field guide will provide the clinching bit of information to solve the day's greatest bird identification mystery. You'll find, however, that as you get more familiar with bird identification, you'll need to refer to the field guide less and less.

IN THIS CHAPTER

» Pinpointing the (many) parts of a bird

» Recognizing field marks

» Working with first impressions

» Watching bird behavior

» Spending your field guide time wisely

Chapter **3**

Identifying Birds ("If It Walks Like a Duck . . .")

All birds have an identity, also known as a *species name*. (See Chapter 1.) Central to the joy of watching birds is identifying those birds you see.

Bird identification is a matter of sifting through various clues to solve the mystery of a bird's identity. It's a process of elimination in which you eliminate all the birds that aren't the one you're looking for. Most of these clues — behavior, size, shape, color, habitat, and important field marks — are visual. Sound plays a role with some birds — bird song, wing whirr, and so on — but your eyes do most of the clue-sifting. (We've yet to see a guide to birding by nose. Perhaps it's just a matter of time.)

The first time you try to identify a strange bird, you may be overwhelmed and confused by all the possibilities. What seems like a perfectly obvious small brown bird sitting on your feeder leads to pages and pages (or screens and screens) of small brown birds to choose from in your field guide. Don't despair. Identifying birds *is* possible, and you don't have to be a genius or devote your life to the study of small brown birds.

Remember, everyone starts out knowing nothing. Millions of bird watchers have mastered the trick of casually throwing a name (sometimes the right one!) on the birds they see. Most of these watchers are no smarter than you. They all started out just like you — appreciating the beauty and wonder of birds and wanting to know more about them. This chapter takes you through the basic steps of identifying a bird.

Before long, that small brown bird at your feeder becomes recognizable as a female house finch. See? You're learning already!

Identifying the Parts of a Bird

Knowing the parts of a bird is very helpful when it comes to bird identification. If you see a strange bird that has some yellow on it, this information is of no use unless you know *where* the yellow is on the bird. If you're new to bird watching, some of the bird parts may also be new to you.

Figure 3-1 shows some of the most common parts used by bird watchers to identify birds. Some parts have more specialized names that are used in bird identification. Notice the various areas of the wings, as shown in Figure 3-2. The length of the *primaries* (again, see Figure 3-2) as seen while the bird is standing on the ground or perched can be a useful ID clue, as can contrasting colors of the various feather groups.

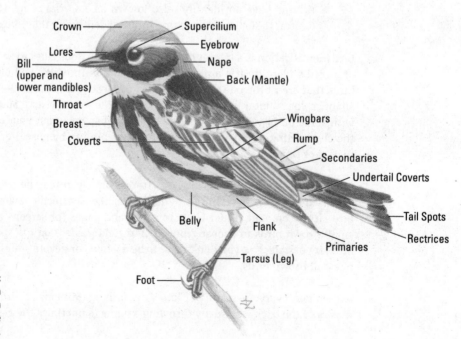

FIGURE 3-1: The parts of a bird as shown on a male magnolia warbler.

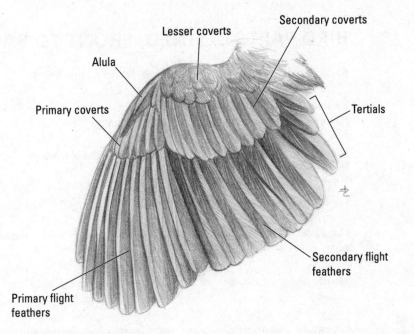

Secondary coverts

Lesser coverts

Alula

Primary coverts

Tertials

Secondary flight
feathers

Primary flight
feathers

If you've ever cooked, eaten, or looked at a chicken, you already know almost all the parts of a bird. (See Figure 3-3.) You don't need to be a bird watcher to know where the legs, breast, head, bill, wings, tail, and feet are. By the time you eliminate all the words and parts you already know, you're left with just a handful of words that are unique to bird watching. Yes, these words may be unfamiliar, but for most people, it takes about 15 minutes to study and learn them — about the time you take to have that morning cup of coffee.

FIGURE 3-3:
A chicken and a
robin: kin
under the skin.

BIRD PARTS DEFINED, FRONT TO BACK

Supercilium: The area above the bird's eye, also called the eyebrow.

Eyeline: A line of contrasting color (usually black or white) that goes through the eye. (The eyeline is lower on the face than a supercilium.)

Eyering: A ring of color (usually white) that encircles the eye. A broken eyering is one that doesn't completely encircle the eye.

Lores: The zone between the bird's eye and its bill.

Mandible: The bird's bill comprises two parts: the upper mandible and the lower mandible.

Mantle: The space between the bird's wings, below the nape; also called its back.

Breast: The area from below the bird's throat to the midway point on its lower body. The area below the breast is the belly.

Coverts: The smaller feathers that overlap the base of the longer feathers of both the wings and the tail.

Wingbar: Contrasting stripes of color on the bird's wing in the shoulder area or mid-wing.

Primary feathers: The longest of the wing feathers; they're the ones that form the pointed edge when the wing is folded.

Secondary feathers: The feathers that form the trailing edge along the middle of a bird's wing. The secondaries are located on a wing, between the bird's body and its primary feathers.

Flank: The area between the bird's side and tail.

Rump: Where the tail connects to the body.

Rectrices: The long feathers of the tail.

Take a few minutes to study the parts of a bird. Once you know what a *flank* and a *supercilium* and a *wingbar* are, and say the words aloud, the terms magically lose their mystique and their ability to cloud your mind when spoken out loud. Not only does the descriptive text in the field guide now make sense, but you can now toss these words casually into bird-watching conversations with others so that you sound like an expert, even if you still have trouble telling a bald eagle from an oven-ready roaster.

Paying Attention to Field Marks

Field marks are those unique characteristics that separate one bird from another. Almost all birds have a distinctive set of field marks that make it possible to tell one species from another. Finding out how to identify a bird is understanding what its field marks are.

REMEMBER

In a very few cases, the field marks are so subtle they can't be seen by the naked eye in the field. Consider those birds a challenge to be tackled at a later date. A good binocular or camera with a long lens or zoom is indispensable in picking up the broadest range of field marks. (See Chapter 10 for tips on using your binocular most effectively, and Chapter 20 for "Birdtography" advice.)

As you progress, you find yourself automatically noticing the field marks of each bird you encounter, much as you would recognize a friend after a while.

TIP

One place that will list all the pertinent field marks for a bird species is a good bird field guide, but before you run out and buy or download one, take this simple test of your observation skills. This exercise calibrates your visual settings and forces you to look at each bird in an analytical way. You can do this exercise even if you don't have a field guide.

1. **Pick a common bird, one you can easily see in your yard or neighborhood, such as a cardinal, robin, or chickadee.** (Already being familiar with the species of the bird helps.)

    For this example, we use the male cardinal. (Forgive us if you aren't familiar with this species. Every time we write "cardinal," please just mentally fill in the blank with your choice of a familiar bird, okay?)

2. **Look at the familiar bird and make written notes about its appearance. Note anything you feel may be a clue to its identity.**

    If you use "cardinal," what you write probably looks something like this:

A bright red bird with a red point of feathers on its head. A black face and a big, orange bill. Medium size, not small, but not huge. Hopping around beneath the bird feeder and eating sunflower seeds. Vocalizes every so often with a loud chip.

Here's what a field guide may say about the cardinal:

Adult males are bright crimson all over with a prominent red crest. Females are also crested, but are a dull rosy brown, lacking the males' bright red coloring. Both have a large, triangular orange bill. Common in woodland edges, along roadsides, and in backyards in the eastern two-thirds of the U.S., southeastern Canada, and south into Mexico. Frequents bird feeders where it eats sunflower seed. Both sexes emit a loud ringing chip!

See how similar the two descriptions are? As you get more experience, you remember more things about the birds you know and automatically look for more things on the birds you don't know. Such observation skills are what identifying birds is all about. (See the section "Focusing on Field Marks," later in this chapter for more about using field marks to help identify birds.)

TIP

Many songbirds and others emit a *chip note* as an alarm or contact call, or maybe they're just talking to themselves. Some are a *squeak*, a *chirp*, a *pip*, a *peep*, or some other quick note.

Look at the bird, not the field guide

Sooner or later, all bird watchers get a field guide, either as a book or an app. It's part of the trio of things that make up the activity called bird watching: **bird, optical device, field guide,** oh, and **you.** (Looks like that's four things — a quartet!)

The traditional steps you take to identify a bird go like this:

1. **See a bird.**

2. **Watch the bird for as long as you can, making notes (mental, digital, or physical) about its appearance and behavior.**

   A good binocular helps immensely.

3. **Consult a field guide** to confirm or find an identity for the bird.

TIP

One of the pitfalls in using a field guide is the tendency on the part of the beginning bird watcher to rely too heavily on the guide. Resist the temptation! Look at the bird for as long as you can. The picture of the bird in the book will always be there, but the actual living bird may linger for only a moment. Catch it while you can!

This method of identifying birds helps you learn and remember the field marks of species you see. Apps such as Merlin can do the heavy lifting of identification for you, but will you remember that species when you see it weeks, months, or years later? The act of figuring out the name of a species is part of the learning process. Figuring it out successfully is a rewarding and fun part of birding. Besides, sometimes apps — like humans — make mistakes.

The following sections should help you remember what you see.

Keep a mental checklist

TIP

Experienced bird watchers go through a mental checklist when looking at an unidentified bird: What is it doing? What size is it? What shape is it? What color? What are its main field marks? Does it have wingbars, an eyeline, a long tail?

You can do the same thing. Take a logical approach to looking at a bird. The first 10 or 20 times you'll have to make a conscious effort to remember all the things to look for, but after that, the checklist becomes automatic.

Talk to yourself

Ask yourself this question first: *What is most noticeable, most obvious about this bird?* Go ahead and talk to yourself. Memory is a leaky cup. When you're looking at the bird, you naturally believe you'll remember all the key points. It ain't so. By the time you get to the field guide, you may not remember whether the bird had wingbars or an eyering.

TIP

A useful trick is to recite the bird's features (field marks) out loud (but softly) while you mentally tick them off. This process works best if no one else is around, of course, although it can be helpful if you're sharing the moment with another observer who is as new to the game as you. By repeating the field marks out loud, you simplify later access to your memory bank. By discussing field marks with your birding companions, you might discover overlooked features. After all, four eyes are better than two.

After you discover the *most* obvious clue to the bird's identity, look at the next most obvious clue, and then the next, and so on. As you gain experience, you mumble to yourself less and less. Experience makes much of the process so fast and automatic that vocal reminders aren't necessary. Until you reach that point, the social downside of being seen as a mutterer is offset by the advantage of being able to identify more birds.

Make notes, sketches, recordings . . .

Being a quick sketch artist is one way to help your brain remember the field marks of a mystery bird. This sketch requires no artistic skill whatsoever. Simply carry a small notepad and a pencil (with an eraser). Use these tools to jot down as much information as you can while the bird is still in front of you. Better yet, draw the outline of the bird, labeling the pertinent field marks as you go.

TIP

If sketching isn't your thing, jot down some quick notes, such as "white wing-bars," or "pink legs," or "yellow rump." You can even use your phone's voice recorder to describe what you're seeing. Later, play back the recording (and relive the moment) as you use your field guide to find the bird with the field marks you noted.

Leveraging Your First Impressions

First impressions are important. A small yellow bird is not a big gray bird and isn't even a small gray bird. The first impression is the outline that you use to organize the specifics.

Sometimes the impression is enough by itself, but most often it serves to get you to the right place in the field guide, at which point you can start to nail down the bird's ID.

TIP

The first impression is made up of several fairly obvious steps. Look at the bird and note your impressions of the following features:

>> The bird's most obvious characteristic (or two)

>> The bird's behavior (What is the bird doing?)

>> The bird's size, shape, color

>> Whether it's a landbird or waterbird

Pay attention to *where* you see the bird. The *where* is often a good clue to *what* the bird actually is. These things take a lot of time to explain (but less than a few seconds to do when you're actually looking at a bird).

The most obvious characteristic, simply stated, is what stands out about the bird. What made you notice it? The following sections cover bird characteristics that provide clues to a bird's identity.

Size — bigger than a softball?

TIP

Size matters. In birding lingo, *size* refers to the measurement of the bird from the tip of the bill to the tip of the tail. Make a quick judgment, using whatever standard is familiar and comfortable.

>> Is it bigger than a softball?

>> Is it about six inches, or is it more than a foot long?

>> Is it shorter than your binoculars, or bigger than a small child?

Which method you use doesn't matter — as long as you have a reasonable idea of how big the bird is. Figure 3-4 compares relative sizes of birds.

REMEMBER

You don't need to be precise. The difference between a six-inch bird and a five-and-a-half-inch bird in the field is beyond most observers. Just get in the ball-park. (We've never seen a field guide organized by size, but knowing how big or small the bird is helps to eliminate a lot of choices.)

FIGURE 3-4: How big is big? From left to top right, comparing the sizes of a wild turkey, American crow, American robin, house finch, and ruby-throated hummingbird.

TIP

Pick a common bird — one you're very familiar with — as a size reference point: rock pigeon, starling, or robin, for example. Then you can discern if a mystery bird is "smaller than a robin." Size is an important clue to identification.

Shape

By looking at a bird, even one silhouetted in poor light, you can make out its general shape. Shape also is an important ID clue. You can use the same descriptive terms you use for humans: tall, lanky, thin, leggy, fat, squat, chunky, round, small-headed, pointy-headed, and egotistical . . . oops, er, uh, big-headed! You get the picture.

With a good idea of the bird's shape, you can narrow the possibilities, throwing out those species that the bird cannot possibly be.

WARNING

Be aware that birds can and do change their shape. In cold weather, birds may puff out their feathers to increase heat retention. This puffing out process makes them appear larger than they actually are. Herons can fold their necks up until they appear to have no neck at all. A careful look at the bird helps you avoid being fooled.

Color

TIP

Color is one of the most easily grasped clues to a bird's identity. But color is not a foolproof, one-step ID tool. Why not? Because light can alter our perception of color. We occasionally hear reports of black hummingbirds — but there are no black hummingbirds in the U.S. or Canada. In shadow, the ruby-throated hummingbird and others, despite being bright and colorful in better lighting, can appear solid black.

Variation exists among young (immature) and adult birds, among some males and females (called sexual dimorphism), and even among same-age, same-sex individuals. Further clouding the issue is the seasonal changing of plumage (feathers) that most birds go through: *molt*.

An adult male American goldfinch in June looks like a brilliant yellow and black jewel. The same bird in January wears colors of dull brownish yellow like a faded color photograph of the summer version. Furthermore, not all individual birds of a given species are the same color. Warblers such as the Cape May can range from brilliant yellow, olive, and chestnut (breeding adult male) to the drabbest imaginable gray-green (fall immature female).

TIP

Even with the confusing variables, you can use color to your advantage. When you see an unfamiliar bird, describe the color to yourself. Don't be afraid to mix the colors together. If the bird looks yellowish-greenish-brown to you, that's great! Better yet, try to remember what parts of the bird have a distinctive or contrasting color. Does the bird have a dark cap? A rusty belly? White wingbars?

Remembering colors and where they appear on the bird is a great start when it comes to understanding field marks and their countless variations, which also helps when figuring out the name of the bird you've observed.

Wet or dry?

Birds are commonly separated into groups.

One of the easiest distinctions is between landbirds and waterbirds. If the bird is swimming around in the middle of the lake, it probably isn't a sparrow. If the bird is hanging on your bird feeder, it probably isn't a duck.

Waterbirds include loons, grebes, seabirds, pelicans, cormorants, shorebirds (such as plovers and sandpipers), ducks, geese, swans, herons, egrets, ibises, cranes, rails, gulls, and terns, among others. Most of the waterbirds are located in the front of most field guides, whether print or digital.

Landbirds include all the other birds you can think of.

In a very few instances, this process of elimination (wet or dry?) won't work, but this method is always worth a try.

Focusing on Field Marks

When it comes to field marks, you have to start somewhere. We recommend starting at the front end of the bird — the one with the bill — and working your way over the bird to the back end (the one without the bill). On many birds, key field marks are found on the head. At the very least, the marks found on the head eliminate a lot of similar-looking birds. Starting at the front/top end and working toward the tail is logical and helps you keep the information organized.

Paying (attention to) the bill

The bill is important. Birds are adapted to a specific way of life, and one of the most obvious adaptations is the bill. Bird bills come in a remarkable variety of shapes and sizes, each designed for a specific lifestyle. Is the bill long or short? Thick or thin? Hooked? Flattened? Broad? For example, sparrows have short, thick bills used for cracking seeds. Hawks have strong, hooked bills for tearing flesh. Herons have long, dagger-like bills for spearing fish. Figure 3-5 shows how different bills can be.

FIGURE 3-5: Bird bills with their different shapes resemble the tools named. Use the tool names to help you identify the shape of a bill.

The bill usually gives you a good idea of which group your bird belongs to. With a little practice, you can look at a bird's bill and say, automatically: "That's a chickadee." On some birds, such as pelicans and spoonbills, seeing the bill is virtually all you need to identify the species. On others, the bill gets you to the right group of birds.

Going head(first)

Especially for small songbirds, field marks appear on the head more than on any other body part. Birds' heads can have eyerings, eyelines, supercilia (that's the plural of supercilium), and ear patches (on the side of the bird's head — birds' ears are usually concealed by feathers). In most cases, the field marks that matter most on the head are stripes on the top (crown) and supercilium.

Look for obvious patterns, such as the crown stripes of a *white-crowned sparrow*, or the dark cap of a *black-capped chickadee*. Later, if the bird is still around, you can go back and look for subtleties.

TIP

Dozens of other field marks are associated with the head. Birds can be bald, bar-headed, beardless, bridled, browed, capped, crested, crowned, cheeked, chinned, collared, eared, eyed, faced, hooded, horned, masked, naped, necked (even red-necked!), nosed, plumed, polled, ringed, spectacled, striped, throated, tufted, and whiskered. And that's just the head.

Moving on to body parts

Many birds are named for their most noticeable body part, such as the *yellow-throated* warbler, or the *black-headed* grosbeak. Some birds are (strangely) named for a marking that can be seen only on a bird held in the hand: *red-bellied* wood-pecker and *ring-necked* duck are two examples. You rarely see either of these subtle field marks unless you happen to be bird watching with the Hubble telescope.

Any reasonable person would notice that a bird's body is one solid object, but for identification purposes, bird bodies have connected sections: the upperparts and the underparts.

Upperparts

The upperparts are the *back* (mantle) and top surface of the *wings*, plus the top surface area extending down to the base of the tail. The key field marks, if any exist on the upperparts, are often found on the wings.

TIP

Many groups of birds (vireos and warblers, for instance) are divided into those that have wingbars and those that don't. Wingbars are pale stripes across the shoulder of the wing. On some birds, subtle distinctions exist in the size, width, and color of the wingbars, but you can be content simply to notice whether the wing has bars — or not.

The back isn't usually too important in determining a bird's identity, but whether the back is streaked, plain, or a contrasting color is worth noting. If you can see the rump — the patch of feathers on the lower back just above the tail — try to notice its color, too. You're in for a surprise the first time you see a yellow-rumped warbler!

Underparts

The underparts are the *breast, belly, vent* (also called *undertail coverts*), and the underside of the tail. In many birds, such as sparrows, noticing whether the breast is plain or streaked is important. In some hawks, the breast is *barred* (the streaks go sideways). Some birds have a breast that's one color and the belly another.

The underparts are, shall we say, distinctly unimportant for identification purposes when it comes to certain birds. Ducks are a good example — ducks are usually seen swimming on a body of water and the underparts can be described only as, well, wet.

The tail

The tail can be a very helpful clue to a bird's identity, and not only by its coloration. You most often note the tail on flying birds, but you can sometimes see the tail clearly when a bird is perched in a tree or hopping on the ground. For some species, a wagging or flicking movement of the tail is a diagnostic field mark. Tails can be relatively long or short, forked, notched, or square. On some birds, such as the *scissor-tailed* flycatcher, the tail is *the* field mark.

The legs

The legs are often overlooked, but there are times when they can be important for identification purposes. Bird feet aren't as helpful as ID tools, but they do tell you something about how the bird makes its living (see Figure 3-6). For example, hawks and owls have sharp, taloned feet used for grabbing and killing their prey. Ducks have short legs and webbed feet for swimming.

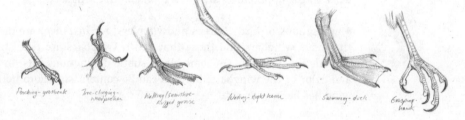

FIGURE 3-6:
Birds' feet can do specific tasks and offer clues to a bird's identity.

Look for the length and color of the legs. Herons, for example, have proportionately long legs for wading in deep water and long toes for support and balance, whereas most landbirds have short legs. As for leg color, it can often be more important than length when trying to identify a bird — so much so that some birds, like lesser yellowlegs, are even named for their leg color.

The lesser yellowlegs is a medium-sized shorebird. This bird is one of a half dozen medium-sized shorebirds with yellow legs (including the confusingly similar greater yellowlegs), but then, the naming of birds isn't always logical.

Be careful with leg color. Birds that have been walking around in mud may appear to have black or brown legs.

WHY DO BIRDS' LEGS BEND BACKWARD?

Go back to Figure 3-1 and look for the bird's tarsus, which you might think is its calf. Actually, that long bone is part of its foot, and the joint behind it is comparable to a heel. Birds' legs don't bend backward; rather, they walk on tiptoes. If you take another look at Figure 3-3, you'll see that the joint between the chicken's thigh and leg is its knee — just like yours and mine.

Parsing plumage

REMEMBER

Birds' feathers, collectively called *plumage*, are what make birds different from all other animals on Earth. And it's their feathers, or rather the color or configuration of their feathers, that make birds so compelling and so beautiful.

Because birds replace feathers as they wear out, you may see the same birds with different plumage at different times during the year, just as you change from a parka in winter to a T-shirt when the weather is hot. Or not. Some birds, once they attain their adult plumage, retain the same appearance throughout the year for the rest of their lives.

Because worn-out feathers provide little protection from cold and don't help much when a bird needs to fly, birds replace most of the feathers on their body every year. They do this by a process called *molting*. When birds molt, the old feathers fall out and a set of healthy new feathers grows in. (Actually, it's the new feathers that push out the old ones.)

REMEMBER

Most birds molt all of their body feathers in the fall and a few feathers in the spring. The long feathers of the wings and tail (together called the *flight feathers*) are replaced annually in smaller bird species, but less frequently for large birds. Growing new feathers, especially long ones, takes a lot of energy, so raptors — hawks and eagles, for example — stagger replacement of their primaries, secondaries, and rectrices, or tail feathers.

For some species, after molting, the bird's appearance changes drastically. Prior to their northward migration in spring, greenish male scarlet tanagers lose their drab, nonbreeding feathers by growing in a set of brilliant red ones, offset by black wings. In late summer, many adult warblers begin a molt that makes them less boldly colored than they were just a few weeks prior.

Some birds, such as the males of many duck species, look different in the winter than in the summer. After breeding, they molt into a dull "eclipse plumage" that they wear for a month or so — and they are flightless! They molt again into breeding plumage prior to fall migration. Bird molts provide another opportunity for bird watchers to study (and be frustrated by) birds.

In almost all birds, immature birds look different from the adult of the species. Their plumage is usually duller and streakier. Although this difference typically lasts less than a year, in some cases (such as gulls and bald eagles), young birds can look different from adult birds for several years. The following plumage stages are typical of most bird species, but the duration of each varies:

>> **Downy:** The fluffy feathers most baby birds have while they're still in the nest. Adult birds retain some down feathers beneath their main contour (body) feathers. This down helps insulate the birds, as it does in a down coat.

>> **Juvenal:** The first real feathers a bird has after leaving the nest. These feathers usually last about a month. Juvenile birds wear juvenal plumage.

>> **Immature:** The feathers a bird wears for much of the first year of its life.

>> **Adult:** The feathers the bird has after its first full year. This is the plumage commonly shown in field guides. For many species, adult plumage coincides with a bird's first breeding season. Reaching full adult plumage can take as little as nine months, or, in the case of bald and golden eagles and many gull species, several years.

Here are some seasonal plumages that adult birds have:

>> **Breeding:** Breeding plumage is the equivalent of courting clothes. This plumage is often the bird's most colorful, especially in birds such as tanagers, many warblers, and ducks. Breeding plumage is commonly associated with adult males, whose bright feathers and loud song serve as an advertisement for a mate during the spring breeding season. Adult female birds, by and large, get the short end of the stick when it comes to flashy spring plumage. Female birds *do* get a new set of feathers each spring, but not eye-catchingly brilliant ones. A brightly colored female bird sitting on a nest would be easier for a predator to spot, so evolution has pushed female birds away from fashionably bright avian attire. Breeding plumage is also called *alternate plumage*.

>> **Non-breeding:** Generically speaking, this is the bird's everyday dress — the plumage that birds are in when not in breeding season. It's also known as fall plumage, *basic plumage*, and winter plumage. Birds that look the same throughout the year are always in basic plumage.

These plumage terms are not something you need to memorize, but when you are using a field guide to identify a bird, you need to understand that some bird species have different appearances throughout the year. Field guides show many different plumages for each bird species — based on age, gender, region, and season — so knowing some of the related terminology can be a big help.

REMEMBER

Most ducks and many songbirds, such as cardinals and house finches, are *sexually dimorphic,* that is, the males and females look different from each other. Most hawks, gulls, shorebirds, and sparrows, however, aren't sexually dimorphic, meaning that males and females resemble each other. Although exceptions do occur, knowing about sexual dimorphism is helpful when watching birds. Although the female cardinal isn't bright red like the male, other important clues tell you it's a cardinal. And as long as birds can tell the difference (and they can), identifying the male or female of a species adds to the challenge that bird watchers embrace.

Among species that are sexually dimorphic, males are usually (but not always) brighter or more colorful than their female counterparts, and so you may hear about "dull females." This is a statement about their coloration, not their intelligence or charisma. It's not sexist, either, but evolutionary: A muted color provides camouflage for the female while she is incubating or attending to her nestlings.

Keeping an Eye on Behavior

Behavior (the bird's, not yours) can assist with identification, too. Chances are, the reason you're looking at a bird is because some aspect of its behavior attracted your attention. The bird flew past you, you heard it sing, or you saw it move high up on a branch. Because bird behavior is so easily observed, it's an excellent first-impression clue to a bird's identity.

The world of bird behavior encompasses a lot of interesting information. For identification purposes, here's a taste (an appetizer, if you will) of how behavior can be useful. (For a full course on bird behavior, see Chapter 5.)

Identifying birds through behavioral clues

Some birds constantly wag their tails (palm warblers and phoebes, for example); some (such as ruby-crowned kinglets) constantly flick their wings. Some birds hop, some walk, some creep, and some flutter. Some ducks dive while others feed by tipping over and sticking their backsides straight up in the air. Woodpeckers and nuthatches hop and scoot along tree trunks and branches searching for food. Hummingbirds hover over flowers to drink nectar. All are examples of bird behavior that provide helpful clues to the bird's identity.

When gathering your first impression, ask yourself: *What is this bird doing?*

Listening in on bird conversations

Bird noises are an entirely separate area of endeavor (see Chapter 6 for more about bird sounds). Birds have a wonderful and bewildering variety of sounds — from songs to calls to alarm notes to wing whirrs. Some warblers have as many as eight or ten different types of vocalizations, depending on who they're talking to and what mood they're in. This barely skims the surface of this topic, but prepare yourself: learning to hear and recognize bird sounds can be as important in identification as seeing birds. That's why some of us prefer the term "birding" to "bird watching." We use our eyes and ears to identify and enjoy birds.

It's worth noting any distinctive noises the bird is making. Is the bird cawing like a crow? Croaking like a raven? Screaming like a jay? Mewing like a catbird?

PLEASED TO MEETCHA, MISS BEECHER!

Bill Thompson III shared the following strategy for learning bird sounds in the first edition of *Bird Watching For Dummies*:

Growing up in southeastern Ohio, I looked forward to spring each year and the return of the colorful warblers, orioles, tanagers, and other migrants. Because this part of Ohio is thickly wooded, making even these brightly colored birds hard to find, most area bird watchers are forced to use bird vocalizations as a means of finding and identifying these birds. To this day I still use lots of the clues I was taught as a kid for remembering bird songs. For example: the chestnut-sided warbler sings, "Pleased to meetcha, Miss Beecher!" The black-throated blue warbler sings, "I am so lay-zeee!" These tricks have stuck with me for decades, and they've never let me down. You can come up with your own devices for remembering bird songs — just remember to remember!

Field Guide Time, at Last!

Okay, you've stared at the bird until you're glassy-eyed; you've cataloged (out loud or in writing) important field marks; you've watched the bird stretch, hop, and wiggle; and you've listened to the bird chip, warble, sing and whirr. You've got enough evidence to solve this identification mystery. It's time to open the field guide and put a name on this thing.

When going to the field guide with a bird in mind that you hope to identify, you have two choices:

>> If you have a general idea of the *kind* of bird you're looking for, you turn to the part of the guide that deals with that kind of bird. Use what you know about avian taxonomy! Chapter 4 will boost your skills on that topic.

>> If you have *no clue* of what you're looking for, you have to flip through the whole guide page by page or screen by screen.

Option one — figuring out the kind of bird and searching for that type of bird in the guide — is the way to do it! Flip, scroll, or search for the group in which you think this bird belongs, such as ducks, woodpeckers, or sparrows.

Option two is time-consuming, and your memory slowly goes south on you with every page that passes. Before long, you have trouble distinguishing between what you actually saw in the field and what you're seeing in the book. (For help with using and understanding your field guide, see Chapter 11.)

Because waterbirds are generally in the first half of the field guide and landbirds are mostly in the second half, start by cutting the problem down.

Suppose that you've found the right group, and three or four pages of the birds look pretty much alike. Glance quickly at each set of pictures to find one with matching field marks and see if one of them jumps (hops or flies) off the page or screen, yelling, "It's me. It's me!" You've completed the journey, accomplishing the task at the heart of the bird-watching experience. You've put a name on the bird. Now you're ready to move on to the next challenge, and the next bird.

Not so fast!

A lot of people, including experts, make the mistake of stopping here. You need to take a few backup steps:

1. **Keep looking!**

   A lot of people find a bird in the field guide that looks like the one in the field and quit on the spot. They don't realize that there's another bird, two screens or pages later in the guide that looks even *more* like the one they saw. Make sure you consider *all* the possibilities.

2. **Don't cram the bird into the picture!**

   Well, the bird you saw looks a lot like one you found in the field guide, except you didn't notice any big white patch on the wings of the bird you saw. Oh well, you may think, you probably just overlooked it. Sorry, that won't hold up in court. It's likely that you're looking at the wrong bird in the field guide.

WARNING

   If you find yourself working too hard to explain away field marks that aren't there or don't quite fit, you probably have made a mistake.

3. **Look at the map!**

   You may not know which birds are likely to be in your backyard and which ones are only found on the other side of the continent (or which ones visit your area only during a certain season of the year). That's why field guides have range maps. Isn't that brilliant? What's not clear is why so many people fail to look at them. Maybe it's the same phenomenon as to why some people refuse to ask directions when they're lost.

Home on the range

Range can solve a lot of identification problems. If you have a chickadee coming to your feeder, and you live in California, you can take one glance at the map for that species in the field guide and eliminate Carolina chickadee. If you confidently have identified the small brown bird in your Virginia backyard as a wrentit (a western bird), you probably made a mistake. So, after you think you know what you're looking at, check the map and make sure the bird is one likely to be seen in your area. If the bird doesn't occur in your area, go back to the pictures and try again.

REMEMBER

Birds have wings and tend to use them. They are very mobile creatures.

Just because your field guide's map says the bird you've identified shouldn't occur where you're seeing it, that doesn't mean that it can't happen. Either you've misidentified the bird or the bird misread the map. A bird far from its normal range is called a *vagrant* or an *accidental*. If you think your bird is one of these, ask a more experienced bird watcher to help you confirm the identification. Finding a vagrant bird is an exciting experience, but a rare one for beginning birders. A much more common experience is for a beginning birder to misidentify a bird, thinking it's a rarity.

TIP

Don't ever be afraid to ask questions of other bird watchers, particularly if they're more experienced than you. Ask for help with a tricky bird ID, or ask "How did you know that was a . . . ?" You pick up lots of great ID tips this way. And you'll probably make a few friends, too. Just don't become too reliant on other people to identify the birds for you, or you'll never improve your ID skills.

If All Else Fails . . .

If all else fails, start over. You may find it frustrating, but go back and look at the bird again, assuming it's still around. If it isn't, go on to the next bird. You don't have to identify every bird you see. No one does, and no one is keeping score. This process is supposed to be fun! Smile! Do what every other bird watcher does — grade yourself on a very generous curve. Mistakes happen. Big deal!

Three outcomes are possible when you attempt to identify a bird:

>> **You get it right — you correctly identify the bird.** It may take a while before you're absolutely sure, but you *will* get it right.

>> **You don't figure it out, and the bird takes off before you can solve the mystery.** You don't forget the one that gets away. When you see it again, you'll be more prepared.

>> **You get it wrong — you (gasp!) misidentify the bird.** You may not realize it at first, but as you see more birds and become more confident in your identification, you know that you got it wrong.

The newer you are to bird watching, the more likely the result will be #2 or #3. Because we all hate to admit failure, #3 will be more common than #2, whether you know it or not. You will — and this is an absolute certainty — misidentify birds when you first start out. In fact, you'll do it for the rest of your bird-watching life.

You would be shocked at the number of experienced birders who identify distant white plastic bags as snowy owls every winter. It's embarrassing — we know from personal experience — but even longtime birders make mistakes, and sometimes we end up with humorous stories to share. There's an adage you should know: "No one has misidentified more birds than a lifelong birder."

REMEMBER

Don't worry about it if you misidentify a bird. The Fate of the Free World doesn't hang in the balance. Misidentifying birds isn't a social crime equivalent to dipping into the collection plate or throwing recyclables into the trash can. Misidentifying birds is part of the process of becoming a bird watcher. Eventually, you'll correctly identify almost all the birds that you see.

TIP

If you're still stumped on a bird ID, you can use Merlin or some other app that uses algorithms or artificial intelligence to come up with likely species from the information you give it: the date, location, size, color, habitat, behavior, and so on. We saved this for later because working to identify a bird helps you learn, helps you hone your observational skills, and helps you remember the species you struggle to figure out. Plus, it usually ends up providing the genuine satisfaction of hard work paying off — without computer assistance.

IN THIS CHAPTER

» **This is too deep for a For Dummies guide (. . .not!)**

» **Taxonomy 101**

» **King Philip came over for WHAT???**

» **Nomenclature, also known as bird names**

» **Taxonomy 102: We're not going there**

Chapter **4**

Taxonomy and Nomenclature

I n this chapter, we're going to focus on *groupings* of birds — some of which you already know. Understanding the scientific groupings of birds will help you narrow your search as you seek to identify a bird that's new to you. Field guides are arranged by such groupings, so learning a bit about them will allow you to use your field guide and other birding apps more efficiently.

You are familiar with at least a few bird groups. For example, you can probably recognize a duck, a pigeon, or an owl. You're likely aware that there are lots of kinds of ducks and pigeons and owls. Recognizing a bird as a member of a group is elementary taxonomy. Is the bird a duck? If so, you can find it in the beginning pages of your book-format field guide or search your field guide app for "duck."

More than that, though: Thinking about the basics of *avian* (also known as "bird") *taxonomy* (also known as relational groupings) will help you understand birds better — that owls have similar head shapes and bill and foot types; what makes a woodpecker a woodpecker; why suddenly, yellow-breasted chat, once considered an oddball warbler, is now an oddball blackbird (sort of) even though it's not black; and why Baltimore oriole and Bullock's oriole were "lumped" into one species (called the northern oriole) and a few years later "split" again into separate species with their previous names.

If you see a three-foot-tall, long-legged gray bird with a long bill, is it a great blue heron or a sandhill crane? Just knowing that there are herons and there are cranes will help with the ID, and if you have a feel for what herons look like, how they behave, and their preferred habitat, you'll probably be able to figure out the species of this bird without even consulting your field guide.

TIP

Speaking of field guides, although most birders have one (or more) installed on their mobile phones and refer to them frequently, for the purposes of this chapter, it would be helpful to have a book-format field guide to refer to. Sure, you can compare one species to another with a field guide app, but it's easier and more instructive to look at birds on facing or adjacent pages than on a small screen. The layout of your field guide book will help clarify taxonomic relationships.

This Is Too Deep for a Dummies Guide (. . .Not!)

Classifying birds into groups is no simple matter. Scientists have done this for hundreds of years and they're still making new discoveries. Your task (if you choose to accept it) is to get a feel for what the groups are, and the basic characteristics of the various groups.

REMEMBER

We're not going to do a deep dive here. A superficial understanding of bird groups and the relationships between and within them is all you need to start out.

TIP

Bird taxonomy got a boost when genetic testing became part of ornithological field research. Nowadays, it's not just appearance, anatomy, behavior, habitat, and visible characteristics (if it has a bill like a duck, it's a duck) that define the various groups of birds. Genetics either confirms long-established relationships or disproves them, requiring a reordering of the taxonomy.

Bird watchers don't need to know nuthin' about DNA, though. (Thank goodness!) We just need to know where to look in our field guides for the various groups or the group name to search on. It helps a lot to be even a little bit familiar with the various groups. That's where we're heading.

Is this too deep? Nah.

NOT ALL RAPTORS ARE HAWKS

Here is an example of why recreational bird watchers need to understand basic taxonomy. If you look at an <u>older</u> field guide (the book form), you'll find falcons, eagles, hawks, and similar flying predators on adjacent pages, possibly with the heading "Raptors," or maybe "Diurnal Raptors," (meaning they hunt in the daytime, unlike nocturnal raptors: owls). And it's true: Hawks, eagles, and falcons are all diurnal raptors. But page or scroll through newer field guides and you'll find hawks, eagles, and other diurnal raptors in the first half, just after water birds. The falcons, however, are listed separately — close to the middle section, between woodpeckers and parrots.

This relocation freaked out a lot of birders! Why did it happen? DNA! Falcons are still considered diurnal raptors, but genetically, they don't have much in common with hawks and eagles. In fact, falcons are more closely related to parrots than to hawks! And when you think about it, the wing shape, the overall sleek, aerodynamic shape of falcons is quite different from hawks and eagles. "Diurnal raptor" describes feeding behavior, but it doesn't describe genetic relationships, and it is not a taxonomic group.

In older field guides, loons will be the first birds described. In more recent field guides, waterfowl — geese, ducks, and swans, but not loons — will be at the top of the list or in the front of the book.

These rearrangements were based on science (not whim!) as ornithologists learn more about birds and how they are related to each other (or not). Understanding why field guides get rearranged, why birds get booted from one group and into another, or get placed in a brand-new, previously unrecognized group may seem arbitrary, but it is based on science, and that is reflected in each new version of the field guides.

Taxonomy 101

The simplest definition of *taxonomy* is "the branch of science concerned with the classification of organisms." Classification means assigning similar organisms into groups. But also, *taxonomy* can refer to the classification itself. For example, we can talk about how the taxonomy of the yellow-breasted chat changed drastically in 2017. Field guides are arranged on the framework of taxonomy.

Taxonomy isn't limited to birds. Think about trees. You've got your evergreens, such as pines and spruces, and your deciduous trees, such as oaks and maples. Trees can be grouped, and field guides to trees are taxonomically based, as are field guides for mammals, insects, and other organisms.

ALTERNATIVE ARRANGEMENTS

There are several established, official ways of grouping birds. In this book we're going to follow the Clements taxonomy (*Clements Checklist of the Birds of the World*), which has been around since 1975, and has been updated many times. This arrangement is the basis for the taxonomy used by the American Birding Association (ABA) and the Cornell Lab of Ornithology, including its apps, such as eBird and Merlin, which many birders use. There are others, though, including Sibley–Ahlquist, Howard and Moore, the Handbook of Birds of the World, BirdLife International, the International Ornithological Committee, and the American Ornithological Society. They are all similar in their groupings, but the arrangements of those groups can be quite different. The American Ornithological Society is the organization of taxonomic ornithologists that establishes the official common and scientific names of North American birds, and this group also decides upon "lumps" and "splits," which we'll get to later in this chapter. Every taxonomic system is updated regularly as new discoveries are made about the relationships between and within bird groups and as new species are recognized. The fact that there is more than one avian taxonomy system is worth knowing because the arrangement of bird groupings is often inconsistent between various online resources, field guides, and apps.

King Philip Came Over for WHAT???

A simplified version of the taxonomy of birds uses this traditional framework: King Philip Came Over For Good Sex.

Who is King Philip? Came over from where? And, um, excuse me?

That's all irrelevant. There have been a few King Philips of Spain, and a Wampanoag (Native American) tribal leader who adopted the name King Philip, but the King Philip of taxonomy is just a *mnemonic device* — a way to help you remember bird taxonomy terminology, in other words. It is not a real person who traveled for carnal pleasure. And if you are offended by why he came over, use the S-word of your choice — salad or spaghetti if you prefer.

REMEMBER

Please don't memorize this:

King	Kingdom
Philip	Phylum
Came	Class

Over	Order
For	Family
Good	Genus
S-something	Species

WARNING

This is a grossly simplified version of animal taxonomy, but it's all a recreational bird watcher needs to know — and you don't need to know it well, but just enough to understand the concepts.

Kingdom

You've heard of "the animal kingdom." It is filled with animals. There is also a plant kingdom and a fungus kingdom and several others, including the protist and monera kingdoms. Fungi are either delicious or deadly. Protists and monera are, um, beyond the realm of this book. Search the internet for them if you're genuinely interested.

The formal name of the animal kingdom is *Animalia.* Birds are just one type of animal. See how much you already know about taxonomy?!

Phylum

The top-level grouping within the animal kingdom, for our purposes, is backbone versus no backbone. If it has a backbone, it is in the phylum Chordata. There are a whole bunch of phyla (that's the plural of *phylum)* of organisms that don't have backbones, and you know many of them: arthropods (insects and spiders), mollusks, and starfish, to name just a few. Birds have backbones, so, the phylum we're talking about is Chordata. Birds are vertebrates.

Birds are a <u>class</u> act!

Within the phylum of organisms with backbones are classes: fish, amphibians, reptiles, mammals, and birds. The animals within each of those classes have characteristics that are unique to the class. For example, all mammals — and only mammals — have fur and mammary glands that produce milk for their babies.

REMEMBER

Birds are literally in a class of their own, with the official name of Aves. The Latin word for bird is *avis* — which explains the word "avian." Here we are in the middle of Chapter 4, and we haven't even provided a full definition of *bird* yet. All birds are warm-blooded vertebrates with toothless bills. They lay hard-shelled eggs, have a strong, lightweight skeleton, and a speedy metabolism. All birds have two legs and two wings, although not all birds can fly. The wings of some flightless birds, such as kiwis, emus, and a few others, have wings so small that they can't be seen!

The true defining characteristic of birds, though, is feathers. All birds — and only birds — have feathers. If it has feathers, an animal is a bird. Consider Australia's platypus. It has a bill like that of a duck, and it lays eggs. Does it have feathers? No, it has fur. It is not a bird, but a mammal (although a bizarre one).

Nearly all birds have a vocal organ, called a syrinx, at the base of the trachea. The syrinx's structure varies widely among bird groups, and this will be a grouping factor when we get further into the branches of the taxonomic tree. Hold that thought.

Birds <u>orders</u> (not the same as putting our ducks in a row)

This is where things get really interesting and useful: classifying class Aves. The paragraphs above were an introduction to the concepts of taxonomy, much of which you already knew, perhaps without realizing it. Class Aves is divided into orders.

TIP

You already know some bird orders: waterfowl, pigeons, owls, and falcons, for example. (See the *Bird Watching For Dummies* cheat sheet at dummies.com for a list of all the orders and families of birds regularly found in the continental United States and Canada.) There are only 23 such orders, but there's no need to memorize them. It will be enough for you to become familiar with the grouping names and their arrangement.

Other bird orders you probably know include flamingos, woodpeckers, hummingbirds, gulls, parrots, and probably a few others. If you are bird watching and you see a woodpecker, open your field guide app and search for "woodpecker." Doing so will narrow the possible IDs from more than 500 to fewer than 25. See what a little taxonomical understanding can do for you?

Let's consider a few of the familiar orders of birds.

>> **Waterfowl (Anseriformes):** You know what ducks, geese, and swans look like, and where to find them. They generally have longish, flattish bills; longish necks, and webbed feet — great for paddling on water, which is what waterfowl do. "Waterfowl" is an obvious, logical grouping of birds.

Loons are in a different order. Loons are water birds, but they aren't waterfowl — their bill and body are shaped differently, they behave differently, and so on. Same with grebes, if you are familiar with grebes (or even if you are not). "Water birds," like "raptors" is a grouping based on behavior, rather than taxonomy. "Water birds" includes waterfowl, loons, grebes, shorebirds, *pelagic* (oceanic) species, and others.

» **Owls (Strigiformes):** You recognize owls when you see them, right? Owls have a disproportionately big, round head. They have a flatter face than most birds, and proportionally bigger eyes — eyes that face forward rather than toward the sides.

Here's a tidbit you probably don't know: On each foot, all owls have two toes that point forward, one that points backward, and one toe — the outside one (also known as the pinky) — that is reversible. It can point forward or backward depending on whether the owl is perching, hunting, carrying prey, or eating. On top of these visible characteristics, the DNA of all owls is similar. That is what makes an owl an owl. If a bird has all of these characteristics, it belongs in the owl order, Strigiformes.

» **Pigeons and Doves (Columbiformes):** If you see a pigeon or a dove you know what it is because, compared with most other birds, it has a small head and a plump body, short legs, a relatively long tail, and a distinctive bopping gait as it walks on the ground, which it often does.

» **Perching birds (Passeriformes):** Many of the birds that visit backyards and bird feeders are passerines, including jays, American robins, bluebirds, northern cardinals, finches, nuthatches, chickadees, wrens, sparrows, and so on. All of those birds are in the order Passeriformes.

This group is more complex than others. If you have a book version of a field guide, the first 20-some orders of birds take up the first half. The final order, Passeriformes, takes up nearly all of the second half of the book! In fact, half of the species of birds in Canada and the U.S. are passerines, also known as perching birds. It's the largest and arguably the most diverse order of birds on Earth. All passerines have four toes, three of which point forward and one that points backward.

TECHNICAL STUFF

The term "songbird" is sometimes used interchangeably with "perching bird," but that's not quite right. A few pages back, we noted that nearly all birds have a vocal organ called a syrinx. All passerines have a syrinx, but not all passerines are songbirds. If you want more information on this, it's in Taxonomy 102, below. In your field guide, if you scroll through the screens or leaf through the pages, passerines immediately follow parrots. All the birds in the front of the field guide up through the end of parrots are technically not perching birds, although most of them do perch! Perching alone does not make a bird a passerine.

THE ORDER OF FIELD GUIDES

The arrangement of field guides follows the taxonomic order of birds. The first order listed is the waterfowl. If you need to identify a duck, look for it in the beginning of your field guide. After the waterfowl come chicken-like birds, such as grouse, quail, and pheasants. Next come the grebes. The first half of the book is mostly (but not entirely) water birds. If you become familiar with the arrangement of your field guide, it will save you time as you flip pages or scroll screens to find a mystery bird.

In the middle of your field guide you'll find woodpeckers. Just before woodpeckers are kingfishers, and before kingfishers, hummingbirds. Just after woodpeckers are falcons, then parrots. And the remainder of the field guide is passerines. You don't have to memorize the order of bird orders, but, for example, knowing that gulls and hawks are in the first half of the guide will narrow your search.

All in the families

King Philip Came Over . . . For = Family.

Within orders are families of birds. Some orders, such as passerines, include numerous families. Some orders have only one family. Once again, please see the online cheat sheet for a list of all the orders and families of birds found in Canada and the U.S. (except Hawaii). (Sorry, Hawaii.) Very few people, even the best bird watchers in North America, have memorized the names of all 80 or so families, but strong birders are familiar with the common names of all of them. There's no rush to do that.

Notice that ducks, geese, and swans are not only in the same order (Anseriformes) but they're also in the same family (Anatidae). Swifts and hummingbirds are in the same order (Caprimulgiformes) but not the same family (Apodidae and Trochilidae, respectively). Same with gulls and sandpipers: Both are Charadriiformes, but sandpipers are in the family Scolopacidae, while gulls are in Laridae. Cranes and herons aren't in the same family — or even the same order!

Finches aren't sparrows, and mockingbirds aren't thrushes (even though they are sometimes called "mimic thrushes"), but all of those are in various families within the order of perching birds, Passeriformes. Birds within each family are pretty similar, and families within an order are similar, too.

Note that family names all have the suffix -*idae*, which is pronounced "eh day." Bird groups ending with -*idae* are families.

Earlier in the chapter we discussed a few examples of bird orders (waterfowl; owls; pigeons and doves; and perching birds). Let's look at a few bird families.

>> **Anatidae** is the family of waterfowl: ducks, geese, and swans. In the U.S. and Canada, it is the only family within the order Anseriformes, but there are two other families of waterfowl elsewhere in the world. Anatidae are unique among birds by having reproductive anatomy similar to mammals. Other birds, both male and female, have one waste-elimination and reproductive orifice called a cloaca. Sex is a quick "cloacal kiss" in which sperm passes from the male to the female. Not so with Anatidae, though. Male ducks, geese, and swans have testes and a corkscrew-shaped penis. Their mates have a spiraling vagina. And that's as far as we're going to take this topic. The point is, ducks, geese, and swans have common characteristics (and DNA) that make them one family: Anatidae.

>> **Apodidae** is the family of swifts. Its name is interesting. The prefix *a* can mean "without," as in *asymmetry* (without symmetry). The root *pod* means "foot," as in podiatrist. So *apod* means "without feet." Centuries ago, the earliest taxonomists believed that swifts didn't have feet! After all, swifts don't — can't — perch on horizontal surfaces; they are either in flight or clinging to vertical walls. They do have tiny feet, though. New bird watchers can easily confuse swifts and swallows in flight. They both flutter with long, thin wings. But swifts and swallows are not close cousins; they're in separate families, and even separate orders. Swifts aren't passerines (perching birds), but swallows are. You've probably seen swallows resting on a wire, but you'll never see swifts on a wire — they can't perch!

>> **Gruidae** is the family of cranes. Cranes have proportionally small heads, long, straight bills, long necks, heavy bodies, and drooping feathers that look like a "bustle" above the tail. (These are actually upper tail coverts, which cover the base of the tail feathers.) When cranes fly, their necks stretch straight out. Their preferred habitat is grassland or shallow water. In North America, most cranes are migratory and travel in large, noisy, V-shaped formations. Courtship involves an elaborate dance, with both male and female leaping into the air, flapping their wings, and stomping. Cranes are in the same order (Gruiformes) as coots and rails (Rallidae) and limpkin (Aramidae). You will not be quizzed on this.

>> **Ardeidae** is the family of herons, egrets, and bitterns: long-legged waders with long, pointed bills and long necks. They are dependent upon shallow water — whether fresh, brackish, or saltwater. In flight and often while resting, their necks curve back into an *S* shape, unlike cranes, and they are not known to dance. This family is in the order Pelicaniformes, along with pelicans (Pelecanidae) and ibises and spoonbills (Threskiornithidae).

Take a look at Figure 4-1 and note the differences between herons and cranes. The next time you see a three-foot-tall, long-legged gray bird with a long bill, you'll be able to make an educated guess as to whether it is a great blue heron or a sandhill crane.

Courtesy of Bruce Wunderlich

Now for some examples of families of passerines (Passeriformes), the most complex order, the second half of the field guide.

» **Tyrannidae** is the family of flycatchers, including phoebes, pewees, kingbirds, and empids. (Empids? Hold that thought.)

Globally, this family includes more species than any other. Flycatchers are primarily insectivores, and many zero in on flying insects by perching on a branch, sallying off to nab a tasty morsel in midair, and then returning to the same branch. Several birds in this family are named for their vocalizations, including pewees, phoebes, and kiskadees.

» **Corvidae** is the family of crows, ravens, magpies, and jays. Corvids are among the most intelligent of birds: some can make and use tools for foraging, some can recognize individual human faces, some can mimic human speech, and all have an excellent memory, especially for where they have cached food. Corvids are large relative to most passerines, with sturdy, straight, relatively long bills, and round-tipped wings. Males and females appear similar. ***Note:*** Although North American crows and ravens are black birds, they are not blackbirds (Icteridae).

» **Paridae** is the family of chickadees and titmice. The common name of this family is *parid* or *tit*. All birds in this family are small but plump, many with relatively large heads and small, strong, bills. They nest in cavities (holes in trees or human-provided nest boxes). Most parids are relatively trusting of humans — sharing our yards, visiting bird feeders, or even accepting seeds directly from a hand.

» **Icteridae** is the family of blackbirds, orioles, and meadowlarks. Male and female icterids are often dissimilar, with males being large and often more brightly colored than their mates. All have sharply pointed, conical bills, but of varying lengths. It was noted above that although crows and ravens are black birds, they are not Icteridae (blackbirds). Conversely, meadowlarks and orioles are blackbirds (Icteridae) but they are not black birds. Grackles, however, are both black birds and blackbirds!

» **Parulidae** is the family of wood-warblers, which is different from Old World warblers. For convenience, we'll just call Parulidae "warblers." Warblers are small, active birds with pointed beaks. Most species are highly migratory, and most migrate at night! Many are brightly colored, but those that nest on the ground have camouflaging plumage. Most warblers are highly insectivorous, especially when feeding their young, but many also eat fruit. Especially during breeding season, warblers are highly vocal, with distinctive, mostly memorable songs. One would think that being warblers, this family of birds would have the most melodious songs, but that distinction (arguably) goes to Turdidae, the family of thrushes.

Genus is good (but not necessary to know)

For Taxonomy 101, the groupings order and family are helpful for purposes of narrowing your search for an ID on an unfamiliar bird. Within families, the next grouping is genus.

We Interrupt King Philip's Adventures for a Discussion of Nomenclature

TIP

Nomenclature? Nomenclature is how organisms are named, usually referring to the scientific name. Birds (and other organisms) have unique, official, two-part, scientific names (binomial nomenclature), composed of the animal's genus and species. (We'll get to species soon!)

American goldfinch, yellowbird, wild canary, *jilguero Yanqui*, *jilguerito amarillo*, *jilguerito canario*, and *chardonneret jaune* all refer to the same species. Its scientific name in all languages is *Spinus tristis*; its official English common name in the U.S. and Canada is American goldfinch. Its colloquial names here include yellowbird and wild canary. The others are common or colloquial names in Spanish and French. Scientific names are italicized (as are words in other languages), and the official common names of birds are set by the American Ornithological Society. The American goldfinch is in the genus *Spinus*, along with Lawrence's goldfinches, lesser goldfinches, pine siskins, and several other bird species not found in the U.S. or Canada. If you look up the scientific names of those species, you'll see that they all begin with *Spinus*.

House finches and purple finches are in a different genus, *Haemorhous*. The scientific name for the house finch is *Haemorhous mexicanus*, and the scientific name for the purple finch is *Haemorhous purpureus*.

REMEMBER

A bird's genus is part of its scientific name. Birds within a taxonomic family are similar, but birds within a genus are even more similar. As your birding skills advance, you might notice that, for example, the white-crowned sparrow and the white-throated sparrow are more similar to each other than they are to song sparrows (even though all three are in the sparrow family, Passerellidae). If so, you're noticing differences at the genus level. White-throated and white-crowned sparrows are in the genus *Zonotrichia*, while the song sparrow is in the genus *Melospiza*. There is no need for you to remember these genus names.

Within the flycatcher family (Tyrannidae) is the genus *Empidonax*, and birds in this genus are called empids. These birds look nearly identical and are often distinguished only by geography, habitat, or vocalization. During spring or fall migration (when birds can be found in many locations and habitats), if an empid is silent it is nearly impossible to identify it.

There are ten empid flycatcher species in Canada and the U.S., and they're challenging to tell apart. Birders often just call them *empids*. That is one genus worth knowing.

A beginning birder does not need to know whether a northern parula is in the genus *Oreothlypis*, *Setophaga*, or *Vermivora*, but if you get serious with this hobby, you might realize that birds within each of those warbler genera have similar bill shapes and tail lengths. Oops! TMI.

Enough about genus. We've accidentally dipped our toes into Taxonomy 102. Sorry.

Finally, the S-word: Sex, salad, spaghetti, <u>species</u>

Most birders enjoy seeing new species. For some, adding new species to their life list (of species) is an important goal of bird watching. That means we need to define species, and it ain't easy.

It would be so helpful if we could define species as "a group of organisms consisting of individuals capable of interbreeding and producing fertile offspring." Unfortunately, it's just not that simple.

Birds of different but related species often mate with each other where their breeding ranges overlap, and some even produce fertile offspring. For example, black-capped and Carolina chickadees often pair up, and their offspring can mate successfully with either parent species or with other hybrids. So, does that mean that black-capped and Carolina species are really just one species? No, even though they are similar in appearance. It is only where their ranges overlap that these two species interbreed.

American black ducks have mated with mallards so often and for so long that nearly all American black ducks have mallard genes. But they're separate species, right? Yes.

Golden-winged and blue-winged warblers really don't look much alike, but they are in the same genus, and they frequently interbreed. Their offspring bear the field marks of both parents and can breed with either species or other hybrids. This happens so commonly that there are names for these hybrids: Lawrence's warbler and Brewster's warbler. So, do the hybrids count on one's life list? Well, you make the rules for your own list, but the American Birding Association and eBird do not count hybrids as species.

Various gull species hybridize, as do some ducks, warblers, hummingbirds, and others. But the two species most likely to hybridize 1) usually have overlapping ranges during breeding season, and 2) are genetically (and therefore taxonomi-cally) similar — that is, related. Most commonly, hybrids occur within the same genus, but not always.

Charles Darwin's birds

If you ever have the chance to visit the Galapagos Islands, go! Odds are high that you will find both mockingbirds and finches there, birds that inspired Charles Darwin to propose that a species, when geographically isolated from its kin, evolves in different ways to produce new species better adapted to its environ-ment. There are four endemic species of mockingbirds on the islands and 18 or so endemic species of Darwin's finches. (*Endemic* means found in the wild there and nowhere else.) Darwin noticed that the mockingbirds look very similar to each other, and also to the Chilean mockingbird, a species he encountered in South America. He proposed that the four mockingbird species found on the Galapagos Islands share a common ancestor, but because of geographic isolation, adapted to their new habitats and, thousands of years later, evolved into distinct species.

Same thing with the finches of the Galapagos Islands (which actually are tanagers, not finches, but for this discussion, that's beside the point). (See Figure 4-2.) The thing is, this demonstration of evolution is still happening! In 2017, researchers published a report of two species of Darwin's finches mating, the first such matchup on record, on a particularly remote island in the archipelago. The offspring were fertile, distinct from their parents, and they interbred. The researchers concluded that creation of a new species can occur in as little as two generations. Birds (and other organisms) are continuing to adapt and evolve, and that's part of the reason that it's so challenging to define *species*.

FIGURE 4-2: An illustration depicting several Darwin's finches.

1. Geospiza magnirostris.
3. Geospiza parvula.
2. Geospiza fortis.
4. Certhidea olivasea.

Lumps and splits

While introducing taxonomy and explaining why it's worth understanding the basics, we mentioned that once upon a time, Baltimore orioles and Bullock's orioles were considered separate species: The Baltimore resides in the East, and the Bullock's in the West. But they hybridize where their breeding ranges overlap, so in 1983 they were officially reclassified (also known as "lumped") into one species: the northern oriole. Birders who keep a life list had to erase those two species and replace them with one. It made them sad to see their life list shrink. But in 1995, ornithologists realized that even though these two species hybridize, they're genetically distinct. The northern oriole was split into its original two species, and bird listers got their species tally restored. That made them happy.

Since North American birds were initially cataloged centuries ago, there were two species of crossbills: white-winged and red. (Crossbills are really cool birds, by the way.) Then, a few years ago, somebody noticed that red crossbills in one county of

Idaho have a song that is different from other red crossbills in the neighborhood. The bill is a little bit thicker, too. Furthermore, most red crossbills are notoriously nomadic — but not the crossbills in Cassia County, Idaho. They never leave home, and they don't interbreed with the nomadic, thinner-billed red crossbills that sing differently. Well, as of 2017, there are officially three crossbill species in North America: white-winged, red, and Cassia.

But there's more! The Cassia crossbill was just one of ten recognized types of red crossbill. Someday there might be even more species of crossbill in North America!

Such lumps and splits happen surprisingly frequently. The red-shafted flicker and the yellow-shafted flicker were lumped into the northern flicker. Myrtle warbler and Audubon's warbler were lumped into the yellow-rumped warbler — and it is possible that it will be split one of these years. Hoary and common redpoll were lumped in 2024.

REMEMBER

All of this is to say that not only is *species* difficult to define, the number of bird species changes frequently as evolution results in new species, and as new species are recognized hiding within other species.

So, how many bird species are there in the world, or even in the U.S. and Canada? In the same way that it's challenging to define *species*, it's also difficult to count them. Different taxonomic systems provide different answers. Does the pink-footed goose or Steller's sea-eagle count as North American species? Both species have shown up in recent years along the coasts of southeastern Canada and New England, far from their normal breeding and wintering ranges. What about the non-native birds that breed here, but only in the past decade or so? Anyway, Table 4-1 gives our best guesstimate of where things stand in 2025.

TABLE 4-1

Bird Groups by Number

	North America	Globally
Bird orders	23	41
Bird families	about 80	250ish
Bird genera	roughly 350	roughly 2,045
Bird species	roughly 1,000	10,857 (plus 160 extinct)

REMEMBER

Note that other taxonomy systems have different numbers.

Subspecies

Now we're really getting into the weeds, but you should know that *species* isn't the caboose of taxonomy. Many species — especially those with a large geographic range — contain subspecies. The American robin has seven subspecies in various locations. The dark-eyed junco has 15! The song sparrow has 24! Subspecies can look similar or remarkably different, so be prepared for species you are familiar with to look or sound different elsewhere.

Taxonomy 102: We're Not Going There

There's a lot we're not going to cover. The taxonomy we've presented here is a simplified version. We opted against mentioning suborders or superfamilies or clades here (because that would mess up the King Philip mnemonic that you accidentally memorized, and also because it's beyond the basics). You've read all you're going to read about DNA and genetic testing.

TIP

But here's one thing that will help you use your field guide more efficiently. Since Passeriformes is such a huge order with so many families, it's helpful to get a handle on the arrangement of those families so you can find them more efficiently in your field guide.

A few pages back you found out that not all passerines are songbirds. Simplifying a bit, passerines can be grouped as *oscine* or *suboscine*. Oscines have a complex syrinx that allows them to make complex vocalizations. Suboscines' syrinxes have a different design, and birds in this group just aren't songbirds.

In your field guide, if you scroll or flip halfway through to the order Passeriformes, the first family you'll come to are the suboscines. In Canada and the U.S., that family is Tyrannidae — the tyrant flycatchers, which are known for relatively simple, not very musical vocalizations that include phrases like *pee-a-wee*, *fee-bee*, *kiss-ka-dee*, *che-beck*, *fitz-bew*, *threeep*, *quick-three beers*, or *Jose Maria* — not nearly as musical or complex as most of the oscines, which are songbirds. Remember, there are more species in the family Tyrannidae — roughly 1,000 globally — than in any other bird family. They are all passerines, but they are not songbirds. So, the first group of passerines are the flycatchers.

After the flycatchers come the songbirds. First, you'll come to the shrikes, which are oscines even though their vocalizations aren't very elaborate. There are only three shrike species in North America, so you might not even notice that family in your field guide.

The third family of passerines, taxonomically, is the vireos, and now we're getting into songbirds that actually have some musical talent —most of them anyhow. After the vireos come the corvids — ravens, crows, and jays.

REMEMBER

If you have a good memory, you can remember the arrangement of more than these four families at the beginning of Passeriformes (flycatchers, shrikes, vireos, and corvids). It's also helpful to remember that toward the end of the field guide you'll find warblers, finches, sparrows, blackbirds, and grosbeaks (including cardinals) but not necessarily in that order because of various taxonomic systems. For most birders, this useful knowledge comes with experience, and not from book learnin'.

TIP

Just as being familiar with the arrangement of bird orders helps you find birds in the first half of your field guide, being familiar with the arrangement of families within passerines will help you narrow your search in the second half.

Now that you've made it to the end of this chapter, you'll be much more efficient and adept at finding birds in your field guide. Just as important, though, you now have a better understanding of bird groups, especially those found in the U.S. and Canada. The next time you find a mystery bird, you'll be prepared to make an educated guess about its taxonomic group and where that group can be found in your field guide.

Chapter **5**

Watching Bird Behavior

Anything that a bird does can be considered part of its behavior, and when you think about it, birds do a lot. They fly, sing, forage for food, perform mating displays, select mates, breed, fight, build nests, lay eggs, preen, bathe, mob predators, and do lots of other stuff.

Bird behavior provides you, the bird watcher, with two primary things: entertainment and information. The entertainment part is self-evident: it's neat to watch birds do their thing. The information aspect of bird behavior provides clues to a bird's identity and gives us insight into their lives.

Viewing the Variety of Bird Behaviors

Bird behavior, at its most basic, is simply a bird being a bird. Anything and everything a bird does is bird behavior. Even a bird, say a song sparrow, sitting still for a moment on a sun-drenched perch on a chilly spring morning — apparently doing nothing — provides an example of bird behavior. The bird might be sunbathing, catching some solar warmth, just as humans do on a sunny day.

Birds behave more like humans than you may think. Some form reasonably loyal pairs between males and females (though studies show that in most species there is considerable avian hanky-panky), raise mostly helpless young (babies that cannot immediately feed and fend for themselves), defend their home territories, have food preferences, and so on. Some ornithologists speculate that it's because birds form loyal pair bonds that we humans are so fascinated with their lives. If you've ever watched a pair of birds nest in your backyard, you'll know what we mean. You get pretty attached to those birds. They become *your* birds!

Some common (and easily observed) examples of bird behavior include foraging, bathing and preening, singing, territoriality, courtship, nest building, roosting, flocking behavior, and migration. Of course, you can observe many, many other aspects of bird behavior.

Figuring out why birds behave as they do

Bird behavior is easy to observe once you realize that birds are always doing something interesting and settle down to watch. When you see a bird's activity that attracts you, try to figure out what the behavior is. Birds are not aimless creatures. Everything they do has a reason behind it. The fun is in trying to figure out *why* a bird is doing what it's doing.

A bird's behavior is what allows it to survive life in a harsh environment. Don't you wonder how birds survive in extreme weather? How would *you* like to spend all day in the freezing rain and then have to keep warm all night as it all freezes into ice? Under such conditions, birds change their behavior to improve their chances of survival:

>> They move around less to save energy.

>> They spend more time at a reliable food source, whether natural or artificial (such as a bird feeder).

>> They puff up their feathers to trap and retain body heat.

>> They seek shelter.

These changes in behavior are not decisions they make; these behavior changes are instinctual. They're a response to the stimulus of the weather.

Assessing bird intelligence

You've no doubt heard the phrase *bird-brained* used to describe someone or something that's not very smart, or that's even pretty stupid. Having raised and rehabilitated nearly 30 different species of common birds, Julie can tell you that birds have a lot more going on in those little craniums than we ever could suspect. That said, a house finch would likely fare poorly in a battle of wits against a raven.

Although not all birds receive an equal share in the smarts department, designating one species as dull while another is smart is not really accurate. What's most impressive about birds is their ability to learn, retain information, and alter their behavior accordingly. In other words, a bird is exactly as smart as it needs to be. A house finch has only to find seeds, pair up, and raise a family, while a raven takes sustenance from a nearly unlimited range of plant and animal sources and has an intricate social hierarchy to boot. It needs complex problem-solving capacity, while a house finch doesn't.

Mourning doves may seem stupid when they build a flimsy stick nest on a slender branch high in a tree. The wind blows, the eggs fall through the bottom of the nest, and the female dove loses her investment in one gust of wind. Because these doves are so prolific (and capable of nesting in any month of the year), they really have no reason to alter their behavior. The female dove will just build another flimsy nest and lay more eggs. It may seem that the doves lack insight, but it's the way evolution has shaped their breeding biology. The system they've evolved works for them. Try many times with a limited number of eggs — two to a clutch — and you're going to be successful.

Ravens, on the other hand, are champion problem-solvers, showing insightful behavior and a keen sense of cause and effect. Consequently, they've been studied by ornithologists and behaviorists for a long time. One particular study was conducted to see if ravens could solve a problem:

> A hunk of suet was suspended by a string from a horizontal branch. Ravens attempted to get at the suet, which was suspended far enough below the perch to prevent the ravens' reaching it by simply leaning down. Because ravens are large and heavy birds, hovering to get the food wasn't an option. Before long, several ravens discovered how to pull the string up in stages by holding the slack string under their feet. (See Figure 5-1.) Once a raven solved this problem, it had no trouble repeating the process when faced with the situation again. Dummy strings that had no suet attached were largely ignored. And ravens observe each other solving problems and copy successful behaviors. They have the rudiments of culture.

Such trial-and-error and observational learning is extremely valuable to birds in the wild. This process is how birds come to know about predators, prey and food, and other skills necessary for survival.

Some birds can count, which helps them keep track of the eggs in their nests. Other birds that hide food in secret places, such as jays, crows, titmice, and chickadees, can remember the location of these caches months later, when they return to consume the food. Researchers have documented that such food-storing species actually produce more brain cells in autumn, as if they're making room in their memory banks for all the additional location information! Humans often wish we could add to our brain cells, but, sadly, they seem to diminish with time.

FIGURE 5-1:
A common raven, pulling up its food reward in stages.

REMEMBER

Birds are incredibly adaptable creatures who can change their behavior to suit a situation and thus enhance their chances of survival. To us, that equates with intelligence.

Interesting bird behavior is happening right now, outside your windows, in your own backyard. The following sections describe some of the most easily observed, everyday examples of bird behavior.

Foraging

Foraging is the act of finding food. All birds have a distinct means of getting food. Robins scamper along on the lawn looking for earthworms, swallows swoop through the air catching flying insects, and woodpeckers hitch up tree trunks and branches looking for insects to excavate from under bark or deep in the wood.

Birds can be generalists in their foraging, looking anywhere and everywhere for food. Good examples of generalists are European starlings and ring-billed gulls, both of which can be found seeking food in a variety of places, from shorelines to city parks to fast-food-restaurant dumpsters.

Birds can also be very specific in their foraging techniques. Sapsuckers have an interesting foraging method. These woodpeckers drill a series of holes in tree trunks or branches. These holes cause the tree to produce protective sap, which oozes out of the holes in small amounts. (It's the same concept that humans use to tap maple trees to make maple syrup.) Later, the sapsuckers return to consume the sap. Other birds have learned about sapsucker holes, too. Many warblers, hummingbirds, and other small songbirds visit the holes for sap and to dine upon the insects that the sweet, sticky sap attracts.

Even closely related bird species can have very different foraging behavior. Take pelicans, for example. White pelicans forage cooperatively in groups, floating along the water's surface, herding fish in front of them, and scooping them up in their pouched bills. Brown pelicans, on the other hand, forage by diving into the water from a height. They may dive in loosely grouped flocks, but each individual is seeking its own targeted fish. If you've been to the beach in the southern portion of North America, you've probably seen brown pelicans flying high above the water looking for fish. When a fish is spotted, a brown pelican wheels and dives headlong into the water.

Singing and Sound-Making

Bird sounds play an important role in courtship and territoriality among birds (which we discuss later in this chapter). Although the males do the singing in some, but not all, bird species (to attract a female as a mate), all birds make other sounds, too, such as chip notes, alarm notes, scolding notes, and even non-vocal sounds such as wing whistling (a sound made by air passing through a flying bird's wing feathers). If you've ever heard a mourning dove launch suddenly into flight (as when scared), you've probably heard the twittering sound the dove's wings make.

Some wren species keep the sexes equal when it comes to vocalizations by performing duet singing. These songs, performed in tandem from separate locations, are thought to help maintain the pair's bond. Wrens also have many contact calls — short whistles or peeps that serve to say:

"Are you okay? Where are you now?"

"I'm fine, dear. I'm over here eating spider eggs in the wood pile."

Sort of like calling home just to check in.

Vocal mimicry among birds is a fascinating thing. One of North America's best mimics is the northern mockingbird, which has been recorded imitating the songs and calls of more than 30 other bird species within a ten-minute span. If you have mockingbirds near you, you may have been lucky enough to hear the male sing his full repertoire all night long during a full moon. (If you're a light sleeper, this can be pretty annoying.) Mockers are thought to imitate the songs of other birds as a means of fueling their need for continuous song, which is part of their intensely territorial behavior. They borrow bits and snippets of other birds' songs and blab day and night. If you watch a singing mocker long enough, you may see him catapult vertically from his perch, fluttering back down on flashing black-and-white wings, never missing a beat in the music.

Another neat example of birds using vocalizations is the blue jay's crafty method of clearing the bird feeder. We've seen this at our feeders. A jay (or several jays) sees a feeding station crowded with birds. Instead of flying in and muscling its way to the seed, one of the jays gives an alarm call. Some jays even imitate the scream of a hawk. The effect this has on the smaller feeder visitors is akin to that of a person yelling "Fire!" in a packed movie theater. The little birds scram, and the jays take over the feeder. How's that for bird brains?

For more information on bird sounds, see Chapter 6.

Bathing/Preening

If you were to go without a bath for a few days — make that a *phew* — or few weeks, your family and friends would start making comments about it, such as "Plumbing not working at your house?" If a bird were to avoid bathing for the same amount of time, it may not survive. The personal hygiene of birds is a matter of life and death. Feathers that aren't clean don't function efficiently, either in flight or in protecting the body from weather and wear and tear. And let's not forget looks. Gaudy-plumaged males need to look good if they hope to attract a mate.

Several kinds of bathing behavior exist among birds, but the most common are water bathing, dust bathing, and sunbathing.

Water bathing

Water bathing is the most common behavior, and it can be easily observed if you offer water to birds in your yard. (See Figure 5-2; for additional information on bird baths, see Chapter 7.)

Birds don't bathe like humans do. Most birds that bathe in water prefer to wade into water that's a few inches deep and then dip their heads and flutter their wings to splash the water onto their bodies. After bathing for a few minutes and getting thoroughly soaked, a bird flies to a safe perch to preen.

FIGURE 5-2:
An American robin, luxuriating in the bath.

Preening is just like a bird combing its hair, but instead of using a comb or brush, birds use their bills. Preening smooths down the feathers and feather edges and removes dirt and parasites from the feathers. Preening also allows the bird to distribute natural oil over its feathers. This oil, which comes from a gland located at the base of the tail, helps give feathers durability and a certain amount of water resistance.

REMEMBER

Birds don't rely exclusively on our bird baths for bathing. They use any shallow or splashing source of water, including puddles, ponds, sprinklers, and even the water caught in leaves after a rainstorm. In fact, many bird species use a rainstorm as an opportunity to take a shower.

Dust bathing

Certain species of birds, such as quail, pheasants, grouse, and turkeys, prefer to dust bathe, using fine dust or loose dirt to help keep their feathers clean. Among the smaller songbirds, sparrows and brown thrashers are particularly enthusiastic dust bathers.

"But how can they get clean in the dirt?" you ask. Ornithological studies have shown that dust bathing improves feather fluffiness and also discourages or dislodges parasites, along with reducing excess moisture and oil.

Julie reflects:

> On our farm, I love to walk along the dirt road to the well during hot summer afternoons. If I'm lucky, I'll see dust-bathing birds in action. The road is dried red clay, which is very fine-grained — excellent for dust bathing. Our wild turkeys love

to scratch out a shallow depression in the roadbed. The clay cooperates by breaking down into a fine dusty powder quite easily. The birds then fluff their feathers until the dust thoroughly covers them. We find dozens of molted feathers near these dust wallows every few days. Other birds take advantage of these wallows to dust bathe, too, including brown thrashers, Carolina wrens, cardinals, blue jays, and even indigo buntings.

Sunbathing

Birds also enjoy bathing in bright, hot sunlight (just as humans do). If you watch some of your familiar backyard birds during warm, sunny weather, particularly following a cloudy, rainy, or cool spell, you may see this behavior.

A sunbathing bird doesn't get out the shades and suntan lotion. Instead, it spreads its wings and tail and raises its feathers so that the sunlight strikes its bare skin in several places. Sunbathing birds often sprawl on the ground, looking dazed, their bills agape. Humans theorize about what birds get from this; these theories include increased vitamin production from the sunlight and a benefit in driving parasites from the bird's back to its breast, where these pests can be preened away.

ANTING

One fascinating and poorly understood behavior is called *anting*. There are two types of anting: active anting and passive anting. In active anting, birds crush ants with their bills and wipe the crushed ants through their feathers. It's long been thought that the formic acid produced by the crushed ants helps the birds ward off feather mites, lice, and other parasites. In passive anting, a bird lies down on the ground on or near an anthill, with wings and feathers spread apart, and lets the ants crawl all over it. Occasionally, a bird engaging in passive anting will crush and preen with an ant.

Birds Julie has observed anting enter a slightly stuporous state and often topple over with a glassy look in their eyes. Perhaps they are getting a contact high from the formic acid. Worldwide, more than 200 bird species have been recorded as engaging in anting behavior. Among the North American species that engage in anting are American robins, American crows, blue jays, northern cardinals, evening grosbeaks, and purple finches. Black-throated green, bay-breasted, and blackpoll warblers come to Julie's birches every fall to pick ants off the trunks and party a bit. It's a yearly phenomenon she looks forward to seeing.

Dating and Mating: Courtship

Remember your first date? Remember wanting to look your best and hoping you didn't say or do anything stupid? Well, looking and sounding their best is part of bird courtship, too.

Bird courtship is a spring phenomenon across most of North America, except for the southernmost reaches where the climate is warm year-round. Most of what birds do in the spring involves courtship, either directly or indirectly, including setting up territories, singing, performing visual displays, and taking off in hot pursuit.

Male ruby-throated hummingbirds perform an interesting courtship display flight. When they locate a female hummer perched nearby, the males zoom above her in a swooping, U-shaped arc. This is called the *pendulum display* because the pattern resembles the path of a clock's pendulum. During the display, the male chatters, his beating wings buzz, and he positions himself so the tiny feathers on his *gorget* (throat) catch the sunlight and show off his ruby-colored throat to the watching female. At the end of the flight he may perform a *shuttle display*, zipping side to side directly in front of the perched female, his ruby gorget flared. (See Figure 5-3.) Now that's sexy!

FIGURE 5-3: The shuttle display flight of a male ruby-throated hummingbird, performed after the pendulum flight.

Have you ever noticed how, on warm days during the late winter and early spring, the birds seem to get much more active? This activity is caused by the birds' raised hormone levels, which are affected by warmer temperatures and increased sunlight. It's a kind of avian spring fever.

Signs of spring on Julie's farm are first apparent in early February when the red-shouldered hawks begin forming pairs. American woodcocks begin to voice their distinctive, nasal *peent* in the meadow at dusk by mid-February, calling for females. Soon after, the bluebirds begin peeking into their nest boxes, singing and waving their wings in courtship display.

The first things a neotropical migrant songbird (a male yellow warbler, for example) does upon returning to its nesting grounds is select a territory and begin singing. Singing serves to attract a mate and to repel potential challengers for both mate and territory.

REMEMBER

Among some bird species, courtship displays are designed to show off the male's color and markings to his best advantage: The male American redstart fans its wings and tail to show off the bright orange patches that would otherwise be concealed. Male meadowlarks puff out their bright yellow breast feathers and sing from an exposed perch. Even male city pigeons put on a show, bowing, circling, and cooing while fanning their tails and inflating their necks to show off iridescent feathers.

At your backyard feeder, you may observe another type of courtship behavior, especially if you have cardinals. The male cardinal selects a seed (it has to be just right) and feeds it to his mate in what is sometimes called a *courtship kiss*. When receiving the seed, the female cardinal quivers her wings in excitement, just like a fledgling bird begging for food. The male cardinal continues to feed his mate while she incubates her eggs, as do many male songbirds.

COURTSHIP OF THE TIMBERDOODLE

If you know the time and place in spring to look, the courtship display of the male American woodcock is one of the most charming displays of all North American birds. Beginning as early as February, these comical-looking birds (which are also known as timberdoodles and bogsuckers) seek out brushy meadows and old fields from which to launch their nightly display flights, as shown in the figure.

Just as dusk turns to darkness, these portly woodland shorebirds begin to call — a short, nasal *peent!* After several minutes of *peent*ing, the male woodcock begins a circular, ascending flight over his chosen display area. As he flies, his wings whistle with each beat, a sound caused by specially evolved, narrowed primary feathers on the front edge of each wing. At the top of his ascent, the woodcock begins a freefall toward the ground, his wings whirring, all the while voicing a liquid warble. No one is sure how a woodcock manages to voice both a *peent* and a warble, but he does! Near the ground, the male swoops to a soft landing and begins the peenting process all over again.

This entire display is done to attract the attention of any female woodcock that happens to be listening. The male mates with as many females as will visit him during his spring displaying time.

TIP

If you ever get the chance to witness the courtship display of a grouse or prairie-chicken, jump on it! The males of these chickenlike birds fluff up their feathers, strike a crazy pose, inflate colorful air sacs on their breast, make strange sounds, stomp their feet, dance, and even fight, just to attract a potential mate.

Nest Building

Birds can be classified by their nest types:

>> **Ground nesters** make their nests on the ground; some come up with something that looks like an actual nest, some use just a shallow scrape, and some don't improve the nest site at all. Nighthawks, killdeer, and terns build no nests at all; rather, they rely on the natural camouflage of their speckled eggs to protect the nest, which may be no more than a shallow scrape in rocky or sandy soil. Other ground-nesting birds are turkeys, grouse, most ducks, larks, towhees, some warblers, and most shorebirds.

>> **Open-cup nesters** create the stereotypical bird's nest woven out of plant materials. Most North American bird species construct open-cup nests. Examples of cup nesters are thrushes, most warblers, tanagers, most flycatchers, sparrows, and hummingbirds.

>> **Platform nesters** include crows, hawks, and eagles that construct flat platforms of sticks with a lined cup at the center.

>> **Cavity nesters** use hollow, enclosed areas, such as a hollow tree, for nesting. Woodpeckers create their own cavities by excavating holes in trees. The excavation of a nest hole is an important part of woodpecker courtship, so woodpeckers create new cavities each spring for nesting. Old woodpecker nests are used in subsequent years by many other cavity-nesting species, such as titmice, chickadees, bluebirds, great crested flycatchers, some ducks, and owls.

Nests aren't bedrooms, for the most part; they're nurseries. With a few exceptions, almost all birds build structures for nesting, often using specific materials. Robins use mud in their nests, chickadees use moss, tree swallows use straw and feathers, gnatcatchers and hummingbirds use lichens and spiderwebs, while chipping sparrows line their grass nests with hair.

If you visit Florida in late winter, especially in the Everglades or another very birdy area, you'll see herons, egrets, and even ospreys flying through the air carrying sticks and branches in their beaks or feet. They're not spring cleaning! They're nest-building, a behavior that's a big part of the courtship and bonding of these species.

Nest-building behavior can include many activities. Gathering of materials, such as grass or sticks, site selection by mated pairs, and the actual building of the nest are all readily observable examples of this behavior. Find a bird that you know nests in your part of the continent and watch its activity during the spring months. See if you can pick up clues that tell you if it's nesting in your immediate area.

WEIRD NEST MATERIALS

Here are some examples of unusual nest construction and unusual materials used by birds in their nests:

- **Great crested flycatchers,** which are cavity-nesters, often place shed snake skins trailing out of the nest hole. Scientists theorize that this may ward off potential avian predators or nest hole competitors. Great cresteds may use cellophane or even fiberglass insulation if snakeskins are scarce.

- **Rock pigeon:** A nest near a metal factory was composed entirely of metal shavings.

- **A mourning dove** nest was found to be made of multicolored electrical wire.

- **Ravens** have constructed nests of barbed wire pieces!

- **Chimney swifts** use their own saliva, which dries like shiny lacquer, to bind their twig nests to the inside walls of chimneys. They break the short twigs off by grabbing them with their bill while in flight!

- **Baltimore orioles** make a baglike nest of plant fibers suspended from a thin branch, sometimes over water. This thwarts most climbing predators.

- **Belted kingfishers** excavate a hole extending as much as six feet straight back into a riverbank or earthen hillside. Their chicks' droppings whitewash its interior, creating a surprisingly clean, adobe-like surface.

The wooded hillsides on Julie's farm are home to several pairs of ovenbirds, a ground-nesting warbler that's named for the way its nest is constructed. Ovenbird nests resemble tiny Dutch ovens — a domed cup with a small entrance on one side. (See Figure 5-4.) Ovenbirds build these nests on the ground, often near a woodland path or road. The materials include moss, twigs, dead grasses, rootlets, and animal fur. A roof of dead leaves helps both to conceal the nest on the forest floor and to keep out the rain. Julie watched an ovenbird nest one spring from egg-laying through fledging of the young. She had one tiny window between leaves that allowed her to peek into the domed nest through her 10-power binoculars from 20 feet away. It was such a thrill to see the chicks grow and eventually fledge, without approaching or disturbing them.

WARNING

Always be careful not to leave your scent around nests. Once you stumble upon one, give it a wide berth and resist the urge to look into it, or you may lead predators to the treasure within.

FIGURE 5-4:
An ovenbird at its
Dutch-oven-
shaped nest.

You can watch birds in your yard collect nesting material by offering them short pieces of soft natural fiber, wool, or alpaca fleece. Never offer dryer lint — it absorbs water and can chill eggs and young in the rain. You can scatter nesting material about your yard in obvious places or offer it in a mesh fruit bag or an unused, wire basket suet feeder, and watch the birds investigate.

Female birds are the nest builders in most species, with little or no help from the male. In some species, such as chickadees, titmice, hawks, and eagles, the males help out with the building. House wrens and some other wren species are different in that the males construct several nests from which the females select their favorite for actual use. The females complete the construction and line the nest with soft material.

For more information on providing nest sites for birds, see Chapter 7.

Defending My Space: Territoriality

Much of the same behavior that birds use in courtship (singing and visual displays) is also associated with territoriality — only this behavior is redirected at interlopers, rivals, and even potential predators rather than at potential mates.

REMEMBER

A bird's *territory* is that physical area that it defends against other members of its own species. Bird territories can be defended year-round by nonmigratory birds, such as mockingbirds, or as temporarily as the small spot of ground that a sand-erling defends while feeding along the ocean beach. Territories can range from vast amounts of land to small zones a few feet square.

You're most likely to notice a bird's territorial behavior during the spring and summer breeding season. This is when males compete for mates, for prime territories, and for dominance over rivals with nearby territories.

Examples of territorial behavior include the males' singing from prominent song perches, such as the top of a tree; fighting among rivals along territorial boundaries; chasing interlopers from a territory; and scolding, which is a harsher, less musical vocalization than singing.

Tips for Watching Bird Behavior

If the definition of bird behavior is anything that a bird does, then behavior watching is defined as *watching* anything that a bird does. It doesn't get much simpler than that.

Behavior watching gains popularity with bird watchers as they become more familiar with certain common bird species. Backyard watchers especially enjoy observing the behavior of those species that regularly appear in their yards and at their feeders.

You can easily give behavior watching a try with the next bird you see. Focus your attention on observing what the bird does, then see if you can guess why it's doing what it's doing.

REMEMBER

Birds aren't little people. Although it's both fun and tempting to *anthropomorphize* — attribute human traits, such as feelings of love, joy, hate, and so on, to birds and other non-human creatures — projecting our feelings on a bird can lead us astray. When behavior watching, try not to superimpose your emotional reaction on the bird's behavior choices. Note what they do, guess why they may have done it, and leave your mind open to the possibility of sentient behavior and rational choices. Birds will always surprise us with their ingenuity and intelligence. Consider the Carolina wren that lined the floor of her nest, built in a hanging basket, with scraps of plastic. Did she understand that it would keep the contents dry during regular waterings? Do not dismiss that notion!

SOUND-OUT AT THE BLUEBIRD CORRAL

At her farm, Julie has bluebird boxes on either side of the house. In late February, especially on warm days, the bluebirds really get fired up. The males begin each dawn singing from their favorite song perches, proclaiming to all other male bluebirds within earshot: "This is MY turf. I'm the king of this section. Don't mess with me or my mate. And stay away from this wonderful house over here. We're already in it, and we're not moving. I DARE you to fly across my territory." Sure enough, a male from the other side can't resist a challenge, so he flies across one tiny corner of male #1's territory, singing, "There ain't enough room in this here yard for both of us! Bring it on, if you think you're so tough. I may just fly over and flirt with your mate!"

A fight ensues, and one male wins, which puts the other one in his place until later in the summer, when both pairs breed a second time. By then, a truce has been worked out, and the pairs take turns at the birdbath with nary a turned feather.

When and where to look

Birds are most active during the early morning hours and in the late afternoon, so naturally these are the times when behavior is most evident. But behavior can happen anytime and anywhere. Nearly all owls are most active at night. Their daytime behavior consists of sleeping. In spring and early summer, male song-birds sing periodically through the day, making them pretty easy to observe and to hear.

TIP

We suggest that you start by looking for bird behavior among your backyard birds. Or look at a nearby park, where a heron might be stalking fish along the edge of a pond where ducks are interacting with each other. Even pigeons in the city have amazing and easy-to-observe behaviors, such as courtship, fancy mate-impressing display flights, territorial fights, and a variety of vocalizations. Bird behavior, like birds, is everywhere.

What to look for

Because almost anything that a bird does can be classified as behavior, choose an easy-to-observe bird and watch it for signs of interesting behavior. For example:

>> Birds at rest may engage in preening, sunbathing while sprawled on the ground, or stretching one wing and leg out to the side in a rather balletic pose.

>> Foraging birds use many methods to get food, including gleaning from tree trunks and branches, flycatching, probing in the ground, excavating in wood,

diving into water, hovering, scraping, prying, and even scaring prey into the open by flashing their tail and wing feathers. Mockingbirds often do this wing-flashing behavior on lawns.

>> Birds in flight can exhibit behaviors such as predator evasion, elaborate courtship displays, migration, and territoriality. Mourning doves, which usually flap rapidly, will set their wings in a shallow arc and glide in a circle, staying shakily aloft as long as they can — a courtship display that always generates a double take, because they look so hawklike!

When you see birds in action, ask yourself what it means. Why is the bird doing that? Lots of bird behavior is repetitive, so you may have more than one chance to catch a certain behavior and figure it out for yourself.

REMEMBER

The busiest time of the year for watching bird behavior is the springtime. This is when the migrants return from the tropics, and all the birds, even locally resident species, become extremely active with the onset of the breeding season. The morning is full of birdsong, and the trees and fields in most every greenspace are alive with all kinds of foraging, preening, singing, and chasing behavior. Pick out one bird and try to watch it for as long as possible. You'll get to peek into this one individual bird's world — watch it live its life — while the bird is totally oblivious to you and the human world. Time spent in this way is both incredibly interesting and wonderfully peaceful.

All three of your authors would rather be out there with the birds than sitting at a computer right now — or anytime, really. Julie has set up her WarblerFall fountain right below her studio window, and she is not making this up: A male indigo bunting hopped up and drank from the fountain as she wrote that line! If she can't get to the birds, she gets the birds to come to her.

Do birds just wanna have fun?

We've often been asked by interested behavior watchers if birds ever like to have fun. The answer is both yes and no.

Birds usually do things for a reason. Swallows swooping to catch a falling feather and then flying higher, only to drop it again, might be maneuvering to catch the feather quill first, so they can insert it in the nest. Tree swallow nests lined with more feathers, and thus better insulated, fledge more young, studies have shown. But when you see this feather-playing behavior repeated over and over, it certainly appears that the swallows are having a great time.

Julie recalls watching a young peregrine falcon playing the same game with an unfortunate monarch butterfly in the strong updrafts over cliffs on Martha's Vineyard. It caught, dropped, and recaptured the butterfly a dozen times. She felt sorry for the butterfly but was equally impressed with the behavior of the falcon. Since monarchs aren't on the falcon's menu, it sure looked like play to her. Videos of Australian magpies stealing clothespins, then dangling upside down from a clothesline are hard to dismiss as purposeful behavior.

A number of years ago, we got a letter at *Bird Watcher's Digest* from a reader in Texas. She explained that she and her husband had seen a dark-eyed junco with two heads at their feeders! Somewhat dubious, the staff of *BWD* wrote back asking if she had any photographs. Well, yes, she did, along with several pages of notes on the bird's behavior and general appearance. We published her observations in the magazine. Afterward, we received calls and letters from several ornithologists asking about this bird. No photographs had ever before been published of a living, apparently healthy, two-headed bird. Our subscriber had made ornithological history by closely watching the birds at her backyard feeder!

And that's what makes bird watching great: Citizen science has always played a big part in bird research. Anyone can contribute to growing knowledge about birds simply by being observant. You can find out how to put your observations to work for science in Chapter 19, "Birding That Makes a Difference."

Keeping notes

An interesting part of behavior watching is keeping notes on what you observe. Our columns and articles on bird behavior are among the most avidly read parts of *BWD Magazine.* Readers love to share their observations and ask resulting questions. Over the years, we've gotten some incredible observations, mostly from careful observers who took notes on what they were seeing.

Keeping notes is very simple. Carry a small notebook with you when you plan to watch birds or have the Notes app on your phone handy. When something unusual occurs, you're ready to record your observations while they're still fresh in your mind. Here are some things to consider when recording your observations:

>> What species is the bird?

>> What sex is the bird or birds (if you can tell)?

>> What is the date?

>> What is the time of day or night?

>> What is the bird doing?

>> What do you think is the cause or purpose of the behavior (mating, courtship, foraging, and so on)?

>> Describe the habitat or location in which the behavior is occurring (fruiting tree, deep woods, at the bird feeders, and so on).

>> Make notes about any other factors that may have affected the behavior (weather, contested food source, presence of predators, and so on).

For more information on keeping records of the birds and behavior you see, see Chapter 12. If you enjoy keeping notes on behavior, you'll really enjoy referring to these notes in the future, long after the actual incident has faded from memory. Your behavior notes provide a wealth of information.

Behavior as an ID Tool

The behavior of birds is very useful in determining a bird's identity. Many bird species have distinctive behavior, such as tail wagging or wing flicking; certain styles or patterns of flight; and varied feeding styles, such as probing in the mud or flycatching in midair. And of course, all types of vocalizations can help identify a bird. Even stray chips, cheeps, and scolds are identifiable to species.

TIP

Suppose that you see a bird that you can't identify right away — perhaps it's a life bird for you (one you've never seen before in your life). You can tell it's a small yellowish warbler. It's spring, so you know that warblers are present as they migrate through your area. This warbler-like bird is flitting from low branches to the grassy ground. All the while it's pumping its tail up and down as it forages. You catch a glimpse of a rusty patch on the bird's head just before the bird flies away. You make a mental note about the bird, particularly about the wagging tail. Later, when you look at your field guide, you find several yellowish warblers that can be found in your area in spring, but only one with a rusty cap and a constantly moving tail. It's a palm warbler. Its behavior was the clinching clue in that bird's identification.

REMEMBER

When you see a strange bird, one that's not immediately recognizable to you, look for signs of distinctive behavior, along with the bird's physical field marks. Behavior is a great ID tool, and one many bird watchers forget to use.

Bird behavior keeps veteran bird watchers interested long after they've exhausted the possibilities for seeing new birds very often. If you're interested in finding out more about bird behavior, here are two suggestions:

>> Settle back to watch what a bird is doing at every opportunity. Careful watchers see lots of amazing behavior.

>> If you are able, make a mobile phone video of the behavior in question. The accompanying vocalizations offer great clues to what might be going on. Now you have concrete evidence of what you've observed, and you can bounce it off knowledgeable friends and social media contacts.

As Julie was writing this, two blue-gray gnatcatchers were sprawled out on a mat of dried grass clippings in her raspberry patch, sunning themselves, and that's something you don't get to see every day. Bird watching is like that! The more attention you pay, the more delightful things you'll see.

Chapter **6**

Bird Sounds: News and Entertainment

B irds are very noisy creatures when they want to be. This fact is both good and bad news for you, the bird watcher. The news is good because when a bird is making noise, you can more easily locate it and perhaps identify the bird without needing to see it.

The bad part about bird sounds is that — to the beginner — the vast array of songs and calls made by birds on a spring morning can be unbelievably daunting. Experiencing bird sounds might make you feel like you'll never figure out who's singing what. But take heart! We'll share some tricks of the trade to help you sort things out.

A bird uses two primary senses, sight and sound, to communicate with other birds. *Sight communication* involves colorful plumage and plumage patterns as well as physical movement such as flight displays. *Sound communication* includes the vast array of sounds that birds can make. Most (but not all) of these sounds are vocalizations, which are generically called *bird song*.

In this chapter we discuss the basic types of bird sounds and how birds use these to communicate. And we'll get you to the point where you'll start understanding bird songs and calls, especially as they pertain to bird identification.

Looking at Types of Bird Sounds

Birds make three basic types of sounds: songs, calls, and non-vocal sounds. All three types have a purpose, but not all birds make all three sounds. Most bird species, however, rely on songs and calls. Some species — such as woodpeckers and some gamebirds, such as the ruffed grouse — lack the vocal skills of, say, the thrushes, and rely on other means to make noise and attract attention. And bird sounds are all about getting noticed.

Singing the avian way

TECHNICAL STUFF

Strictly defined, *bird song* is a repetitive pattern of musical notes or vocalizations. Birds produce their songs using a complex muscular organ called the syrinx, which is roughly analogous to our larynx. The syrinx allows birds to produce beautiful vocal sounds. The syrinx also allows birds to produce several tones at one time, unlike most humans who can only produce a single tone at a time. When recorded and played back at a slow rate, the simple *chickadee-dee-dee* call of the black-capped chickadee is found to be composed of several harmonic tones, all sung at once.

Among North American birds, true song (that is, a complex vocalization designed to attract a mate) is generally performed by adult male birds on, or en route to, their established territories during the spring and summer months, which is the breeding or nesting season. (Female birds may sing as well.) The bird species that perform elaborate vocalizations are known as songbirds (see Figure 6-1), but this label can be a little misleading. A northern bobwhite is not a songbird in a taxonomic sense, but we love listening to this bird's cheery whistle.

It pays to advertise

The primary purpose of bird song is, believe it or not, *advertising*. But a bird's vocal advertisements have nothing to do with Madison Avenue. The songs of male birds advertise two things:

> *"Here I am, females! Check me out! I'm ready for action! All I need is the right female to choose me, and I'm ready to settle down!"*

and

> *"Attention! All other males of my species! This is my territory here! Don't mess with me. Trespass at your own risk!"*

FIGURE 6-1:
A song
sparrow, singing.

These musical messages are how birds sort themselves into pairs for breeding and into territories divided among rival males and rival pairs.

Bird song does have a seasonal nature. Although some species (such as mocking-birds, Carolina wrens, and wrentits) perform songs at all times of the year, most song begins with the longer days and increasingly warm temperatures of early spring. The increased daylight causes changes in the hormonal levels in birds, which in turn affects their behavior. On a cloudy, cold, late-January day in your backyard, the birds may be actively visiting your feeders, uttering chips and scolds at each other. But if the next day dawns clear, sunny, and warmer, some of your backyard visitors begin to sing their spring songs in anticipation of the changing season.

A song of spring

Spring song starts earlier in the southern parts of the continent than it does in the northern parts. Spring song in southern Florida may begin in earnest in late January, while folks in the Rocky Mountain regions of Colorado, or those in New Hampshire, may have to wait until early April for the birds to get going vocally. In other parts of the West, where the seasonal differences in temperature and weather are not as great, the advent of spring song is strung out over many months.

Bird song reaches its crescendo across much of the continent during spring migration, when birds that are already on territories (early arriving migrants and resident or nonmigratory species) are joined by passing migrants. These migrants — thrushes, vireos, warblers, orioles, and tanagers — are singing their way north to their breeding grounds, where they'll establish territories of their own.

TIP

Watch the birds in your backyard in early spring. As they sort out their turf boundaries, the males begin to perform most of their singing from favorite spots within their territories. These prominent locations are called *song perches.* Males use song perches to display themselves to the best advantage, both to potential mates and to nearby rivals. You can find the song perches in your backyard at the tops of trees, at the peak of a roof, or perhaps from the top of a brush pile. Song perches offer a reliable place to look for territorial male birds during the breeding season.

The drive to sing

Most songbirds need to learn their songs by hearing them sung by adult birds. Only a small complement of species, including flycatchers, are born with a preprogrammed song embedded in their DNA. So, a flycatcher's song is an innate, inherited trait, while a wood thrush or an indigo bunting must learn by listening to its father sing.

Imagine sitting in a chair all day listening to the same bird singing the same song over and over again. Could you do it? Some patient souls have done it, and among the things they discovered were:

>> A male red-eyed vireo sang his song 22,197 times in one day between sunrise and sunset.

>> The average songbird sings its song between 1,500 and 3,000 times daily during high breeding season.

>> Songbirds sing most actively from predawn to near midday, and again from late afternoon to before sundown.

REMEMBER

Bird songs are amazingly varied. They range from low-impact squawks and whistles to the long, sweet, trilling melody of the winter wren — the longest continuous song of any North American bird, which can include more than 100 notes. Hearing a bird song can be as pleasing as seeing the visual beauty of birds.

Categorizing bird calls

Not every vocal sound that a bird makes is a song. Many short chips, whistles, trills, twitters, and chirps are uttered by birds. All of these sounds, referred to as *bird calls,* have a communication role among birds.

Calls are used by birds in a variety of ways. Among the uses of calls are:

» To keep contact among the members of a flock, family, or pair of birds

» To announce the presence of predators

» To signal the presence of food

The primary difference between bird songs and bird calls is that calls are much shorter in duration and may be less musical. Some birds, such as the American crow, don't have very musical songs, but they do possess an array of calls. We think of bird calls as being strictly functional, like a tool, whereas true bird song sounds more artistic, more musical.

All birds, including very young birds (nestlings), use call notes for communication. If you listen to the bird sounds in your yard, you can pick out the sounds that are obvious call notes, and those that are actual, full-fledged song.

TIP

Some of the calls you may encounter among the common birds in your area are the *pit-pit-pit!* alarm call of the American robin; the *pick!* call of the downy woodpecker; and the *chicka-dee-dee-dee* call of the black-capped chickadee, or of the very similar Carolina chickadee, found in the southeastern quadrant of the United States.

Recognizing non-vocal sounds

Can you sing? Not everybody can. And if you've been to karaoke night lately, you may have had a painful reminder of this fact. Not all birds can sing, either. Some birds have evolved, over the eons, to make their courtship and territorial points using non-vocal sounds. These sounds may be produced by specialized feather shafts that whistle in flight (woodcocks and some duck species have these feather shafts), or by specialized displays that involve a booming sound produced by flapping wings (the male ruffed grouse's drumming), or by some other specialized behavior, such as a woodpecker's drumming on hollow trees to make noise.

If you have mourning doves at your feeder, you've doubtless heard the loud winnowing twitter that their wings make when they launch into flight. Mourning doves' brown and gray coloring camouflages them on the ground, and they tend to freeze when feeling threatened. Once they've identified the threat, they'll burst into flight with a fanfare of sound, which startles any potential predator and aids their speedy escape.

Non-vocal bird sounds can also serve the same purpose as the most beautiful phrase ever sung by a winter wren. These sounds proclaim: "Available male seeks seasonal female companion!" and "Macho guy lives here. Keep out!"

Mimicry: The Sincerest Form of Flattery

TECHNICAL STUFF

Birds are the only living creatures, other than humans, capable of imitating sounds that they weren't born to produce. This ability to learn and imitate strange sounds is called *vocal mimicry,* and the birds that can do it are called *mimics.*

The almost indisputable champion of vocal mimicry among North American birds is the northern mockingbird. (See Figure 6-2.) The mockingbird, a gray bird with showy white wing and tail panels, is a year-round resident and a year-round singer wherever it's found. Because mockers must eke out a living on the same territory throughout the year, they defend winter feeding territories against intruders, and their song is one weapon in this defense.

How good are mockingbirds at singing and mimicry? One mocker was heard to perform the songs of more than 50 different species in one hour. Most mocking-birds have a repertoire that includes two dozen or more songs and calls. Some have learned to imitate doorbells, ringing telephones, whistles, car alarms, and even the notes of a piano.

What is the purpose of such vocal mastery? The original theory was that mocking-birds, by imitating the songs of many other territorial male birds, would discour-age other birds from choosing that area for their own territories and thus reduce competition for food. Newer studies have indicated that the bigger a male mock-er's song repertoire, the more appealing he is to potential female mates and the more dominating he is to other male mockers. Mockingbirds seem to learn their songs from other birds singing in their vicinity, so a mocker in Southern California learns the songs of birds in that area, while one in New England draws on that area's vocalizers for material.

Other excellent mimics in our midst include the gray catbird, brown thrasher (some bird people believe the thrasher, which can have as many as 1,000 song bits in its repertoire, is the king of the mimics), blue jay, yellow-breasted chat, and the European starling. The mockingbird, thrashers, and catbird are all members of the genus *Mimidae,* which is Latin for *mimic.*

FIGURE 6-2:
A northern
mockingbird
singing.

TIP

"Birder's Sudoku" is Julie's name for one of her favorite pastimes: parking under a singing mockingbird, brown thrasher, or European starling and jotting down all the species she can identify as it mimics. It's great ear training and really fun to get an insight into how the bird organizes its imitations. For instance, a mockingbird will pick one species, like an eastern bluebird, and, in a matter of seconds, run through every call from that species that it knows: baby begging calls, alarm calls, flight calls, contact calls, and angry chitters as well as the bluebird's territorial song. You can almost hear the mockingbird saying, "OK. Eastern bluebird. Here's what I know!" as it unleashes the string of vocalizations. And then it moves on to northern flicker, Carolina wren, or a gray tree frog!

Identifying Birds by Sound

Bird song is a very useful identification tool for bird watchers. We can't count the number of times that bird song has been the clinching clue to a bird's identity, especially when we've had a less-than-perfect look at the bird. We remember the song or call, and later consult a field guide for a description of the song, or better yet, listen to an actual recording of the bird's song.

AN EAR FOR BIRDS

Julie started birding at age eight, without having the slightest idea that anyone else did it, too. Naturally curious, she loved to follow an unfamiliar call or song until she found out which bird was making it. The pattern of chasing down bird song was set early. To this day, she finds birds first by their sounds, and she can picture the community of birds in any given habitat by what she hears. The trick was, and still is, to chase down anything she didn't recognize. That's how a birder finds the outliers, and that's how we learn.

It's always a huge and humbling thrill to wake up in a foreign land, listening to the dawn chorus. Sifting through the calls of tinamous, motmots, toucans, and antbirds in a Costa Rican jungle puts one right back in the beginner's seat, reminds us how far we've come with the calls back home, and whets our appetite to learn a whole new set of them wherever we go. Birding by ear is the bomb!

In fact, some birds are most readily identified by their vocalizations. As mentioned in Chapter 4, one example is the group of drab gray-green birds known as the *Empidonax* flycatchers. *Empidonax* is Greek (the literal translation is "gnat king") for the group of small, indistinctly marked flycatchers. The Acadian, willow, alder, least, and yellow-bellied flycatchers live in the eastern portions of North America. Western bird watchers get to thrill to the calls of the least and willow flycatchers, as well as the Hammond's, dusky, western, buff-breasted, and gray flycatchers.

These flycatchers are so similar in appearance that most bird watchers rely on the calls of each for positive identification. When faced with a non-vocal Empid, as these birds are generically known, birders everywhere do one of three things: make an educated guess, shrug and list the bird as "Empid species," or sit and wait patiently for the bird to make a peep.

REMEMBER

Each bird you encounter is an individual, so don't be surprised if you encounter differences in the songs you hear from two members of the same species — just as each person has a distinctive voice and even an accent. Bird watchers listening to recordings of bird songs often remark, "That doesn't sound like our (wren/warbler/sparrow) at all!" That's because birds from different parts of the continent have different dialects, sometimes even different songs. Listen for common characteristics that give you a composite aural picture of the species' song: pitch, tone, pattern. Is the song ringing? Sibilant? Syncopated? Thin and wiry or rich and chortling?

You'll have lots of situations in which you, fellow bird watcher, will hear but not see birds. At night, owls and nightjars (whip-poor-wills, nighthawks, and their kin) will be calling, but offer you little to look at. There will be thick vegetation, fog, and poor light. There will be treetop-singing warblers. There will be annoyingly persistent singers that you *just can't seem to locate!* The picture we're painting here is that you will greatly benefit from opening your ears to the wonders (and usefulness!) of bird songs. When you know your bird vocalizations, stepping into a scene where a number of birds are singing is like taking roll call — you know who's there without having to track them down and see them! But seeing them is the icing on the cake.

Starting with a Reference Bird

TIP

To begin deciphering and recognizing bird songs, we suggest you pick a *reference bird*. Choose a common species, preferably one that sings regularly in your area. Perhaps this bird is a cardinal if you live in the East, or a white-crowned sparrow if you live in the West. The American robin is reasonably common all across the continent, so maybe the robin works as a reference bird for you.

Listen to your reference bird's call and songs as often as you can. Soon, you become familiar with this species' vocalizations, and you're able to pick them out if they're singing, no matter where you are. This practice establishes a good reference point for your future bird song adventures.

When you next hear a bird song that you can't identify, use the song of your reference bird as a comparison. If your reference bird is a robin, which has a rich, throaty, warbling song, compare the mystery bird's song to that of the robin. Is it thinner-sounding? Is it harsher? More musical? While you're making the comparison, try to make visual contact with the mystery bird.

TIP

If you're just beginning with bird songs, we suggest you start by trying to sort out the early spring songs of common birds in and around your backyard. Get outside and listen before the trees leaf out, all the spring migrants come through, and the summer nesters begin to set up territories. You'll have fewer songs to sort out in the early spring than at the height of migration in your area. The peak period of bird migration varies greatly from north to south and east to west. For much of North America, spring migration starts early in the year — as early as February — and ends in June. Knowing the songs of your locally common and resident (nonmigratory) birds gives you a great head start later when these songs are mixed with dozens of others. Knowing these few songs, you can put them aside and concentrate on the new ones you're hearing.

Remembering phrases

Pleased to meetcha, Miss Beecher! is one of our all-time favorite phrases used to describe a bird song — in this case, a chestnut-sided warbler. The genius of this phrase is that it not only *sounds* like what the bird sings but it's weird enough that you're not going to forget it immediately.

Field guides to the birds invariably include a description of the vocalizations of each species. These descriptions may be straightforward ("a buzzy trill ending on an upward phrase") or poetic ("a melodic series of ethereal, flutelike notes"). But our favorites are the old-fashioned "sounds like the bird is saying" descriptions, such as *Quick! Three beers!* (olive-sided flycatcher), *Drink your tea!* (eastern towhee), and *Spring of the year!* (eastern meadowlark).

Table 6-1 lists some phrases that may help you remember a bird by its song.

TABLE 6-1 **Bird Songs to Remember**

Name of Bird	Sounds Like
Red-eyed vireo	Here I am. Look at me. I'm up here!
Yellow-throated vireo	Three-eight. Cheerio!
Carolina wren	Teakettle, teakettle, teakettle!
Barred owl	Who cooks for you? Who cooks for you-all?
California quail	Chi-ca-go!
Olive-sided flycatcher	Quick! Three beers!
Black-throated blue warbler	I'm so lay-zee!
Yellow warbler	Sweet, sweet, sweet, I'm so sweet!
Indigo bunting	Fire! Fire! Where? Where? There! There! Put it out! Put it out!
Eastern towhee	Drink your tea!
Golden-crowned sparrow	Oh dear me!
White-throated sparrow	Old Sam Peabody, Peabody, Peabody! (or) Oh Sweet Canada, Canada, Canada!

Squeaky wheel: An image of sound

Not all bird songs are translatable into the language of humans. But many that aren't fit for descriptive sentences can be remembered using descriptive *imagery*. A good example is the song of the black-and-white warbler, which is often described as sounding like a squeaky wheel. The ring-necked pheasant's harsh crow sounds like a very rusty gate being opened quickly. The notes of the red-breasted nuthatch's call sound as though they're being played on a tiny tin trumpet.

As you become more familiar with the songs of the birds you hear, feel free to come up with your own descriptions. How goofy they are doesn't matter, as long as they help you to remember.

Finding a pattern

Another method for remembering a bird's song is to tie the rhythm or cadence of the song to a pattern. A good example of this is the description used for the song of the American goldfinch, one often sung in flight: *Po-ta-to chip! Po-ta-to chip!* The goldfinch's song doesn't sound like the actual phrase "potato chip," but the rhythmic pattern of that phrase and the bird's song are unmistakably similar. "Potato chip" is an excellent reminder of the song's pattern. And since potato chips are many a bird watcher's snacking staple when out in the field, the phrase is never far from your mind.

Birding by Ear

With experience, you'll become more comfortable with your ability to identify birds by their songs, calls, and sounds. Getting experience is the same as getting directions on how to get to Carnegie Hall: *practice, practice, practice.*

We know that getting experience sounds boring, but it's not. All you have to do is go out bird watching and remember to take your ears with you. Unless you're Vincent van Gogh, this should be easy to do.

>> While in the field (or in your backyard), listen for bird sounds that you don't recognize.

>> Choose a sound and try to locate its source.

>> Once you find the singer, listen to its song a few times and make mental notes about the song's pattern and quality.

While you're listening, watch the bird carefully; it may do something that cements the moment (and the bird's song) in your mind forever.

Hear it, find it, watch it sing!

As you gain experience in birding by ear, you'll find yourself stopping whenever a strange call or song catches your attention. That's how it's supposed to happen! You'll find many interesting — even unexpected — birds if you use your ears in conjunction with your eyes.

Looking for singers

You hear a strange bird song, but you can't find the bird. What do you do?

Stop. Listen. Look.

SONG ON THE MOUNTAIN

The first Blackburnian warbler Bill Thompson III ever heard was also the first one he ever saw. In early June, he was hiking to the top of a ski run at a West Virginia resort. You know, it's amazing the things that fall out of people's pockets when they're skiing. All that stuff ends up on the ground after the snow is gone. He was richer by about $6.25 in coins, a few combs, a moneyless money clip, and a pair of barely broken sunglasses when he heard an extremely high-pitched bird song coming from the pines at the very top of the mountain. He scrambled to the summit and found himself looking up 10 feet into the fiery gaze of a male Blackburnian warbler. The bird sang again. Bill's heart pounded. He felt light-headed. The bird sang once more and then flew off down the mountain. The high altitude, the high-pitched song, and the Bengal-tiger-like face of the male warbler were the highlight of that entire summer. Bill never forgot that moment or that song. Each time he heard it in the spring, when the Blackburnians pass through on their way north, he was transported.

That's the best way to find a singing bird. Each time the bird sings, try to figure out the direction from which the sound is coming. As you narrow the possibilities, try this trick:

TIP

Turn your head slightly from side to side, as if you're telling someone "no" in slow motion. Your ears will narrow down the directional possibilities as your head turns and the sound hits your eardrums from different angles.

If you have a good idea of the bird's direction, move slowly toward it, stopping to listen each time the bird sings. If you think you have the general location, scan it carefully for signs of movement. Once you find the bird, watch to see if it really is the one making the noise that you're following. Birds can put most human ventriloquists to shame.

TIP

If you're having trouble locating a singing bird, try cupping your hands behind your ears. This cupping helps to scoop the sounds into your ears more efficiently. It's astounding how much better you can hear distant songs with the aid of your hands: two free amplifiers, right in your pockets!

Helping your hearing

If you're even a little hard of hearing, you may have difficulty picking up high-pitched bird songs, such as warbler songs. Many bird watchers, especially men over the age of 50, naturally lose the high-end register of their hearing. This fact can be depressing to longtime birders who can *see* a male warbler singing but can't *hear* the song.

Some help is available for lost hearing, however. The help comes in the form of hearing aids adapted for use outdoors. These products were initially designed for use by hunters, but they work equally well for bird watchers. In some cases, such as with a large group of birders, these hearing devices can amplify normal human conversation to painful volumes, but the fact remains that many a warbler song has been re-found with the help of modern hearing technology.

A quick online search of "hearing aids for birders" nets an impressive array of lightweight, affordable, non-prescription choices.

Using Merlin

You'll notice that our recommendations for learning bird songs and calls are rather old-school. Listening, chasing unfamiliar songs down, and finding the bird while it's singing can't be replaced by technology — or can it? While we would never suggest you walk to school through chest-high snow like we did, it is a good idea to learn your bird calls in person, one at a time, to really cement them in your brain.

There is an app for that, though, and you may already be using it. It's called Merlin, like the wizard (and the falcon). Developed at the Cornell Lab of Ornithology, this bird identification app has a visual component that will walk you through identifying a bird you've seen. But it's the listening feature — which commandeers your cellphone to make a recording of what's singing around you — that's truly revolutionary. The app compares what it picks up with thousands of recordings in its database to identify the birds that are singing, in real time! We'll spend more time discussing Merlin in Chapter 21.

For years and years, Julie was too stubborn to download the app, being proud of her hard-won old-school knowledge and, well, *old.* That changed in the winter of 2024 when she took a hike outside Tucson in a completely unfamiliar Sonoran Desert biome. What was that strange *spichee!* coming from a jumble of red rock?

Julie climbed to a high boulder, picked up a good cell signal, and downloaded Merlin on the spot. The bird called. Merlin listened, then identified the mystery call as a rock wren. Julie squealed like a kindergartner to have instant confirmation. When the wren popped up to do some deep knee bends and say hello, she was sold. For the rest of the hike, she was like a kid in a candy store, merrily identifying each *squeak* and *squirk* coming from the thorny desert vegetation. It would have been flat-out painful to track each one of them down, and besides, her flight was leaving out of Tucson in a few hours!

REMEMBER

Birders who start the old-fashioned way will always have an advantage. They've built their skills slowly, taking it one bird at a time. It's harder to cement a song ID in your brain when you let an app identify it for you. Merlin isn't always right, nor can it hear everything you can hear. So, as magical as it is to have songs effortlessly identified for you, try to resist the temptation to use Merlin to the exclusion of time-tested techniques of listening, stalking, and watching birds as they sing. Enjoy it for corroboration, but don't let it replace the slow, steady absorption of information that fieldcraft gently gives.

2

Backyard Bird Watching

Chapter **7**

Making a Bird-Friendly Yard

The best place to start watching birds is close to home. Even if you have but an apartment balcony, there will be birds nearby. But why settle for the random house sparrow? If you provide birds with a few perks and pleasures, they'll hang around your outdoor space because it's a nice place to be. (We know, you probably believe that it's you they love.)

Think of it this way: Suppose you're faced with choosing between two parties given by the neighbors. One party is held in a large room with no furniture, a few stale crackers, some Cheez-Whiz, flat cola (no glasses), and an AM radio. The other party (in an equally large room) has big, soft sofas, lots of comfy chairs, a huge table of food, a vast selection of beverages in an open bar, and a live band playing Calypso music. Which one would you choose?

Attracting birds to your yard works the same way. Native vegetation, abundant flowers, shrubbery and trees for shelter and nesting, a water source, and lots of handy song perches are the banquet table and comfy chairs birds are looking for. See Figure 7-1 for an example. This chapter gives you tips for turning out a truly hospitable bird environment in your own backyard.

FIGURE 7-1:
Bird-friendly
backyard with
native plants,
birdbath, shrubs,
trees, and birds.

Focusing on the Four Basics

Birds need four basic things to survive: Food, water, shelter, and a place to nest. You can attract birds with these four offerings no matter where you live, even in the urban heart of a large city. The first three — food, water, and shelter — are fairly simple to offer. Places to nest are offered in varying levels of perennial plantings, shrubbery, and trees.

Eating like a bird

Consider your bird feeding to be an ongoing experiment. Use trial and error to determine what foods attract the most interesting birds to your yard. Also experiment with how you offer the foods to birds, because not all birds like to eat in the same way. Not all people like lasagna, or chicken wings, or drive-through windows, or fancy restaurants, and not all birds like all bird foods or all bird feeders.

Where you live in North America has a bearing on what birds you can attract to your yard. The birds at the feeders in Julie's rural Ohio yard are very unlike those in a friend's Arizona yard. She gets Gambel's quail, curve-billed thrashers, and Lucifer hummingbirds; Julie gets northern cardinals, hairy woodpeckers, and blue jays. (Sometimes Julie dreams about a bird trade, but that's not legal.)

Settling on a seed type

In the most general terms, bird feeding involves seeds. Black-oil sunflower seed is the most universally used seed for bird feeding because it's eaten by many feeder visitors, including chickadees, titmice, finches, grosbeaks, cardinals, jays, nuthatches, and woodpeckers, among others. Bird feeding's other popular seeds include sunflower hearts, millet, safflower, cracked corn, peanuts and peanut bits, Nyjer or thistle seed (which the American goldfinches are partaking in Figure 7-2), and mixed seed containing milo, wheat, millet, and cracked corn.

The bottom line on birdseed can be found in Chapter 8.

FIGURE 7-2:
American goldfinches eating seed.

Finding a feeder (or two, or three)

Today, as many feeder types and styles are available as there are sunflower kernels in a 50-pound bag. Let's keep the subject of feeders simple for starters.

The ideal feeding station has:

>> A small hanging platform feeder (or two), for sunflower hearts and safflower

>> A cylindrical mesh feeder or two offering sunflower seed, sunflower hearts, or Nyjer seed

>> A hopper feeder dispensing sunflower seed

>> A cylindrical mesh feeder for shell-less peanuts

>> An area of open ground for scattering mixed seed, with a nearby shelter or brush pile

TIP

Start simply with one or two of the feeders listed above. Expand the feeding operation at your own pace. Once you've got the basics down, you and your birds can move on to other areas of bird feeding, including offering fruits, nuts, suet, and specialized foods and feeders to cater to (or discourage) certain feeder visitors.

Check out Chapter 8 for specifics on feeder types and for more tips on great dining for birds.

WARNING

One note of caution here: If you're going to provide bird feeders, you need to wash them often. Dirty bird feeders are likely to spread disease among the birds who visit them. If you can't commit to keeping your feeders clean, please don't feed the birds.

Getting water

The single best bird attractant for any yard is a reliable source of clean, shallow, preferably moving, water. Birds are perfectly adapted for finding new sources of food, and they rarely actually need supplemental feeding to survive. Water is non-negotiable. Birds need water both for drinking and bathing. Keeping their plumage clean, for birds, is keeping it functional. Dirty feathers don't insulate well, they don't function as well in flight, and, let's face it, dirty feathers don't look good.

Surprisingly, having a fishpond in your yard doesn't necessarily help birds. Songbirds need a specific set of features for a usable bath. (Read on to find out what we're talking about.)

Bird bath basics

Remember the following for an ideal bird bath setup:

>> **Keep it shallow.** Most commercial birdbaths are five inches or deeper. But most songbirds won't enter water that is more than two inches deep.

>> **The surface of the bath offers secure footing.** While plastic basins are fine, you'll need to cover the bottom with a few large, flat stones to make birds feel safe to hop in.

>> **The area immediately around the bath should offer perches, but no thick vegetation where predators could hide.** Chipmunks are the worst offenders — cute but deadly predators to small birds.

>> **Water should be moving.** A trickling sound brings birds in like nothing else. (We'll get to how to do that below.)

If you can't put your bird bath in the shade of a tree, place it within about 15 feet of some type of cover. Birds get nervous when they're all wet. (Wet birds can't fly well.) A nearby bit of cover makes them feel safer and, if shelter is near, they're more likely to stop and bathe than to sip and fly, or not stop at all.

If your bath is in the open, drive a sturdy dead tree branch, preferably a curvy one with both horizontal and vertical perching options, in the ground next to it. (Digging a good deep pilot hole for the branch is the easiest way to make it stand up.) Don't let branches hang directly over the water, as this invites bird droppings in the bath. A sturdy natural perch right alongside the basin can mean the difference between a popular bird bath and one that stands empty.

TIP

Locate your bath where you can see and enjoy it from a convenient vantage point — say, your living room window. Here's another tip: Locate your bird bath where you can reach it easily with a garden hose for regular cleaning and refilling.

A couple of warnings

WARNING

It's imperative to keep the bath clean. A bath in heavy use should be emptied, scrubbed out, and refilled every two to three days. Droppings in the water are a deal breaker for fastidious birds.

Keep an old scrub brush handy to loosen the gunk that inevitably appears and then blast the bath clean with the garden hose. For tough algae and scum, grab a handful of gritty soil or a lump of soil with roots attached and rub it around on the inside of the bath. The soil acts as an abrasive to remove scum.

REMEMBER

Although nearby shelter or cover is important for birds at both feeders and bird baths, you don't want to give the neighbor's cat a hiding place from where it can ambush birds. Keep feeders and baths a cat's leap or two away from dense cover. If you've got chipmunks around, elevate the bath at least a foot (placing it on a large, overturned flowerpot works great) so the rodents can't ambush bathing birds.

Driving birds crazy

Want to really make your bird bath irresistible? Make the water move. Better yet, make it trickle — loudly! Birds key in to the sound of running water.

A QUARANTINE STORY

In the worst of the COVID-19 pandemic shutdown, Julie spent more time than ever look-ing out her studio window, figuring out how to design the perfect bird fountain. At a gar-den shop, she found the ideal basin, and the concept that had been hatching in her mind took wings. Drawing on decades of experience with a variety of water features aimed at birds, Julie designed a homemade bubbling bird fountain she calls the WarblerFall. (See a photo of a brown thrasher using the WarblerFall in the color photo section.) Fifty-four species of birds bathed and drank at Julie's southeastern Ohio WarblerFall in 2023, including 11 warbler species, tanagers, grosbeaks, vireos, and a stunning parade of ruby-crowned kinglets. Who knew kinglets love to soak their tiny feet in running water?

Julie spent quarantine perfecting the WarblerFall so that anyone can construct and enjoy it. No tools required! It's affordable, easy to assemble, and it's the single most potent bird attractant in her yard. Wherever you live, the WarblerFall is sure to attract forest birds and migrants you didn't know were around! Check out https://warblerfall.com/ for instructions on how to build your own.

Gimme shelter

Suppose you're a towhee absent-mindedly kicking through the seeds scattered on the ground below a feeding station. Suddenly, one of those annoyingly perky chickadees sitting on the platform feeder above you gives an alarm call that means a hawk is nearby.

Swooooooosh!

A Cooper's hawk makes a quick pass at the feeder, looking for a victim. (See Figure 7-3.) "Oh man," you say to yourself, "this is a serious bird-eater, and he's just waiting for me to bolt to the woods in a panic."

FIGURE 7-3: Cooper's hawk diving on birds at feeder.

Lucky for you, the kind human owner of this backyard has placed the feeders near several evergreen trees and a nice thick brush pile. Good shelter. That's why you liked this yard and decided to stop here for a bite to eat. Being a denizen of the brushy field edges, you calmly hop into the center of the brush pile and wait for the Coop to get bored (or lucky) and leave.

A backyard can have all the perfect feeders and best bird foods, but the birds will ignore it if no decent shelter (cover) is available nearby. They're not stupid. Like people, birds need shelter from bad weather. And birds and people want a cozy place to sleep, roost, and hide from predators. If the shelter is nice enough, some birds may even decide to nest in your yard.

REMEMBER

Shelter can come in many forms: weedy areas, shrubs and brush, trees, brush piles (see Figure 7-4), woods, and even buildings. (Barn owls and barn swallows got their names in this way.)

TIP

When you look at the setup of your feeding station, try thinking like a bird. If you're a bird at the feeder, think about:

>> Where is the nearest place you can go to hide from danger?

>> What about in bad weather? Are the feeders exposed to direct wind, snow, or rain?

FIGURE 7-4:
This brush pile provides welcome respite for a tree sparrow and an eastern towhee.

If no shelter is convenient to the area of the feeders, create some shelter, such as an instant brush pile. If you're not into brush piles, here's a nice compromise. Julie likes to lay her cut Christmas tree on its side near the feeding station and scatter seed around it. It's an easy, removable shelter that's irresistible to juncos, sparrows, towhees, and cardinals. When spring rolls around and it's time to mow again, it's easy to remove and dispose of this temporary bird haven.

A place to nest

All birds that venture into your yard benefit from a varied habitat. Some species take advantage of human-made shelter — commonly called birdhouses or nest boxes. Birdhouses come in an array of shapes, sizes, and designs.

As you get to know the birds in your yard, you can target the housing you provide to maximize the birds' benefit. Among the species that use housing are bluebirds, tree and violet-green swallows, chickadees, titmice, some wrens, nuthatches, some flycatchers and woodpeckers, and even a few warblers, ducks, kestrels, and owls. But remember, not all birds use birdhouses, just as not all birds visit bird feeders. Most cavity-nesting birds are picky about the size, shape, entrance hole size, height, and direction of human-made nest boxes. If you decide to offer a nest box, please do your research first, and be sure to predator-proof it by using a metal pole and a stovepipe baffle. Providing a nest box properly is more challenging than it sounds and beyond the scope of this book.

Standing dead wood

Though most people believe a dead tree should come down as soon as possible, the birds disagree. Standing dead wood provides valuable nesting habitat for woodpeckers and the myriad cavity-nesting species that use their old nesting cavities. As cities and towns grow, consuming the surrounding countryside, a great deal of nesting habitat is lost. Dead, standing trees may look messy and unkempt to people, but if they present no hazard to people or property where they are, the insects in their decaying wood will feed woodpeckers and nuthatches, and can produce generations of hole-nesting birds, like the eastern bluebirds in Figure 7-5.

Varied habitats are very nice

For those birds that don't use nest cavities, the best thing you can do is create a variety of habitats in your yard. An easy way to plan this is to think about providing habitats (landscaping, plants, trees, and other types of shelter) in a mixture of differing heights and textures. Start with the short stuff like grasses and ground cover, and then move up to flowering plants and a garden area. Next come shrubs, hedges, and small bushes, followed by trees, and even woodlands.

TECHNICAL STUFF

Any experienced bird watcher will tell you that you find the most birds in the *edge habitat*. Edge habitat is the area where two or more habitat types meet, such as where a meadow habitat meets the edge of a woodland habitat, or where a thick, overgrown brushy area abuts a roadway. The greatest variety of habitat occurs where habitat types meet, so it's not just a coincidence that edge habitat is where the birds are. Birds preferring each individual type of habitat can potentially be in the place where these habitats meet. And, with some creative thinking, that place could be in your backyard.

FIGURE 7-5:
Eastern bluebirds
nesting in a
woodpecker
cavity in a
dead tree.

Cultivating Bird-Friendly Plants

If you're a gardener, or plan to landscape your yard, consider planting species that provide both food and shelter to birds. Think of these species as bed-and-breakfast (B+B) plantings for birds.

Chapter 9 goes into greater detail on what plants to choose to enhance your surroundings and attract the greatest variety of birds. The single most important tenet to remember is that plants native to your region will be of greatest benefit to birds, and they pack the most bang for your buck. Birds recognize and readily use these plants, whether for nectar, seed, or fruit. Native plants, in general, will not become invasive and take over your yard because they've evolved in balance with the plant community. (Someone please give the native trumpet vine this memo!) And native plants have evolved to survive local winters and endure drought cycles that will bring non-native ornamentals to their knees. Your local agricultural extension service can be helpful in planning your native plant paradise but go warned: They may also recommend you plant invasive groundcovers such as crown vetch or various clovers. Thanks to this inconsistency, your best bet is to find a native plant nursery in your region and trust their recommendations.

AVOIDING CERTAIN PLANTS

Every part of North America has a list of non-native plants that have invaded from some foreign habitat and taken over. These invaders thrive at the expense of native plant species, and the birds and animals that rely on native plants for food and shelter don't get the same benefits from the invaders. Where Julie lives in Ohio, species such as Japanese honeysuckle, autumn olive, multiflora rose, and ornamental Miscanthus grass take over wherever they are not controlled. Formerly vibrant native fields and woodlands become wildlife deserts. Even deer can't move through multiflora and Miscanthus, and these invasives shade out and kill all native vegetation when they take hold. Before you plant any species in your backyard or garden, find out if it is considered invasive in your region. It takes a few seconds to type, "Is wisteria invasive?" in your favorite search engine. If you stick to native plants and a few non-invasive but useful ornamentals, you can enhance the plant community rather than compromising it. You'll be glad you did your homework!

Backing Backyard Bird Conservation

Providing the four basics to birds (food, water, shelter, and a place to nest) in your backyard is a good start to backyard bird conservation. You're thinking globally and acting locally. Of course, not all birds will visit your feeders or bath, nor will all the birds stay around to nest in your yard, but all birds that pass through your yard will take advantage of whatever the habitat has to offer. The beautiful part is, as you are rewarded by seeing more birds, you'll come up with more ways to spread the welcome mat for them, until your formerly bland backyard is bustling with motion and song.

Poison-free is the way to be

The most responsible thing you can do for birds in your yard is to keep their environment free of harmful, unnatural things such as toxic pesticides and herbicides, human-made trash, and potentially unhealthy bird feeders.

Environmental impact studies done on the effects of poisons on birds have shown that surprisingly low amounts of herbicides and pesticides, such as those used to make beautiful lawns, can be toxic to birds such as robins, bluebirds, and other species that depend on insects as a primary food source. The full impact of the chemical DDT on the environment took years to discover. Today, bald eagles and ospreys — two bird species nearly wiped out by the cumulative effects of

DDT — are doing better because this harmful chemical is banned in North America. But DDT is still widely used in Central and South America, so migrant birds are still exposed to it.

Will the popular lawn and garden chemicals of today be tomorrow's banned substances? Time and time again, we uncover the true impact of supposedly "safe" herbicides and pesticides. In the meantime — if you can manage it — keep your yard as poison-free as possible. If you've got a weedy patio, try using boiling water or undiluted white vinegar in a spray bottle. It can be as effective as herbicide, with little to no collateral damage.

Putting out the welcome mat

Nobody wants to have a silent spring, when no birds sing. Almost all migratory birds are experiencing population declines due to loss of habitat, overuse of toxic pesticides and herbicides, cat and window kills, and other anthropogenic causes. Nonmigratory resident birds, too, are feeling the effects of the growing human population. This is not a call to rally on the White House lawn. You can do your part in your own backyard. Here are some suggestions:

>> **Keep your yard as free from pesticides and herbicides as possible.** Remember: Hawks and owls eat mice. Please don't poison mice.

>> **Mow high and allow some diversity in your lawn.** The finches and butterflies will thank you.

>> **Clean your bird feeders and bird bath regularly.** Doing so helps prevent the spread of disease.

>> **Offer only as much food on platform feeders (or on the ground) as can be eaten in one day.** Old food can get wet, spoil, and carry disease.

>> **Leave standing dead wood for cavity-nesting birds.**

>> **Appreciate insects!** Insect diversity = bird diversity. Caterpillars are a good thing; they're baby bird food.

>> **Keep cats indoors or leashed when outdoors.** Domestic cats kill millions of songbirds annually. This tragic toll is not "natural" because domestic cats are not native to North America. Cat kills are completely preventable.

>> **Prevent window strikes (birds colliding with large windows) by treating problem windows with bird-saving crop netting or closely spaced frosted decals.** The old flying hawk silhouette decals, which never worked in the first place, have recently been replaced by a host of truly effective solutions. It's estimated that window strikes kill a billion birds each year. More on this in Chapter 22. The American Bird Conservancy offers many effective ways to

reduce or eliminate window strikes. Please visit `https://abcbirds.org/blog/truth-about-birds-and-glass-collisions/`

» **Pick up and carry out trash, such as rusty cans, plastic bags, fishing line, and six-pack rings, wherever you go.** Birds and other wildlife can become entangled or even be choked by these unnatural items. Recycle what you can. Before disposing of any plastic ring or wad of monofilament, cut it so it won't end up on a seabird's neck should it find its way to the ocean.

If you realize that you're already doing all these things for birds in your backyard, you should be enjoying plenty of birds already. In that case, you may want to branch out beyond your backyard to find and care for a greater variety of birds. You can definitely go to the head of the class (or skip to a later chapter of this book).

On the other hand, if some or all of these ideas and suggestions are new to you, get ready for some real fun. Your yard is about to become as busy as a shopping mall on December 24. There's nothing like looking outside and seeing happy bird neighbors (and other creatures) everywhere (Figure 7-6)!

FIGURE 7-6:
Dilapidated gate with native vegetation and happy wildlife.

Chapter **8**

Bird Feeding: The Start of It All

When some picture birdwatching, expeditions and long car rides with the back seat bristling with spotting scopes and snacks might come to mind. But watching birds can be a non-taxing, all-day, everyday event, if you just make the effort to bring birds to your yard. Feeding birds is a gateway drug to birdwatching for many of us. And there are all kinds of ways to do it.

There's No Place Like Home

The story is the same for feeding birds as it is for birdwatching in general: start at home. Unless you live on the 108th floor of the Willis Tower in Chicago (or some similarly tall, hermetically sealed building), you, too, can enjoy luring unsuspecting birds in close, where you can ogle them to your heart's content. We'll start off with the *For Dummies*–approved, totally basic and fool-proof method of feeding birds: throw seed on the ground.

From the ground up

Believe it or not, starting a bird feeding station can be as simple as flinging a few handfuls of seed on the ground. We knew a Connecticut Yankee who for 50 years did nothing more than this and had a devoted following of birds, including fox sparrows, towhees, cardinals, chickadees, and a pack of tufted titmice who learned her daily routine. They would peek into her bedroom, bathroom, or kitchen windows and tap on the glass if she was a little late in rising to throw a coffee can full of sunflower seed out the back door!

There are a couple of messages in this little story. First, you really don't have to have expensive bird feeders to feed birds. Second, unexpected joys and surprises await you when you start feeding birds.

No takers

Sometimes people report, "I put up a bird feeder, but no birds will come to it." Julie never really understood why this would be so, until she moved to a rural area with very little tradition of bird feeding. She put up a bird feeder and nobody came! For weeks!

So, she took a fresh look at bird feeders, from the point of view of a wild bird. Your typical tube feeder — all slippery Lucite and shiny metal — is really a pretty scary thing to a naive wild bird. There's nothing natural about it, and even though you can see the seed inside it, a skittish bird may not want to land on it to figure out how to get at the seed.

TIP

It was time to meet the birds where they live. She dragged a hollow log out of the woods, sprinkled seed over it, and built a low, rough plywood and block table — nothing fancy — then stuck a bunch of dead branches into the ground around the whole setup. (See Figures 8-1 and 8-2.) This gave birds some natural surfaces to land on and investigate. They came, they ate, they stayed — and they completely ignored the hanging feeder until the day a bold tufted titmouse landed on it, scolding, and took the first sunflower seed. The other birds watched and learned, and Julie was on her way to hosting a great feeding station.

Feeder freebies

Bird watchers prefer free entertainment. If you don't think so, watch how many of them brown-bag it in favor of eating out while birding, or listen to them hem and haw over purchases of any bird-watching accoutrement.

FIGURE 8-1:
A Carolina wren and a song sparrow find seed in a hollow log.

FIGURE 8-2:
White-throated sparrows and an evening grosbeak on a simple low bird table.

A lot of free materials are available out there that you can use to improve your bird feeding station. We already mentioned hollow logs, which make a natural and attractive stage for ground-feeding birds, and which help keep the seed up off the wet ground. Branches or dead snags (still-standing, broken-off tree trunks or branches — birds like to use them as perches) can immediately enhance the attractiveness of your yard to everyone except your meticulous neighbor. Just take a spade or post-hole digger and stick a few big dead vertical branches in the ground. Voila! You've made a perch where there was none and given woodpeckers and hawks and songbirds a reason to pause in your yard.

Snags are a potent attractant; they can serve as song perches for territorial birds, lookouts for still-hunting insect-eaters like bluebirds and flycatchers, prey-spotting perches for hawks, or drumming boards for woodpeckers. Try a few. They're free, and when they eventually rot and fall down, plenty more are out there in the woods to choose from.

An instant safe haven

Sticks and stones. Think natural, and you'll be thinking like a bird.

Imagine yourself a timorous little sparrow, skulking around the edge of the woods, scratching in the leaf litter for food. Would you fly across a big open green lawn, even if seed was on the ground? Wouldn't you be afraid of hawks and cats, dogs and people? Now, imagine a big, sheltering brush pile with lots of nooks and crannies to hide in smack dab in the middle of that feeding area. Sparrow heaven.

You can spread the welcome mat for timid sparrows, juncos, and towhees by building a brush pile near your feeding station. This gives them a nearby retreat when a hawk zooms over or the back door suddenly opens. It provides an out for the more skittish birds; they'll feel much freer to visit, knowing there's a place to hide nearby. You could even lay your used holiday tree on its side behind the feeding station and layer it with larger sticks and fallen branches — an instant brush pile that's easy to take up when spring comes and the tree starts looking crispy. Julie stands her cut Christmas tree up in a cinder block turned on its side. With mixed seed spread around it, it's a decorative natural feeding station.

High or Low: Knowing Where Birds Feed

There are lots of ways to feed birds. The two basic choices are: on the ground or from a suspended feeder.

Ground feeding

Ground feeding is great — with caveats. Most bird species that come to feeders take all or part of their natural food from the ground anyway. In winter, though, there's snow and rain. That can spoil seed that's scattered on the ground, and spoiled seed can lead to sick birds. Plus, many non-target species, like squirrels, rabbits, and deer, help themselves to food on the ground. To avoid this, clever humans have come up with a variety of feeders that either keep the seed up off the ground, keep it dry by dispensing a little at a time, or both.

The drawback to ground feeding is that the seed is exposed to the weather, so it gets soaked by rain and covered up by snow and ice, and so on. There's the additional problem of hygiene: It's easy for the food to become fouled with droppings. Julie scatters seed on the ground only when conditions are dry, and she constantly changes where she tosses it — never directly under hanging feeders. A few handfuls of seeds thus scattered are wonderful for sparrows, towhees, and juncos, who scratch for their food on the ground. With the price of seed, though, it's hard to watch much of it go to fatten the squirrels. The answer is to offer food in raised or hanging feeders.

Suspended or raised feeders

Most forest birds that feed in the tree canopy, such as finches, grosbeaks, woodpeckers, chickadees, titmice, and nuthatches, readily use hanging feeders. You can use elevation and a squirrel-proof suspension system to keep that expensive seed clean, dry, and accessible only to the birds you wish to attract. Setting things up right from the get-go will save you lots of time, money, and frustration going forward. Read on to find out which feeder designs we recommend as being the simplest, and most hygienic out there, perfect for those who are just getting started in the bird catering business.

Feeder types

There are hundreds of bird feeders on the market, everything from tiny ones meant to be suction-cupped to a window to battery-powered ones that spin madly when a squirrel jumps onto them to "smart feeders" that take close-up photos and videos of bird visitors, send the images to your smartphone, and even identify species for you! The array is truly dizzying, but it really doesn't need to be. Because this is *Bird Watching For Dummies*, we're going to keep it really simple, and help you set up a feeding station that covers all the bases for convenience, ease of cleaning, and safety for the birds.

A word about hygiene

Wherever birds concentrate, the potential for disease follows them. (See Figure 8-3.) Feeding birds results in lots of droppings, and germs multiply around busy feeding stations. A conscientious host watches for signs of disease. Should you see birds huddled, puffed up, with eyes closed, in your yard, be prepared to pull in the feeders and discontinue feeding the birds for a couple of weeks. You don't want to spread disease while subsidizing the birds you love.

The most common diseases around feeders include:

>> **House finch disease (*Mycoplasma gallisepticum* and others):** Causes swollen, red, inflamed eyes, lethargy, and blindness. Bacteria carried by house finches. Highly contagious; infects more than 30 other species.

>> **Salmonella:** Symptoms include lethargy, puffed feathers, trouble swallowing. Commonly breaks out in pine siskins throughout the West but can occur anywhere. Bacterial.

>> **Avian flu:** Lethargy is yet again a sign of the disease, as are puffed feathers and (tragically) rapid death. Rapidly evolving virus. May be spread by wild birds to the detriment of domestic waterfowl and poultry.

>> **Avian pox:** You'll notice fleshy nodules and growths around eyes, bill, and feet, which may impair sight and feeding. Highly contagious, viral.

FIGURE 8-3:
A sick redpoll huddles near a busy tube feeder, a possible source of infection.

First, do no harm

REMEMBER

Because of the potential for spreading disease, we recommend only certain types of feeders: those least likely to harbor and spread infection. Unfortunately, the popular *tube feeder*, an acrylic cylinder equipped with ports that dispense food, is also likely to spread disease, because birds brush against the ports while feeding. We'll describe and recommend feeders that are safer for birds.

Safer feeder: Hopper

Hopper feeders have a lot of different styles, but the old favorite looks like a little barn or covered bridge, minus the young lovers and graffiti. The sides are usually panels of acrylic that allow you to see how much seed remains, and it is usually filled through the top. (See Figure 8-4.)

FIGURE 8-4: Hopper feeders are old favorites. A downy woodpecker (left) and a male rosebreasted grosbeak are at this one. A pole-mounted baffle keeps squirrels from climbing up.

A good hopper feeder can be completely disassembled to be cleaned. (More on this later.) Hoppers can be pole-mounted, often with a threaded sleeve that screws onto the threaded top of a plumber's galvanized pipe. They can be suspended, too.

The two best features of hoppers are:

>> They hold a lot of seed, so you don't have to go out every day to refill them.

>> They're big and bird-friendly. Shy birds, or big birds, like doves, jays, and woodpeckers, are able to land and feed from them comfortably.

When we've had unusual species (rose-breasted grosbeaks, for example) at our feeders, they've come to hopper feeders. Birds that are reluctant to perch on smaller, swinging feeders will happily come to a hopper feeder.

You can feed any kind of seed in a hopper feeder because the seed comes out of slots at the bottom of the acrylic panels. Sunflower seed is a favorite of many hopper feeder visitors, but seed mixes containing shelled sunflower, millet, corn, and peanut hearts can be fed in these feeders, too.

Safer feeder: Cylindrical mesh

Cylindrical mesh feeders are super simple. They're basically two metal pans with a rolled cylinder of metal mesh, like hardware cloth, in between. The wire mesh dispenses seed over its entire surface area. The beauty of this is that there are no ports for birds to contact; they simply pull seeds out of the mesh wherever they wish. The metal pan on top keeps the seed dry, and the one on the bottom provides a place for birds to perch. Droppings don't accumulate on the feeder but fall below.

Cylindrical mesh feeders are easy to disassemble and hose clean. Not only that, they're inexpensive. It's nice when the best, safest option is also the least expensive!

The size of the holes in the mesh determines what kind of food cylindrical mesh feeders can dispense. You can find very fine mesh for Nyjer (thistle) that's great for attracting goldfinches; small mesh that works for shell-less sunflower hearts; diamond-shaped mesh that dispenses black-oil sunflower seed; and larger round holes that work for peanut halves — a powerful woodpecker attractant. Feeder labels should indicate which foods they are designed to dispense.

Safer feeder: Screened platform feeder

Small screen-bottomed platform feeders, designed for hanging, are a recent and wonderful innovation for safer bird feeding. You can offer any kind of food in them, or a variety of seeds and nuts.

To keep the food dry, accessorize with an acrylic dome or shield suspended above the feeder. These are often sold as squirrel baffles, but they also make wonderful weather guards for feeders.

With smaller hanging platform feeders, birds tend to perch on their raised sides, and droppings fall to the ground rather than going into the seed. Acrylic domes keep droppings from above from fouling the seed. The steel mesh floor of the feeder is easy to clean and allows moisture to run through.

Suet feeder

Suet is beef fat. Our favorite kind is raw suet, available at some grocery stores but mostly at butcher shops. Lots of folks like to offer commercial suet cakes to their bird visitors instead. Whichever kind you offer, you'll need a special suet feeder. They're usually a simple vinyl-coated wire cage, designed to hang.

TIP

When buying a suet feeder, make sure you can easily scrub it, or even put it in the dishwasher to clean it.

Because animal fat is attractive to raccoons, opossums, and bears, you might want to invest in a feeder called the Lifelong Suet Feeder. It's made of two industrial-strength aluminum plates, perforated by holes, held together by a steel frame. Only birds can peck suet out of it; it's impervious to mammalian raiders. Julie has two Lifelongs going all winter long, with a parade of woodpeckers and sapsuckers lining up to cling and eat.

What to look for when buying a feeder

Many feeder styles are on the market, but any feeder you buy should be easily filled, emptied, and cleaned.

>> You should be able to pour seed into your feeder from a scoop or bag.

Beware of feeders that require you to use a funnel to fill them. You'll quickly tire of lugging a funnel out every time you have to replenish the seed.

>> Recycled plastic is a great innovation for feeders, as it is much easier to clean and it doesn't rot. Mesh should be powder-coated enamel or stainless steel.

TIP

Because you may be looking at a feeder for a decade or more, it pays to buy the sturdiest and most easily maintained one you can.

>> Make sure you can take the feeder apart to scrub and clean it relatively easily. Beware of small crevices or ledges.

TIP

If it looks like you'll need a screwdriver or a fancy bottle brush to get a feeder clean, pick one of a simpler design.

>> If you're buying a cylindrical mesh feeder, make sure that the seed you are feeding will fit through the mesh before buying.

Mount it right, because: squirrels and raccoons

We've presented a small array of feeders so far in this section: hopper, cylindrical mesh, hanging platform, and suet feeder. Those should be all you need to offer a nice variety of food to the birds. Now comes the all-important step of properly hanging those feeders so as to avoid donating hundreds of dollars' worth of seed to the local squirrels and raccoons. With one simple purchase, you can save money and stave off a *lot* of frustration.

We highly recommend suspending your feeders from a single sturdy metal pole with long arms ending in hooks at the top. The central pole must be equipped with a squirrel baffle, preferably one that slides on a spring when the animal attempts to climb it. (A sliding baffle is a tapered cylindrical metal sheath that makes it difficult for an animal to gain purchase and climb.) These baffled hanging systems are not cheap, but when compared to the cost of replacing chewed and broken feeders and the massive amount of expensive seed that squirrels and raccoons consume daily, they are a screaming bargain.

A gray squirrel can jump 3½ feet high from a standing start, broad jump with a running start of 10 feet or more, and it can crawl down thin limbs or tightrope on wire to drop down on your feeders. So, trust us here: start with a baffled pole and spare yourself the spectacle of seeing your every preventive move thwarted.

This sliding baffle and pole system works to deter raccoons as well — well-known destroyers of many a feeding station. However, a sliding baffle and pole system is powerless in the face of a larger and far more formidable feeding station foe: black bears. Those who live within the rapidly expanding range of black bears must wait to start feeding until the bears go into hibernation, and then pull their feeders in as soon as the bears awaken, very early in spring. Bear-proof birding stations are possible to construct, but complicated, very tall, and beyond the scope of this book.

You'll need to find an open area in your yard, away from overhanging limbs, in which to erect the feeder pole. Julie finds that, as the years go by, she must keep trimming key tree limbs from which squirrels can launch themselves to land atop the pole. It's worth it to cut the trees back and maintain a squirrel-free zone where the birds alone get fed!

To get the most enjoyment from your feeders, be sure to mount the pole near a window where you spend a lot of time.

Feeding Times: When to Start, When to Stop

The vast majority of people feed birds only in winter, when it's truly tough out there and the birds look so pitiful all puffed up against the cold. We recommend waiting until the weather turns cold and frost has laid its hand upon the land to start feeding. When insects, wild fruits, and weed seeds are still abundant in fall, there's no need to supplement food.

TIP

It's a good idea to start your feeding program before the weather turns really nasty. This way, you'll entice birds into including your feeder in their winter-feeding routes. Think of the flocks using your feeder as an ever-changing river of birds and you'll have a good idea how it works. You may think you have the same five chickadees all day long, but it's more likely that you have 30 or 40 chickadees who stop in for a few minutes every day, and then go on their merry way looking for caterpillar cocoons, scale insects, and spiders hiding under tree bark.

REMEMBER

Bird feeding is mostly for people. Birds have winter survival skills we can only dream about. That said, it's really nice to have your feeder clientele coming regularly before the temperatures plummet and truly rotten weather sets in.

The birds give you clues

Each spring is different. Some are early and warm, but others are late, cold, and wet. Long after the grass has greened up, you'll still have lots of birds at your feeder. Even after the weather has warmed up, nights can still drop below freezing, which keeps the insects inactive. But one fine April or May day, as the leaves are unfurling, it occurs to you that the feeders just aren't emptying as fast as usual, and you aren't going out quite as often to fill them. It's time to taper off. In Julie's yard, this is quite dramatic, because she has a flock of about a hundred American goldfinches that patronize the feeders all winter. By late April, the males have shed their dull winter plumage for brilliant yellow, trimmed with black wings, cap, and tail. They're singing like crazy in every treetop; it can be deafening. And all of a sudden, they leave, dispersing to the surrounding countryside to pair up and eventually breed. It's quiet. And by then, Julie really doesn't miss them at all!

TIP

As the weather warms, slowly reduce the amount of food you put out and the frequency with which you fill the feeders. In the event of that freak April cold snap, you can always put out more food.

Migratory birds follow their instincts

Birds are happy to desert your feeders when it's time to migrate, or when protein-rich insects become available. You don't need to worry about getting them addicted to seed or keeping them from their normal migratory behavior. But this leads to another question.

A SPRING TO REMEMBER — OR
TRY TO FORGET

Julie will never forget the spring of 2020, when a string of May days in the 30s and 40s, with nighttime lows dipping to the 20s, at her home in Southeast Ohio sent colorful migrant orioles, rose-breasted grosbeaks, and even tanagers, bluebirds, and kingbirds down to her feeding station. Julie had never seen such a diversity of unusual feeder visitors. Rose-breasted grosbeaks and even a summer tanager were eating peanuts; orioles were diving into bunches of grapes and cut oranges. She'd wake up around 3:30 a.m., thinking about what she needed to do, and be up by 5. She was buying oranges and grapefruit by the 10-pound bag, halving them and impaling them on tree branches and feeder hooks for the orioles. She was mail-ordering mealworms, 40,000 at a time, to put out for the insectivorous birds that could find no food in the cold rain. She was keeping the seed feeders stocked for the regular clientele and making her special recipe Zick Dough in quadruple batches. Social media was full of people posting excitedly about the colorful migrant birds coming to backyard feeding stations, but those celebrating the event seemed unaware just how dire the situation was. Julie was deeply concerned for all the birds that were caught out by the horrible weather, just when the leaves should have been unfolding and the caterpillars hatching out. Bird feeding is usually merely recreational in nature. But in unseasonal weather events, like days of freezing temperatures and cold rain in mid-spring, bird feeding can save a lot of beautiful birds' lives.

Suppose that Aunt Reba just called. The condo in Florida is free for ten days. You take a look at the 20-pound icicles hanging from the eaves and say, YES. Only as you're locking the door behind you does it occur to you: who's going to feed the birds? Will they die without the handouts they've grown accustomed to?

There's no clear-cut answer to this because a lot depends on whether other feeding stations are nearby. Here's a story:

> When Julie lived on a nature preserve in New England, she had an annoyingly huge flock of perhaps 70 house finches who camped on the feeders all day long, mowing through 50-pound bags of shell-less sunflower hearts at a pocket-emptying pace. A friend who lived, as the finch flies, two miles away often gloated to Julie that the house finches that once plagued her feeders had disappeared once Julie moved in. Well, one fine day Julie was called away on business, and her feeders went empty for two days. Guess where the flock went? Back to Barbara's house. After that, Julie sometimes waited to refill her feeders until midday and could barely suppress a cackle when Barbara would call to scold her for foisting the flock back on her. It was humbling to realize that the house finches had feeders scoped out over a space of two miles, and likely much more!

Color-banding lets researchers identify individual birds by harmlessly placing colored plastic markers on the legs. Such studies have shown that chickadees take, on average, only one-quarter of their daily food from feeders. Flocking species, like goldfinches, siskins, and house finches, though, seem more inclined to camp out at feeders, relying more heavily on them for their daily meals. As Julie's house finch experience shows, though, birds are intelligent and resourceful enough to move elsewhere when a food source is exhausted.

Resident birds need continuity

Some bird species keep winter territories from which they don't wander. Cardinals and Carolina wrens are two examples. For them, a stop-and-start feeding program can be worse than none at all.

When you have a successful feeding station, populations of birds can explode. And even though the birds may be taking most of their food from your feeders, the natural food supply in the immediate vicinity of the feeders is bound to be exhausted soon. There's not much for the birds to fall back on should the feeding stop. Pulling the rug out from under territorial species who live right around your yard is unfair, at best.

TIP

If you're going away for only a couple of days, fill all your feeders, and scatter a lot of seed on the ground and under shrubbery. For longer vacations in winter, you might consider paying a neighbor to fill your feeders while watering your plants and feeding your indoor pets. Some of us look at feeding birds as having a couple hundred outdoor pets!

IS FEEDING GOOD OR BAD FOR BIRDS?

Let's face it: Bird feeding is really more for people than birds. Birds have been getting by for eons without the artificial supplementation of millions of tons of sunflower, millet, corn, and other things we throw at them all winter. Time was when people just threw a few crusts of stale bread out on a particularly nasty day and called it bird feeding.

The craze we're part of really got started in the 1960s and has been growing ever since, along with the populations of birds that use feeders. The fact is, we know comparatively little about the relative benefits and drawbacks of bird feeding, but it makes for some interesting discussion among bird feeding proponents and opponents.

(continued)

(continued)

Wisconsin researchers Margaret Brittingham and Stanley Temple studied black-capped chickadees that had access to feeders and compared them to chickadee flocks that did not. Although chickadees take, on average, only 20 to 25 percent of their daily food from feeders, the researchers found that feeder-using birds had a higher winter survival rate than their unsubsidized counterparts. Chickadees using feeders had a month-to-month survival rate of 95 percent, compared to 87 percent for birds in the wild with no access to feeders. And get this: 69 percent of feeder-using chickadees survived the winter, while a paltry 37 percent of the feeder-deprived birds made it through.

Maintaining Your Feeding Station

Okay now, it's time to have The Talk about feeder hygiene.

REMEMBER

We discussed earlier in this chapter the merits of acrylic domes, suspended over your hanging feeders. We also talked about safer feeder types that will help keep your feeding station from becoming ground zero for infectious diseases. It's hard to overstress how important it is to keep bird droppings out of the food! When you feed several hundred individual birds, as Julie does at her rural feeding station, things can get whitewashed in a hurry, and it's not nice — for the birds or for their poor human servants who have to refill the feeders.

Give it a shake!

TIP

One simple tip to keep things moving along at the feeder is to pop out and give your feeders a good shake once or twice a day. When birds are busy extracting all the easier-to-get seeds from a large wire mesh cylinder feeder, for instance, things can come to a standstill. The solution is to invert the feeder and give it a good shake. That will re-sort the seeds and open up a lot more opportunities for hungry clients.

Keep cleaning stuff handy

TIP

Julie keeps a pair of low rubber boots by the front door that she wears to fill the feeders, so that stuff doesn't get tracked all through the house. At the feeding station, she keeps an old spatula, a couple of chopsticks, and a couple of scrub brushes. The spatula is great for clearing away seed hulls on table and hopper feeders. The chopsticks can quickly ream out drainage holes. The scrub brush, with a bucket of hot soapy water, takes care of that sickly sweet-smelling sunflower gunk that accumulates in wet weather. It's made up of bits of uneaten sunflower meats, hulls, and goodness knows what else. Phew. One thing you can say for the arid western climate is it's a lot easier to keep feeders clean there. The rainy eastern winters require vigilance!

Periodically, Julie breaks out the Clorox and makes a solution of one part bleach to nine parts hot water. She soaks the feeders in this, scrubs them out, douses the platforms, and scrubs them. It's wet, sloppy work, best done on a warmish day, but it's essential to keep buildup and droppings from fouling the feeding station. It's wonderful to have clean feeders standing ready to swap out while the dirty ones are soaking in bleach!

Always, always wash your hands immediately after servicing the feeding station and bird bath!

Clean up for healthy birds

There are good reasons other than personal fastidiousness to keep your feeders well-cleaned. Disease. Yup. You can do a whole lot of good by feeding birds. But you can also do harm by inviting so many guests to one table because, unlike most human dinner guests over two years of age, birds poop while they eat. Being birds, they don't pay a whole lot of attention to where, either. It's not something birds have to deal with when they're flying around free, but when you get a couple hundred birds in maybe 20 square feet, you have a poopfest. And along with this goes the potential for spreading disease in your feeder flock.

Watch where the food falls

To get around the poop problem, you can start by keeping your ground feeding out from under the hanging feeders and perches. Julie usually throws seed for ground-feeders in a wide circle outside the immediate feeder area, and she keeps changing where she throws it. Enough seed will fall out of the feeders that you'll always have birds directly under the feeders, too. That brush pile or discarded Christmas tree you provided for shelter will show the effects of its popularity and will need to be disposed of in spring.

When Julie first started feeding, she hung the feeders right off her deck. Hoo, boy. The flocks sat up on her television antenna in between meals and made a real mess of her deck. If you're into hosing and scrubbing a lot, feeding birds over your deck may be an option, but it's better to hang the feeders over grass where you won't be walking.

TIP

Here's an idea that may work for you. Because the grass under heavily used feeders takes a beating, try spreading bark mulch under your feeders. When it gets full of hulls and droppings, rake it up, compost it, and put down a fresh layer of mulch.

Looking at Bird Seed Types

There is quite an array of seed and grain, and it can be confusing to visit a bird-feeding store and wonder which kind to buy. Table 8-1 provides the general food preferences for the most common feeder birds of North America. Foods are listed in approximate order of preference. Check out Figure 8-5 to see what the seeds look like.

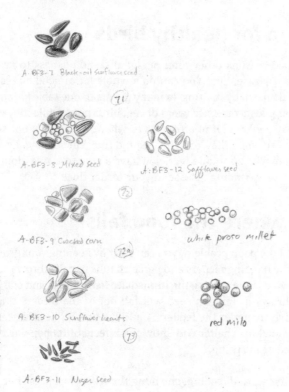

FIGURE 8-5:
Commonly fed seeds: black-oil sunflower, mixed seed, cracked corn, sunflower hearts, Nyjer seed, and safflower seed.

TABLE 8-1   ## Bird Food Preference Chart

Species	Preferred Foods
Quail, pheasants	Cracked corn, millet, wheat, milo
Pigeons, doves	Millet, cracked corn, wheat, milo, Nyjer, buckwheat, sunflower, safflower
Roadrunner	Meat scraps, hamburger, suet, Zick Dough*
Hummingbirds	Plant nectar, small insects, sugar solution
Woodpeckers	Suet, sunflower hearts/seed, cracked corn, peanuts, fruits, nectar, mealworms
Jays	Peanuts (in or out of the shell), sunflower, suet, cracked corn, mealworms
Crows, magpies, nutcracker	Meat scraps, suet, cracked corn, peanuts (in or out of the shell), dog kibble
Titmice, chickadees	Peanut halves, sunflower, safflower, suet, peanut butter, Zick Dough*, mealworms
Nuthatches	Suet, sunflower hearts and seed, peanut halves, peanut butter, Zick Dough*, mealworms
Wrens, creepers	Suet, peanut butter, peanut bits, Zick Dough*, mealworms
Mockingbirds, thrashers, catbird	Halved apple, chopped fruits, suet, nutmeats, millet (thrashers), soaked raisins, currants, sunflower hearts, Zick Dough*, mealworms
Robins, bluebirds, other thrushes	Suet, berries, chopped fruits, soaked raisins, currants, nutmeats, sunflower hearts, Zick Dough*, mealworms
Kinglets	Suet, suet mixes, Zick Dough*
Warblers	Suet, suet mixes, fruit, chopped nutmeats, Zick Dough*, mealworms
Tanagers	Suet, fruits, sugar solution, mealworms, Zick Dough*
Cardinals, grosbeaks, pyrrhuloxia (a type of cardinal)	Sunflower, safflower, cracked corn, peanut halves, fruit, Zick Dough*
Towhees, juncos	Millet, sunflower, safflower, cracked corn, peanut halves
Sparrows, buntings	Millet, sunflower hearts, black-oil sunflower, cracked corn
Blackbirds, starlings	Cracked corn, milo, wheat, table scraps, baked goods, suet
Orioles	Halved oranges, apples, berries, sugar solution, grape jelly, suet, suet mixes, soaked raisins, currants
Finches, siskins	Nyjer, sunflower hearts, black-oil sunflower, millet, canary seed, peanut bits, suet mixes

A recipe for Julie's popular lard-based concoction, Zick Dough, is at the end of this chapter.

In a nutshell, sunflower seed is a great place to start — attractive to the widest array of birds. So, if you're just starting out in feeding, we suggest you buy some black-oil sunflower seed at a local hardware store, feed store, specialty bird store, or even at a major retail chain store. But you need to watch out for certain things when buying seed. The following sections point you in the right direction by describing the best kinds of seed.

Black-oil sunflower

Riding across northern Wisconsin as a kid, Julie was delighted by mile after mile of golden sunflowers nodding in the breeze, heralds of a quiet revolution in bird feeding. She's old enough to remember when bird feeding meant throwing stale bread out in the yard! Then, there was sunflower seed, the gray-striped or white-striped kind, with thick, woody shells accessible only to heavy-billed cardinals and grosbeaks as well as birds like jays, chickadees, and titmice, which can hammer the thick shell open with their bill as they hold the seed in their toes. Since then, black-oil sunflower seed, such as she saw growing in Wisconsin, has completely overtaken gray-striped seed in bird feeding popularity and sales.

Smaller than gray-striped sunflower seed, with a thin, all-black, papery shell, black-oil sunflower seed can be cracked by sparrows, juncos, and even the small-billed goldfinches (though it's a bridge too far for pine siskins). It's a better buy, too, because 70 percent of each seed is meat, compared to only 57 percent for striped sunflower. Its high oil and fat content helps birds get through cold winter nights. Black-oil sunflower seed is the heart of any feeding program because it's the seed accepted by the greatest variety of birds. You can feed it out of hanging feeders, put it in hoppers or on tables, or scatter it on the ground — preferably all of the above.

Have a sunflower heart

TIP

If Julie were to pick only one food to offer at a feeding station, it would be sunflower hearts. Yes, they're expensive, but a bag of sunflower hearts (no shells, just the meat of the seed) lasts more than three times as long as a bag of seeds with shells. Not only this, but every species that comes to a feeding station eats them. Being hull-less, hearts are accessible to weaker-billed birds like siskins, redpolls, and Carolina wrens. Goldfinches love them, and even bluebirds can develop a taste for them.

Keep it dry

Compared to seeds with hulls, hearts are relatively free of waste and of the messy shells that pile up to smother grass and rot decks. The only drawback is that the hearts shouldn't be exposed to wet weather; they rot quickly when damp. As such, they should be fed only from feeders that protect them from moisture.

REMEMBER

On dry days, it's fine to spread a handful on the deck railing or bird table, but otherwise, stick to weatherproof feeders. You'll be surprised how little it takes to feed a lot of birds.

Getting a good mix

Mixed seed, often generically referred to as "wild bird seed," is a good addition to any feeding program. Not all mixes are created equal, however, and what is eagerly eaten in Arizona can go to waste in New York.

Millet

Despite certain regional preferences, birds everywhere will eat some foods. Try a mix that contains white proso millet — a little, round, shiny, cream-colored seed. It's a staple for most sparrows and juncos, and birds as diverse as doves, Carolina wrens, thrashers, and cardinals will eat it, too.

Cracked corn

The second foolproof ingredient of a mix is cracked corn, which is accepted by a surprising array of birds. Cracked corn is the cheapest and best offering for quail, pheasants, and doves, but jays, cardinals, and towhees love it, too. Keep in mind that it's irresistible to cowbirds, grackles, and house sparrows. If you're inundated by these less-desirable birds, you may want to pull in your corn horns.

THE MALARKEY ABOUT MILO

Bird Watcher's Digest once published an article about bird feeding that really Illustrates how vastly different bird food preferences can be from region to region. The author of the article pointed out how the birds at his feeders never touched the milo seeds, making them a waste as a bird food. Alongside the article, we ran a cartoon that showed one bird saying to another "Real birds don't eat milo."

(continued)

(continued)

As soon as the article and cartoon appeared, *BWD* received several letters from readers in Arizona, New Mexico, and California singing the praises of milo. Doves, quail, towhees, and other ground-feeding birds of the Southwest loved milo. These folks wouldn't part with their milo for a second. And just who did we think we were?

As astute journalists, we investigated further and discovered that, indeed, milo was readily eaten by many western species while eastern birds largely ignored it. That makes sense, since bird feeders out West are likely to be frequented by larger seed-eaters, like flocks of quail, blackbirds, a number of dove and pigeon species, and several species of towhees (a ground-scratching tribe of oversized sparrows) — all able to swallow whole or otherwise handle these larger seeds and grains that our small eastern sparrows and juncos struggle to consume. Suffice it to say that bird tastes and preferences (like those of people) vary widely from place to place.

Sunflower seed and other ingredients

The third ingredient of a good mix is our old buddy, black-oil sunflower seed. Peanut hearts, which are small, rather bitter byproducts of peanut processing, make birdseed mixes smell good (which is nice for us), boost the price (which is nice for retailers), and may appeal to chickadees, titmice, jays, and wrens. Peanut hearts are not vital and, in our experience, the sunflower always goes first anyway. This isn't to devalue whole peanuts as a food — they can be great if offered in the right feeder.

DON'T LOOK FOR IT AT THE GROCERY STORE!

Grocery stores may have lots to offer people, but they're mostly in the Dark Ages where birds are concerned. The wild bird feed offered at the supermarket is usually of the lowest quality available, and sometimes at the highest price! Packed in five- or ten-pound bags, grocery store mixes are usually full of wheat, barley, and milo, seeds that most birds, at least in the eastern half of the country, ignore.

To find better prices on better bird seed, go to a feed store, a hardware store, or a specialty wild bird store that carries bird feed and feeders — and buy it in bulk. It pays to know what you're after. If your local grocery store has good mixtures of readily eaten seed types, that's great! You're lucky.

Peanuts

Peanuts are a vital part of a good feeding program. Offered in the shell, only crows, jays, and the occasional clever titmouse can really exploit them, because peanuts are just too big and cumbersome for most birds to crack open. Better feed and birdseed stores, though, sell raw, shelled peanuts in bulk.

Offer these peanuts in a feeder that keeps larger birds from carrying them away whole. Special cylindrical steel or wire mesh peanut feeders have large, 5/16-inch openings that allow birds to peck the peanuts into bits. (See Figure 8-6.) The idea is to allow birds to peck small bits out of the peanuts, not carry entire halves off. Peanuts offer a great, high-protein boost to winter-weary birds and help insect-eaters like wrens, woodpeckers, and sapsuckers make it through. Nuthatches, titmice, chickadees, cardinals, and rose-breasted grosbeaks love peanuts, too. Either roasted or raw is fine.

FIGURE 8-6:
A cylindrical mesh feeder designed for peanut halves. White-breasted nuthatch approves.

WARNING

Peanuts can be subject to mold in hot, wet weather. Check them often for signs of black mold or the darkening in color that can mean they've gone rancid. Offer only as many peanuts as the birds will eat in a few days in warmer weather conditions, doling them out like the gold they are. And make sure the peanut feeder is protected by an acrylic dome that will keep them clean and dry.

Other options: thistle and safflower

A couple of the more obscure seeds have their adherents:

WARNING

>> **Nyjer** (also known as *thistle seed*) is imported from Africa and Asia. The seed is sterilized, so it won't germinate and take over backyards all over North America. Lots of people are under the misapprehension that Nyjer seed is the only thing American goldfinches eat. Contrary to this belief, goldfinches do just fine on black-oil sunflower, either with or without shells.

In addition to being expensive, Nyjer is subject to mold, especially in hot, damp weather, and you have to shake your feeders every time you fill them to be sure the seed is coming out of the ports properly. If the seed clumps, you'll have to dump it out in your trash and wash and dry your feeder before refilling it. Fine mesh "thistle socks" are a cheap way to feed Nyjer, and they let air circulate around the seed. We hear from a lot of people about batches of Nyjer that the birds just won't eat; it looks fine, smells fine, but probably tastes bad.

Dawn learned this the hard way. Her local wild bird store was having a big sale. She bought 80 pounds of Nyjer seed, which she hoped would last through the fall and winter. For the first month, she had a finch bonanza in her yard. But that diminished no matter how often she shook the feeder or replaced the seed. She ended up throwing away more than half of it — in unopened bags — because it just didn't keep. Even with the discount, it wasn't a bargain after all.

For all these reasons, black-oil sunflower and sunflower hearts are a better all-around choice.

>> **Safflower** is a white, shiny, conical seed that's gained popularity among people who find that cardinals and many other birds that eat sunflower seed also like it, and some squirrels and grackles don't. (Some squirrels *do* eat safflower seed, however; you may want to try it and see.) Safflower seed is usually found in bulk at better feed stores. You can offer it in any feeder that dispenses sunflower seed.

REMEMBER

Safflower seed is nice to offer, but not vital; any bird that eats safflower will also take sunflower seed. Part of the fun of feeding birds is seeing who likes what!

Exploring Other Bird Foods

You can offer birds a vast array of other foods besides bird seed — some advisable, some not. Here are a few of the most commonly offered parts of the birds' smorgasbord.

Bready or not

Birds and bread just seem to go together in most people's minds. As children, the first food many of us ever offered birds was stale white bread. We've come a long way, though, and bread is now recognized as a bad choice for any bird, most obviously for waterfowl at city parks. The truth is, bread is high in carbohydrates and low in nutritional value. Birds don't know any better, however. Bread fills up their stomachs quite nicely, so they feel satisfied, but now there's no room for healthier foods. Poor nutrition caused by a bread diet can cause birth defects from malnutrition, which often can render birds flightless. So, a word the wise: Don't feed bread to birds.

Suet is fat city

Suet is the dense, white fat that collects around beef kidneys and loins. Don't confuse it with meat trimmings, which are slippery and tough and spoil quickly. Only true suet — kidney and loin fat — will do. While suet was once commonly sold in grocery store meat cases, that's no longer the case, now that fewer and fewer stores employ butchers to cut meat. To get raw suet now, Julie heads to her local small meat-processing plant for bulk prices. She cuts it up into feeder-sized chunks and freezes them in resealable plastic bags.

You'll be surprised at how many different species of birds go for suet, including some you may need to look up in the field guide. All the regular seed-eaters — chickadees, titmice, nuthatches, woodpeckers ((see Figure 8-7) — eat suet, as well as wrens, sapsuckers, warblers, orioles, catbirds, creepers, and other birds. A little suet goes a long way.

WARNING

Like most good things, suet comes with caveats:

>> Check your suet feeder often. It disappears faster than you'd expect.

>> Be sure not to mistake the inedible white rind left when all the fat is pecked away for edible suet.

>> Suet is only for cold-weather feeding. Having contact with melted suet fouls bird feathers and destroys their waterproofing.

>> Do not feed raw suet after the weather warms up in spring.

>> Rancid suet, it goes without saying, is to be avoided!

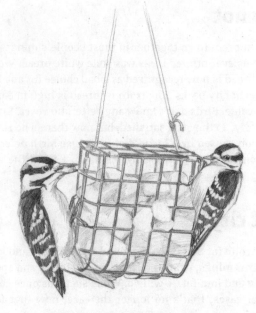

FIGURE 8-7:
A hairy woodpecker (left) and a downy woodpecker share raw suet at a hanging wire cage feeder.

About suet blocks

Lots of people take convenience a step further and buy commercial suet blocks. Some of these blocks are good; some aren't so good. Here's what to look for.

TIP

Avoid commercial blocks that have whole seed, like sunflower and millet seed, melted into them. They look great, but are practically useless to the birds, who can't crack the fat-soaked seed shells. They wind up just picking the seeds out of the suet and discarding them or pecking the suet away from the seeds. Such blocks are a waste of money.

If you buy blocks, buy only those with 100-percent-edible ingredients like peanut hearts, sunflower hearts, dried mealworms, chopped raisins, or cornmeal. No seeds with shells on them!

In Julie's experience, the expense of buying blocks isn't justified by any greater enthusiasm on the part of the birds who eat fat. They're crazy about raw suet. But should you decide to offer suet as part of your feeding program, you'll be rewarded by lots of interesting woodpecker visitors. Maybe you'll get a chance to compare hairy and downy woodpeckers side-by-side! (See Figure 8-7.)

A special recipe

Here's a winter treat for your birds that Julie popularized on her blog. The recipe has been around for years, but the addition of chick starter (a crumbly pellet for raising young chickens) gives this rich food a nutritional boost.

ZICK DOUGH, IMPROVED

2 cups chick starter, unmedicated (available at any feed store, check label for antibiotics)

2 cups quick oats

1 cup flour

1 cup yellow cornmeal

1 cup lard

1 cup peanut butter

1 **Combine the dry ingredients.**

2 **Melt together the lard and peanut butter in a microwave.**

3 **Slowly add liquid fats to dry mixture while stirring or mixing on low until dough forms.**

If it's too gummy, add a little more flour and cornmeal until it's soft, dry, and crumbly.

4 **Serve as a treat in a small dish with an acrylic dome to protect from rain. Store at room temperature in jars.**

Zick Dough is a very rich food, and it should not be fed at all in late spring and summer or any time when average daytime temperatures rise above 55 degrees. It's best for the birds to reserve it for winter, as a once-daily treat. It's wonderful nutrition during ice storms, when their usual fruit and insect foods are locked away. Feed it in early spring when the weather turns vile and migrating birds face starvation. And enjoy the relationships you'll cultivate when you serve this premium food to your small, feathery neighbors.

Settling in for the Summer

The joy of bird feeding doesn't have to *entirely* stop when the weather turns warmer and many of your winter feeder visitors vamoose. But summer is the time of year both to pull in your horns and to switch gears, to tailor your offerings to suit the tastes and preferences of a new set of visitors. We'll get to those in a moment. Here are the best reasons for taking a feeding vacation for the summer.

>> **They don't need it.** Even most of the resident or year-round birds that are feeder regulars change their dining habits in the warmer months. Why? Because they have an abundance of natural food available: insects, fruits, and new plant growth such as buds, nuts, and seeds. Most feeder birds, with the exception of doves and finches, switch to insects in summer. That's what they feed their young, too. And that's what they *should* be eating and feeding their young in summer! So, there's no need to offer mass quantities of seed, peanuts, and suet.

>> **Disease runs rampant in hot weather.** Seed goes rancid and spoils, suet melts, and the germs that cause house finch disease, avian pox, salmonella, and botulism multiply and spread much faster in warm weather. It's much better for birds to disperse and find natural food than to hang around feeding stations.

>> **Mammals take over in summer.** Summer feeding encourages mice, chipmunks, squirrels, rabbits, deer, and raccoons — all of whom love bird seed — to put your yard on their must-visit list. While they're at it, the rodents will gladly dig up and tunnel through your flowerbeds; the rabbits will chew your favorite plants to the ground; deer will decimate shrubbery and ornamental plantings; and raccoons will do a combination of all those things, and poop on your doorstep for good measure.

It took Julie more than 25 years to figure out the host of problems that unfold when one feeds birds all summer long. But now she quits as soon as night temperatures hit the 50s, and she is a much happier gardener, with healthier birds, for abstaining in summer.

Now for the good news about summer feeding. And that good news is: hummingbirds!

Hummingbirds

North America's smallest birds are not only beautiful to look at, but they have near-mythic flying abilities. Unique rotating joints close to the body let hummingbirds swivel their wings through figure-eight arcs and do outrageous aerobatics. They need this maneuverability because hummingbirds feed by hovering and drinking nectar from flowers. (See Figure 8-8.) It's a good thing they can fly so well, because hummingbirds have such tiny, weak legs and feet that they aren't able to walk at all. They fly everywhere, even if they only have to go a few inches.

FIGURE 8-8:
Ruby-throated hummingbird feeding at trumpet vine.

If you're lucky enough to live along the Gulf of Mexico, in southern Florida, in South Texas, Arizona, Southern California, or along the temperate Pacific coast, you get to see hummingbirds all year long. For the rest of us, the poor hummerless masses, it's a long wait from each fall to spring when the hummingbirds return to our midst. And for those of us east of the Rocky Mountains, we're waiting for only one species (the ruby-throated hummingbird) to return.

Why are hummingbirds so fascinating to us?

>> Humans find it hard to believe that something so tiny, something almost insect-like in its appearance and habits, can possibly be a bird.

>> We can easily attract hummingbirds to our yards, porches, patios, and windowsills using feeders and a simple nectar solution. With hummers in our midst, we can observe their fascinating behaviors and high-energy lifestyles.

Most any yard in North America can attract hummingbirds during the warmer months of the year. And, most of the hummingbirds native to this continent are reliable visitors to hummer feeders in some part of their range.

TIP

What attracts a hummer's attention better than anything are bright flowers. To attract and keep hummingbirds in your yard, plant masses of the flowers they love in beds, hanging baskets, and planters. (See Chapter 9 for more on strategies to attract specific bird species.)

Hummingbird feeders

A good hummingbird feeder is easy to clean. The best hummingbird feeders can be taken apart completely in seconds and have no nooks and crannies accessible only by cotton swabs or bottle brushes. You should be able to scrub out the feeding ports and reservoir completely without special tools. Look for wide, two-part bases that come completely apart, and wide-necked bottle reservoirs.

Feeders that have feeding ports facing up toward the sky can't drip; those with feeding ports off the side or pointed down toward the ground invariably drip, attracting insects and often emptying themselves without help from the birds! Look for feeder designs that minimize drippage. The "Little Beginner" feeder in Figure 8-9 may drip in hot weather, but it's handy for early spring when hummingbirds are just arriving and not drinking much.

FIGURE 8-9:
A simple "Little Beginner" feeder, good for early spring when hummingbirds are just arriving.

Almost all the good feeders on the market feature bright red parts. This is to attract the attention of thirsty hummers, just as red flowers do. Other bright colors may work, but red is the most eye-catching for hummingbirds.

If you're starting a new hummingbird feeding station and you don't have blooming flowers already attracting hummingbirds, try hanging a bright red or orange ribbon below the feeder. This flash of bright color improves the feeder's chances of catching the eye of a passing hummingbird.

To keep ants out, invest in an ant moat — a water cup with a hook above and below, suspended above the feeder that keeps ants from accessing the feeder, because ants can't swim.

Nectar — A recipe for happy hummers

A mixture with a four-to-one (4:1) ratio of water to sugar most closely matches the sugar and energy content of the natural nectar that hummingbirds drink from blooming flowers.

More is not better for these tiny birds, so don't assume that you're doing your hummingbirds a favor by putting more sugar into the mixture. It can tax their liver and cause health problems!

When making the nectar mixture, use refined white sugar (one part), and add it to boiling tap water (four parts). Stir in the sugar until it's dissolved, and then let the mixture cool before offering it to hummingbirds. Julie likes to use filtered water for making nectar; it does not promote the growth of molds or bacteria and doesn't need to be boiled.

Do not be seduced by the jugs of ruby-red commercial "hummingbird food" on the market. It contains artificial dyes like Red #40, which has been shown to be harmful to hummingbirds, and the "vitamins and minerals" are a red herring. Don't use anything other than white table sugar when making hummingbird nectar. Molasses, honey, brown sugar, and artificial sweeteners do not match the level of sucrose that hummingbirds get from natural nectars.

Putting red food coloring in your hummingbird nectar is totally unnecessary. If your feeder has red parts, that's enough to attract hummingbirds. You can revive a faded hummer feeder with bright red nail polish applied around the ports. We do this frequently with our older feeders. Be sure to let the polish dry thoroughly before filling and hanging the feeder.

We dream of hygiene

After getting the 4:1 water-to-sugar ratio right, the most important thing you can do is keep your feeders scrupulously clean. Here's where feeder design comes in. Our favorite feeders disassemble in seconds, with as few small parts as possible. In hot, humid weather, we take it down every other day, dump out any remaining sugar solution, and wash it thoroughly in hot, soapy water, rinsing well.

You know it's past time to wash your feeders when the solution turns cloudy, emitting a yeasty smell, or (heaven forbid) begins to grow clumps of gelatinous mold or black scuzz. This reaction can happen in as few as three days in the heat of summer, so err on the side of cleanliness and make washing and scrubbing your feeders in hot, soapy water a regular habit. Rinse well and wash each time you refill the feeders. Spoiled solution can harm hummingbirds.

Orioles

Among the most colorful of all the North American birds are the orioles. (Although related to blackbirds, they outdo their cousins in the style department by accessorizing with brilliant yellow and orange plumage.) These birds spend the winter months in Central and South America, where they feed on fruit and insects. When they return to our midst in the spring, crafty feeder operators have halved fresh oranges and grapefruit prominently displayed where curious birds can spot them. It can be as easy as impaling the citrus halves on tall dowels, stuck into the ground near overhanging tree branches, as shown in Figure 8-10.

FIGURE 8-10:
Baltimore oriole on an orange half, which is offered on a dowel stuck into the ground.

TIP

Orioles are nectar-lovers, too, though most hummingbird feeders aren't suited to the orioles' large size and lack of hovering skills. Offer nectar for orioles in small, wide-mouthed jars, hung by a wire looped around the neck of the jar. Tie a bright orange ribbon or silk flower to the top of the jar and hang the jar from a sturdy branch in the outer canopy of a small tree, where an oriole is sure to spot it. Don't add artificial color to the nectar; just make it with four parts water to one part sugar.

There's a bit of a fad going around: feeding grape jelly to orioles. Some people buy huge jars at bulk food stores to keep "their" orioles supplied. We take strong exception to this! As an avian rehabilitator, Julie doesn't feed anything to wild birds that she wouldn't feed to a captive pet bird. The deciding factor: could a wild oriole find any natural food that's literally half sugar by weight? One tablespoon of grape jelly (20 grams) has 10 grams of sugar. That's too much sugar for any small bird to take in. Stick to orange halves and a one part sugar, four parts water nectar solution.

EEK! A worm!

Another trend to watch is feeding live and freeze-dried mealworms to backyard birds. Live mealworms are available via mail order from a number of reputable suppliers. (Don't even think about buying them at a pet store, where you'll pay a premium for tiny, half-dead larvae that have been refrigerated for weeks.) Mealworms are a valuable food for birds in times of hardship. We're talking about winter ice and snowstorms and cold spring rains here. Be sure to offer them in a domed or covered hanging feeder; they drown and die if rained upon.

People who feed mealworms, especially to bluebirds, throughout the year are making a big mistake. Having a supply of live larvae in midwinter isn't natural, and can lead to dependency, especially on the part of bluebirds. It can make them try to nest too early and raise too many broods of young. It can throw off their molt schedules and tax their reproductive systems. Mealworms are very high in fat and phosphorus and are bad for birds if they're being offered 24/7. If you must feed mealworms to birds, keep it to no more than eight worms per bird per day. That's treat-level feeding, no more.

Dried mealworms are a nice winter supplement for birds. Juncos seem to especially appreciate them. You'll find prices vary widely. Packaged for wild bird feeding, they tend to be quite expensive. Step over to the chicken section of the same feed supply store, and you'll find much better deals in bulk. The fat/phosphorus caveat holds; keep even dried mealworms a treat for your birds.

Walking on eggshells

Here's a cool offering that birds love, and it's free! As you make your morning omelet, rinse and save the eggshells. Put them on a cookie sheet and bake them in a 250-degree oven until they're just beginning to brown. This disinfects them and makes them easier to digest. Store them in jars. Crumble them into small bits and scatter them on table feeders, deck railings, flat rocks, sidewalks, or bare ground. Julie throws handfuls of eggshells up on the garage roof for a flock of 17 barn swallows who've been flying from neighboring farms to her yard for 33 years, just for eggshells! (See Figure 8-11.) You'll be amazed at the array of birds that come to eat them! Female birds need calcium to replace that lost in egg-laying, and you may get rare looks at secretive woodland species attracted by the bright white shells. Barn and tree swallows, purple martins, goldfinches, and blue jays seem to be the most enthusiastic takers, but female birds of many species appreciate the calcium boost.

FIGURE 8-11: Barn swallows are enthusiastic consumers of eggshells, tossed up onto a garage roof or scattered on a sidewalk.

Chapter **9**

Gardening for the Birds

No matter where you live, it's a sure bet that you can attract more birds to your yard, garden, or immediate surroundings by including the kinds of plants, shrubs, trees, and other vegetation that birds love. Beyond providing food to birds, plants provide shelter, nesting material, and nesting sites. And — best of all — trees and plants make your yard and garden more beautiful and diverse.

Throughout this chapter, we list many plants that are exceptionally good for birds. The names of these plants are in **bold-faced type.** Because you may live in a part of the continent where certain plants thrive while others die (such as the desert), we suggest you check with a local garden center, landscaping firm, or your regional agricultural or soil-conservation office for specific recommendations on plants that do well in your growing zone.

Lose the Lawn, Lose the Yawns

Here in Ohio where we live, the lawn is king. Many people spend most of a day each week mowing vast expanses of bluegrass and fescue, tracing endless back-and-forth paths with lawnmowers. Here and there, a small tree may stand, wrapped in white tape and supported by guy wires. Carefully clipped shrubs march in rows along the house foundations. This scene is fine, but no birds flit about these cookie-cutter yards, except perhaps the odd robin out prospecting for earthworms on the shaven greensward.

Why are these classic mid-American yards so devoid of birdlife? Because, in a word, these yards are boring. When you plant a lawn, you're tying up the landscape with one or two species of grass. If you mow regularly, these grasses are never allowed to go to seed, and thus have little to offer a bird in the way of food.

Why not rethink things? Plan your yard with a variety of species and types of plant life, from grasses to flowers to shrubs and trees.

But how? We've given it some thought and have come up with some rules in the next section that should do the trick.

Cardinal rules for a bird-friendly yard

Creating a bird-friendly yard is easy if you obey these five, basic, birdwatcher-tested rules. We call these the cardinal rules for a bird-friendly yard, but they work for robins and bluebirds, as well. Many kinds of birds, actually.

Rule one: Be diverse!

The first rule of planting for birds is: Be diverse! Move beyond the clipped lawn and neat ranks of non-native shrubbery lined up along the foundation. Plant lots of different kinds of plants — annual and perennial flowers, vines, shrubs, and trees. Look at any natural habitat popping with birds, and you see a mixture, even a jumble, of different kinds of plants, with different heights and growth habits. That doesn't mean your yard has to look like a Tarzan film set. You can lay things out in a nice, orderly way and still create a paradise for birds.

Rule two: Choose plants that have something birds like

Precious few plants don't have anything to offer some species of birds, but one that comes to mind as a loser for birds is a hybrid tea rose. Lovely to look at, this rose offers no nectar for hummingbirds and rarely sets fruit that a mockingbird or another fruit-eater may enjoy. Because many people who are serious about tea roses find it necessary to defend them chemically against insect pests, these plants may even be dangerous to birds! Another bird-unfriendly plant is nandina, whose beautiful red drupes are toxic to fruit-eating birds. Now that you know our prejudices, let us be quick to say that we have lawns, and Julie even has roses, but she plants a whole lot of other stuff, too! And some roses are better than others for birds. (See the list at the end of this chapter.)

A quick scan down the tables in any gardening book shows an endless array of useful and attractive plants you can use to create a bird paradise. Everything from annual flowers, such as zinnias — which attract hummingbirds with their nectar and lure goldfinches with their seeds — to the stately oak, with its sheltering branches and nourishing acorns, can be of use to birds. The secret is to offer a lot of options for food, shelter, and nesting. A dense shrub like an arborvitae or Chamaecyparis may not have flashy flowers or fleshy fruit, but it's perfect for a nesting chipping sparrow or a roosting junco. The more options, the more birds you can attract.

Rule three: Plant lots!

Julie shares: "When I first started gardening at about age ten, I used to plant a single specimen of every flower I was interested in, all in a neat little row. I still have that penchant for diversity, but I've learned to plant flowers and shrubs in groups. This is just good gardening sense, but it's also good for the birds." (See Figure 9-1.)

FIGURE 9-1:
Plan to watch birds while gardening.

A goldfinch may not give a single native **Coreopsis** plant a passing look, but a drift of Coreopsis in a bed gets you a flock of goldfinches, busily stripping seeds from the old flower heads. Flowers planted in masses attract attention with their color. Besides, we think flowers look best that way. This is especially important in a hummingbird garden. Hummers need lots and lots of flowers to feed on so that some flowers are always offering nectar while others recharge their supply. A major side bonus is the butterflies that are attracted to your display.

Rule four: Don't worry, be messy!

Along about March, Julie says her flower and vegetable gardens start looking really awful. "That's because I don't clean them up in the fall. I have a couple of reasons for this. First, I'm lazy. Second, I get a lot of pleasure out of watching how the birds use the standing dead stalks of annuals and perennials all winter long. Leaving dead stalks also leaves butterfly and moth chrysalides undisturbed, making more food for birds."

A bed of flowers left standing after frost is an abundant seed source for sparrows, finches, and juncos all winter. Even with feeding stations going full bore in February, old trashy flower beds are still full of birds every morning, stripping the last seeds of zinnias, primroses, sunflowers, and even lettuce plants left to bolt. The birds always drop some seeds, too, providing the added pleasure of seeing volunteers come up from seed in spring.

We wait until the weather warms up and new growth starts before cleaning all the beds. By then, the birds hardly miss the old stalks, as they've had all winter to strip them of seeds.

Rule five: Native plants are best

REMEMBER

Native plants are adapted to the conditions at hand; they tend not to need coddling. More than this, local birds recognize their food value and readily exploit them. Going native in your plantings means you'll be fostering native insects, which serve as food for the birds you wish to attract. As just one example, a native oak can support up to 534 different species of butterfly and moth caterpillars, according to Douglas Tallamy in his excellent book *Bringing Nature Home.* And caterpillars are the best food for nestling birds.

TIP

Doug Tallamy's books are a great place to start to build a native plant paradise for birds in your own yard, a trend he calls your "Homegrown National Park." Find out more at https://homegrownnationalpark.org.

For Julie, buying an 80-acre farm that was rapidly being taken over by "trash" vegetation — some of it native and desirable; much of it invasive and needing removal, has been an education in the value of trash! Yes, native **staghorn** and **shining sumac** (*Rhus* spp.) look a little gangly as they lean out over the meadow, but we're hard-pressed to think of another plant that has as much to offer birds in the dead of winter. Because their tiny fruits aren't fleshy, they don't ferment, staying edible all winter and remaining just as nutritious in April as they were in October. Warblers migrating in fall gorge on their fruits; northern parulas and Cape May warblers partake of them, as well as eastern bluebirds and hermit thrushes. What sumac fruits lack in fleshiness they make up for in volume. A single sumac shrub can help dozens of birds when the going gets tough in late winter. It's such a thrill to hear the loud yakking of great big pileated woodpeckers (see Figure 9-2) who cling and dangle like chickadees in the sumac as they pluck each crimson fruit.

TIP

The abbreviation *spp.* (pronounced *spuh*) indicates the plural of the word species. When you see it as *Rhus* spp. it indicates that many species are in the genus *Rhus* (the sumac family) that share the same qualities. And when we're describing several plants belonging to the same genus (as for example *Salvia*, we will list subsequent species in this genus with only S., followed by the species name. So: *Salvia coccinea, S. patens, S. guaranitica.*

Bluebirds make an electric statement perched atop maroon sumac heads, and flickers and robins look spectacular in the smooth gray branches as they forage.

TIP

We have a suggestion — one which won't endear us to all of our fellow humans. Consider keeping your lawn all-natural and mowing with the level set high. Watch bees working the white clover and other small plants blooming in an untreated yard and realize that there's far more wildlife value there than in fescue. You can save both bucks and birds by not drenching your lawn in chemicals and fertilizers. In fact, common lawn herbicides — not to mention insecticides — can kill insectivorous birds that ingest them. Nature has this amazing gift for doing just fine on its own — which is in direct contrast to the old axiom "better living through chemistry."

TIP

If you have the space to spare, let one section of your yard or garden go wild; that is, let it grow up and don't impose your gardener's will on it. You may be pleasantly surprised by the bird-friendly plants that appear. Besides, they'll be free!

FIGURE 9-2:
Pileated
woodpeckers
eating sumac and
greenbrier fruit.

Taking Inventory

Even if you don't know the plants you have in your yard, you can do an inventory of the *types* of plants you have. This can be a simple walk around the yard, noting what's there in terms of flowering plants, seed-producing plants, vines, shrubs and bushes, hedgerows, and trees. Do you see birds feeding on the buds, flowers, or fruits of a certain plant, shrub, or tree? Do the birds seem to spend lots more time in and around a certain part of your yard? If so, try to figure out what is attracting them there. Is it a food source? Is it excellent shelter?

It's important to get a handle on what plants are good guys and which ones you should eliminate. You'll hear the term *invasive* to describe any species that isn't native and tends to take over, whether plant or animal. Invasive plants are a huge problem, with a negative impact throughout every aspect of an ecosystem. Your local agricultural extension service should be able to tell you what invasives to remove.

Here in Ohio, Julie spends much of her winter cutting down multiflora rose and pulling Japanese honeysuckle off the native shrubs and trees. These two non-native invaders had smothered most of the bird-friendly native dogwood, spice-bush, and herbaceous plants that are supposed to be here. She got serious about removing the 12-foot-high multiflora rose walls and towers of Japanese honeysuckle, and six years later, she is astounded at the response from nesting birds. Kentucky, blue-winged, black-and-white, and hooded warblers; ovenbirds and American redstarts; white-eyed, red-eyed, and yellow-throated vireos and wood thrushes now nest where hideous tangles once reigned. She can't overemphasize what a difference it's made in the bird population in her orchard and meadow. Consider removing what you don't want so you can see what happens when native vegetation is allowed to flourish.

REMEMBER

Native plants span a wide array, and each has its place in the ecosystem. The blackberry brambles may tear at pant legs, but they offer food in late summer to a great variety of birds, including waxwings, catbirds, brown thrashers, bluebirds, robins, and towhees. Field sparrows, yellowthroats, cardinals, and thrashers nest in their dense tangles. **Blackberries** (*Rubus* spp.) may be a pain in the pants, but they're invaluable to wildlife.

Now we'll really cement ourselves in the lunatic fringe by singing the praises of **poison ivy** (*Toxicodendron radicans*). It's a great food for birds! Woodpeckers of all kinds seem especially fond of its waxy white berries, as do yellow-rumped warblers and waxwings. Why can birds eat the fruits and flit among the leaves without itching? Because poison ivy is not toxic to birds as it is for most humans. And this plant is so common precisely because birds are so good at dispersing the seeds. Poison ivy certainly isn't a plant you want in the dooryard, but it definitely has its place in the back 40, if you're lucky enough to have a back 40.

Our point is simply that you may be tempted to uproot or mow many plants until you take stock of what they offer birds. Always figure out what it is before you decide if it goes or stays. Mobile phone apps like iNaturalist and Seek are incredibly helpful for identifying mystery plants. If it's native, let it grow!

REMEMBER

To a bird looking for a source of tasty seeds, there is no such thing as a weed. Many of the plants that we, as gardeners, love to hate (**dandelions, native thistles, wild native grasses**) are excellent food sources for birds. Consider letting some of these weed species grow in one section of your property.

Praising Meadows

Meadows come in lots of styles, from *au naturel*, dominated by grasses and native wildflowers, to the so-called meadows-in-a-can, which can create spectacular masses of color. Any meadow is a great habitat for birds, if it's properly cared for — that is to say, left wild until it's time to mow.

REMEMBER

Although you need to mow to maintain any meadow (if you don't have grazing livestock or don't tend to do controlled burning), mowing too much can reduce diversity, in both plant species and the birds they attract. And mowing at the wrong time can be devastating to birds that nest on the ground or in low meadow vegetation.

TIP

If you're catering to birds, it's best to mow as little as possible to maintain the clearing. Without mowing, though, there is no meadow; succession will take a meadow to shrubland and then forest in a startlingly short time. It took Julie decades of experimentation to hit on the right time to mow for her large, diverse southern Ohio meadows: yearly, in early November. Vegetation is left standing for fall migration, but it gets mowed before winter rain and snows start, which make it impossible to use the tractor. November mowing means no birds' nests are destroyed, and no box turtles or rabbits are hit. "I don't even consider mowing after the woodcocks arrive in February," she says, "and I won't mow until long after the last indigo buntings fledge in September. Mowing in November works for me. When the American woodcocks begin their displays in mid-February, the meadow is cleared and ready for them. Grasses and flowering plants begin to grow in March, and by mid-May, there's enough cover for field sparrows and indigo buntings to feed and begin to nest. The wildflower show goes on all season, with flaming orange butterfly weed, yellow coreopsis, lavender wild bergamot, and the rich yellows of goldenrods. A wildlife meadow in August and September is absolutely throbbing with insect song, and we all know what follows abundant insects: birds!"

Meadows-in-a-can

Having planted both inexpensive "wildflower mix" and the considerably more expensive native prairie seed, we can attest that the ultimate bang for the buck comes from native seed. "Meadows in a can" are composed largely of very showy non-native species like poppies, wallflowers, and dame's rocket, which at best will make a big splash the first year and vanish for good, and at worst (dame's rocket) will become invasive. By contrast, a good native prairie seed mix will give you meadows that increase in beauty and usefulness to birds every year. Deep-rooted perennials like prairie coneflower, wild bergamot, and woodland sunflower just get better each year. When in doubt, go native!

TIP

Julie took the earth-tilling route in preference to the drenched-earth herbicide route recommended by the seed supplier, figuring that the birds would appreciate a toxin-free meadow. She was glad she did, because the moment the seedbed was plowed and prepared, the resident nesting bluebirds were busily foraging in the tilled soil for cutworms and beetle grubs! As her corn-farming uncle Willard always said, "I grow enough for the bugs and me, too!"

Daisies!

Many of the very best plants for attracting birds are in the composite, or **daisy**, family. These include sunflowers, coreopsis, and purple coneflower, as well as the beloved **zinnia**. These plants are popular because they set fairly large seeds that birds such as goldfinches, sparrows, and juncos find tasty. These plants are also ridiculously easy to grow and cultivate. Most germinate if scratched into the soil as soon as the ground is warm and frost-free. The following list highlights some of our favorite composites:

>> **Sunflowers:** When we think of sunflowers (*Helianthus* spp.), most of us picture the giant ones standing taller than us. But there are many native sunflowers that can be found in a good prairie mix that have multiple smaller heads and abundant seeds for a great array of birds. Our Ohio meadows have Maximilian sunflowers, woodland sunflowers, and gray sunflowers: all natives with a lot more bird appeal than the commercial seed type. Goldfinches and cardinals love to pull the maturing, milky seeds from the heads; they fill the garden with color, motion, and sound as they flutter and cling. Cardinals often bring broods of young to sit atop the drooping seed heads as they forage.

>> **Coneflowers:** Julie admits that she used to think purple coneflowers (*Echinacea purpurea*) were a bit gangly — ugly even! That was until she was gifted with two gallon pots full of the big, lanky plants. When they bloomed, the butterflies fought for position, and when they went to seed, the gold-finches did the same. Purple coneflowers are wonderful for attracting birds and butterflies, and they make a great statement in the border or the meadow. Just give them room, and they'll do the work for wildlife in your garden. (By the way, that's the same Echinacea that herbalists tout as a cold remedy.)

REMEMBER

Don't be a plant snob if you want to garden with the birds in mind. Chances are, what you think is beautiful may not fit with what the birds prefer to eat. Birds may be attracted to the bright colors of the plants, but it's not because they seek beauty. They want to EAT! Don't be afraid to challenge your gardening prejudices. You, too, might become a convert to coneflowers!

>> **Zinnias:** Zinnias (*Zinnia* spp.) are lovely old-fashioned flowers with brilliant color that lure hummingbirds to probe the tiny yellow "true flowers" ringing their middles. When zinnias go to seed, goldfinches love to strip the petals off and feast. There's no better flower for attracting a wide variety of butterflies, either. Zinnias are one non-native composite that is a must in our gardens. The more you plant, the better the show. Make a long strip, a mound, or a big patch for them, and direct sow right in the soil.

>> **Coreopsis:** Several species in the genus *Coreopsis* (which includes many species of daisy, and several species of coreopsis) are great bird attractants, too. Hardy and easy to grow, they are a major component in many of the wildflower meadow mixes and are much appreciated by finches, sparrows, and butterflies. There's nothing like seeing a flock of lemon-yellow goldfinches lift up out of a meadow where they've been harvesting coreopsis seeds. All told, the daisy family has treasures aplenty for bird gardeners.

Hummingbirds and Blossoms

Seed-producing plants in the daisy family are terrific for seed-eating birds. But what about birds that depend on flowers for food? In North America, we're blessed with a number of species of hummingbirds, tiny wonders that feed largely on the nectar of flowering annuals, perennials, shrubs, and trees. The main thing to remember when selecting plants for hummingbirds is: *red*. True, hummingbirds come to blue, white, pink, yellow, and orange flowers, but red really turns them on. It's no coincidence that many red flowers are tubular in shape (to fit the hummingbirds' long bills) and have stamens that dangle pollen outside the petals to dab on hummingbird foreheads!

If you have only a little room or want to simplify things and plant a few flowers that really appeal to hummingbirds, you can't go wrong with these:

>> **Salvias** are the queens of hummingbird gardens. Their tubular flowers come in a wide array of colors, and all have appeal to the tiny buzzers. Among the best are *Salvia greggii* ("Cherry Chief") and *S. guaranitica* ("Black and Blue.")

>> **Cardinal flower** (*Lobelia cardinalis*) is a free-seeding native that bursts into bloom in July, as long as it's kept damp. The flower is brilliant red, (which explains its name). Hummingbirds can't resist it. Julie plants it near her bubbling "WarblerFall" bird fountain so she is sure the plant gets watered each time she cleans the fountain.

>> **Bee balm** (*Monarda* spp.) is a hotly contested resource with its tangy nectar. Male hummers will set up a territory around bee balm, keeping all others away. It's best planted in shades of red or purple (*M. didyma*); the pink and white varieties (*M. fistulosa*) don't seem so popular with hummingbirds, though they are terrific swallowtail butterfly attractants.

TIP

When selecting hummingbird flowers, always choose *single-flowered* varieties. Beware of the fancy, ruffled flowers loaded with petals; these often conceal or block nectar-producing parts of the flower, or they simply don't produce nectar at all.

Columbines and agastaches (also known as giant hyssops) as well as penstemons and annual larkspur are popular with hummingbirds, to the point of battle!

Vines that bear watching

Any discussion of hummingbird plants eventually twines 'round to vines. One native vine is **trumpet creeper** (*Campsis radicans*). It has big orange or yellow tubular flowers that hummingbirds literally dive into for abundant nectar, but we do not recommend planting it — trumpet creeper is one of the few native plants that becomes an absolute thug, making carpets of itself in your lawn and coming up right through your sidewalk or patio.

Another irresistible vine is **honeysuckle** (*Lonicera* spp.). Heads up, though — not all honeysuckles are created equal! Hummingbird fans sometimes comment that their regular feeder visitors disappear in late spring and early summer. This mysterious vanishing act coincides with the appearance of Japanese honeysuckle blossoms (*L. japonica*), which can cause mass desertion of hummingbird feeders when they come into bloom, so abundant and enticing is their nectar. That said, do not plant this overbearing invasive vine! A native, well-behaved, and much more beautiful choice is **coral honeysuckle** (*Lonicera sempervirens*), whose tubular red flowers will delight both you and the hummingbirds.

Hanging gardens

For the urbanite with little ground to call garden, hanging baskets can bring hummingbirds in. Coupled with a few feeders, hanging baskets can attract and keep hummers coming. Baskets loaded with single-flowered fuchsias and cupheas are always a hit with hummingbirds. Avoid the double fuchsias that look like frilly tutus; their nectar is hard to get to. A favorite hummingbird fuchsia is "Gartenmeister," with its long, dangling clusters of coral-red flowers. And the red *Cupheas* "Batface" and "Tiny Mice" are beloved, but the simple Mexican firecracker *Cuphea* is a strong attractant as well.

A Tree, a Bush, or a Shrub

Some of you may remember Lady Bird Johnson's Texas drawl as she encouraged the gardening public simply to plant "a tree, a booosh, or a shhrruhb" for the betterment of the landscape. (For the undated among us, Lady Bird was the wildflower-loving wife of U.S. President Lyndon Johnson.) We owe much of Americans' fervor for planting to Lady Bird and her campaign to beautify the country, one shhrruhb at a time. Think of birds, and you think of bushes. Birds love thick shrubbery in which to hide themselves, their nests, and their young. Even better is shrubbery with something to offer in the form of flowers or fruit.

Stumping for shrubbery

Viburnums offer both flowers and fruit; one is even called the **highbush cranberry** (*Viburnum triloburri*). Lots of native species form a graceful understory to shade trees, such as hobblebush (*V. alnifolium*). Seek out those that set fruit, and you'll please birds. The **dogwood** family is loaded with useful fruiting shrubs and small trees. The familiar flowering dogwood (*Cornus florida*) calls bluebirds, robins, and other thrushes, as well as woodpeckers, catbirds, thrashers, and starlings, with its fiery red fruit in the autumn. Some of the less well-known small dogwoods like red osier (*C. sericea*), silky (*C. amomum*), and gray (*C. racemosa*) are beloved by fruit-loving birds as well.

Hollies are well-known for their fruits. One of our very favorites is the native **common winterberry** (*Ilex verticillata*). It is deciduous, and its bare branches are laden with brilliant clusters of round scarlet fruits all winter. (That is, before the birds finally strip them.) Bluebirds especially love them. The American holly tree (*Ilex opaca*) is as native as its name, and a fruiting female tree will fill up with robins and cedar waxwings in early winter.

Spicebush (*Lindera benzoin*) is a graceful, spreading native shrub that bears beautiful shiny scarlet drupes to tempt birds in fall.

Allegheny serviceberry (*Amelanchier laevis*) falls somewhere in between a shrub and a small tree. It's wonderful in that it is among the first to bloom, with clouds of white flowers, in early spring, and it bears delicious, sweet fruits by early June, at a time of year when fruit-eating birds are hard-pressed to find what they need. It's highly recommended for attracting waxwings and robins, among many others. About 20 native serviceberry species grow across North America. They all bear fleshy fruit that attracts birds. A best bet for your yard would be a species native to your region.

Evergreens, like **yews** (*Taxus* spp.) and **arborvitaes** (*Thuja* spp.), as well as **junipers** (*Juniperus* spp.), are almost as varied in their form and color as birds and people. The ones we've mentioned, though, offer seeds or fleshy fruits and dense cover for roosting and nesting birds. They stop the cold winter wind and the prying eyes of predators and make birds feel safe at night. Planted up against the shelter of buildings, evergreens can mean the difference between life and death for a bird on a night that's 20 below.

When I see birches . . .

Everyone knows birds need trees to forage, sing, roost, and nest in. There's hardly a tree you could plant that wouldn't attract some bird. Some, though, have so much to offer that we have to point them out.

When I see birches bend to left and right

Along the lines of straighter, darker trees

I like to think some boy's been swinging on them . . .

TIP

Robert Frost loved birches, and so do we, perhaps more than any other tree. If they'll grow in your area, **birch trees** (*Betula* spp.) along with oaks, are highly prized bird attractors. (In southern climes, **river birch** works best.) Julie planted eight native gray birch clumps in a staggered ring around her Ohio home. On a single fall morning, seven species of warblers and a couple of Philadelphia vireos combed through their small triangular leaves, picking sweet aphid treats from the undersides. Small looper caterpillars, datana moth caterpillars; scale insects; leaf miners . . . all the insects love to chew on birches and, as a result, all the birds flock to those much-beset trees! Planting for insects: It's a thing! When you plant for insects, you plant for birds, and native is the very best way to go. The other great thing about birches is their abundant seed crop. American goldfinches, pine siskins, and redpolls will ignore the feeders to gorge on the seeds, which are available from June through early spring. They're like seed dispensers! And get this: You can plant birches close to your house and never fear that these rather delicate trees are going to fall on it and smash the roof.

Sassafras (*Sassafras albidum*) is a common species in the eastern half of the continent. It produces small blue fruits that are loved by thrushes, waxwings, bluebirds, and other berry eaters. Sassafras also seems to be a favorite drilling tree for species such as downy, hairy, and pileated woodpeckers, who are after the carpenter ants that chew galleries in the soft wood. Another reason to love sassafras trees is because you can pluck a twig from one at any time of year and get a flavorful stick to chew on. Pioneers used sassafras twigs as toothbrushes. Maybe that's why George Washington had wooden teeth.

While they're kind of a mess, **red mulberry trees** (*Morus rubra* is the native species) are unbelievably effective bird magnets. The watery, purple berries slide easily down the throats of almost every bird that eats fruit. And the watery, purple . . . well, just don't plant a mulberry over your sidewalk or driveway, or near your clothesline. Really, it's a treat to watch birds bring their just-fledged young to a mulberry tree, poke a few fruits in the gaping mouth, and leave them to figure it out for themselves. This tree's great advantage is fruiting in early summer, when not much else is available, fruitwise.

It almost goes without saying that the larger shade trees — **oak, maple, hickory, elm,** and others—have lots to offer in the bird garden. They are the framework around which you can build your garden. You can attract lots of birds without big trees, it's true, but mature plantings offer lots of nest sites for both open-cup and cavity-nesting birds, and they make seeds, from acorns to the winged seeds of maple, that birds as diverse as jays and grosbeaks relish. Just make sure you plant only native species, avoiding invasive Norway maples especially.

Julie has been pleasantly surprised by the unusual birds found breeding in the mature **sycamores, maples, oaks,** and **gums** planted all around her medium-sized Ohio hometown. Yellow-throated warblers don't mind the traffic roaring beneath them; they're too busy feeding young in cup-shaped nests high in the canopy of the sycamores lining Third Street! Wood duck hens, wooed by the same syca-mores' nest holes, can be seen parading tiny ducklings in heavy traffic on their perilous way to the Ohio River each spring. And yellow-throated vireos believe the town green, with its massive deciduous trees, is a perfectly acceptable forest in which to hang their little basket-like nests. Plant them, and they will come.

Get the Picture?

By now, we hope you have a picture of a bird garden that's diverse, colorful, strat-ified in height, and limited only by your imagination. The key is to design your garden around plants that have something to offer birds. Give each plant room to grow and the light it needs, whether full sun or shade, and let it do its work.

Bill Thompson III, author of the first edition of *Bird Watching For Dummies*, recalled visiting an acquaintance who had a new house on the edge of a huge woodland. The builders had cleared the lot right up to the edge of the woods, where the great forest trees made a dark wall. A lawn stretched between the house and woods, innocent of plantings, without a birdbath, feeder, or even a twig to perch on. He sat, making conversation with the homeowners for three hours, but what he was secretly doing was looking over their shoulders and designing a bird garden in his mind. He could see birds flitting through the woods and imagined luring them with plantings and feeders and baths right up to that big (and totally wasted) pic-ture window.

Once you know the joy of having birds at hand, you'll wonder how you survived without your bird-friendly yard.

In the tables that follow, we list some of the trees (Table 9-1), shrubs (Table 9-2), vines (Table 9-3), and flowering plants (Table 9-4) that are good for birds. The information under the "Good for" heading tells you what these plant species provide for birds. Remember this list is not exhaustive. Many other species exist that may be more appropriate for your climate and soil type. Check with a local garden center or garden club for suggestions specific to your region.

TABLE 9-1 **Trees for a Bird-Friendly Yard**

Common Name	Latin Name	Height/Size	Good for/Other Notes
Aspen, quaking	*Populus tremuloides*	60'	Seeds, insects, cover, cavities
Birch, gray	*Betula populifolia*	30'	Seeds, insects, cover
Birch, paper	*Betula papyrifera*	40'	Seeds, insects, cover
Birch, sweet	*Betula lenta*	60'	Seeds, insects, cover
Cedar, eastern red	*Juniperus virginiana*	50'	Fruit, year-round cover
Cedar, Rocky Mountain	*Juniperus scopulorum*	50'	Fruit, year-round cover
Cherry, black	*Prunus serotina*	50'	Fruit attracts 50 species
Cherry, pin	*Prunus pennsylvanica*	25'	Fruit attracts 50 species
Chokecherry, common	*Prunus virginiana*	25'	Fruit attracts 50 species
Dogwood, alternate-leaf	*Cornus alternifolia*	30'	Fruit attracts 35 species
Dogwood, flowering	*Cornus florida*	30'	Fruit attracts 40 species
Hackberry, common	*Celtis occidentalis*	50'	Fruit, cover
Hawthorn	*Crataegus* spp.	20'	Fruit, cover, nesting
Holly, American	*Ilex opaca*	50'	Fruit, year-round cover
Maple, red	*Acer rubrum*	80'	Seeds, cover
Maple, silver	*Acer saccharinum*	80'	Seeds, cover, cavities
Maple, sugar	*Acer saccharum*	100'	Seeds, cover
Mountain ash, American	*Sorbus americana*	30'	Fruit attracts many species
Mulberry, red	*Morus rubra*	70'	Fruit attracts 40 species
Oak, pin	*Quercus palustris*	75'	Acorns, cover, insects
Oak, red	*Quercus rubrum*	80'	Acorns, cover, insects

(continued)

TABLE 9-1 *(continued)*

Common Name	Latin Name	Height/Size	Good for/Other Notes
Oak, white	*Quercus alba*	100'	Acorns, cover, insects
Oak, willow	*Quercus phellos*	100'	Acorns, cover, insects
Sassafras	*Sassafras albidum*	100'	Fruit, cover, cavities, insects
Shadbush, serviceberry	*Amelanchier laevis*	30'	Fruit, flowers
Tupelo, black	*Nyssa sylvatica*	100'	Fruit (male and female needed for fruit), cover

TABLE 9-2   **Shrubs for a Bird-Friendly Yard**

Common Name	Latin Name	Height/ Size	Good for/ Other Notes
Arrowwood viburnum	*Viburnum dentatum*	20'	Fruit, tolerates shade
Bayberry, northern	*Myrica pensylvanica*	8'	Fruit (male and female needed for fruit)
Blackberry, American	*Rubus allegheniensis*	8'	Fruit, dense cover, nesting
Blueberry, highbush	*Vaccinium corymbosum*	15'	Fruit, flowers, cover, acid soil
Chokeberry, red	*Aronia arbutifolia*	8'	Fruit, moist soil preferred
Cranberry, highbush	*Viburnum trilobum*	12'	Fruit, shade tolerant, ornamental
Dogwood, gray	*Cornus racemosa*	10'	Fruit, dense cover
Dogwood, red-osier	*Cornus stolonifera*	15'	Fruit, dense cover
Dogwood, silky	*Cornus amomum*	10'	Fruit, ornamental, wet soil
Elderberry, American	*Sambucus canadensis*	12'	Fruit, dense cover
Hercules' club	*Aralia spinosa*	15'	Fruit attracts warblers, thrushes
Hobblebush	*Viburnum alnifolium*	5'	Fruit, shade tolerant
Holly, deciduous	*Ilex decidua*	30'	Fruit (male and female needed for fruit)
Huckleberry, black	*Gaylussacia baccata*	3'	Fruit, sandy soil preferred
Inkberry	*Ilex glabra*	10'	Fruit, thicket-forming, acid soil
Mahonia	*Mahonia aquifolium*	10'	Fruit, year-round cover
Nannyberry	*Viburnum lentago*	30'	Fruit, shade-tolerant
Pokeweed	*Phytolacca americana*	12'	Fruit, perennial herb

Common Name	Latin Name	Height/ Size	Good for/ Other Notes
Rose, pasture	*Rosa carolina*	7'	Fruit, many related species
Spicebush	*Lindera benzoin*	20'	Fruit, moist soil
Sumac, smooth	*Rhus glabra*	20'	Fruit, available all winter
Sumac, staghorn	*Rhus typhina*	30'	Fruit, available all winter
Winterberry, common	*Ilex verticillata*	15'	Fruit, ornamental (male and female needed for fruit)

TABLE 9-3 ## Vines for a Bird-Friendly Yard

	Latin Name	Good for/Other Notes
Bittersweet, American	*Celastrus scandens*	Fruit, avoid Oriental species
Grape, wild	*Vitis* spp.	Fruit attracts 100 species, cover, insects
Virginia creeper	*Parthenocissus quinquefolia*	Fruit attracts 40 species

TABLE 9-4 ## Flowers for a Bird-Friendly Yard

Common Name	Latin Name	Good for/Other Notes
Bee balm	*Monarda* spp.	Nectar for hummingbirds
Black-eyed Susan	*Rudbeckia hirta*	Seed
Blazing star	*Liatris* spp.	Seed; flowers attract butterflies
Brown-eyed Susan	*Rudbeckia triloba*	Seed
California poppy	*Eschscholzia californica*	Seed
Cardinal flower	*Lobelia cardinalis*	Nectar for hummingbirds
Coneflower, purple	*Echinacea purpurea*	Seed; flowers attract butterflies
Coreopsis	*Coreopsis* spp.	Seed; flowers attract butterflies
Cosmos	*Cosmos* spp.	Seed
Marigold**	*Tagetes* spp.	Seed
Primrose	*Oenothera* spp.	Seed
Salvia	*Salvia* spp.	Nectar for hummingbirds
Sunflowers	*Helianthus* spp.	Seed
Zinnia**	*Zinnia elegans*	Seed; flowers attract hummingbirds, butterflies

**Not native to North America, but beneficial for birds and not invasive.*

3

Bird Sighting 101: Using Your Tools

Chapter **10**

Binoculars and How to Use Them

The binocular has long been the tool of the bird-watching trade. When digital cameras hit the market, some birders began opting for a camera with a zoom or long fixed lens instead of a binocular for bird watching. Using a camera has its advantages, but trying to find birds using only one eye and a long lens is a fool's errand. Face it: A binocular is easier to use and more affordable. In this chapter, we focus (pun intended) on using binoculars. Chapter 20 focuses (yes, the very same pun) on cameras. Take your pick, but to truly enjoy bird watching, you'll need some sort of magnifying glass. You can watch birds without "bins" or a camera with a long lens, but you often won't get a satisfactory look at the birds.

A myth about binoculars is that they're expensive. They can be, but they don't have to be. Recent advances in lens technology and the manufacturing process have resulted in affordable binoculars for bird watchers.

In this chapter, we discuss what binoculars are, how they work, how to choose them, and how to use them most effectively for watching birds. Plus, we offer some tips on cleaning and loving your binoculars, because if you have decent binoculars, you *will* learn to love them, especially if they show you lots of cool birds.

Optics Defined: What You See Is What You Get

When birders talk about their *optics,* they're referring to their binoculars, camera, or spotting scope. Because the majority of the bird-watching public has binoculars (also known as *binocs, bins, or binos*), this is usually what is meant by the term optics.

Spotting scopes — higher-powered, single-tube (telescope) viewing devices — are used primarily for viewing distant birds, such as waterfowl, shorebirds, or soaring hawks. These high-powered scopes are becoming more popular as the number of avid bird watchers grows. But almost no one starts out with just a spotting scope — however, everyone starts out with binocs or a camera with a long lens.

Binoculars are composed of two optical tubes, joined side by side, much like two miniature telescopes. Inside each tube is a series of lenses and prisms that reflect, magnify, and transmit light. (Refer to Figure 2-1.) When binoculars are held up to your eyes and pointed at a distant object, a magnified image of that object is transmitted to your eyes — it looks bigger and closer than if you had no binoculars. Because you are using both eyes, the result is a better sense of depth and dimension than with a telescope (or other monocular) one-barrel, one-eyed view.

SPOTTING SCOPES

For 85 percent of the bird watching you do, your binoculars likely give you adequate performance in magnification and image clarity. However, for some birding situations where the birds are quite distant, you can enjoy better looks at birds by using a spotting scope. A spotting scope is one optical tube (binoculars have two) that generally offers greater magnification (above 20 power) than binoculars (usually between 7 and 10 power). Your first exposure to a scope will likely be with a guide who totes one along on a bird walk or field trip for participants to use. This is also a good way to practice using one and try out different models if you are interested in taking your hobby further and purchasing one of your own.

Comparing the Different Types of Binoculars

Two basic types of binoculars are used by modern bird watchers: Porro prism and roof prism. You can tell them apart by how they're constructed.

Porro-prism binocs

Porro-prism binoculars were first designed in the mid-1800s by some Italian fellow named Ignazio Porro. His concept of placing two right-angled prisms in each barrel of a set of binoculars (see Figure 10-1) is still used today. Porro-prism binocs have an angled-body design. When standing on their barrels, or hanging from a strap around someone's neck, Porro-prism binoculars appear to form an M shape.

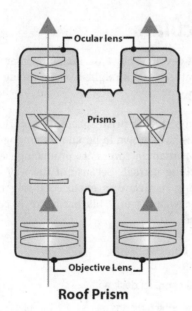

Ocular lens

Prisms

Objective Lens

Roof Prism

FIGURE 10-1:
Porro-prism
binoculars.

Porros focus by relying upon an external focus wheel that, when turned, causes the eyepieces for both sides to slide forward or backward along an external tube. This type of focusing allows for precise focusing and sharp images of close birds and other objects.

The advantages of this binocular design are:

» Brighter images due to greater transmission of light

» Fast focusing

» Usually less expensive

» Wider *field of view* (side-to-side distance you see when looking through the binocular)

The disadvantages are weight (the better transmission of light is due to large prisms, which are heavy) and bulkiness, which can make Porros hard to use for small-handed folks. In addition, the external focusing mechanisms of many Porros can make for less-durable binoculars; that is, ones that can be more easily jarred out of alignment. The external focusing mechanism also means that Porro-prism bins are rarely waterproof.

Roof-prism binoculars

Roof-prism binoculars were first developed by a German binocular manufacturer in the late 1800s. This design features two straight barrels, giving it an H-shaped appearance when upright.

The design reflects light through smaller prisms, arranged more compactly. (See Figure 10-2) Roof-prism binocs have grown in popularity among birders primarily because many leading optics manufacturers are producing excellent optics in this format for the bird-watching market. Because of the way roof-prisms are designed, most of the focusing hardware is enclosed inside the body of the binocular, making it easier to waterproof. This hardware is adjusted with an external focusing knob or wheel.

The advantages of roof-prism binoculars are:

» Ease of handling because of compact design

» Fewer external moving parts (which means increased durability)

» A better ratio of power-to-weight; that is, in general, a 10x roof-prism weighs less than a 10x Porro

Roof-prisms dominate the mid- to high-price range for binoculars.

The disadvantages are that roof-prisms tend to be more expensive than Porros. The most affordable ones may not focus as closely, making it hard to see nearby objects clearly. At the low-price end, roof prisms often do not offer as bright an image as Porros.

Welcome to the color section of *Bird Watching For Dummies!*

Let's be honest. We wanted to give you some eye candy, to remind you how coming to know the birds, and learning how to find them, will enrich your life.

The next two pages, referenced in Chapter 15, suggest what birds you might hope to find hidden in various habitats. Birding by habitat makes a walk through the natural world more like a personal mini-safari.

Enjoy the remaining photos, many of which have appeared in *BWD* magazine. We added a little text about each to pique your curiosity.

A male eastern towhee — one of the largest and flashiest sparrows — opens up with his "Drink your tea!" song.

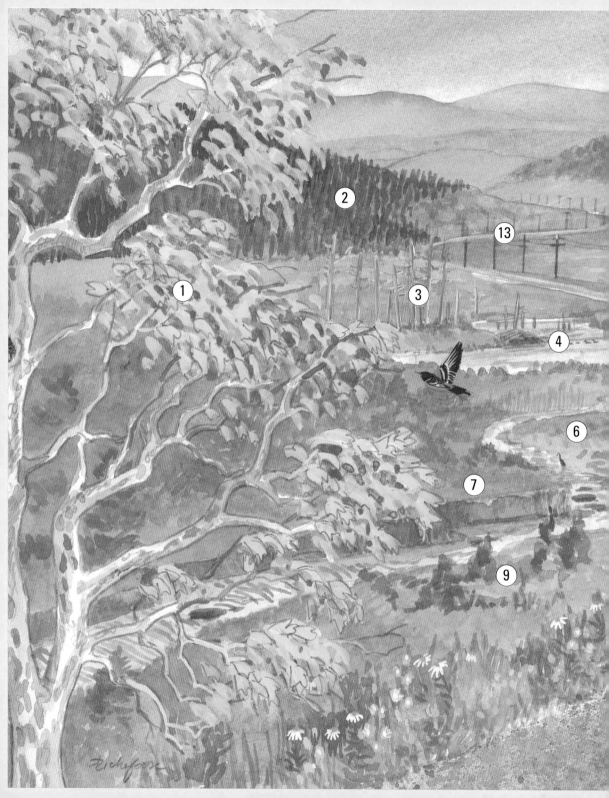

© JULIE ZICKEFOOSE

Birding by Habitat

When you look at a landscape as a bird watcher, you can predict what species will be found in each habitat. This southern Ohio scene is fairly typical, and will get you thinking in those terms. For more about birding by habitat, see Chapter 15.

1. Sycamore
Orioles
Yellow-throated warblers
Wood ducks

2. Conifer plantation
Owl roosts, nests
Heron nests
Raptor nests
Black-throated green warblers
Pine warblers

3. Beaver swamp
Swallow nests
Ducks
Woodpeckers
Herons
Flycatchers

4. Beaver pond
Ducks
Swallows
Herons
Grebes
Shorebirds

5. Cattail marsh
Rails
Blackbirds
Marsh wrens

6. Tussock (sedge) marsh
Sedge wrens
Swamp sparrows

7. Cut bank of stream
Nesting kingfishers
Nesting bank swallows
Rough-winged swallows
Spotted sandpipers

8. Roadside
Bluebirds
Hummingbirds
Indigo buntings
Sparrows
Killdeer

9. Old field
Common yellowthroats
Prairie warblers
Song sparrows
Brown thrashers
Yellow-breasted chats
Cardinals
Blue-winged warblers

10. Farmyard
Barn swallow nests
Eastern phoebe nests
Barn owl nests
American kestrel nests
House sparrows
Starlings
Cowbirds
Rock pigeons

11. Hardwood Forest
Tanagers
Warblers
Thrushes
Flycatchers
Cuckoos
Whip-poor-wills
Woodpeckers

12. Haymeadow
Meadowlarks
Blackbirds
Field sparrows
Grasshopper sparrows
Bobolinks

13. Power lines
Hawks
Bluebirds
Indigo buntings
Meadowlarks
Blackbirds
Doves
Kingbirds

14. Pasture
Killdeer
Meadowlarks
Cowbirds
Starlings
Bluebirds
Prairie warblers
Field sparrows

15. Sky
Soaring raptors
Vultures

A passing pickup truck's reflection on a lake lends color and motion to Bruce Wunderlich's photo of a female common merganser. See Chapter 20 to learn more about taking advantage of fleeting moments like this.

The WarblerFall bird fountain has a magnetic attraction to all birds, from tiny kinglets and warblers to this brown thrasher, bringing them in close for delightful viewing. Find simple DIY plans and instructions at https://warblerfall.com/.

Bald eagle rises over the Muskingum River with its morning catch. Marietta, Ohio.

**A migrating male bay-breasted warbler about to launch after a
flying insect. Magee Marsh, Ohio.**

Brown marks on the breast distinguish a female osprey, carrying an enormous dead limb to her nest at Seneca Lake in Ohio.

A male scarlet tanager processes a small wasp, its large, strong bill keeping it safe from stings.

A juvenile male ruby-throated hummingbird, its bill coated with pollen, feeds at Salvia "Black and Blue" in an Ohio garden.

A rare Ross's goose stands in front of a greater snow goose at Bosque del Apache NWR, New Mexico. The Ross's goose is half the snow goose's size, has a rounded forehead, and its stubby bill lacks the black "grin mark" shown by the snow goose.

A purple gallinule navigates floating lotus leaves with ease, its long toes spreading its weight so it rarely falls in. Orlando Wetlands, Florida.

Male pileated woodpecker feeds ant larvae to its clamoring young in a dead bigtooth aspen. Digiscoped from a pop-up blind in Whipple, Ohio.

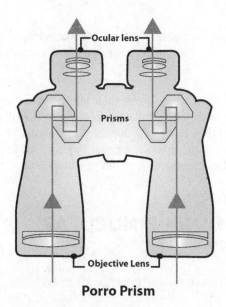

FIGURE 10-2:
Roof-prism
binoculars.

Ocular lens

Prisms

Objective Lens

Porro Prism

Reverse Porro binoculars

You might happen upon odd-looking binoculars that are widest at the eyepiece and narrow at the objective lens, with the barrels hidden within the tapering body. These are reverse Porro models, and they are compact, lightweight, and affordable. By design they have small objective lenses (less surface area for light entry), which necessarily makes them less than ideal for bird watching. The models at the lowest end are (dare we say it) junk, both optically and in terms of durability. Top-of-the-line reverse Porros might be higher quality, but we still don't recommend them as a primary binocular for birding.

Choosing Binoculars

You need to consider several factors when choosing binoculars, but the four most important ones are *cost, power* (or magnification), *size,* and *comfort.* When selecting binoculars for yourself, bear these four factors in mind. Neglect any one of them, and you'll almost certainly regret your decision later.

For example, if you decide to buy an inexpensive pair of binoculars even though you like a pricier pair better, you may find at a later date that you wished you'd made the additional investment. Or if you purchase a large pair of bins that seem heavy when hanging around your neck in the store, imagine your agony months later when you're out on a long bird walk. Talk about a pain in the neck!

TIP

Before you buy, we suggest you gather all the information you can about binoculars. The best sources for information and advice on bird-watching optics are your fellow bird watchers.

Ask your friends and fellow birders about their binocs. What brand, power, and size do they have? What do they like about them? What do they dislike? How much did they pay? Where did they buy them? Would they do anything differently the next time they buy binoculars? If you can get answers to these questions, you'll begin to get a picture of what *you* would prefer in a binocular.

WADING THROUGH BINOCULAR TERMINOLOGY

TECHNICAL STUFF

These terms are helpful to know if you wish to be fluent in binocular-speak.

- **Armoring:** An outer coating, often rubber or synthetic, that makes binoculars more water-resistant (or even waterproof), more durable, and easier to hold.

- **Close focus:** How closely a pair of binoculars can focus (between 6 and 12 feet is ideal). Less-expensive high-magnification binoculars usually can't focus on objects that are nearer than 20 feet. This limitation is a disadvantage for birders wishing to look at nearby birds or butterflies. To determine the close focus of a binocular, try to focus on your feet, or another nearby object. The distance to the closest object upon which you can focus clearly is the close-focus value of your binocular. If you're a butterfly watcher, good close focus is desirable.

- **Eye relief:** The distance from the outer surfaces of the ocular (eyepiece) lenses to the point where the optimal image is formed. You don't want your eyes or eyelashes to touch the lenses, but if the distance between the lens and your eyeball is too great, you lose field of view. Imagine peeking through a hole in a fence: the closer your eye gets to the hole, the more area you can see through the hole.

- **Field of view:** The amount of area that can be seen when looking through a binocular. A larger field of view makes finding a distant bird through your binocular easier. Higher powered binocs (10x and up) have a narrower field of view. Consider that when a camera zooms in on an object, objects on the periphery fall out of view.

- **Lens coatings:** Treatments applied to binocular lenses to increase image clarity, brightness, and color quality. Coated lenses are one of the things that make expensive binoculars expensive, but also give a better image.

- **Objective lens:** The lens nearest the object at which you're looking. The diameter of the objective lens, measured in millimeters, is the second number in the two numbers used to describe optics (like the "35" in "7x35").

- **Ocular lens,** also known as the **eyepiece:** The lens nearest your eyes (the end of the binoculars that you look into).

- **Power:** The amount of magnification provided by the binoculars. Usually listed as 7x, 8x, or 10x.

- **7x35, 8x42, 10x40:** Pronounced "7 by 35," and so on. This is the common model designation for binoculars. The first number is the power or magnification (a 7x or 7-power binocular magnifies a distant bird 7 times, making it appear 7 times larger). The second number indicates the diameter of the objective lens measured in millimeters. The larger this number, the larger the objective lens (and wider the field of view), and thus the more light enters your binoculars. More light means a clearer, brighter image.

After you get answers to these questions (and if you feel you can pester your friends a bit more without endangering your friendship), ask to try their binoculars for a few minutes. Try to avoid asking for the binocs just as a peregrine falcon flies overhead — your friend may get cranky. While trying your friend's bins, it's time to ask yourself a few questions: How do they feel in your hands? Are they easy to focus? Are they too heavy for you to hold steady?

Cost

It may seem hard to believe, but binoculars are one of those few items for which a higher price actually means higher quality. Another way to say this is: You get what you pay for. So, the guiding rule for binocular-buying birders has been: "Buy the best binocular you can afford."

But what's the price range for good binoculars? We're glad you asked that question. The answer depends on you and how you use the binoculars.

The low end of the price range for new birding binoculars is $100. You can get some compact (small and lightweight) binocs for slightly less than that, but such models are not ideal for in-the-field bird watching. The high end of the price range for binoculars is in the thousands of dollars! But you need not spend this much to get good optics.

Why not shoot for the mid-range? In this price range, you can get a binocular that will be well-suited to you and your mode of watching birds. Dozens of binocular brands and models are available to choose from in the mid-price range. If you choose to get mid-priced binoculars, you can always invest in a better (more expensive) pair at a later date. When birders upgrade their binoculars, their old ones often become car bins, or kitchen-window bins, extending their useful life.

"But," you ask, "isn't a $100 7x35 bin the same as a $500 7x35?" In terms of magnification and size of the objective lens, yes. But in optical terms and durability terms, probably not. The more expensive 7x35 has higher-quality glass, coated lenses, more rugged armoring, is water-resistant, and comes with a manufacturer's warranty of several years.

Here's an interesting thought: A new mid-price binocular, costing, say, $750 would, over the course of a year, average out to only about $2.05 per day. Over five years, the figure becomes $0.41 per day. Not much to pay for what you get in return.

WARNING

Don't, under any circumstances, buy any binoculars that lack a familiar and respected brand name or that are offered at unbelievably low prices. These optics stink! You'll be sorry. One warning sign of El Cheapo binoculars is a prism-like halo of colors around any object you view. This effect is caused by inferior optics inside the binoculars. As Bill used to say, "You'll never be sorry you bought the best binoculars you could afford."

Power and size

The magnification of binoculars best suited for bird watching are in the 7x to 10x range (that's 7-power to 10-power). This number is the first one listed (for example, 7x35, refers to 7-power). Binocs in this range provide enough magnification to make distant birds look bigger without being too heavy to hold steady. Three of the most common powers are 7x, 8x, and 10x.

Power is as much a matter of personal preference as anything. You may like the high magnification of 10x binoculars, but they have a narrower field of view. Add some jiggling, and it can be harder to find birds in higher-powered bins. Try several different binocs, either at a camera/optics store or at a gathering of bird watchers. Binoculars above 10-power are likely to be challenging to hold steady but can be used successfully when mounted on a tripod.

The magnification of a binocular is generally not related to its weight. Within a brand and model, an 8x will probably weigh the same as a 10x. Remember, though: As magnification increases, field of view decreases. Which is more important to you? The mantra is "Try before you buy!"

REMEMBER

The first number in a binocular description (8x32) refers to the power or magnification of the binocular. The higher the number, the more powerful the binoculars (which means a 10x binoc makes a distant bird appear closer than a 7x one does). The second number in the description refers to the size (in millimeters) of the diameter of the objective lens. The larger this number is, the more light is allowed into the optics. Lots of light means a bright, clear image is presented to your eyes.

Using the logic that more is better, wouldn't a 12x50 binocular be great? Lots of magnification and lots of light? The answer is an emphatic *no!* Such powerful binocs require large lenses and internal prisms, which makes them almost impossibly heavy to use without mounting them on a tripod.

Birding binoculars typically have a magnification of 6, 7, 7.5, 8, or 10, and an objective lens size of 25, 30, 32, 35, 40, or 42 millimeters. Pocket binoculars are the smallest, with objective lenses of less than 30. Compact bins have an objective lens size of 30 to 35. Full-size binoculars have 40- or 42-mm objective lenses. Many birders find 8x42 or 10x42 to be a sweet spot. Top-of-the-line binoculars, however, have such powerful light-gathering ability that 8x32 bins are gaining popularity because of their significantly lighter weight. Julie winds up grabbing her 8x32 for everyday birding because, when fitted with a shoulder harness, she barely notices she's wearing them until she sees a bird!

WARNING

Never look directly at the sun through binoculars. Magnified sunlight can seriously damage your eyes. When bird watching, always be aware of the sun's position so you don't inadvertently point at or swing your binocs past the sun. Ouch!

Comfort

"The best binoculars," an optics expert once wrote, "will disappear from your awareness while you are using them."

When you try binoculars, ask yourself if they feel comfortable to use. Comfort is a combination of factors: Are they easy to raise to your eyes? Does your forefinger automatically rest on the focus wheel? Can you easily adjust the settings to fit your needs? Do the binocs feel very heavy around your neck? Do they feel good in your hands?

You can have the best optics money can buy, but if you're not comfortable using them, they may as well be a lead doorstop.

TIP

If you have trouble holding a binocular steady (if the image is constantly moving and jiggling), the binocs may be too big and heavy or have too much magnification for you to use. Try using a smaller binocular, or one with lower power, and see if you have a more stable image.

Other considerations

If we haven't confused you yet about how to choose binoculars, here are some other things to think about:

>> **Eye space (also known as inter-pupillary distance):** Eye space is an important consideration in finding the best binocular for you. If your eyes are exceptionally close-set or far apart, some binocular models might not work for you. The average adult inter-pupillary distance (IPD) is 63 mm, with a range of 50 to 77. Small children can have an IPD as small as 40! Many binoculars have a minimum IPD of 58. If your eyes are wide-set or close, it is especially important to find out a binocular's IPD range before making that purchase. Minimum IPD is reported in the specifications of all respectable binocular brands and models. To discover the minimum IPD, simply squeeze the two barrels together.

>> **Field of view:** Make sure the binoculars you choose have a reasonable *field of view* (the amount of side-to-side area you can see at one time when looking through the binocs). Binoculars with narrow fields of view make it hard to find the bird when you raise the optics to your eyes. Among various makes and models, the field of view can vary substantially even within the same power and size specs. That is, Brand A binocular in 8x42 might have a much wider field of view than Brand B's 8x42. Shop around and try to notice the field of view among your top choices.

>> **Close focus:** An ideal binocular focuses on objects 12 feet away or closer. Most top-of-the-line binoculars focus to less than 10 feet. When a warbler perches 10 feet away, you can enjoy it with your naked eye, but you'll get a much more detailed view through your binocular — if it has a short close focus. For butterfly watching (a natural spin-off of birding), close-focusing is a must. No one wants to *back up* to get a binocular view of a resting butterfly!

>> **Brightness:** The level of image brightness produced by your binoculars is a factor of how large the objective lenses are (25, 32, 40, 42, and so on) combined with the quality and coatings of the optical elements (lenses and prisms). Larger objective lenses in general allow more light to enter and so produce brighter images. High-quality coatings, however, can compensate for smaller objective lenses.

>> **Lens coatings:** Coated lenses and high-quality prisms reduce the amount of light lost as an image passes through the glass inside the barrels of a binocular. High-quality glass and coatings can improve the transmission of light, which sends a brighter image to your eyes. The better the coatings, the more expensive the binocular is likely to be. How much is a bright view worth to you?

>> **Armoring/waterproofing:** Despite our best efforts to avoid such events, a binocular that is frequently used is inevitably dropped or otherwise knocked around. Armoring is a protective external coating that encases the binocular's barrels (but not the lenses), providing protection from bumps and knocks, as well as providing some protection from moisture. Only the most expensive binocs are waterproof (its openings are hermetically sealed to keep moisture out), but mid-priced bins from quality manufacturers are water *resistant* (sealed to withstand precipitation or waves splashing but may leak if exposure to water is prolonged). A rain shower won't harm a good binocular, and most top-shelf models can even withstand brief full submersion. The details of a binocular's water resistance are typically listed in the owner's manual or on the manufacturer's website.

Binoculars to avoid

TIP

As this book goes to press, a few models of zoom binoculars are on the market, ranging from cheap to expensive. Standard binoculars have a fixed magnification of 7, 8, or 10. Zoom binoculars have a lever that allows the user to rapidly increase the magnification. That might sound helpful, but zooming in decreases the field of view, making it difficult to stay on your target, especially if it is moving, since you'll also have to refocus. Zooming in on a moving object while hand-holding the binocular is next to impossible, and birds are frequently in motion. We do not recommend zoom binoculars for birding.

Likewise, avoid fixed-focus field glasses, created for marine or military use, which are simply impractical for watching birds. We also don't recommend image-stabilized binoculars as your primary optics for bird watching. On stationary objects, image-stabilized binoculars can overcome hand tremor from wind, high magnification, and vibration. They are great for a bird perched on a branch on a windy day, or a bird floating on the waves while you are on a boat. They are less useful with moving objects, however, such as birds in flight or otherwise changing distance from the observer.

Using Binoculars

Many binocular owners either neglect to read the owner's manual or forget its instructions for use. Learning how to set up and focus your bins will make all the difference in the world for a clear, 3D view — and no headaches from your eyes trying and failing to focus.

TIP

Please review "Using binoculars" in Chapter 2. It's important.

Each time you use your binoculars, remember to:

1. Adjust the spacing of the barrels (apart or together) to match the distance between your eyes.

2. Make sure the eye cups are in your preferred position (usually down for glasses wearers and extended for those who don't wear glasses).

3. Make sure the diopter is set for your eyes. That is, make sure you can see a focused, crystal-clear image with both eyes. If not, follow the instructions in Chapter 2 to reset the diopter.

Properly focused, your binoculars will give you a sharp, almost 3D image.

Lifting and holding your binoculars

TIP

Beginners often lift their binoculars to their eyes and then search for something interesting, such as a bird that someone has pointed out. With their bins in place, they turn their head left and right, up and down, searching for that object — and probably making themselves nauseated while failing to find the bird. It's a beginner's mistake.

Instead, try this: Before lifting your binoculars, fix your eyes on the object you wish to see. Do not look away or even blink. Now, without moving your head, lift your bins to your eyes, aligning them with your target. If your eyes are still glued to it, you will now be seeing it magnified! Now, focus!

To provide the most stable support for your binocular, hold it with both hands, elbows tight to the sides of your chest. (See Figure 10-3.)

TIP

It's worth practicing with your binoculars, both finding your target quickly and focusing quickly.

Wearing glasses — or not — is up to you

Folks who wear glasses all the time wear them when using binoculars, too — including those of us who wear bifocals. We find it natural and easy. Some glasses-wearers, however, lift their spectacles to their forehead as they lift their binoculars to their eyes. They, apparently, get used to that, too. It really is a personal matter of choice. For glasses-wearers new to using binoculars: With a little practice you can raise your binocs to your glasses without jamming your glasses into your nose.

FIGURE 10-3:
Fix your eyes on an object you wish to see through your binoculars, then lift them to your eyes. Hold your bins with both hands, elbows against your sides for steady support.

Trouble in Paradise: Balky Bins

If you're new to this binocular-toting hobby called bird watching, you may be having some less-than-heavenly experiences using your optics. This is normal, even for veteran birders! The happy news is that all these problems are easy to remedy.

Focus problems

If you can't seem to get your birds in focus, even after carefully following the steps in Chapter 2, here are two suggestions:

>> Clean your binoculars thoroughly and try again.

>> Take or send your binoculars to a trained optics repair professional and ask that the alignment be checked.

Binoculars, especially Porro models, go out of alignment from a hard bump or knock, just like the tires on your car. Out-of-alignment binocs are impossible to focus precisely, so your eyes try to adjust to make up for the lack of focus. The result is headache, dizziness, and frustration for you.

To find a person trained to fix optics, call your binoculars' manufacturer, ask the company that sold you the optics, or inquire at your local camera store.

Dizzy eyes

If your binoculars are not truly in focus, or if they're out of alignment, you may experience a moment of dizziness after you lower the binocs from your eyes. Believe us, it's better to resolve this problem than to continue to use the binocs as they are. If you can't eliminate the problem by refocusing or by resetting your diopter adjustment, take your binoculars to someone who can adjust the alignment. If you don't have an optics specialty store in your area, call the manufacturer of your binoculars and inquire about certified repair shops. High-end manufacturers have in-house repair shops, and some provide free repairs (another good reason to invest in top-of-the-line optics). Yes, it's hard to send them in and wait, but when they come back fixed, cleaned, and sometimes re-armored, it's well worth the wait!

TIP

Here's a quick way to check the alignment of your binoculars. Look at a horizontal line, such as a telephone wire. Slowly move the binoculars away from your eyes while keeping them level and watch to see if the lines in the two eyepieces stay lined up. If one appears higher than the other, get thee to an optics repair shop— your bins are out of whack.

Warbler neck

Warbler neck can happen with or without binoculars. It's caused by looking up for long periods, perhaps at some treetop warblers or soaring hawks. To avoid it, stretch out on the ground. This way you can scan the skies while your aching neck gets a rest.

Can't find the bird

It takes practice to find birds and other targets through your bins. This is by far the most commonly made rookie mistake: they see a bird, then lift their binoculars to their eyes, and then start moving their head around crazily looking for the bird. Relax, will ya?

TIP

Here's a trick. See a bird before lifting your bins. Note where the bird is in relation to a landmark near it, such as a red leaf, a crooked branch, a clod of dirt, or whatever. *Lock your eyes on the bird and don't move them!* Bring your binocs up to your eyes. Line up the binocs on the landmark that you spotted, and the bird should be easy to find — unless it has flown.

Practice this important skill: Find a stationary object and lock your eyes on it. Don't blink. Using both hands, lift your bins to your eyes, and keeping your head still, adjust the angle you are holding your bins until you see clearly. If your eyes haven't moved, you'll have that very object in view (although it might not be in focus).

REMEMBER

The goal is to find the object before you lift your bins, lock your view, and then put your bins precisely in front of your eyes, aligned with that object. It becomes easier, even second nature, with practice and experience. Trying to find an object through your binoculars without spotting it first is often an exercise in futility and dizziness.

If someone says, "The bird is two feet above the broken branch," find the broken branch before lifting your binoculars. When you see the branch through your bins, the bird will probably be within the field of view and a breeze to spot.

Also practice this: After you are comfortable locking your eyes on an object, then finding it immediately when you lift your binoculars, work on focusing your binoculars on that object quickly. Lower your binoculars, pick a more distant object, lock on it, find it through your bins, and focus on it. Lower your bins, and pick a close object, lock on it, find it through your bins, and focus on it.

This exercise will help you pick up speed at locating objects near and far and near again, finding them immediately through your bins, and getting them quickly in focus. It does take practice and familiarity with your binocular to focus quickly. Practice.

Fogging

There are certain times when you just have to put up with your bins fogging up, such as when you walk into a warm house after being outside in very cold weather. But if your binoculars fog up all the time, try cleaning them and then using some anti-fogging lens fluid. This fluid is available at any camera store and at many pharmacies.

If your binocs fog up on the inside, you need to seek professional help (for them). Good binoculars don't fog internally. Binoculars with internal fog have not been properly sealed, allowing moisture inside them. There is nothing you can do to clear them. Get them looked at by the manufacturer or by an authorized repair shop. If they fog because they're cheap and unsealed, it's time for an upgrade.

Carrying Your Bins

Strap it up, I'll take it! *Always, always, always* use some kind of strap with your binoculars. If you don't — mark our words—you'll be sorry. And even if you do have a strap on your bins, but you tend to get lazy and hand carry them by the strap, beware! You will drop them at some point.

With that dire warning, we strongly recommend that you have a strap or harness for your binoculars and that you wear it around your neck or shoulders. These carrying devices are not just convenient, hands-free ways of carrying your bins; they are also a kind of safety belt for them.

If you buy a good-quality binocular, a decent strap will be included in the package. Not everyone loves the "kit" strap, though, especially if it is narrow. Excellent straps are available online or in any store that sells optical equipment. Camera straps fit most binocs. Invest in a strap that is comfortable for you. Be sure to adjust it to your length preference.

An alternative to a neck strap that is hugely popular is a binocular harness, sometimes called a "bino bra" by birders. These units spread out the weight of the binocular by means of crisscrossing shoulder straps. The weight is off the neck and spread out across the shoulders and back. Like neck straps, they are adjustable and come in various widths and styles. Find them online or wherever outdoor optics are sold. Julie loves hers, which is made of stretchy parachute cord. Sometimes she goes looking for her binoculars only to discover she's already wearing them!

TIP

If your binoculars bounce around and pound against your chest or stomach when you walk, here are three solutions:

» Change the way you walk or quit birding from a pogo stick. If this isn't practical . . .

» Shorten your binocular strap; most straps have a slip-through buckle for making this adjustment on either end, near where they connect to the binoculars. Don't let them swing around at waist level! Or . . .

» Purchase one of the harness-type straps that holds your optics snugly against your body. The added benefit is that a good harness distributes the weight evenly across your back and shoulders.

Cleaning and Caring

Clean binoculars are happy binoculars. You don't want to be able to recall practically every meal you've ever eaten over them. The hard-to-reach areas around the lenses hold a veritable food museum's worth of crumbs and UFOs (unidentifiable food-like objects). There's no time like the present to clean up your act!

Here's how:

1. Get lens-cleaning fluid and lens tissue or a lens-cleaning cloth from a drugstore or camera store.

2. Let gravity help you. Point the objective end of your binocular skyward, with the eyepieces pointed down. Blow forcefully on each ocular lens to loosen bits of dirt, breadcrumbs, or hardened mayonnaise, and watch them fall to the ground.

3. Using a crumpled lens tissue or lens cloth, wipe lightly across each lens.

4. Dampen a clean lens tissue with lens cleaning fluid and lightly wipe each lens in a circular motion.

5. Use a clean and dry lens tissue or a clean, dry corner of the lens cloth to wipe excess moisture from the lenses.

6. Now invert the bins so that the eyepieces are pointing skyward and repeat this process with a fresh lens tissue or lens cloth on the objective lenses.

For especially gunk-covered lenses, two rounds of cleaning may be in order.

To clean the body of your binoculars, which may be coated in french-fry grease, dampen a cloth with water or lens cleaner and wipe. Be careful not to get your binocs too wet and be sure to dry them promptly.

WARNING

Do not wipe your binocular lenses with your shirt tail, T-shirt, handkerchief, or cosmetic tissue. Take the time to clean them properly, and they'll pay you back with great vision for years to come. If you take the sloppy way out and wipe them with a fabric not designed for lens care, you'll put thousands of tiny, light-bending scratches on the glass. This puts you on the road to binocular ruin. Breathing on the lenses and then rubbing them with your shirt tail or a facial tissue is also not good.

TIP

The ocular lens cover that came with your binocular is called a rain guard. It works well as a crumb and mayo guard, too. We recommend using it not only during rain, but also when eating while birding.

Chapter **11**

Choosing and Using Field Guides

The arsenal of the bird watcher includes two primary weapons: binoculars and a field guide. Binoculars (see Chapter 10) let you see a bird well enough to identify it. A field guide helps you identify what you see.

A field guide is a great companion to have alongside you in the field. At home, it can be a rich source of daydreams as you flip through it and fantasize about all the birds you've never seen. A field guide can also be your record book, a place where you note important sightings, dates, and locations.

Looking at Field Guides in Their Infinite Variety

A field guide is a book that has illustrations of all the birds that regularly occur in a given area. Many field guides are also available digitally, accessible as an app on your smartphone, and utilize the same features as a hard copy. Most experienced birders we know use both versions; however, we recommend new bird watchers get comfortable with a physical guide first.

Most field guides used on this continent show all the birds found in North America. A few guides are limited to the eastern or western halves of the continent. You also have scores of regional guides to birds of big, birdy places such as Texas. Which guide you choose depends, in part, on where you live and how much you're going to travel. You can also find field guides to the birds of Europe, Mexico, and most South American, Asian, and African countries. No matter where you live or go — at least on this planet — you can almost certainly find a field guide to the birds of the region.

REMEMBER

A field guide has only one purpose: It enables the user to identify a bird. Nothing else matters if it doesn't fulfill that purpose. A field guide doesn't ID a bird for you. You can't take a field guide, point it at a bird, and expect the guide to fall open to the right page. (But there are apps like Merlin that will point you in the right direction of what bird you might be seeing or hearing; see Chapter 21 for more on getting an assist from bird identification apps.)

Good field guides, like good tools, are designed well. They make the job easier. But just as you're good with some tools and some tools you should never be allowed to touch, different field guides work better or worse depending on the user. If the field guide you're using is not producing results (that is, you aren't able to identify *anything*), don't punish yourself. Get another field guide. You wouldn't use a hammer if the head kept falling off and hitting you on your big toe. Don't use a field guide that leaves you scratching your head and saying, "Well, I wonder what *that* was?" each time you spot an unusual bird.

Determining a field guide's guiding principle

New bird watchers frequently ask why field guides are organized the way they are. Why are the water birds in the front half and land birds in the second half? Well, it's not as arbitrary as it first appears. The answer is *taxonomy*.

The problem is that any sequence is the result of trying to cram a complicated set of relationships into a linear format. Taxonomists (the scientists) do this because field guides and other books are two-dimensional (flat page, words) rather than three-dimensional, which would allow the scientists to show the many branches of simultaneous evolution. It's like trying to press a many-branched oak tree in a book.

WARNING

Almost all field guides are organized by taxonomy. Be wary of field guides that choose a different system of presenting the birds. At first glance, a guide that organizes birds by habitat or color or size may seem appealing, but first glances can be misleading, and ultimately these guides can prove much harder to use.

For bird watchers, two aspects of taxonomy are important:

>> **Relationships:** Think of this as the avian version of Six Degrees of Kevin Bacon. It's fairly obvious that hummingbirds are not closely related to pelicans, except that they both have feathers and fly. On the other hand, gulls and terns are clearly closely related. One aspect of taxonomy is trying to determine which groups are closely related and which are not. The result serves as the basis for the sequence of birds found in most field guides and checklists.

This sequence — usually starting with waterfowl and usually ending with passerines — is an attempt to put in order our best understanding of those relationships between and among species. It's an imperfect and constantly changing system. If you look at the order of birds in your field guide, you might find that the hawks are next to the ducks, but the closest relationship between ducks and hawks is that one sometimes eats the other. The problem again is that field guides try to put the oldest bird lineages (ones that evolved long ago to their present form) first and the newest (most recently evolved) at the end of the list. It's generally thought that ducks evolved very early and sparrows evolved more recently. Hawks also evolved fairly early, so they end up near the front of the book.

>> **Species:** The second part of taxonomy is the question of what constitutes a species and what doesn't. Go back to the hummingbird and the pelican in the previous section. It doesn't take a bird scientist to know that these two are different species. It also isn't too hard to see how the two kinds of pelicans that occur in North America are different — one is brown and the other is white. But when you try to tell the differences among the sparrows, the problem gets harder. Why are birds that look almost identical considered separate species? (Again, refer to Chapter 4 Taxonomy for more on this topic.)

Getting to the bottom of names

Bird names can be strange. Beginning bird watchers frequently ask why birds are called pipits, warblers, or loons. They also wonder why, for example, a certain sparrow is called Henslow's sparrow. Who is Henslow, anyway, and why do they have a bird named after them? And what is a prothonotary warbler? And why is a bird with a red hood, a black-and-white barred back, and a wash of red on the belly called a red-bellied woodpecker? Who thinks up these things?

Bird naming is a quirky and inexact science. In fact, despite the existence of some rules, it's not a science at all. At its best, bird naming is an art. Some of the time it's a mess. Here's how birds get their names.

Playing the name game

First, the scientist who initially discovered a new species got to name it, sort of like a game of finders–keepers. They couldn't name it after themselves, but if they had a friend whom they wished to honor or owed a favor — well, you get the idea.

Second, most bird species were named more than two centuries ago, back in the time when scientists didn't have ready and immediate communication with each other. They were left creatively free when choosing names. A great many of North America's birds were named by early ornithologists and explorers. These guys (they were almost all men) tended to take one of four roads when choosing the name for a bird:

>> **My sponsor's warbler:** One of the most popular ways to name a bird was after a friend or sponsor. A lot of the early ornithologists were poor, and they relied on the largesse of rich patrons to fund the pursuit of their passion. Ornithologists rewarded those patrons by naming birds after them. They also named birds after people to whom they owed money or favors as a way of settling the debt. (They also named birds after wives, girlfriends, and relatives.) So, for example, John James Audubon named a warbler and a sparrow after his good friend and sponsor Reverend Bachman.

>> **Name that feature:** Just as popular was the practice of naming birds after some distinctive characteristic. White pelicans and brown pelicans were named because they are, well, white and brown, respectively. Ditto black-and-white warblers, blue grosbeaks, and vermilion flycatchers. Hundreds of examples exist. Sometimes birds were named for obscure characteristics because early ornithologists, not having binoculars or field guides, carried shotguns in the field so they could capture the bird and study it closely. The ring-necked duck, for example, has a subtle chestnut ring around its purple neck, easy to appreciate in a hand-held bird, but usually invisible in the field. The same goes for the red-bellied woodpecker.

>> **Name that place:** The third large category of bird names consists of habitat and location. The first Cape May warbler known to science was collected in Cape May, New Jersey. The fact that the bird is fairly rare there didn't apply, because nobody knew where it bred then. Ditto Connecticut warbler, which is a rare migrant in Connecticut. The generic form of this type of naming concerns geography and includes names like mountain bluebird (found in the mountains), eastern kingbird (found in the East), western kingbird (guess where) . . . you get the idea.

Habitat is also popular. The seaside sparrow is found along the seaside. The pine warbler is found in pines. Wood ducks nest in tree cavities.

>> **Sounds and symbols:** The fourth category is sounds. Pewees are called pewees because that's the sound they make. Chickadees say *chick-a-dee.* Bobwhites say *bob-white.* A warbling vireo warbles, sort of.

Some names are more imaginative. The prothonotary warbler was so named because its golden color reminded an early scientist of the color of the robes worn by the prothonotary, an officer of the Catholic Church. Harriers were named because they were known to *harry* (harass) poultry and gamebirds in Europe. Limpkins have a halting gait as they move about in the marsh.

Keeping track of name changes

Sometimes bird names change, because of *lumps* and *splits* — new taxonomic research recognizing two species as one, or one species recognized as actually two — or for other reasons. If scientists decide that two species, like Audubon's and myrtle warblers, are really one species, they have to come up with a new name. They chose yellow-rumped warbler (despite the fact that a half-dozen other warbler species have yellow rumps). When ornithologists decide that one species is really two, they have to come up with two new names. What was, until 1989, the brown towhee, is now the canyon towhee and the California towhee. It is likely that the official common names of many bird names will change, especially those named for people.

Dissecting a Field Guide

All field guides are different, but all do have basic components necessary to the bird watcher. These components are

>> **Images** using color artwork or photographs of each species.

>> **Maps** showing each species' range and distribution.

>> **Text** that augments the visual depiction and gives other information unique to each species.

>> **An introduction** that tells you about the guide, how to use it, how to interpret the maps, what the special characteristics of the book are, what unique symbols are used, and so on.

>> **An image** of the parts of a bird that allows you to see quickly what the author meant when talking about primaries or a supercilium (eyebrow stripe).

>> **An index** that enables you to find the right pages quickly if you already know the bird is a hawk, or a duck, or whatever.

Perusing pictures of birds

An image of a bird, whether it's an illustration or photography, is a visual representation of thousands of facts. Each feather (and birds have lots of feathers) is a fact. The color of the bill, the length of the legs, and the shape of the tail are all facts. The more facts the illustration shows, the better the illustration. An illustration that shows only a few key field marks (and this can happen with photographs as well) can leave you frustrated. A field mark may help you decide which bird it is, but you need to see the whole bird, in all its glory, before you get to the field mark stage.

WARNING

Be wary of guides in which the birds look awkward or ill-formed to you. If the artist doesn't have a feel for what a bird looks like, they are likely to get a lot of the facts wrong, too. Of course, photographs, being a frozen moment in time, can present some very distorted views as well. All of us have seen at least one photograph of ourselves that we wish didn't exist.

Using field guide range maps

The maps in a field guide show, in general terms, where each species can be found at different times of the year. The area over which a species can be found is known as its *range*. The easiest-to-use field guides place the range map on the same page as the text and an image of the bird. Maps are terrifically useful, telling you whether the bird is supposed to be in your part of the world.

Not all maps are equally well done, but all maps in field guides are generally accurate. Each guide's maps can be a little different, reflecting the changing state of knowledge and the personal interpretation of the author.

REMEMBER

A map can tell you whether a bird should be in your state, but it can't tell you whether it ought to be in your yard. You discover that fact by watching the birds in your yard.

The field guide may say that a certain bird is common and show it occurring all over your state. But if it's a woodland bird, and you have no woods where you live, the bird is likely to be rare for you. Because they cover a vast area, range maps in field guides simply can't provide that kind of detail. Field guide maps are pictures painted with very broad brushes. For instance, rapidly expanding or contracting bird ranges may not get accurate representation in all guides.

Evaluating field guide text

The text in a field guide interprets the pictures of the birds and tells you which field marks of each species are important. The text also tells you which species are similar and how to tell them apart. Some field guide authors are more adept at this than others, so reading the text for a few species is important before you choose which guide to buy. What you're looking for is text that seems clear and easy for you to understand. If the text confuses you, try a different guide.

TIP

Many people don't read the text, even after they've bought a guide and are using it in the field. Most people trust what they *see* rather than what they *read*. Remember, the text is supposed to be a help, not a hindrance. Eventually, you'll need the text to identify a bird, so get in the habit of reading it.

The text is a detailed guide to the illustration. Not reading the text is like trying to find your way in a strange city without using a map. Sparrows offer a good example because they have a fascinating and subtle collection of streaks, spots, bars, and patterns to their plumage. If you're trying to identify a sparrow that you've seen, you can spend hours poring over several pages of sparrow illustrations trying to figure out what is important. Don't bother. The field guide author has already figured it out and put the information in the text. You paid good money for the information, so go ahead and use it. The information tells you immediately whether the streak on the head, the spot on the breast, or some other field mark matters most when identifying each bird.

APPRECIATING ABUNDANCE TERMS: HOW COMMON IS COMMON?

All field guides use words like *abundant, common, uncommon,* and *rare* to describe how numerous a bird is. These descriptions aren't precise, scientific terms; they're generalizations, and different authors mean different things when using them. The only way to interpret what is meant by *common* in the field guide you're using is to read the author's definition of *common* in the introduction.

These terms are an attempt to relay what we think is known about real bird populations. They have nothing to do with the likelihood of your seeing the bird. For beginning bird watchers, a conversion table is helpful:

- Abundant birds are, at best, common or fairly common, meaning you're apt to see them regularly.

(continued)

(continued)

- Common birds can be uncommon, but you'll probably run across some more often than not.

- Uncommon birds are definitely rare.

- Rare birds don't exist. At least that's how it can seem.

The more experience you have, the more the definitions in the field guide make sense. Seeing an uncommon or rare bird requires experience in finding birds, an understanding of the bird and its habitat requirements, and often, knowing in which pond or field to look. Sometimes luck can compensate for a lack of all that knowledge.

Gauging the Variations Among Field Guides

Unlike humans, not all field guides are created equal. Each guide that's ever been published has one or more traits that set it apart from its competitors.

A field guide is a delicate balancing act between three competing interests: cost, size, and knowledge. Publishers know that they can't sell $100 field guides. They impose limits on the author — limits designed to make the book affordable. Field guides can't be the size of an unabridged dictionary, and they can't come in 10-volume sets. A field guide has to be one book, small and light enough to carry and use in the field.

The information gets distilled to fit the requirements of cost and size. The distiller is the author. Different authors have different ideas about what makes a good field guide, what information is most important, how it should be presented, and what will make users happy.

REMEMBER

The differences among authors, and thus the field guides that they write, are the reason so many bird watchers own more than one. They don't carry them all in the field, but these field guides are great backup references for the library shelf. No matter how attached you get to the field guide that you choose for your go-to, eventually you'll need a piece of information from one of the other guides.

SPECIALTY FIELD GUIDES

In recent decades, a new arena of field guides has emerged, focused on single families or groupings of families of birds. These specialized guides go into great detail on the species they're covering, especially in plumage variations among individuals. Among the new crop of specialized guides are those covering the warblers of North America, seabirds, shorebirds, hawks, owls, hummingbirds, and many others. If you find that you're particularly interested in one bird family or another, a specialized guide can place a vast amount of information about the order or family at your fingertips.

Settling on coverage

The big decision for most bird watchers is whether to choose a guide that shows all the birds found in North America or to go with one that shows only the birds found in either the western half or the eastern half of the continent. Each choice has advantages. If you live in (or are planning a trip to) the mid-continent — the northern parts of the western Great Plains to South Texas —you'll need a field guide to all of North America, or both an eastern and a western field guide. There are no mid-continent field guides. Sorry about that.

What's the advantage to using an eastern guide or a western guide? Well, let's say you live in Salt Lake City, or San Diego. The western guide has almost every bird you'll ever see (except, of course when you're visiting relatives in Miami). But because such a guide covers fewer species than an all-of-North America-guide, it can include more in-depth information about the species it covers.

What's the advantage of owning a field guide that covers the entire continent? Well, eventually you're going to see a bird that isn't in an eastern or western field guide. Sometimes western birds show up in the East, and sometimes eastern birds show up in the West. Few things are as frustrating as seeing a bird and then discovering it isn't in your limited-coverage field guide. So, if you own a western guide or an eastern guide, you'd be wise to own both, even though you'll only be referencing one guide most of the time. On the other hand, if you have a guide that has all the birds, this problem almost never comes up —unless you didn't get a sufficiently good look at the bird to ID it.

Photographs versus illustrations?

This is the *big* question — the hottest argument in the field guide galaxy. Do you choose a guide that uses photographs or one that uses art to depict birds?

Experienced bird watchers overwhelmingly favor guides with art. Beginners over-whelmingly favor guides with photographs. What are the differences, and which should you choose?

A field guide, ignoring for the moment that it includes text, is a collection of bird pictures. The illustrations are supposed to show the birds in a way that demon-strates the characteristics that make each bird distinctive. Both paintings and photographs can accomplish this goal. We open the debate with a statement from the proponent of photographs:

> Photographs show real birds, just like the ones you see in the field. Photographs give a real sense of the bird that an artist can rarely, if ever, capture. This realism inspires confidence in the field guide user. Photographs don't filter the image of the bird through the artist's eye.

Thank you. And now a word from the proponent of paintings:

> Available photographs often don't show the key field marks. Too often a distortion in the photographic or printing process results in an incorrect coloration shown. Sometimes the only decent photograph available of a given species is blurry, or shows a slightly weird plumage variation, or subspecies. Getting comparable photographs of large groups (such as warblers) is impossible, where all the images are equal in quality, image size, and brightness. An artist can show exactly the same pose, typically in profile, for a large group of similar species. This art allows the user to make direct comparisons between similar species. An artist can create a picture that shows every part of the bird the user needs to see. Artists' renditions are composites, showing the most typical plumage.

Which should you choose? It depends in part on what is available. Some of the most popular field guides are by David Sibley, Kenn Kaufman, Roger Tory Peterson, Ted Floyd, Donald and Lillian Stokes, National Geographic, and Audubon. If you can afford to, choose two, one with photographs and one with illustrations. Over time, one becomes your primary source, and one becomes your backup.

Size does matter

If you're going to be carrying this field guide around with you, consider that two-, three-, and four-volume field guides will turn you from a bird watcher into a pack mule. Worse, you will never know which volume to grab.

A guide that is too big to fit in the pocket of any jacket that you own can be a burden. The only thing you want in your hand when you're watching birds is your binoculars. (And perhaps a snack.) A bigger field guide is useful, though, for reference when you get home.

On the other end of the scale, a variety of compact pocket guides are small enough to fit into any pocket. Most of them cover only a sampling of the birds that you're likely to see, or the information in them is somewhat limited. Try for the middle ground — single volume guides that cover all the birds of the continent, or at least the half of the continent in which you live.

Durability

Do you know what the life expectancy of a poorly made field guide is? Probably about two years of moderate field use. It will be crammed into pockets and backpacks. It'll fall under car seats and into mud puddles. Your field guide will be left out in the rain and baked by the sun. It'll tumble onto the road after being left on the car rooftop. It'll be bent around pencils and forefingers, pressed on flowers, and closed on mosquitoes and bits of tuna fish sandwich. And it'll be opened a thousand times, at least.

TIP

Some guides today come with a coated paper cover. This kind of cover adds some durability and flexibility to the guide. Hardbound field guides put up a noble defense inside backpacks and pockets, but they ultimately lose their covers. Flexible is where it's at.

Also check a field guide's binding (where the pages are glued together and joined to the book's spine). If the binding looks like the pages are barely held in there, put the guide down and back away slowly. If you buy a field guide with a bad binding, plan on chasing those pretty pages of bird pictures across a windblown field in a few months (or years).

Format

Early field guides featured text first; farther along in the book, the color plates (illustrations of the birds) were grouped (which made it cheaper to print), and then in the back came the range maps. This formatting made for clumsy reference. You spent a lot of time flipping from one section to another. Today, most available guides clump all the pertinent information about each bird together on facing pages.

REMEMBER

Field guides that don't have the maps, the text, and the illustrations on the same page may have other virtues, but they're harder to use. If you believe that you have the dexterity to hold a field guide open to two or three different pages using the fingers of one hand, while flipping back and forth, while holding binoculars in the other hand, while looking first at the bird and then at the guide, go ahead. But don't try it while standing over a puddle.

In Search of the Mythical Perfect Field Guide

No such thing as the perfect field guide exists. The search for the perfect field guide is the equivalent of the search for the Holy Grail or the Fountain of Youth. The perfect field guide *for you* is the one that you're comfortable using, the one that you most easily understand, and the one that enables you to identify birds. Your perfect guide may be someone else's nightmare.

TIP

Here is the basic field test for a field guide. It's just you, the guide, and the bird. Consider the following:

» Are the illustrations easy to interpret?

» Are similar species easy to find and compare?

» Is the typeface large enough to be readable?

» Is the text clear and easy to understand?

» Can you read the map quickly? Is it next to the bird's picture?

» Does the bird in the book look like the one in the bush?

The answer may not be yes to every question, but if more than one or two is no, you're headed for frustration and an attempt at breaking the field-guide tossing record.

If you buy a guide and then find that it isn't the right one for you, we suggest you buy another guide. After all, practice makes perfect. The first guide you bought can be a handy reference at home or at the office.

Using Your Field Guide

You have a brand-new field guide. Now it's time to get out in the field and use it. For the first few weeks or months, you'll baby your new guide. That's okay. But soon your guide evolves into a trusted, slightly worn field companion, and you won't leave home without it.

Read the introduction

Field guides are semi-technical. If you're a new bird watcher and have never used a guide before, read the introduction to the guide. Don't worry — introductions are almost always short.

The introduction is the basic operating instructions— the user's manual, if you will. Just as you wouldn't consider operating a new microwave, automobile, or camera without reading the instructions (actually, a lot of us do, with predictable results), you shouldn't consider using a field guide for the first time without making sure how best to use it.

The introduction provides several key pieces of information. It tells you how to interpret the range maps, which can be confusing because all the guides seem bent on using different colors. Some guides use special keys to speed you to the right section or bird family, and the introduction tells you how to make the key work for you. Introductions often provide basic backgrounds on bird families, bird behavior, bird migration, bird finding, and bird identification.

REMEMBER

The introduction is a quick and dirty seminar on birds and bird watching, written for the beginner. Taking a few minutes to read it can save hours later. It's a good investment.

Read the text

Don't just look at the pretty pictures of the birds. Once you've found the bird that you're trying to identify in the field guide, take a moment to read the accompanying text for that species. This step is another way to firm up (or totally negate) your identification of the bird. The text contains many gems of information that can't be conveyed visually in a painting, photograph, or range map, such as descriptions of vocalizations or other sounds. And the text tells you about confusingly similar species, which you may want to check out, just in case your identification sleuthing has led you to the (slightly) wrong bird.

Use the maps

Range maps are key to a bird's identity. They tell you where a bird occurs, or at least where it ought to occur. Often, the final identification of a bird is based on the discovery that the only other species possibility is found in a small area on the opposite coast. It's best, as a beginner, to trust the range map to tell you if what you think you're seeing is even a possibility. A common rookie mistake is to assume you've found a rare bird way out of its normal range. It happens, but not very often. If you hear hoofbeats coming up behind you, don't turn around expecting a zebra.

Range maps typically show where you can expect to find a bird in the summer, in the winter, and year-round. (See Figure 11-1.) Each map appears as a different color or pattern, and the introduction (remember to read the introduction very carefully) provides the key to the colors or patterns. Remember them so that a quick glance lets you know how likely the bird is to be in your area.

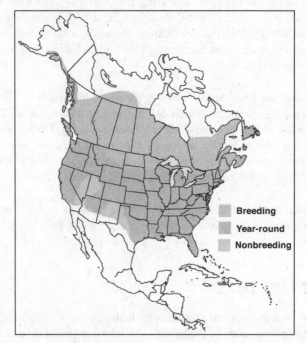

	Breeding
	Year-round
	Nonbreeding

REMEMBER

Range maps are a snapshot, a picture of the range of the bird at the time of the guide's publication. But sometimes ranges change. Use the maps as a guide but be prepared to see changes over time.

Digital Field Guides

When you're comfortable using your printed-on-paper field guide, you might want to download a field guide app to your phone. Most printed field guides have an app version, so if you're satisfied with your book, look for it as an app.

REMEMBER

There are some digital field guides that don't have a book, including the respected iBird Pro. Some field guide apps are free; some are as expensive as their book counterparts.

There is a learning curve to using field guide apps, but they do have advantages over books:

>> They're on your phone, so there's one less thing to carry in your pocket or bag.

>> You can search for species or groups of birds by species or group name, as well as by scrolling.

>> Some include sound recordings of the species, something a book could never do.

>> Some allow side-by-side comparisons, splitting the screen for each species you select.

>> Some have built-in databases and notebooks for recording species you find (although we recommend using eBird, detailed in Chapter 12, for this).

The disadvantages of a field guide app are that the taxonomic relationships among bird groups, and even the groupings themselves, are not always easy to see or understand. Also, the learning curve is usually steeper with an app.

With practice, you'll soon be as comfortable using a field guide app as you have become with your trusty book.

Chapter **12**

Writing It Down

N early all bird watchers are record-keepers — only the level of involvement in record-keeping varies. Some folks are content with the occasional note stuck on the refrigerator saying something like, "I saw a bluebird in the backyard today!" Some bird watchers catalog every bird they see, every day, along with the date, time, location, weather, who they were with, phase of the moon, and whether the coffee was decaf or high test.

Most bird watchers fall somewhere between these two extremes. We make notes about the things that interest us, or about things that we think interest others, or things that we're afraid we'll forget. No experiments prove that people who watch birds have a gene for compulsive record-keeping, but it's widely accepted as truth.

Birders use several formats of record-keeping. First, and the method many new bird watchers start with, is making your own, private list(s) on paper or on your digital device, such as in a spreadsheet. Another is recording your observations digitally, in an app, on the web, often with the intention of sharing. Many birders also keep a birding notebook or journal. (For lots more on birding notebooks, check out the "Keeping Notebook Records" section, later in this chapter.)

Each form has its pleasures and advantages. Which you choose depends on your own interests, and some bird watchers employ all the above. For some, listing becomes a goal, an end in itself. Admittedly, it is rewarding to watch your lists grow. Deriving enjoyment from finding and watching birds is the primary goal of this hobby, of course, but encountering new bird species is usually extra rewarding, and can become addictive. If you stick with bird watching, you *will* see species new to you — possibly many of them — so keeping lists of birds you have seen will be necessary to help you remember whether a species is new to you.

Understanding the Reasons for Record-Keeping

TIP

It is well documented that taking notes by hand (rather than typing or clicking boxes in an app) improves retention of that information. Unless you are the rare bird watcher who is indifferent about seeing species for the first time, you'd be wise to take notes on the birds you see. Many longtime bird watchers have shelves or drawers full of notebooks they've used over the years. It will help you remember, for example, the first time you saw a lark sparrow if you know when and where you were when it happened. Later, even years later, you can look over your trip notes and enjoy that happy memory. The more detailed the notes, the clearer your memory will be.

TIP

If you go on an outing with a bird club, it will reinforce your memory if you take a notebook and record the date, every location you visit, the names of the people you were with, the weather, where you stopped for lunch, and so on. Include a list of every bird species you saw, and even tally the numbers of each species at each location if you want. Note interesting bird behaviors you witnessed, or mnemonics you learned to describe a vocal pattern. All of this is optional, but taking notes fortifies memories.

REMEMBER

Bird watchers can and do contribute to citizen science by sharing their observation records with researchers. Apps make it easy to do, and because so many birders participate, our hobby has helped reveal insights about the ecology of birds, including population dynamics, distribution and range changes, behavior, and more. See Chapter 19 to learn more about birding that makes a difference.

Maintaining the Life List

Bird watchers can become obsessive about keeping lists. The number of lists is limited only by your imagination, as you'll see below.

The list, the one nearly every bird watcher keeps — even if only mentally — is the life list. All other lists are secondary. To bird watchers, there are two kinds of birds: bird species we've seen before and bird species we haven't seen yet. If you see a species and you're unsure whether you've seen it or not, you may consider keeping lists more reliably.

REMEMBER

A *life list* is a list of all the species of birds you've seen (or heard, or both). Some cynics claim that this list is really a list of all the birds you *think* you've seen and is therefore a lot longer than the list of birds you actually *have* seen. Ignore those people. They're just jealous.

A life list is a very personal construct that can add richness and meaning to your life. It can be a source of pride in several ways:

>> If the total number is large.

>> If the total recently jumped.

>> It can reflect that you have traveled to interesting places.

>> It can be the source of interesting stories, such as "nemesis birds" that you work and struggle to find, but have, to date, "dipped on" (birding lingo for "struck out").

REMEMBER

A *life bird* is a bird you encounter for the first time, one you've never seen before in your life. When you encounter one, a life bird gets added to your life list.

Bill Thompson III, author of the first edition of *Bird Watching For Dummies*, often encouraged people to do "the life bird dance" upon "getting a lifer." As he instructed: "You put your hands in the air like you just don't care and wiggle your hips like no one is watching." It is tempting to whoop and holler when you get a lifer, but Rule #1 in birding is "Do not disturb the birds." So, save that audible expression of joy for afterward!

When you see a wild bald eagle for the first time (those in zoos or appearing in TV commercials don't count), you will know it's a new bird for you, something that you've not seen before. That's a life bird for you, and it is now on your life list. Remembering your lifer bald eagle is an unforgettable experience for most bird-ers, especially those old enough to remember when bald eagles were rare and an endangered species in the Lower 48.

On the other hand, do you remember the first time and place you saw an American robin or an American crow? Do you know for certain that you've seen a song sparrow or a hairy woodpecker? More than 1,000 bird species can be found in the U.S., Canada, and Mexico. How many have you seen? As you pay more attention to birds, you might forget some or get confused. Taking notes on what you see will improve the accuracy of your life list.

Starting a life list

The simplest form of a life list is just a list of the birds you've seen, either written down somewhere, checked off on a pre-printed list, or entered into a spreadsheet or database. Most people like to add a little more information, such as the date and the location of the sighting. This information allows them to check not only what they've seen, but when and where.

If you haven't started keeping a life list, we encourage you to start right away. Surely you've seen an American robin already — maybe hundreds of them throughout your life. Time to put that bird on your list, either the next time you see one, or as a historical record, without including an exact date or location.

Maybe you remember seeing a bald eagle on a vacation with your family when you were a child, long before you knew that bird watching was a thing. You can choose to use that bald eagle as your lifer, even without knowing the exact date or location of that experience. Or you can wait until you see the next bald eagle and record that as your lifer, now that you're a genuine birder. It's your life list; it's your choice.

Same for American crow, house sparrow, European starling — all the species you can likely identify and have seen. These "early birds" on your list will be different from many to come. These birds are ones you took for granted previously, and the date you record for them may not be the first time you spotted each one. That's okay. If you record the date and location of the next ones you see, the date will reflect when these species became more meaningful to you.

Deciding where to keep your list

There is no right way or place to keep a life list. You can use a notebook, a sheet of paper, a book, a spreadsheet, or computer software designed for just such record-keeping.

Many new birders jot the date and location directly into their (book version) field guide next to the image or description of each new species they see. The problem is, to count the total of your life list requires flipping through each page of the field guide. Some field guides provide lines or little boxes in the index that can be used to check off the birds after you've spotted and identified them, or even provide a checklist for your life list. That's more convenient for tallying, but such pages leave little room for notes.

TIP

If you decide to keep your life list in your printed field guide, write notes on the pages next to the image or description of the species, and also make a checkmark beside that species in the index.

Just remember that bird names and even species change. (See Chapter 4 for more about bird taxonomy and nomenclature.) Printed field guides can become out of date surprisingly quickly.

If you decide against using your (book version) field guide as your notes repository, here are some other options to consider:

» Set aside a dedicated notebook to use as your life list of birds or dedicate just a page or two of a notebook you carry with you when you are watching birds.

Leave plenty of room, though. You'll be surprised how quickly your life list can grow to 100 species or more with just a little bit of (enjoyable) effort. And don't misplace the notebook!

» Create a document file or spreadsheet on your computer of each new bird species you see, including the date and location of your observation.

TIP

Try searching the Internet for "North American bird species checklist," and you can find several versions that list all the birds of North America in editable spreadsheet form.

» Check out online or brick-and-mortar nature or wild bird stores for notebooks specifically designed to be used as life lists or trip lists. Some include a taxonomic list of all the birds in North America. Others are relatively blank, so you can record your life birds chronologically. These notebooks are often 50 to 100 pages long and include space to record additional information.

» The Cornell Lab of Ornithology offers a free app that can keep your life list for you. It's called eBird, and it will automatically arrange your life list into numerous additional lists for you. Because eBird is way more than list-keeping software, we'll spend more time on it a few pages from now and in upcoming chapters.

REMEMBER

Typing detailed notes about your observations on your phone, however, is not convenient for those of us with fat fingers. It is not a good substitute for writing notes on your birding observations and adventures.

Going with your own list rules

A few bird organizations and some (overly competitive?) birders have come up with some "rules" for list-keeping that they believe should be followed. Two examples of these are:

» If you only *hear* a bird, but don't see it, you cannot count the bird on your life list, no matter how certain you are of the species' song or call.

DAWN'S CONNECTICUT WARBLER

Many Junes ago, while Dawn and her birding pal Greg were helping with Indiana's second Breeding Bird Atlas, Dawn heard a Connecticut warbler. She had been studying the songs of 35 eastern warblers, and she distinctly and certainly heard a Connecticut. This species isn't known to breed in southern Indiana, but it does pass through late in the spring. It wouldn't count on the Breeding Bird Atlas, but it would count on Dawn's life list! The pair circled the small wetland. They knew the bird was on or close to the ground, and they knew precisely where, but the vegetation was dense. They spent an hour or more, waiting and watching, listening to it sing, trying to get a better angle, and hoping that bird would show itself. It never did. Still, Dawn counts that bird on her life list. It wasn't a satisfying find, but so it goes sometimes.

Years later, while attending the Biggest Week in American Birding in northwestern Ohio, word spread that a Connecticut warbler was found in a particular location. Dawn and hundreds of other birders flocked to that spot. Again, she heard the Connecticut. Through the crowd, she scoured the ground where the bird's call of *wheat, a winter wheat, a winter wheat* was coming from and got a quick but clear glimpse of its feet. Only its feet. Again, it wasn't satisfying. To this day, Dawn has not had a full, satisfying look at a Connecticut warbler, but she sure has had fun trying. And that's the thing: Even though she counts Connecticut warbler on her life list, she still wants a good, long look at one. Sure, the list is important to her, but the experience and the memory are every bit as worthy a goal.

>> If you're bird watching with another person or persons and somebody else identifies a bird and points it out to you, you cannot count it on your life list. You did not identify it yourself.

We think both of these rules are for people who are a tad obsessive-compulsive about how long their bird list is. When bird watching starts imposing rules, it begins to lose its appeal as a relaxing, enjoyable activity. If you want to count birds that you have heard but not seen, and you want to count the obscure shorebird that somebody ID'd for you, do it. But if you don't feel right about counting a bird you did not see well or did not ID yourself, that's okay, too. It's all about what works for you.

TIP

In general, you make the rules regarding whether you can include a bird on your life list. Most people, however, would agree on these rules:

>> The bird must be alive when you see it.

>> The bird must be wild and free (not in a zoo, mist-net, or the hands of a falconer, and not on a TV or movie screen).

>> You must be certain of its identification, whether by sight or sound.

>> Eggs do not count as birds, but nestlings and fledglings do.

>> Pets, zoo animals (even escapees), and farm animals don't count.

Lists Breed Lists

Once you've started your life list, you'll probably begin other lists. This process is natural. The trick is to not let it get out of hand — unless you really want it to, that is. Listing can become an obsession that dominates your bird watching and even your life! A few lists are a good idea, and most people are sufficiently balanced to keep lists in perspective. If you have an addictive personality, however, you'll want to keep a close watch on the tendency to create additional lists. Or just indulge it and enjoy this fascinating new cranny in your personality.

What additional lists do birders keep? We cover the countless ways birders keep lists so you can consider which lists best fit your goals for bird watching.

Yard list

After the life list, the second list that almost every bird watcher keeps is a *yard list*. This list is exactly what it sounds like: a list of all the birds that you've seen in your yard. Yard lists are popular because they're simple and rewarding. Yard lists cover an area you're in almost every day, and they're a way of documenting the diversity of bird life in your area. Yard lists can be kept the same way as life lists, except that the list of birds is likely to be much shorter and include mostly familiar species. Many bird watchers keep their yard lists on a sheet of paper or printed checklist and stick it to the refrigerator door along with shopping lists, drawings by small children, and curly photos.

TIP

Search the Internet for a "printable bird checklist" for your state and print it, if you want a professional-looking checklist.

Bird watchers who don't have yards (and even some who do) sometimes keep a window list of bird species they've seen at home while they were indoors!

Keeping a yard list has one tricky part. Even if you have several bird feeders, a bird bath, and a brush pile, the list stops growing rapidly after a year or two. After that, each new addition becomes a red-letter event because you've already seen all the common and regularly occurring birds. Some birders keep not only a yard list, but a yard-year list. They keep a master yard list, but every January they start a new yard list.

WHAT COUNTS AS "IN" A YARD

Anywhere in North America you can go outdoors, look up, and see a vulture or a hawk flying over. The bird flying overhead definitely was not in your yard, but you were. Should you count it? Yes, of course — if you want to!

Unless you've entered a contest with one of your friends over who has the largest yard list and have negotiated a complicated set of rules over what counts and what doesn't (don't laugh — it happens), the answer is entirely up to you. It's no one else's business. Do whatever brings you the most pleasure or what you think is right. Most birders keep a yard list that includes anything they can see or hear while they (the observers) are standing in the yard. They do this because it's easier and because it means a bigger list. Other bird watchers like to do it the hard way, where each bird has to be physically in the yard. Some keep a list of all the birds they have seen or heard in or from their yard — so the bird can be in or above their yard even if the observer is next door or down the street. Or, the observer can be in their yard and observe a bird in the park across the street. You can define the boundaries as you see fit.

Remember, a bird watcher's yard is a bird watcher's castle. You make the rules.

A list of lists

After the life list and the yard list, the sky is the limit. Commonly kept lists include state lists, county lists, and North American lists. Some people keep lists for their favorite bird-watching sites — places like national wildlife refuges and local parks. The number and type of lists is limited only by your imagination, interests, and places you visit.

To see how varied lists can be, and how far some people can go, here's an annotated list of some lists that bird watchers keep. Some of these lists are not so common, but they give you an idea of the possibilities:

>> **County list:** All the birds that you've seen in one county, usually the one in which you live. Our friend Margaret keeps a list of all the birds she has seen in every county of Ohio. She worked hard to see at least 100 birds in every Ohio county. (Ohio has 88 counties!)

>> **State list:** All the birds that you've seen in one state, usually the one in which you live, but some well-traveled bird watchers keep a list for every state.

>> **Lower 48 list:** All the birds that you've seen in the lower 48 states. Popular with bird watchers who travel but are unable to get to Alaska or Hawaii, where many birds exist that you cannot see anywhere else on this continent.

- » **U.S. list:** All the birds that you've seen in all 50 U.S. states. (Or, for our Canadian readers, a **Canada list** for all the birds seen in the 10 provinces and three territories.)

- » **North American list:** All the birds that you've seen in North America.

- » **ABA Area list:** The American Birding Association Checklist includes all 50 states, Canada, the French islands of St Pierre and Miquelon, and waters 200 miles from those land areas.

- » **World list:** This list is important for folks with the resources, time, opportunity, or obsession to travel often to other continents. Remember, there are about 10,000 bird species on this planet, but only about one-tenth of them are possible in North America. Anytime you venture outside the USA, you can add to your world life list.

- » **Country list:** Like state lists, but for each country you've visited.

- » **Regional list:** For less far-ranging bird watchers, typically covering several states; for example, a Midwest list.

- » **Day list:** All the birds that you've seen each day. If you keep your lists on paper, this is time-consuming. Still, many bird watchers keep day lists, at least for the days they spend actively bird watching. One advantage of day lists is that they reveal the change of the seasons. You can look back at them and tell exactly what day the first migrating dark-eyed juncos showed up in the fall, and what day the hummingbirds or chipping sparrows returned in the spring.

- » **Year list:** A list of all the birds seen in a year, in any locality you choose. Year lists are popular because they allow you to start over every January 1. These lists can also be compared from year to year. Did you see more birds this year than last? It's a question you'll probably ask yourself someday, and a year list is the only way to answer it. If you want to know whether your new native-plant landscaping attracted more birds, you'll need a baseline "before" yard/year list, and an "after" yard/year list in subsequent years.

- » **Workplace list:** If you find yourself noticing birds as you arrive at work, leave from work, or out your office window, consider keeping a workplace list.

- » **Birdbath list:** A list of all the birds that use your birdbath. Julie's birdbath list starts over every January 1. Her all-time bath list for her Ohio yard has grown to a whopping 81 species since she started counting in 2005!

- » **Television list:** Now we're getting into some of the stranger lists. This one includes all the birds you've seen or heard on television. Some bird watchers watch golf tournaments solely to increase their TV bird lists. The advantage is that golf tournaments are held outdoors, with trees around, and everyone is quiet. It's amazing how many bird species you can identify by sound if you're familiar with the songs. Nature shows are another popular source for TV birding. Some purists won't count any bird that the announcer identifies for them, while others count them all.

» **Sports list:** Speaking of sports, this list includes birds observed while attending outdoor sporting events. If you have season tickets for your local minor league baseball team, you could rack up a nice little count between innings. Jessica keeps a list of birds seen and heard at her children's sporting events. With four active kiddos, she spends a lot of time outside cheering, watching, and listening — her kids and the birds.

» **Heard-only list:** This is a list of birds that the observer has heard but never seen. Usually it contains owls, rails, and a few other night birds. The primary purpose of this list is to target birds that you need (or want) to see — like Dawn's Connecticut warbler.

» **Dream list:** Some people dream about birds. This is not a cause for concern. Some people dream about birds constantly. (This may be a cause for concern, but that's between those people and their therapists.) Some people keep lists of birds they have dreamt about. You can decide for yourself what that means.

Many more lists do exist, of course, some of which are too strange for a family publication such as this. Feel free to invent your own. If it brings you pleasure, keep a list of all the birds you've seen while at baseball games, or while lying in bed. (Heard-only species count.) It's probably not a good idea to share these lists with other bird watchers until you know them well.

Printed lists

Printed or printable checklists are available at many birding hot spots and online. Most states and many local bird clubs produce a checklist for the region or local area. National parks and wildlife refuges have bird checklists available, too. Printed checklists are often inexpensive or even free at the visitor center. They're great to document the species you see while visiting, say, Everglades National Park. If you are planning a trip, search the Internet for "printable bird checklist" of that place, and then print it. If you have time as you travel to this destination, you can use it as a study guide: scan the list for species you aren't familiar with, and then look them up in your field guide.

TIP

Just for kicks (and for practice) do an Internet search for "printable bird checklist" for your state. Print it, and tape it to your refrigerator. Use it as your yard list — or your yard list for this year.

eBird Makes Listing So Much Easier

Cornell Lab of Ornithology has created an app called eBird that will keep track of all your birding observations for you and sort them into your life list, lists for every county of every state, and every country you visit, every year, and more — as long as you actually use it to record your data. It is so much more than an app, really — it's a database of global birding records, and each time you enter your bird observations, you are contributing to that important knowledge base. We'll discuss the myriad ways birders and researchers can use the output of eBird later, but for now, we're going to focus on entering your observations into eBird.

REMEMBER

eBird is a free app, and you can download it to your mobile device from your favorite app store. It is not a field guide; its primary purpose is not to help you identify birds. The app exists to collect data from birders all over the world (including your data!) — and then make it available for others to use.

Installing eBird on your mobile phone

After you have downloaded eBird and fired it up for the first time, you'll be prompted to sign in or create an account at Cornell Lab. (This account is free.) As usually happens when creating an online account, you'll be required to enter your e-mail address and then to create a username — which can be the same as your e-mail address or something shorter and simpler (but unique). (Dawn has been using eBird for so long that her last name was available as her eBird username!) A short, memorable username is useful for when you are birding with others; one person enters the data into eBird, and then can share that data with the eBirders in the group. You'll also have to come up with a password. When you have submitted that information, go to your e-mail and confirm that you have requested this account. This activates your eBird account.

TIP

If you already have a Cornell Lab of Ornithology account, perhaps because you participate in their Project FeederWatch or another such activity, you can use the same login to access eBird, even for the first time.

The first time you log in to eBird on your mobile device using your personal account, you'll be asked for personal preferences — your preferred language, whether you'd like species' common or scientific name, whether you prefer distances in miles or kilometers, whether you'd like to be given the opportunity to enter data about subspecies, and so on. (*Note:* We three longtime birders have declined the opportunity to enter subspecies data because that's beyond our interest level.)

Next, eBird will ask if it may use your location. If you deny this request, you'll have to pinpoint your exact location on a map each time you enter your birding observations. This can be a hassle. If you permit eBird to use your location while you are using the app, it will use GPS to locate where you birded. It can even track your travel route if you want it to. If this seems creepy to you, you can disable it, but most birders think it's cool and useful. Jessica especially enjoys seeing her travel route when she's birding by kayak — it's quite satisfying to see the long squiggly route and cumulative miles slowly paddled over the course of the day!

Finally, eBird will offer you geographic "packs," which are lists of birds possible in various locations around the world. Initially, it will suggest the most appropriate pack for you based on your current location. Many people download only the pack for their state or province of residence.

TIP

If you frequently travel to far-off places, you'd be wise to download the packs for those places before you depart. This could take a few minutes and require a reliable Internet connection. This data is stored on your phone, not in the cloud, and some packs require several megabytes of storage space. You can, however, delete packs when your travels are over. Doing so does not delete your data — just the template for the regional bird list.

Now you're ready to enter data! Since eBird knows this is your maiden voyage, it will offer you a quick and easy tutorial of how to enter data. We highly recommend taking this tutorial and paying attention!

Recording your observations in eBird

The nutshell version of using eBird to record your bird observations is:

1. **Launch the eBird app.**

2. **Click the Start Checklist button, (See Figure 12-1.)**

3. **Click on the + Add Observation or Find Species option. (See Figure 12-2.)**

4. **When you see a bird, enter how many of that species you saw in the Numbers Observed field and start typing its name.**

   If you see three American robins in your yard, enter 3 and start typing **American robin.** Many birds whose name begins with *Amer . . .* will display.

   When you see *American robin* on that list, tap the name of the bird, and *3* will magically appear next to it. If another robin flies over your house, tap on that *3* and it will increase to 4. If a flock of 10 robins lands in a tree, you can tap on the number 10 times or tap on the name *American robin*. The latter will take you into a form, where you can type in your tally so far.

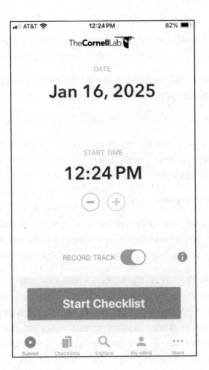

FIGURE 12-1:
Starting a
checklist in eBird.

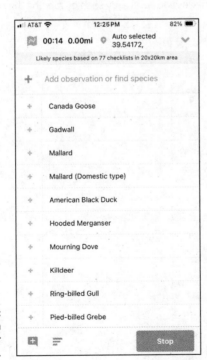

FIGURE 12-2:
Adding an
observation or
finding a species.

Note: If you want to add a add a note or two, there's room for that as well, as shown in Figure 12-3.

5. **After recording your sighting, clicking Cancel will allow you to exit that screen — but it won't erase your new observation.**

   It feels strange, but trust us — in eBird, Cancel works just like Exit.

   But don't overcount. If it's likely that the three robins you saw at first are part of the 10 you saw landing in the tree, add 7, not 10. (In other words, don't count the first 3 robins again.) Judgment is required. Better to undercount than to overcount.

6. **Repeat for each species you see.**

   eBird stays in a mode ready for a new number and species, or a tap to increase the number of a species you've already found. If you click Cancel, it will allow you to scroll through the whole list of possible species for your region.

TIP

Note the checkmark at the bottom of the screen — the one with a number on it. (See Figure 12-4.) That number indicates the number of species you've seen since you started this checklist. If you tap that checkmark, the list of birds shown will change from all birds possible in your location to just the ones you've already seen. You can still start typing in a number and the name of new species you see, but if you are birding on the kind of day where species diversity is low, it's convenient to just add to the tally of a species you've already seen by tapping the number.

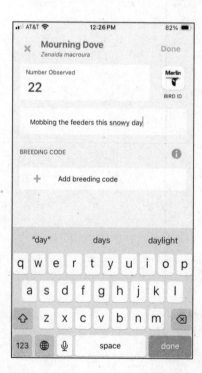

FIGURE 12-3:
There's room to add notes!

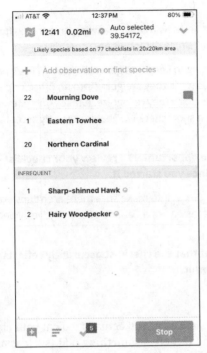

FIGURE 12-4:
The Checkmark
icon keeps a
running tally.

7. **When you are done birding at this time and place and are ready to submit this checklist, click Cancel and then click Stop.**

   It will ask if you are done birding, confirming that you did intend to tap "Stop."

8. **If you are done, click Stop Track and then click Choose Location.**

   If your location is enabled on your mobile device, eBird will suggest your current location, as well as nearby birding hotspots (if there are any).

9. **It will guess the "type" of observation — whether you were stationary or traveling, but other options include taking part in research and entering an "incidental" observation.**

TIP

   Help is available by clicking the *i* button next to most fields. The app will ask for the number of observers and display both the duration since you started this checklist, as well as the distance you traveled — if you were traveling. You'll also have the option to add comments about this checklist.

10. **eBird will ask you if this is a complete checklist of all the birds you were able to identify.**

    We generally click "Yes," because we pay attention to all the birds we see when making a checklist. If you answer "No," your list will be considered "incidental," which indicates that you did not give birding your full attention. Perhaps you were going to the dentist and saw a cedar waxwing on a tree in front of the office. It's fine to enter this single datapoint on a checklist.

TIP

Birders who are just starting to keep lists generally rack up lifers quickly and in unusual locations, such as while they are going into an office or parking their car and happen to notice a bird they recognize. It takes only a few minutes to fire up eBird and submit a short checklist. That is perfectly acceptable — and encouraged — behavior.

11. **eBird now gives you the opportunity to review your checklist — all the species you reported since you started it.**

   It's a good idea to take a look at it to make sure there aren't any errors, such as entering a cackling goose instead of a Canada goose. (We've all been guilty of mistakes like this.)

12. **When you are confident that the checklist accurately reflects your observations, press Submit.**

   Congratulations!

Within several days, an eBird reviewer will actually look at your checklist to make sure it seems reasonable, and if there's something odd (such as a cackling goose in southeastern Ohio in July), they will e-mail you to verify what you saw. If it was a mistake, you can edit your checklist, even months or years after submitting it.

REMEMBER

If you submit a checklist and suddenly remember leaving out that turkey vulture you saw drifting over, it's easy to pull up the checklist (choose Submitted from the bottom bar of the home eBird screen), click Edit, and add the vulture.

Once upon a time, Dawn spotted a glossy ibis near Parkersburg, West Virginia, far from its normal range. Of course she reported it via eBird. A few days later, she got an e-mail from the local eBird reviewer (whom some birders call the eBird police) asking for more details on the observation. Dawn did *not* think "How rude of them to doubt me" — because she knows that verifying questionable observations ensures the accuracy of the database.

The more frequently you use eBird to enter your observations, the easier and more intuitive it will become for you. There's lots of help online at https://ebird.org/home, many ways of doing things, shortcuts, editing tools, and so much more. For now, the best way to learn the eBird app is to figure it out for yourself. If you make mistakes, you can edit them, both immediately and even after you've submitted the checklist. You can even delete checklists.

TIP

Lots of experienced birders use eBird. If you run into problems, odds are high that a birding pal or your birding mentor can help you figure it out.

Looking at your lists in eBird

When you are logged in to eBird, either on your mobile app, or at eBird.org on your computer, you'll see a link to My eBird. Go there and hold on to your hat. Depending upon your setup, it will show you the tally of all the bird species you've seen in your life and provide you with that list of species names and the date and location you first saw each one. Or it will show you all the birds you've seen in the current year, in your current location, or in the current month. You can ask it to show you all the birds you saw in a particular state in a particular year or all the birds you saw in a certain month in a certain county, or a certain country. As you enter more checklists into eBird, your lists will grow.

WARNING

Listing via eBird can be addictive. Some birders, however, find that using eBird while in the field interrupts their birding Zen. Such folks don't enter each bird as they see it but rather enter a batch every few minutes or even at the end of their outing. Retaining a mental bird list may result in a few omissions, and certainly the tally won't be as accurate for species you see again and again. You could keep a notebook and transfer that data to eBird. In time, you will find your own eBird rhythm and style.

Listers, Twitchers, and Just Plain Birders

Listing has become an obsession with some bird watchers. They live for the chance to add a bird to any or all of their various lists. They frequently venture far afield with the intention of pumping up their list. Such *listers* represent a significant portion of the bird-watching community. Everyone keeps lists, but a few let it take over their lives.

How do you know lists have gotten out of hand? Well, here's a true story. One lister (now completely recovered) reached the point where he had to create a list of his lists because he had so many lists that he could not keep track. eBird does not accommodate heard-only lists, or dream lists, birdbath lists, or TV lists, so if you wish to keep those, you'll need to use a notebook or spreadsheet. That helps limit the number of lists you keep.

On the other hand, eBird keeps all the geographic and time-specific lists you can think of with only data entry required on your part. Watching those lists grow can be motivation enough to find species of birds you haven't seen before. When you see you have 99 birds on your life list (or 199 . . .) the pull to see one more is strong. And again, listing via eBird contributes to our understanding of wild birds, which is also motivating. Again, more on that in Chapter 19.

For many birders who keep lists, the real joy comes not from the length of one's list, but from seeing new species in unfamiliar locations. There is pleasure in the quest for new species, pleasure in encountering them, and pleasure in watching them. Hardcore birders study up on birds when they can't be out there with the birds and fantasize about trips to birdy locations. Sure, there is joy in growing a long life list, but the real joy comes from experiencing and appreciating the diversity of birds.

Twitchers

Birders who drop what they are doing because of a report of a rare species — either nearby or on the other side of the continent — are called *twitchers*. That's originally a British term, derived from the uncontrollable excitement that takes over their bodies at the prospect of seeing a new species — and adding a new bird to their list.

Listers and twitchers take themselves very seriously, which is good because if they didn't, who would?

Listers are collectors, no different from collectors of baseball cards, salt shakers, or beer cans. Their pleasure is both in experiencing the birds themselves, and in adding to their collection. It's easy to recognize obsessive listers. They see a new bird and immediately begin to gush: "Wow, that's not only a state and county bird, it's my first March record, a new park bird, a new bird seen only in flight . . ." When the list of lists gets too long, it's time to break away, lie down, and have a cool drink.

We admit, we sometimes travel a great distance chasing a bird we haven't seen in a long time, such as a snowy owl. Finding it will add to our year and county and state lists, but we travel to see the owl, not to grow the list. We enjoy listing, but we enjoy seeing and watching birds even more. Enjoyment of the birds is why we list. Try leaving the list at home once in a while and go back to looking at birds — familiar birds, common birds. They can be a source of joy, just in the watching without collecting data.

Obsessive listing is not contagious unless you hang out too long with listers. The vast majority of bird watchers handle lists the way the vast majority of people handle drinking adult beverages — in moderation and with easy control. A yard list is a nice glass of wine with dinner. Ten or twenty lists is binge listing and can lead to blackouts.

Real birders versus listers-only

Bird watchers fed up with the obsessiveness — and occasional nuttiness — of out-of-control listers sometimes try to argue that listers aren't really bird watchers. They even claim that they themselves never keep lists. This attitude is the opposite extreme. Avoid list-aversion as determinedly as you would avoid list mania. But if you don't want to keep a written or digital list, that's your choice. Odds are, though, you won't remember the details of the species you see.

REMEMBER

Lists are merely a way of organizing information. They are catalogs and reminders. Make them work for you.

Don't let a fear of being obsessive interfere with the pleasure of seeing a new or rare bird. If, very rarely, you arise at three in the morning, drive for several hours, and stand around a garbage dump in freezing weather to see a rare bird, you are not, by definition, a compulsive lister. Some would call you a twitcher, though. Rare birds are fun to see, mostly because they are rare. Going the extra mile once in a while is not nutty. On the other hand, if you do all that to see a bird you've seen many times before, and you do it only because it's a new bird for your Friday the 13th list . . .

Two lists that you can get fairly nutty about without raising other bird watchers' eyebrows are the life list and the yard list.

Keeping Notebook Records

Notebooks can serve as a birding journal that enhances list-keeping. Many bird watchers keep notebooks in which they record a variety of observations about the birds they see, and their birding experiences in general. Notebooks can include lists, but also sketches, stories, and your emotional reactions. Years later, such information can be more rewarding to read than a collection of lists.

What goes into a notebook is entirely up to you. Notebooks are by nature quirky, reflecting the interest of you, their author. They can be full of unanswered questions, speculations, humorous stories, the names of people that you've met, descriptions of places you've been, where you stopped for lunch, and what you ate.

Most bird watchers who keep notebooks use them to record descriptions of unusual birds they've seen or birds that they've had a difficult time identifying.

These entries include notes about birds in unusual plumage, or interesting bird behavior. Later, when at home, these notes are valuable in helping the bird watcher recall the field marks of hard-to-identify birds. There's nothing like a quick sketch or a few observations jotted down to help refresh your memory long after the bird is gone.

Deciding which kind of notebook is best for you

Whatever you like, but consider the following requirements:

>> It should be large enough to write in easily, to sketch in, and to draw maps.

>> It should be portable enough to travel with you, both on business trips and for a day in the field. The large, loose-leaf binders that kids used to lug to school are just too bulky, and the paper tears and falls out.

>> It should be durable. Flimsy covers eventually tear. You can even find some waterproof notebooks designed specifically for birders in specialty stores and online.

Many birders use one of the hard-back diaries found in stationery sections of stores or online. They usually measure about 5x8 inches and hold 100 to 200 pages. These diaries are small enough to fit in a suitcase, briefcase, or even a large coat pocket. They are hardy enough to tolerate the occasional splash of coffee or blob of doughnut icing. The hard covers make writing in them easy when you're sitting in the car or standing in a field.

TIP

Use a pencil, rather than a pen, when you are writing in your notebook. Pencil withstands rain, coffee, even mud puddles. Ink runs when it gets wet.

Remembering just what's worth remembering

Keeping a notebook is what you want it to be. Just as with keeping your lists, no rules exist. The notebook is yours and should accomplish what you want with it. Try keeping one, because it will boost your long-term memories of your experiences with birding and individual birds, but don't let it become a burden. There is no obligation here. There is no need to take notes on birds you see when you walk your dog in the morning or take your garbage to the curb. (But you might want to get into the habit of taking your binoculars with you when you walk your dog, and for longer strolls with Poochie, even firing up eBird on your phone to record species you encounter.)

TIP

For most people, keeping track of what you've seen and where you've been enhances the pleasure of bird watching. Even if you're just starting out, try keeping at least a simple list and a few notes. If keeping records is not your thing, quitting is easy. But if your notes turn out to be a source of pleasure, you cannot go back and recreate them a year or two later. Too many bird watchers don't start keeping lists and notes until they've been bird watching for several years, and they usually regret not having started sooner.

4

Beyond the Backyard

Chapter **13**

Migration: When Birds and Birders Get Moving

N ot all birds stay put year-round. The cast changes with the season. When spring arrives in temperate zones, a whole new bunch of species that weren't here in winter arrives to set up housekeeping, mark out territory, nest, and raise young. Now, some birds, like northern cardinals, woodpeckers, chickadees, titmice, and nuthatches, do stay put year-round. These are the birds with winter survival skills. The ones that don't have those skills, or those that depend on insect prey throughout the year, have to get packing and head south before cold weather comes in autumn.

Of all the weird things birds do, flying hundreds or thousands of miles twice each year is one of the weirdest. Look at the hummingbird at your front porch feeder. Now consider that it may have made a nonstop flight across the Gulf of Mexico — 18 hours in good weather; 24 hours in bad — then buzzed several thousand more miles to get to your porch. And then, come September, it'll make the trip in reverse! How did something like that even get started?

Solving the Migration Mystery

Migration began as a way for birds to exploit seasonally abundant food resources in northern latitudes. If you've ever stood by a Maine streamside, arms moving like a human windmill, swatting blackflies, mosquitoes, and deerflies, you have a good concept of the staggering abundance of insects in northern forests. What you're experiencing is a compressed seasonal flush of insects in the short boreal summer. And exploiting that flush of insect food is what songbird migration is all about. As the ice sheet retreated north in the Pleistocene, birds that originated in tropical latitudes followed its edge, finding more and better food resources the farther north they went. Over time, the ice retreated farther and farther north, to the Arctic Circle. And some tropical birds made longer and longer flights to exploit those food resources. The Cape May warbler in Figure 13-1 has found so many spruce budworms in her Canadian breeding territory that she was able to lay seven eggs!

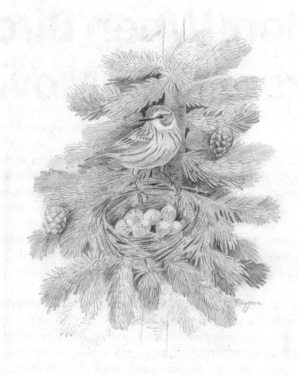

FIGURE 13-1:
Cape May warbler
nest with seven
eggs, female.

When autumn comes, insect abundance falls, and birds dependent upon insects head south, seeking warmer climes, and insects. Though you may think about your warblers, tanagers, vireos, and flycatchers as "your" breeding birds who fly south for a winter vacation, they are in truth tropical birds that come north to breed, then fly home for the winter!

TIP

Some thrushes, grosbeaks, and many more join the cuckoos, orioles, tanagers, vireos, warblers, and hummingbirds in this great seasonal mass movement. It is one of the greatest spectacles on Earth, and it goes on all around us. Once you've tuned into it with the new eyes and ears of a bird watcher, spring and fall will never be boring!

Looking at the three types of migration

The phenomenon we've just described is *complete migration,* meaning virtually all individuals of these species leave their breeding grounds for the winter. Some species may go only as far as the Gulf Coast, but some keep flying to Central and South America, logging many thousands of miles round trip.

More common is *partial migration,* where some, but not all members of a given species move from their breeding range. These birds are taking advantage of seasonal food abundance, too, but they're more flexible than complete migrants. Eastern bluebirds are a good example of a partial migrant. Some stay in northern latitudes; some head for the sunny Southeast, and some linger somewhere in between. Red-tailed hawks are partial migrants, too: you can see them sunning along winter highways in northern climes and streaming south in autumn at hawk-watching lookouts.

Then there's *irruptive migration,* which gets birders' hearts beating faster. Irruptive migrants are unpredictable, because they come south only in years when they get short of food in their normal wintering grounds. Some of us chase fabulous phantoms like snowy and great gray owls, which come south only when their favorite prey (voles and lemmings) becomes scarce in the Far North. Bill Thompson III, author of the first edition of *Bird Watching For Dummies,* once drove 11 hours with his friend Geoff to catch a Bohemian waxwing irruption in Michigan. It sounds crazy — unless you've ever seen Bohemian waxwings: devastatingly plump, impossibly sleek units trimmed in scarlet, black, yellow, and white.

Birders talk about "finch years" with a wistful sigh. That's when irruptive migrants like purple finches, pine grosbeaks, evening grosbeaks, and crossbills, like the red crossbill in Figure 13-2, have trouble finding conifer seeds and move far south of their normal winter range. Julie will never forget the flock of 60 mustard-yellow, black, and white evening grosbeaks that piled into a trough-like feeder her dad built for her in the mid-1960s in Richmond, Virginia. Far, far south of their normal winter range, these wandering visitors might as well have been parrots for how excited she was. As scarce as evening grosbeaks have become, we're pretty sure we'll never see such an event again.

FIGURE 13-2:
Red crossbill on spruce cone.

Debunking the "First Robin of Spring" myth

Many people consider the reappearance of the American robin a harbinger of spring, and for those who live in the northern tier of states and Canada, they are. But for folks who live in the southernmost tier of states, robins are a harbinger of "snowbirds" — humans who head south to avoid cold weather. For the rest of us Yanks, robins are year-round residents of our country, from coast to coast. Robins that breed up north might spend the winters farther south, but from Northern California to the Chesapeake Bay, robins are shivering not far from us. We don't see them as often because 1) we're indoors keeping warm, and 2) their behavior changes when the ground freezes and their invertebrate diet becomes inaccessible. In cold months, the robin's diet changes to frozen fruit — things like wild grape, chokecherry, honeysuckle, hawthorn, holly, and dogwood, still hanging frozen or dried on the vines. Here in Ohio, we have seen huge flocks of robins in frigid weather in January merrily feasting on fruit-bearing ornamental trees. When the ground thaws, earthworms and other such delectable critters become available again, and we begin to notice robins in our yards once again — but they've been nearby for most of the winter. The first robin of spring is actually the first one you see on the day of the vernal equinox.

Detailing the Logistics of Migration

Birds are aware of the seasons. When nesting and caring for their young winds down, the hours of daylight shorten, and birds instinctively sense that it's time for a change. They don't, however, just wake up one morning and decide to go. Rather, they pack for the trip.

Getting fat is a good thing!

Prior to migration, birds that have a long way to fly must quickly build up stores of fat. Fat is a bird's metabolic fuel. It is light and energy-dense, and a good fat deposit can propel a red knot from the Eastern seaboard to the Canadian Arctic! A red knot (sandpiper) can land on a New Jersey beach weighing as little as 90 grams, having exhausted its reserves flying from its wintering grounds in Chile. (See the image on the left in Figure 13-3.) At coastal stopovers in springtime, exactly timed to coincide with horseshoe crab spawning, red knots gorge on the tiny crab eggs, gaining from 8 to 15 grams per day. Knots look visibly bulbous when they have bulked up to as much as 200 grams, having stored enough fat to fly on to the Arctic. (Check out the image on the right in Figure 13-3.) Imagine doubling your weight in only two weeks! We can't even picture it . . . but here's a painting Julie did of two knots, one thin and one fat. Fat is good for migrating birds!

FIGURE 13-3:
Red knot emaciated and bulked up.

Songbirds, which average a 20 to 40 percent weight gain before migration, gorge on fruits and insects to build themselves up. A worm-eating warbler, which weighs 15 grams, can fly 125 miles on one gram of fat. Hummingbirds stock up at feeders and grab small insects out of the air. Fat fuels the ruby-throated hummingbird through a 600-mile, up to 24-hour nonstop flight across the Gulf of Mexico. Needless to say, migratory stopovers with ample habitat and food are vital to the survival of these tired travelers.

Clocking flight speed

The speed at which birds fly during migration depends on their body size. In general, the bigger the bird, the faster it can fly. Birds weighing less than 20 grams, including vireos, sparrows, wrens, and warblers, fly around 10 to 30 mph. Shorebirds weighing up to 200 grams average 22 to 42 mph. Ducks and geese clock 28 to 50 mph on average. Julie has a hobby of clocking birds while driving, something she can safely do only on deserted backroads and occasionally on highways. She'll match her car's speed with that of birds flying overhead. She once clocked a flock of migrating red-throated loons at a sustained 53 mph for a couple of miles over I-95 in Connecticut. They might have had a good tailwind, but their speed was impressive nonetheless!

REMEMBER

Birds are sensitive to wind direction, and they take advantage of tailwinds that strong cold fronts can provide in autumn. Likewise, they may choose not to fly at all if faced with a headwind, hunkering down to wait for more favorable weather before resuming their journey.

Sticking to the time-distance plan

It boggles the mind to think of a young bird that has never flown anywhere, suddenly undertaking a long migration to a place it's never been. How in the world do they know what to do? Laboratory experiments have shown that some birds, such as Europe's garden warbler, have a genetically determined program in their brains. They fly in one direction for a predetermined amount of time, then reorient and fly in a different direction for another set span of time. Young, naïve garden warblers kept in "orientation cages" hopped and fluttered facing one direction for a set number of hours, then changed and hopped and fluttered in another direction, exactly corresponding to the directions and time they would have flown in the wild to reach their African wintering grounds. This is called the "time-distance plan," and it's one way some birds find their way south, and then back north again in springtime. It seems that this innate plan guides young, naïve birds entirely, while adult birds are able to navigate using both time-distance and geographic cues to find the place they wish to be.

Flying in the dark

Lest you think that birds are born encoded with everything they need to make marathon flights into unknown territory, know that there are many more cues birds use to navigate. Genetically predetermined flights are just a starting point. Birds note the plane of polarized light coming from the setting sun to set their internal compasses for the night's flight. Yes! Many birds, particularly smaller songbirds that must use powered, flapping flight, migrate at night, as shown in

Figure 13-4. (Soaring raptors depend largely on rising thermal currents to lift them in passive, long-distance gliding, and must fly in daytime, when thermals can buoy them.)

REMEMBER

So why fly at night? There are good reasons for this. Migratory flight is extremely hot, tiring, and thirsty work, and cooler night temperatures are kinder to these endurance athletes. Night air is usually smoother and less turbulent, easing their passage. Furthermore, hawks and falcons are sleeping then, and no threat to migrants.

FIGURE 13-4:
Black-billed cuckoos with lighthouse.

It's written in the stars

A songbird flying at night uses a variety of cues to find its way. Laboratory experiments using caged birds in planetariums have demonstrated that birds can navigate by the stars, like the blackpoll warbler in Figure 13-5. But sensitivity to Earth's magnetic field can guide birds when clouds obscure the moon and stars. It was at first assumed that magnetite deposits in a bird's head would move and send directional signals — but newer research has shown that a bird exposed to red wavelengths instead of natural white light cannot orient magnetically, magnetite bits or not. We're oversimplifying greatly here, since the explanation veers into quantum physics, but a bird's eye can apparently map magnetic fields, using a chemical called cryptochrome.

REMEMBER

"Seeing" the planet's magnetic field certainly qualifies as a superpower in our minds, but it's only one of the things birds routinely do that we humans can barely even imagine.

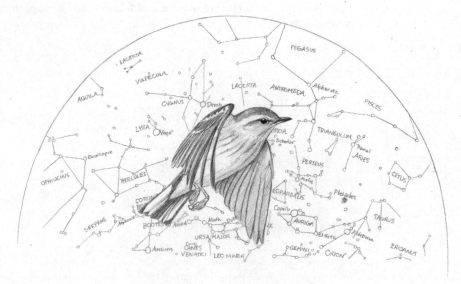

FIGURE 13-5:
Blackpoll warbler
with star map.

Exploring the Research behind Bird Migration

Most everyone has heard of bird banding, the oldest and most basic way of marking and tracking birds' movements. Banders are licensed by the U.S. Fish & Wildlife Service to catch birds, usually with ranks of fine mist nets, and then place numbered aluminum rings on the birds' legs. Each bird's number is stored and curated in a computer database. When a bird is recaptured or found dead, which seems like a very chancy and random thing, we get a data point on its travels. Roughly 1 to 3 percent of banded birds are ever recovered. But band enough birds over enough decades, and you can build a pretty good picture of where they start and where they end up. Banding was all we had before other technologies stepped in, and it continues to generate a goldmine of information for researchers.

Laboratory studies (if you give a bunting an inkpad)

Some of the controlled laboratory experiments scientists have devised to learn about bird navigation are diabolically clever. In one famous study, Stephen Emlen placed indigo buntings in "Emlen funnels," which consist of a cone of white paper with an inkpad at the bottom. The bird inks its feet, then hops up against the cone in the direction it wants to fly — all night long. When researchers change external stimuli, exposing them to the natural night sky, a planetarium sky with selected orientations, a changed magnetic field, or polarized light, for instance, the resultant scratches from its inked feet record the bird's changed orientation to a given stimulus. In this way, scientists could determine which cues birds are using to orient themselves.

Radar revelations

The advent of radar in the 1940s was a big breakthrough for migration studies. Migrating birds, by virtue of radar waves bouncing off the water in their cells, show up as bursts of green, and big nocturnal flocks can appear almost like storms and fireworks spangled across the map. Tracking radar can lock onto an individual migrating bird as long as it is in range.

Radar reveals valuable data such as altitude, flight speed, and direction of flight, but it cannot identify species. For that to happen, researchers have to look to other cues. Radar can give us advance warning of big flights and fallouts of migrants, telling us when and where the bulk of birds are traveling on any given night or day.

New technology: Motus

We've discussed bird banding, which is a labor-intensive and somewhat scatter-shot way of receiving data points and depends on banding large numbers of individuals to get a relatively small number of returns. Radio-tracking birds was the next innovation, but only birds large and strong enough to carry the transmitters could be tracked. Over the years, the species scientists can track have gotten smaller and smaller as the transmitter technology permits. Comparatively bulky packs placed on waterfowl and owls in the earlier days of wildlife tracking have been replaced by feather-light transmitters with a brand-new system of tracking, first deployed in 2014. Conceived by Birds Canada, Motus (Latin for "motion") involves miniature VHF transmitters, some weighing a fraction of a gram, that can broadcast unique identification codes that are picked up by automated receiver stations nearly worldwide. Since Motus tracking was first conceived, more than

37,000 individual birds, bats, and even *insects* such as monarch butterflies and dragonflies have been tagged with these micro-transmitters, which have collectively generated billions of data points on the movements of the organisms under study.

Clicking "Explore Data" at `https://motus.org/` reveals an absolutely staggering database, rich with maps showing receiver tower locations as well as all the organisms (mostly birds) that have been tracked at each one. Researchers can locate their subjects and parse out their moments down to the second. Species maps show all the Motus detections of each bird worldwide. With breathtaking accuracy and speed, the migration routes and sometimes surprising migratory stopovers and wintering areas for species have been revealed, and anyone can access all this data!

In the words of migration biologist, renowned writer, and *BWD* magazine columnist Scott Weidensaul, "Every age of science thinks it's a Golden Age, but there's something about this explosion in tracking technology that feels fundamentally different — and which, just maybe, has arrived in the nick of time . . . We've never had such a precise and continuous window into the lives of wild birds . . . to see where and exactly what they need at each point of their lives. The birds can finally show us what foods, what habitats, what routes, what wintering areas are important to them."

Migration and You

Paying attention to bird migration, being ready to catch its magic, is a fast track to birding delight, while also giving us a deeper understanding of what makes birds so special. Spring becomes much more than cherry blossoms and balmy breezes. It's when feathered jewels arrive from their tropical wintering grounds and flit through the treetops. Be ready to position yourself to enjoy spring migration, seeking birds wherever you go.

Spring is for migration lovers

Here in Ohio, spring starts for us in chilly mid-February, when the American woodcocks arrive from their wintering grounds in the southeastern U.S. and begin to voice a weird beeping *peent!* from soggy meadows. Bird arrivals slowly pick up through March and accelerate in April. Louisiana waterthrushes voice their ringing song from rushing woodland streams in late March. The first eastern meadowlark's song on a cold March morning tells us spring is truly on its way. By April, buds are swelling, and early warblers such as pine, yellow-rumped, palm, and yellow-throated are poking through the treetops. Migration is like an accelerating train from mid-April through mid-May. We never know what we might see on a given morning: the flame-orange of a Blackburnian warbler in young oak leaves; an American redstart tumble-fluttering after a flying insect (Figure 13-6); the jaw-dropping fire-engine red of a scarlet tanager against a soft spring sky — they all make our hearts race and enrich our lives immeasurably.

FIGURE 13-6: American redstart leaping after a hopper.

Fall is mighty fine

Much as we love the colorful parade of spring migration, some of us love fall migration even more. It's long and protracted, and the fun begins in late July and continues through October! As juvenile birds disperse from all around, we're always ready for a conundrum, and a surprise. And there's something about the muted fall plumage of warblers that delights us — we love figuring out who each one might be in its camouflage costume. Even though Julie's been doing it since she was eight, birding has so many levels of enjoyment, so many opportunities for challenge. There's always another level to explore.

GET BIRDING, GET WRITING!

One of the very best ways to begin to get a feel for migration is to keep a list of the new birds you see as they arrive in springtime (and fall as well). Julie has been doing this for decades, and it's the best way she knows to get a feel for the rhythm and pacing of migration, and which species you can expect to see in your area. In the past few years, her list-keeping, once kept in spiral-bound notebooks, then on cardboard taped to the studio wall, then curated on her laptop, has migrated over to eBird, where her daily checklists during migration times provide an accurately archived and searchable database of arrivals. However you do it, write it down, and you'll be on the way to getting a real feel for how migration proceeds in your region. A few other things you should consider (to make the most of your migration experience) are weather, geography, and tech resources. See Chapter 12 for more about keeping track of your bird observations and using eBird.

Donning Your Meteorologist Hat

TIP

Just like sailors, birds keep a keen eye on the weather before setting off, so it behooves us to do that as well. Birds heading south respond strongly to cold fronts sweeping down from the north, and they try to ride those strong tailwinds as long as they can. As a result, the morning after a cold front has come through can be exciting, with lots of new migrants singing from the trees, brought in on a fresh Canadian wind.

Days of northerly winds in springtime can inhibit migration, as birds stack up, unwilling to fight a headwind to continue north. Surprisingly, dull, foggy weather during spring migration can be thrilling for birders, as birds descend from the skies to wait out the damp and mist. Julie will never forget a foggy late April morning along the Connecticut shore, when warblers, vireos, and tanagers hopped practically underfoot in a thin strip of woodland behind the marsh she often birded. She always says to watch out for those dull gray days, as they can gift you with great surprises!

TIP

Extreme birders head out to the coasts immediately after hurricanes, hoping for storm-blown waifs, and are often richly rewarded. Hurricanes can pick up tropical seabirds like boobies and noddy terns and can deposit them almost anywhere. Hurricane Idalia's 2023 unprecedented shipment and delivery of hundreds of American flamingoes from the Yucatán Peninsula of Mexico to northern latitudes from Wisconsin to Cape Cod and all down the Eastern Seaboard won't soon be forgotten by anyone who sought out these storm-tossed pink waifs wading in unfamiliar waters.

Taking the Lay of the Land into Account

Migrating birds can show up just about anywhere, but some locales see more action than others. Why? Geography, including terrain, obstacles, habitat, and other such terrestrial factors.

Fear of flying

Big bodies of water have a big influence on migratory pathways for a couple of reasons. Birds like hawks and eagles, which are passive soaring birds that need thermal updrafts to give them lift, avoid crossing large bodies of water. They will detour around them to avoid having to flap their wings to exhaustion and possibly wind up in the water. Fall and spring migrations along the Texas coast offer fabulous hawk-watching opportunities, as a river of raptors skirts the Gulf and hugs the nearest land. Imagine 10,000 birds passing per hour at some South Texas hawk-watching hotspots, for a total of 100,000 plus raptors per day. (See Figure 13-7.)

FIGURE 13-7:
Broad-winged hawks in a kettle (a soaring flock).

For the same reasons, narrow land bridges with ocean on either side can be spectacular bird funnels. Most of North America's broad-winged hawks and vultures, neither of which are fans of flapping, funnel through the Central American land bridge, with Veracruz, Mexico, taking the prize for massive numbers of raptors streaming through. How about seeing 75,000 birds in a single hour? Seems kind of like cheating!

Julie will never forget the serendipity of seeing Point Pelee in Lake Erie from the air. This finely tapered little snippet of Ontario juts 15 kilometers south into Lake Erie along its north shore, pointing toward Ohio. Her eyes widened as she beheld the narrow finger of land in a vast inland sea, and she understood viscerally why, each spring, migrating songbirds crossing Lake Erie, headed for Canadian forest, make a mad dash for this first bit of sand that they see. And just like the exhausted songbirds, excited birders stack up to watch them make landfall after their long water crossing. Cape May, New Jersey, has a similar land-finger, where southbound birds stack up in fall migration, waiting for calm weather before crossing Delaware Bay. Such geographical funnel points draw both birds and birders in great numbers.

Flyways are flightpaths

Even without maps, apps, or road signs to guide them, most migrating birds follow long-established flightpaths from their wintering grounds to their breeding grounds and back again. This is especially true and well documented for waterfowl, cranes, and shorebirds, but not so clear for passerines. These flyways don't have clear boundaries, and different species follow different routes.

In general, North America has four major avian superhighways, each with bountiful stopover spots along the way:

The Atlantic Coast

Many birds follow the East Coast, from northern Quebec and Labrador to the Florida Keys. The western edge isn't rigid, but this flyway encompasses the eastern Great Lakes, and the Appalachian Mountains may be a barrier to some birds. Many birds that follow the Atlantic Flyway cross the Gulf of Mexico to spend the winter on Caribbean islands or in South America.

The great Midwestern rivers

The Mississippi, Missouri, and Ohio Rivers and their watersheds provide a clear path for birds to follow. Called the Mississippi Flyway, this aerial highway extends north to Hudson Bay and includes the western Great Lakes. Birds that head south on this route generally skirt the Gulf of Mexico, rather than flying over, and winter in Central and South America.

The Central U.S.

From northernmost Nunavut, where millions of shorebirds breed, through the Great Plains and south to Mexico's southernmost state (Chiapas), the Central Flyway includes the Prairie Pothole Region (also known as the duck factory). More than half of North America's migratory waterfowl population travels on this route, as do great flocks of sandhill cranes. Visiting Nebraska's Platte River — a migratory bottleneck where hundreds of thousands of sandhill cranes (and as many as 300 species of other birds) stop over in late March and early April — should be on every birder's to-do list.

The Pacific region

From Alaska, south along the Pacific Coast, east to the Rocky Mountains and including the desert Southwest, and south into southern South America, the Pacific Flyway is the primary route for the millions of shorebirds that nest in Alaska's coastal plains, hummingbirds, and western passerines.

Exceptions

Not all migrating birds follow these flyways. For example, the blackpoll warbler takes a direct route from its wintering range in northern South America, hops over the Gulf of Mexico, and heads north to disperse in the boreal forest, where it nests. But in the fall, tracking data shows that this tiny bird takes the scenic route home to its wintering grounds, flying generally east to the northeast coast, out above the Atlantic Ocean, and then south, bypassing the West Indies, then southwest to Venezuela and Colombia. Why it has evolved to take this circular route is still being researched. If we had a choice to avoid flying thousands of miles over open ocean, we'd choose land!

Hie Thee to a Hotspot!

By now, we hope we've whetted your appetite for making a migration of your own in spring or fall, to see this spectacle for yourself. There are many time-tested places to go — see Chapter 16 for a listing. If you go, make plans and book your lodging early — many bird watchers time their vacations and travel to migration hotspots during spring and fall.

Migration depends on so many factors, weather being primary, that it can be hit or miss, but you're sure to see some wonderful new birds and meet new friends at a migration hotspot. Birders are generally friendly folks and quite welcoming to newcomers, so don't be intimidated. Invite a friend or plan a solo adventure; take your best optics, camera, and field guide, and see what you can find!

Falling for a fallout

You'll hear birders refer to a "fallout," and we hope you get to experience one. Fallouts can happen when birds hit adverse weather and wind conditions and decide to set down right where they are — usually at one of the aforementioned geographical pinch points, often near a large body of water. Perhaps they have just crossed it and are making landfall for the first time in many hours. Maybe they are hoping to cross and are stacking up as they wait for the winds to change in their favor. The upshot for birders is tired or unnaturally tame birds all around, perched low and even underfoot, resting and looking for what food they can find. You may see the first five sedge wrens you've ever seen in your life, crowded in a small hedge along the Chicago lakefront. Or a mess of Swainson's thrushes, hopping everywhere like small robins. Fallouts are like Christmas morning for birders, with birds dripping from the trees. Of course, this makes for great photo ops, but please remember that a bird with a choice wouldn't pal around with people, so give them some space and don't crowd them!

Using online tools to get the most from migration

There's a really cool website, `birdcast.info`, that is tailored to help birders visualize migration and be prepared for waves of migratory birds. Administered by the Cornell Lab of Ornithology in collaboration with many other academic and scientific contributors, BirdCast develops and maintains tools that predict and monitor bird migration. There are forecast bird migration maps that predict how much, where, and when bird migration will occur. Very exciting are their live bird migration maps that show migration occurring in real time. You can subscribe to migration alerts to learn when intense bird migration will occur. There's also a dashboard that provides radar-based measurements of nocturnal bird migration at county and state levels in the contiguous U.S. Data from weather surveillance radar are essential for developing and maintaining these tools. It's a thrill to see your county lit up white-hot on the BirdCast map, and to get up and head out the next morning, eager to ground-truth that prediction.

These are heady times to be a birder, with such astounding research findings and easily accessible online tools to guide us in our pursuit of these feathered beauties. Don't let migration pass you by!

Chapter **14**

Taking a Field Trip

A field trip — it's what makes bird watching exciting, especially when you visit new places in search of new birds. Depending on the extent of your trip and the type of habitat you plan to visit, a field excursion can be as simple as throwing your binocs in the car and going to a new spot to watch birds, or it can be something akin to the Lewis and Clark Expedition. It's up to you.

In this chapter, we cover the basic stuff that you need to consider when taking a bird-watching field trip, whether you go alone or with your local bird club. Over the years, we've discovered the hard way what to take and what to leave when setting out on a birding adventure. Some of our experience may be helpful to you. If nothing else, you can laugh at our examples of learning the hard way.

So, What's a Field Trip Exactly?

A *field trip* is defined as going afield — that is, beyond your immediate home surroundings or backyard. For many beginning bird watchers, their first organized field trip is with a bird club. This field trip can be an educational experience as you observe how other bird watchers act in the field, how they spot and identify birds, and where they go to find birds.

Our definition of a field trip is loading the car with food, coats, boots, and other gear, more food, drinks of all types, optics, a field guide, and ourselves, if we can fit. Then we head off to see what we can see. Sometimes we go for a couple hours, sometimes all day — however long we have time for, or until we are worn out and happy.

TIP

Sometimes your luck just runs out and you get to a birding spot that has *no birds!* This can happen in the heat of a midsummer's day or in the dead of winter. We have a suggestion for keeping yourself interested on a birdless summer day. If it's sunny, look for butterflies or dragonflies or other things with wings. If it's the middle of winter, we suggest you go find a warm diner and get a cup of hot chocolate. You can count the days until spring.

Planning Your Field Trip

If you've got common sense, you can plan a field trip just fine. Here's a quick checklist to help you:

>> Plan where you want to go.

>> Plot your route and determine your schedule (early wake-up and departure to get there for prime dawn birding, and so on). Map apps, which supply distances, suggest the best routes, and estimate driving time, make getting there easier than ever.

>> Gather binoculars and other gear such as spotting scope, camera, field guide, and bird checklist.

>> Check the weather and plan the clothing and outerwear you'll need. Then take one extra layer. Windproof clothing is key. Cotton hoodies are practically useless for birding.

>> Make sure that you have the right footwear (boots, rubber boots, extra socks).

>> Pack or wear a hat that can cover your ears.

>> Add food, glorious food. Take some snacks even if you plan to eat in restaurants or at quickie-marts. Where the best birds are, restaurants often aren't!

>> Bring water and/or favorite beverages. You'll be thirsty more often than not.

>> Take money. You may need cash for an emergency.

>> Include other gear for comfort or necessity. Depending on the weather, the gear can include sunscreen, lip balm, sunglasses, binocular rain guard, emergency survival kit, and other stuff.

>> Tell someone where you're going. You can't be too safe.

ACCESS FOR EVERYBODY

TIP

For information on areas that are accessible for bird watchers who use wheelchairs, motorized carts, and other devices that facilitate mobility, visit the National Park Service webpage devoted to accessibility: www.nps.gov/aboutus/accessibility.htm. Each national park's website also has its own accessibility section to help plan a trip for those with accessibility needs. Another excellent resource is www.birdability.org/, offering a crowdsourced map describing accessibility features of birding locations all over the world.

Dressing for Birding Success

Do you recall the scene in the classic movie *The Graduate* where a friend of the family is telling Dustin Hoffman that the key to his future is one word, "Plastics!"? Well, the key to your bird-watching comfort is just as easy: layers. As in, dress in layers of clothing.

There's little that's more miserable than being underdressed in cold or damp weather or overdressed when the sun and temps rise higher and higher. Take our many years of experience in wearing the wrong thing to go bird watching and put it to good use for yourself.

There are things we always wear or take no matter the season when we go bird watching.

Layers

Dressing in layers is always a good idea, whether it's 110 degrees or –10 degrees. Layers allow you to peel off or add on clothing as needed. In winter, we recommend layers, starting with thermal underwear — long johns — top and bottom and ending with a wind-and-waterproof outer shell. Lightweight nylon snow pants over leggings are a terrific combo. In summer, upper body layers are a T-shirt and a light-colored (reflects the sun), lightweight, long-sleeved shirt with a collar. Many shirts on the market today even offer UPF 50 sun protection. Your arms and neck will thank you!

Hat

Some bird watchers swear by the wide-brimmed Tilley hat or a similar Australian or African bush hat. Those hats are nice looking on some heads, but others of us prefer a simple ball cap to protect our scalp and shield our eyes from the sun. In winter, an insulated hat is key for keeping your body heat from escaping. Whatever the weather, and whatever your hat preference, it's a good idea to bring one along. And you can't have too many ear-warmers!

Comfy footwear

You do experience times when you can get away with wearing tennis shoes for bird watching — heck, there are even times when you can get away with loafers or sandals. But our experience has shown that the best way to stay comfy while birding is to have warm, dry, comfortable feet (as in, not sore!). Flip-flops are a big no. Close-toed shoes are a must to guard against brambles, random pointed sticks, and insect bites. That's why we usually wear sturdy but lightweight hiking boots when on a field trip.

Hiking boots have come a long way and come in countless styles, materials, and weights to suit your preference. We recommend you get a pair of lightweight hikers and break them in well before you wear them for any extensive hiking or walking. The best hiking boots for birding are also waterproof, and they have stiff ankle support, rugged shock-absorbent soles, and sufficient tread to help you clamber up a muddy hillside.

TIP

If you wear athletic shoes to bird, consider high-tops. These give much-needed ankle support. Believe us, you need ankle support if you do any off-road bird watching. All it takes is one molehill to make you aware of inadequate footwear.

Rain boots or waders that cover your calves are a good idea to bring along if rain is in the forecast, or if there's been precipitation lately and there's a good chance you'll encounter puddles and mud on your field trip. An added bonus of such boots is their impenetrability to things other than rain and oozy mud: thorns, ticks, and snakes are three things you can laugh off when wearing your wellies. We know field biologists who wear nothing else, year-round.

Sunscreen/lip balm/lotion

The sun is a dangerous thing, even in small amounts. All avid bird watchers can take precaution against overexposure to sunlight by using sunscreen. If you plan to be out in the sun for any length of time, dab some sunscreen on your ears, neck, face, and hands, and any other parts not covered with clothing.

Chapped lips are a regular thing for field birders. But you can stay kissable by regularly protecting your lips with lip balm. We carry some in our bird-watching coats and backpacks.

If you're on an extended trip and are outside birding a lot, you'll notice the effects of sun and wind on your skin as a whole. Don't forget to lotion up! Why shed your skin like a snake?

Pockets

There's a funny stereotype about bird watchers wearing clothes with lots of pockets — and many of us do. Notebook, pens, pencils, snacks, owl pellets, somebody else's litter — all kinds of stuff ends up in our pockets. Pockets hold our stuff and keep our hands free for holding a binocular and/or camera.

You may find that you don't need pockets, or you may find that a birding or safari vest is your thing. It's up to you to find your own comfort level.

Other stuff we always take

Just because you're dressed to go birding doesn't mean that you're ready for action. Being ready for anything means taking along a few extra things. Here are some of the items we choose to tote:

>> **Small waist pack or backpack:** Jessica likes to carry a small crossbody bag on shorter field trips, and her trusty hiking backpack for longer ones. Even with numerous bird identification apps on her phone, she still likes to bring along a field guide for easy page-flipping when confronted with confusing fall warblers or look-alike flycatchers, for example. Plus, it's good to have a place to throw in your phone, car keys, and other assorted items like those below.

>> **Trek stick:** There's nothing Julie appreciates more than a lightweight, telescoping metal trek stick when she's hiking steep, rocky trails. A trek stick acts like a third limb, catching her when she's even the slightest bit off-balance. It also increases walking speed up and downhill, making it easier to keep up with a group. If you get in a steep situation and have forgotten your stick, the woods are full of them. Just be sure to test it well and break it to the proper length before putting weight on it!

>> **Pen or pencil and paper:** Writing notes is part of bird watching, and while many of us do that in our phone these days, some folks still prefer to keep physical notes about the birds, people, or places they encounter. A pen with waterproof ink (in case of rain) or pencil and a small notebook will do the trick. (You can even find waterproof notepads marketed toward birders!)

>> **Pocketknife:** We've done everything from fixing eyeglasses to cutting open watermelons with a pocketknife. Everybody has the occasional screw loose. A pocketknife — so useful, so outdoorsy. Sterilize your knife blade over a match and you're almost ready to remove somebody's appendix.

>> **Pocket munchies:** You can work up quite an appetite while birding! After a predawn start, 10 a.m. feels like lunchtime, and you'll be ravenous for dinner by 3 p.m.

>> **Tissues:** You have every chance that you'll see some bird that is so beautiful that it reduces you to tears. You have an even better chance that you'll have a runny nose. In either case, having tissues handy is a good thing. Not to mention, well-stocked public restrooms aren't available at every bird-watching spot you'll visit.

>> **Bandanna:** The bandanna cleans your glasses! It dries your sweaty brow! It keeps the black flies from biting the back of your neck! It wipes the mayonnaise off the windshield after you sneeze! You get the idea. (Please don't use it on your binocular or camera lenses, though.)

>> **Wallet:** You may think that you won't want to risk losing your wallet while out bird watching. But you may get pulled over for speeding to a birding hotspot (we do not endorse this!) or you may be stopped in a routine round-up of suspicious binocular-toting characters. In such a situation, it's good to have a photo ID on your person. ***Bonus:*** A credit card can come in handy for scraping ice off your windshield.

Where the Birds Are

The whole point of taking a field trip is to find birds. If you don't have a local bird club with which you can take field trips, you'll have to find the birds yourself. Here are some places to look for information:

>> **Check out your own county:** Get a county map and check out all the places that have water, extensive woodland, or preserved natural areas. Some birds are bound to be in some of these places. Use the Explore function of eBird to discover lesser-known birding hotspots in your county or one nearby. (For more on using eBird in this way, see Chapter 16.)

>> **Pile in for a few hours' drive:** State or provincial parks, preserves, and wildlife management areas are great places to explore for birds and to find information about birds. Scan a map of your area or search the internet to find government-run sites that can offer you assistance. Apply what you know about bird habitat preferences to your searching.

>> **Ask around:** Your birding acquaintances may have suggestions for good birdy places. If you don't know any other birders, call your local extension office, conservation office, or department of natural resources. They may even be able to put you in touch with other bird clubs or bird watchers in your area.

>> **Join a birding group on social media:** You can find loads of social media groups devoted to birding — everywhere from local metro parks to towns to counties to regions of a state and beyond. Follow any of these birding groups for a short time, and you'll get a feel for where folks are going to look at birds in your area or a location you plan to visit.

>> **Visit the big hotspots:** Feel thwarted by the lack of field trip sites in your region? It can happen. That's when you need to pack up and head for a really big hotspot. Entire books are written just on North American bird-watching hotspots, and *BWD* magazine features at least one prime location in each issue (sometimes written by one of us!). Cornell Lab of Ornithology's eBird is an excellent website to reference for finding hotspots and learn what people have seen at them recently. See Chapter 16 for more about birding hotspots, including using eBird to find them.

For more suggestions on how to find birds when you get there, see Chapter 15.

Using Your Field Skills

When you encounter birds on a field trip, you need to get your binoculars on them, listen to their calls or songs, and then, with any luck, identify them. This is the time that your field skills as a bird watcher come into play. More experienced birders get their binoculars on the bird by first hearing a call or sound, and then scanning for the source.

Nothing substitutes for years of experience finding birds in the field. But if you're a beginner, you can make major strides in your field skills with just a bit of practice. (For more on general birding field skills, see Chapter 21.) Here are some field-trip-specific things you can do to improve your performance in the field:

>> **Anticipate and study:** If you plan to go to a place known for its spring migrant fallouts, where warblers, orioles, tanagers, grosbeaks, and the like are dripping from the trees, you can prepare by reviewing what you know about the species you're likely to see. Jessica still does this every May before heading to northwestern Ohio to lead field trips at the Biggest Week in American Birding. When it's been several months since seeing many of these songbirds, it's good to re-familiarize yourself with old friends!

Reading through the species accounts in her field guide sparks rusty memories of the previous spring. She's made notes in her guide over the years — things that help her remember something about a particular species. Then once her eyes and brain are synched up, she moves on to another sense: hearing. (For more on birding by ear, see Chapter 6.)

>> **Scout the spot:** If you plan to go on a field trip with a bird club and you want to have a bit of a head start over the other participants, visit the location a day or two ahead of the trip and scout it for birds. Scouting helps you gain valuable insight into what to expect in terms of terrain, climate, birds, and other important information, such as where to eat or where to get a cold drink.

Field Trip Etiquette

Believe it or not, there are rules of etiquette — both written and unwritten — that guide the behavior of bird watchers. The American Birding Association offers some widely followed written guidelines, called the Code of Birding Ethics, on their website. We've also put it in the Cheat Sheet for this book, available at www.dummies.com. Search for "Bird Watching For Dummies."

In some ways, the unwritten rules are more important. Nearly all of them deal with common-sense notions and modes of polite conduct. You probably remember all those types of rules either from your mom or some strict schoolteacher. (Figure 14-1 shows how good manners ensures harmony.)

Following are a few helpful hints from us — and we are not perfect and have likely broken most rules of the hobby somewhere along the way. But we do better now.

Following the leader

When out with a group that's being led, by all means follow the leader. It's pretty annoying for everyone else if one person decides to forge ahead of the group to find "the good birds." What ends up happening, usually, is that all the birds — good or bad — get scared away.

TIP

If you want to get away from the group, stay behind and wait for the birds to reappear. But don't move ahead. Let the leader lead. Besides, you may miss something good if you wander off.

FIGURE 14-1:
Being polite and mindful of your fellow field trip participants makes for a more enjoyable birding experience for all.

Calling out birds

Sooner or later, you'll get good enough to identify most of the birds you encounter. On many field trips, particularly those organized outings with a trip leader, you may not need to call out the identities of the birds you spot. In some cases, your fellow bird watchers may not *want* you to call out the IDs because they want to try their own hand at reaching a conclusion. The proper tactic for you is to hold back until you see how the trip is going. If folks are calling out birds left and right, there's no reason you can't, too.

PISHING

On a field trip, ask the leader, or your fellow bird watchers, how they feel about pishing before you commence. *Pishing* is a bird-attracting sound birders make by hissing through closed teeth. It mimics predator alarm calls of small birds, sparking curiosity and sometimes better views of previously hidden birds. If your fellow watchers don't endorse this activity, don't pish. If they're pro-pishing, pish away, but do so with moderation, and not all at once. One pisher at a time is plenty.

On Bill Thompson III's first trip to Costa Rica, he and Julie were anticipating lots of new birds. Even though Julie had been to Costa Rica several times before, she told him that she was not going to call out the birds but was going to let him try to ID them himself. "There's more satisfaction that way," she said. Just their luck, on a guided part of their trip, they were stuck with a very knowledgeable guide who called out every bird he saw and every bird song he heard. They may as well have stayed home and watched a nature special about Costa Rica on TV. They soon peeled away and made their own outings. They did encounter some mystery birds with which they could have used some help (and Bill did ask Julie to reactivate her bird-ID-calling), but they enjoyed being their own guides. The experience was much richer that way!

Pointing out others' incorrect IDs

Somebody on a field trip with you sees a red-tailed hawk soaring overhead but calls out, "Immature bald eagle!" What do you do? You have three choices:

>> Say nothing.

>> Say: "I don't see your eagle, but there's a red-tailed hawk soaring overhead."

>> Say: "What field marks are you seeing?"

How you respond depends on the tone of the field trip and the level of expertise of the participants. It can come across as rude to point out somebody else's misiden-tifications out loud and potentially embarrass them. Any of the above responses could be fine if expressed properly.

REMEMBER

Be sensitive to the other person's feelings. What goes around comes around, and if you make somebody else feel stupid, you can bet that your turn will come soon.

Sometimes the best thing to do is to get everybody else looking at the bird. "OK, let's all look at this raptor and see what we can find out about it." Then the col-lective skill of the group can come to a conclusion as to the bird's ID in a non-threatening forum.

Asking questions

When we were beginning birders, we made it a point to ask questions of the better bird watchers we were in the field with to learn from them. Now we are often the people who are asked questions — but we still ask questions ourselves, especially when we're with someone who knows more about a bird, plant, butterfly, or some other natural phenomenon than we do.

Never be shy about asking questions of others on a field trip. Almost everyone you encounter is thrilled to pass along the information you seek. If you get rebuffed, you just received a very important answer to the question *Is this a nice person to go bird watching with?* Answer: *No!*

Providing gas money

An unwritten rule of the bird-watching field trip is this: When riding as a passenger on a long field trip in another birder's car, offer to help defray the cost of gasoline. Or you can treat for an ice cream cone, or lunch, or something. Even if your driver accepts nothing, offering to help with expenses is the right thing to do.

Dealing with the jerk

Most field trips you go on are trouble-free. Once in a great while — about as often as a rare bird shows up at your bird feeder — you find yourself on a field trip that's cursed with a jerk. This jerk can be somebody who's having a bad day, who's crotchety by nature, or who's simply hard to be around.

Knowing what to do is difficult when you've got a jerk on your hands. Confrontation is not always helpful, nor is ridicule. If at all possible, hint to the jerk that they are being unpleasant. You can do this with a stare, without a word. If the message isn't received, you may have to put up with the jerk until the trip is over. Then make sure that you don't include this person again. If you're on an expensive, prepaid bird-watching tour, ask the leader to deal with the situation.

We've been on a few trips with a jerk — not the same jerk each time, mind you. And we've tried all the obvious tactics. Once Bill even told a jerk that she was being a jerk, and the transformation was amazing. But that's not always going to be a magic solution.

Taking Precautions

Some people argue that bird watching is not a sport. Well, maybe it's not a *contact* sport, but, like any other sport, bird watching can take a lot out of your body. Not only do you, the bird watcher, have to concentrate on locating your quarry, but you must also deal with the natural elements in all their fierce glory.

Here are some of the dangerous and painful things that may await you and the precautions you can take to avoid them.

Sun

If the ozone layer is getting thinner, our sunscreen lotions should be getting more powerful. And they are. Even on cloudy days the sun can burn your skin, so you can't be too careful about applying sunscreen — at least SPF 30 — to exposed areas of your skin.

REMEMBER

It's also always a good idea to wear a hat when you go out birding. The sun is our friend in that it gives us light with which to see birds. But the sun is not our skin's friend, and we should protect it accordingly.

Temperature extremes

Too cold at dawn, too hot at noon, too cold at night. This is the pattern of temperatures that bird watchers encounter across much of North America between April and October. In some areas (Arizona, South Texas, Southern California), the pattern is hot, hot, hot, though desert nights can dip into the 20s, even as daytime highs soar to the 90s. And in winter the temperature can be cold everywhere. This variation in temperature is why the concept of dressing in layers was invented.

When you're birding afield in these so-called warm locales, remember to have adequate clothing for the conditions. No bird, no matter how rare, is worth getting frostbite or risking your life to heat exhaustion.

WARNING

Always drink plenty of liquids (water is best) whenever you're out bird watching. You can be overcome by heat exhaustion or dehydration very quickly, even on seemingly balmy days. On hot days and in desert areas, be sure to add electrolytes to your water bottle to replace the minerals and salts you lose in dehydration. Powdered electrolyte packets are very handy. Look for those without artificial sweeteners or colors.

Insects

Of all the insects that can really get at a bird watcher, ticks, mosquitoes, biting flies, and chiggers are the four worst pests. We have used chemical deterrents to ward off biting insects with mixed results. Some bird watchers swear by a certain brand of spray or bug-repellent clothing or their own natural concoction. Remember that some of us are allergic to DEET and walk well away from the group to spray your clothing, never spraying inside a vehicle. Our strategy with the aerial biters is to cover up as much exposed skin with clothing as possible. Of course, in some places where you seek birds — in a swamp, for example — biting insects are unavoidable and you're vastly outnumbered. In this case, you can put up with it or not go.

Chiggers

Chiggers are tiny biting mites most often encountered in areas of tall grass. Some chiggers only bite you. Other chiggers crawl up your legs and embed themselves beneath the surface of your skin, particularly in areas where they can push against your clothing to dig in, such as waistbands and around the tops of elasticized socks. Once embedded, chiggers (and chigger bites) can cause weeks of intense itching. Getting rid of chiggers once they're embedded is difficult. One method used by Texas birders, where chiggers are fairly common, is to soak your legs and torso in a hot bath. The hot water kills the chiggers. So will clear nail polish applied to the bites (or, more properly, burrows).

Ticks

The problem with ticks is that they can carry an array of harmful diseases: Rocky Mountain spotted fever, Lyme disease, babesiosis, and Ehrlichiosis being only a few. For both ticks and chiggers (which are too small to see), you can use the trusted and oh-so-stylish tuck-the-pant-legs-in-the-socks method. This forces these critters to crawl all the way up your pant legs to get to their beloved goal: skin. You should regularly look over your pant legs to see if you can find any ticks before they find you. Once home, change clothes right away, leaving your field clothes outside until laundered, so any unseen pests cannot find their way to your flesh. Permethrin is a spray that can be applied to pant legs, and it remains effective through a number of washings. Follow label directions and allow sprayed clothing to dry completely before wearing it.

WARNING

If we know an area is heavily infested with ticks or harbors chiggers, we stay out. This may mean staying on a road or path, avoiding nearby brushy or grassy areas. Or it may mean avoiding the areas altogether. After visiting an area where ticks are present, always check yourself thoroughly for these small, dark insects. If you find a tick embedded, use tweezers or your fingernails to pull the tick out, head and all. Any fever or soreness that results should send you to your doctor to be tested and treated for tick-borne diseases. Many can be headed off by antibiotics administered right away. If your doctor seems unaware or dubious of tick-borne diseases, find another doctor.

Fire ants

In some areas of the South, a burning source of pain for bird watchers is the fire ant. Fire ants are aggressive colonial ants from Central and South America that have invaded North America. When their large, conical earthen nest is disturbed, fire ants swarm the perceived threat and deliver an exceedingly painful sting. If you plan to visit a southern state, ask local officials about fire ants. Ask a local to point out a fire ant mound, so you know what to avoid. Jessica did this backwards on a trip to Texas. First, she stepped on a small fire ant mound and got stung, and then she found out about fire ants and what to avoid. And she still forgets on occasion and has been painfully reminded to look down at where your feet are before you stop to look up at a bird.

REMEMBER

This all sounds horrible, but it really isn't. Most insects you encounter while bird watching do nothing more than annoy you. Hundreds of insect repellents, insect-proof suits, and even folklore cures (eat a banana the night before and the bugs won't bite you) are available. You can find one that suits you.

Trespassing

We have one rule about trespassing: *don't*. Wandering onto somebody's property without asking permission is never okay. That you're only bird watching won't make a difference to a landowner who decides to be a hard case about their property lines. Bill learned this lesson the hard way:

> One June, I was with a group doing a Breeding Bird Survey high in the mountains of West Virginia when we came upon an old barn alongside the remote road we were covering. I thought the barn looked like a prime spot for barn owls and said as much as I walked over to the barn and then through the open doorway. What I saw inside was a neatly arranged line of glass jugs and plastic buckets. Steam was coming up through the floorboards. Copper tubing was running to a large vat. I was putting all this together when one of my colleagues said, "Bill. Come out slowly as if nothing unusual is going on. We've got to get out of here." I did so. Only after we were down the road a mile did he tell me that, in scanning the hillside opposite the barn, he had seen another ramshackle building. Only this one had a man sitting in the doorway, with a rifle pointed at me, ready to shoot the people who'd discovered his moonshine still! In some states, it's legal to shoot trespassers. I never unthinkingly trespassed after that.

Hunting seasons

Speaking of rifles . . . A hunting season exists for almost everything. In some cases, this coincides with good times of the year for bird watching. Check your state's environment and wildlife department website for any active hunting seasons and active hunting areas. It's as easy as Googling "Ohio hunting seasons" (or, you know, whatever state or province you're planning to visit).

When Things Go Wrong

Sometimes things just go wrong. What starts out as a bird-watching adventure can become a nightmare, or at least no fun at all. A twist of fate may be unavoidable, but you do have ways to cope when things go wrong.

Lost

If you're lost in the wilderness and can't retrace your steps, the best thing to do is to stay put. If you have your cellphone on you (and you should, with your location enabled!) and cell service is available, you can use the map feature to determine your location and possibly search up a trail map. Or you can phone a friend or the authorities for help. But if your phone is out of the service area or the battery is dead, don't panic. Sooner or later, somebody will come looking for you, or someone will happen along the same path you took. If you keep wandering aimlessly, you may be making it tougher for someone to track you down.

Foul weather

Not to sound like a nagging parent, but please don't go outside to watch birds when a major storm is either happening or about to happen. Especially avoid lightning, hail, blizzards, tornadoes, and hurricanes. You can go look for birds *afterwards*. Don't make us have to say, "We told you so!"

TIP

If you're going to be out in the rain, you may wish to have something to cover your binoculars (as well as your phone). A hasty binocular rain guard can be fashioned out of a zippable plastic sandwich bag. You can use the one in which you packed your snack. It's cheap and it works. Keep a few such plastic bags in your backpack for just such moments. They're weightless and indispensable.

A moderately priced raincoat, like those sold at camping stores or outdoor outfitters, can be very handy for foul-weather birding. Jessica once went to "sunny San Diego" for a birding festival, where it rained the entire week. The birds didn't mind the weather, and she didn't either, all dry inside her raincoat. (She still managed to see over 100 species on one particularly drenched day!)

WARNING

Flash floods are deadly and happen unbelievably fast. Do not, under any circumstances, attempt to drive your car or walk through rapidly moving water, particularly if you're in a flash flood zone.

Sickness

If you start feeling ill when you're out in the field, don't keep pressing onward thinking that it will go away. Seek help or get home as soon as you can.

If you're feeling dizzy or have a headache, stop using your binoculars for a while. Sometimes you can give yourself a headache by straining to see through binoculars for long periods. And if your binocs are even a little out of alignment, your eyes work extra hard to keep the images aligned and in focus. This extra effort gives you the feeling of wearing someone else's prescription glasses.

TIP

If the problem goes away while you're not using your optics, consider getting your binocs checked out by an optics professional. The optics may be out of alignment. Realignment is simple and usually inexpensive.

Accidents

WARNING

It's a good idea to let somebody know where you're going before you leave for a long field trip. If you're unfortunate enough to have an accident, someone can eventually come looking for you. You could even share your location on your phone with friends or family for a little extra assurance that someone knows where you are, at least when you are in a cell service area, which is more places than not these days.

Most birders take precautions against accidents: wearing ankle-supporting hiking boots to guard against injuries to ankles or feet; carrying a trek stick for rocky trails; avoiding areas of unsafe footing; balancing periods of strenuous walking with periods of rest. Common sense can be your guide.

It's also good practice to carry an emergency kit in your car in case of a breakdown. Better to be overprepared, especially when traveling in remote areas (where birds tend to lure us) and when birding solo.

Lining Up a Special Trip

Field trips take on new meaning when you have target birds. Target birds are birds that may be the goal of a given field trip. Certain groups of birds can be relied upon (usually) to put on a show at certain times of the year. Here are a few of our favorites.

Warblers and migrants in spring

Spring migration is arguably the best time of the year to be a bird watcher. On a good fallout day, when brilliantly colored birds are everywhere, having seemingly *fallen out* of the sky in large numbers, and their songs are filling the air, you thank your lucky stars that you're there with your bins. And you'll wonder how you ever ignored birds before you became a bird watcher.

TIP

Legendary spring migration hotspots exist, such as Point Pelee in Canada and High Island in Texas, but you can also do quite well near your home. You need to find a prime habitat to which migrant birds are attracted. Wooded areas along large bodies of water, or high points of the landscape, such as ridges, are likely spots for migrants, as are geographical features such as islands and peninsulas that concentrate migrating birds.

You also need to have cooperation from the weather. The relationship between the weather and bird migration is not entirely understood. But, put simply, in spring, northbound migrants tend to move when they have a strong tailwind — winds from the south, southeast, or southwest. This pattern makes sense. The wind helps the migrants on their way. Many species won't migrate northward if faced with a southbound wind.

TIP

Monitor how the weather in your area affects local migration spots. This information can help you predict the best mornings in late March, April, May, or early June (depending on where you live) to be outside looking for migrants.

Checking BirdCast (https://birdcast.info/) will show you where the flocks are with continually updated color maps, revealing migrating birds on radar. (For more about this cool website, check out Chapter 13.)

Hawks in fall

September, October, and November are peak months for fall hawk migration. Many bird clubs and other nature groups organize special hawk-watching field trips at this time of year. Many important hawk migration observation sites have been established all over North America. (Visit https://hawkcount.org/ to view the Hawk Migration Association of North America's database profiling over 300 hawkwatches.) Even at places where official hawk counts are being conducted the public is almost always welcome. Do yourself a favor and get to a hawk watch in the fall. You'll learn a lot and gain a new appreciation for birds of prey and the people who spend their lives honing incredible identification skills.

Shorebirds in late summer

The only good thing about the end of summer (besides the fact that the kids get to go back to school) is that this is when the majority of Arctic-nesting shorebirds migrate southward through North America toward their wintering grounds. If you're within driving distance of any shoreline on a large body of water, July and August are the prime months for watching shorebirds, many of which are still in breeding plumage as they migrate from their breeding grounds in the Far North. If you want to study shorebirds and improve your ID skills on this often-confusing group of birds, late summer is the best time of year to do so.

Owling

Owling is cool. It helps you to get to know *whoooo's whoooo* in the woods at night. Most bird clubs run owling trips, sometimes called *owl prowls*. These prowls are usually held in mid-to-late winter when the owls are at their most vocal, during courtship, just prior to settling down to breed.

You can do your own mini owl prowl if you have a suitable wooded habitat near your house. Go outside late at night in midwinter and listen for the low hoots of the barred or great-horned owl, or the whinnying whistle of the members of the screech-owl family.

REMEMBER

Not all owls are denizens of the woods. Some owls prefer prairie, or desert, or tundra. Your field guide can help you determine which owls may be found in your area.

If you're curious about owl sounds, check out recordings of their various — and quite varied — calls. Soon you'll know which owl wants to "cook for you-all" (barred owl) and which one will scare the bejeezus out of you with its rasping screams (barn owl).

Pelagic trips

Get on a boat in the wee hours of the morning. Head out to sea in search of sea-birds. Maybe you'll see thousands, maybe you'll see none. You may get seasick. What is it that bird watchers find so fascinating about pelagic trips? The birds!

TECHNICAL
STUFF

Pelagic is a word derived from Greek that means "of the open sea." There are many seabird species — called *pelagic birds* — that come to land only to nest. These birds spend the majority of their lives roaming the surface of the briny sea.

If you're interested in building a long life list of birds, sooner or later you'll hear the siren call of the sea. On the East Coast, most pelagic trips are aimed at getting out as far as the Gulf Stream — the warm ocean current in which seabirds find abundant food. Because this trip can be quite far offshore, you can spend several hours getting there, do a bit of birding, and spend several more hours getting back.

The West Coast is blessed with rich, life-sustaining ocean currents near to shore, so the pelagic trips get to the birds faster. But the Pacific Ocean, some would say, is misnamed. It can have mighty large swells, which are anything but peaceful on your stomach.

TIP

If you wish to go on a pelagic trip, by all means go on an organized one for birders. Don't ride along on a fishing charter boat. You'll see far more birds and smell fewer fishes and tackle boxes on the all-birder trip.

Taking your first field trip could be the start of a lifelong passion for birds. On land or on sea, you may soon find that you enjoy nothing more than your friends of the air.

Chapter **15**

Birding by Habitat

I magine yourself as a bird, flying high in the sky. You're a spring migrant song-bird, returning from the mountains of Costa Rica where you spent the winter. Instinct is propelling you to the place where you were born so that you can seek a mate and produce offspring yourself. But how do you know when you get there? You're a bird and can neither read a roadmap, nor stop to ask for directions. (Of course, we all know that *male* birds never stop to ask directions. Hmmm . . .)

The answer for a bird is that home can be wherever the habitat is — but the habitat must be right or the bird may not survive. Being extremely mobile creatures, flying around in search of a suitable place to rest, feed, seek shelter, and repro-duce is pretty easy for birds.

For you, the bird watcher, bird habitat preferences are an excellent clue to help you know what species to expect in certain types of habitats. This chapter helps you make the connection between habitat type and bird type.

TIP

When looking at a particular piece of habitat, ask yourself: "If I were a bird, where would I go within this area? Where's the best shelter? Where am I likely to find food? Water? If I wanted to hide from nosy bird watchers, where would I go?"

See the color section in this book for an example of how to view a landscape (as a human) when you're birding by habitat.

Birding by Habitat

Birding by habitat (BBH) is not only a neat way to find birds, it's also easy. Here's a test to check your BBH IQ: In which of these two habitats would you most likely find a wood duck: Along a river? Or in a tree in the woods?

If you said along a river, your score is 75 out of 100. If you said in a tree in the woods, you score 25 out of 100. But if you said **both,** you scored a perfect 100! Wood ducks feed along rivers and streams, but they nest in hollow trees (hence their name)!

Focusing on preferred habitats

Every bird species has habitat preferences, and some of them are very specific. Bird families have broad habitat preferences, which makes generalizing about ducks preferring water to land easy. As you become more familiar with the habitat preferences of birds, you begin to see some of the specifics among bird habitat preferences as well.

Birding by habitat allows you to know what to expect in a given habitat before you enter it. This knowledge gives you a distinct advantage. You won't be fooled or surprised to hear a yellow warbler singing from a willow tree on the edge of a wetland. You know that this species loves willow trees and wet areas, and so, during certain times of the year, you expect to find a yellow warbler in this area. (Yellow warblers breed throughout most of North America and migrate through areas where they don't breed. See Chapter 13 for more on bird migration.)

But when something unexpected shows up, you're ready. If a bird isn't in your mental reference for this habitat, you know you'd better take a closer look.

Knowing your wheres and whens

Another advantage of being able to bird by habitat is knowing where birds can be found during different times of year, as many birds use different habitats at different times. That yellow warbler in the willow tree may not be there from December through April, but you know that it is likely to be around from May through July.

If you're like us, from time to time you get an urge to see a certain species. For example, in the summer, we delight in seeing cerulean warblers; in winter, short-eared owls are always a treat. Neither species is common here in Ohio, so we have to know when and where to look. In both cases, we know precisely where the best habitats are for these species (ceruleans love stands of big, old deciduous trees; short-eared owls love large rough grasslands), so we can get our annual fix if we visit these spots at the right time of year.

REMEMBER

Birds need four basic things to survive: food, water, shelter, and a place to reproduce. Look for these things when you're birding by habitat, and you'll find birds.

Habitat Types and the Birds That Love Them

What follows is a very general list of some common North American habitat types and the bird families and species you commonly find in them. Remember that the birds in your part of the world may differ somewhat from those listed here, depending on factors of climate, available habitat type, and season. This list is not all-inclusive, but it does contain some representative species for each habitat type.

You can use this general round-up of bird habitats to help form your own ideas of what birds to expect in the habitats in your region.

Lakes, rivers, and wetlands

Anywhere in North America where you find water may be considered a wetland. Where there's water, there are bound to be birds. Why? Because wet habitats support a vast diversity of life, from microscopic aquatic insects to huge animals such as humans, bears, and the Loch Ness Monster.

Bird watchers are drawn to water because birds are drawn there, too. All birds need water to survive, but some birds prefer to make their homes in, on, or near water. These are the species and families of birds that you can expect to find in wetland habitats:

>> **In open water:** Ducks, geese, swans, loons, grebes, cormorants, phalaropes

>> **Along the water's edge:** Herons, egrets, shorebirds (sandpipers, plovers, and the like)

>> **In the marsh vegetation:** Bitterns, rails, boat-tailed grackles, marsh wrens, swamp sparrows, common yellowthroats, blackbirds (yellow-headed, tricolored or red-winged, rusty, Brewer's)

>> **In wooded edges and flooded bottomland:** Willow flycatchers, alder flycatchers, Acadian flycatchers, prothonotary warblers, yellow warblers, woodpeckers, kingfishers, red-shouldered hawks, barred owls

>> **Flying overhead:** Osprey, swallows, swifts, flocks of waterfowl

SPECIAL PLACES: DAMS AND RESERVOIRS

In winter, when much of the fresh water may be frozen, birds congregate wherever the unfrozen water is, such as directly below a dam or reservoir — anywhere that has moving water, or a heated outflow, as from a power plant. Ducks, geese, swans, loons, grebes, gulls, and other waterbirds will congregate in winter on open water. Hanging around nearby may be several bald or golden eagles, or possibly red-tailed hawks, looking for an easy meal among the many waterbirds.

The key to success: Sneaking up on 'em

Finding birds in habitats with water can require some stealth on your part. Ducks feeding and resting on a wooded pond won't stick around long if you appear suddenly on the shore. Nor will any other species on or near the water.

TIP

Find a distant vantage point from which to scan the pond and then choose a discreet route to get closer for a better look. We've had amazing luck watching birds from a canoe or kayak. For some reason, a pair of slow-moving kayaks with bird watchers in them doesn't seem to threaten waterbirds as much as if those same two birders popped out of a car and walked to the edge of the water. (Make sure you observe all boating safety rules. Just because you're a bird watcher in the middle of a calm lake doesn't mean you can't tip over if you get too excited about that osprey flying over your head!)

Woodlands: From clearings to deep, thick forests

Four hundred or so years ago, the eastern half of North America was so thickly forested in virgin old-growth timber, it's said that a single squirrel could have traveled from Maine to the eastern edge of the Great Plains without ever touching the ground. Although this is no longer the case (due to the effects of human industry and agriculture on the landscape), many parts of the continent are more tree-covered than they were 100 years ago. Besides, all the squirrels are too busy raiding our bird feeders to attempt a historical reenactment of this epic mammalian trek.

These are some species and families of birds that you can expect to find in various woodland habitats:

>> **Clearings and cut or burned-over areas:** Flycatchers, bluebirds, kestrels, flickers, robins, swallows

>> **Scrubby zones, with a few saplings:** Warblers (such as prairie, yellow, orange-crowned), white-eyed vireos, sparrows, grouse

>> **Riparian areas (wooded waterways):** Wood ducks, hooded mergansers, herons, woodcocks, barred owls, red-shouldered hawks, magpies, crows, some warbler species (such as prothonotary, American redstart, water-thrushes), phoebes, flycatchers

>> **Secondary growth (medium-sized trees, with thick underbrush):** Towhees, sparrows, gray catbirds, thrashers, northern cardinals, buntings, warblers (such as mourning, hooded, Kentucky, MacGillivray's)

>> **Deciduous forest:** Red-eyed vireos, many warblers, tanagers, grosbeaks, thrushes, grouse, turkey, nightjars, jays, woodpeckers, great-horned owls, screech owls, broad-winged hawks, white-breasted nuthatches, black-capped or Carolina chickadees, titmice

>> **Coniferous forest (pine, spruce, fir):** Crossbills, grouse, finches, nuthatches (red-breasted, pygmy, and brown-headed), chickadees (mountain, boreal, and chestnut-backed), warblers (Blackburnian, pine, yellow-rumped, Townsend's, black-throated green)

>> **Mixed coniferous/deciduous forest:** Solitary vireos, chuck-will's-widows, woodpeckers, jays, many warbler species

SUCCESSION: THE PROCESS OF REGROWTH

After a thickly wooded area is cut or otherwise destroyed, regrowth begins in a process called *succession*. Each stage of succession has certain characteristics that set it apart from other stages, just as each stage has particular bird, animal, and plant species associated with it. For example, golden-winged warblers prefer to nest in old, neglected fields where brush and saplings have begun to grow. A farm field, if left alone, goes through these stages: grassy meadow, brushy meadow, overgrown meadow (brushy with some saplings), secondary woodland (medium-sized trees, thick underbrush), climax forest (large trees, sparse undergrowth). The first few stages can occur over just a few years. The last two stages take longer, even centuries. For the golden-winged warbler, the habitat may be suitable for only two or three years before it becomes too wooded. Then it's time to move on to another old meadow.

SPECIAL PLACES: EDGE HABITAT AND WASTE SPACES

An *edge habitat* occurs where an open habitat (a meadow, for example) meets a different type of habitat (such as woods). This mix of habitats is very attractive to birds of both areas and is almost always productive for bird watching. Plus, the birds are easier to see than if they're deep in the woods. Test this theory out the next time you're in an edge habitat. See if it isn't birdier than either the meadow or woods habitat alone.

Believe it or not, *waste spaces* — areas that are unsightly or even ugly — can be very good places to find birds. Old abandoned farmland, clearcuts, old cemeteries, and even old industrial land can have lots of birds simply because they have successional habitats and no people.

The key to success: Listen up

TIP

Use your ears when birding in wooded habitats and you greatly increase your chances of finding birds. Even if you don't know what the bird is that's singing, that's okay. Use its song to help you locate it. With visual and audio clues, you can identify the bird accurately. For information on identifying birds by their songs, see Chapter 6.

Grasslands, prairies, and farmlands

Before the central portions of North America fell under the plow, they were part of a vast sea of grass stretching from present-day Ohio to Colorado, and from north-western Canada to Mexico. It was the proverbial "home where the buffalo roam." Patches of the native prairies remain, and in these patches you can see what the trip list of a Westward Ho pioneer may have included: prairie-chickens, bobwhite, several grouse species, sandhill crane, longspurs, bobolink, many sparrows, larks, and so on.

But even in areas that are heavily farmed, you can see many birds. Some birds are prairie species that have adapted to take advantage of available habitats, while other birds are immigrants that prefer living in this altered habitat.

These are the species and families of birds that you can expect to find in various grassland habitats:

>> **Native grasslands/prairies:** Special sparrows (such as LeConte's, grasshopper, vesper, Henslow's, and others), lark buntings, horned larks, longspurs,

pipits, willets, upland sandpipers, mountain plovers, long-billed curlews, ferruginous hawks, golden eagles, short-eared owls

>> **Fences and roadsides:** *On fences* — dickcissels, lark buntings, bluebirds, nighthawks, meadowlarks, sparrows, upland plovers, burrowing owls; *along roadsides* — killdeer, horned larks, longspurs, quail, pheasants

>> **Telephone/electric poles and wires:** *Used for hunting, eating, and resting* — hawks, eagles, vultures, kingbirds, shrikes, swallows, flycatchers; *used as song perches* — meadowlarks, bluebirds, buntings, sparrows

>> **Farm fields:** *Plowed fields* — killdeer, some plovers (mountain, golden, and black-bellied), snow buntings, Lapland longspur, horned larks, gulls, black-birds; *pastures/cultivated fields* — crows, blackbirds, swallows, sparrows, goldfinches, kestrel

>> **Woodlots and windbreaks:** Great horned owls, barn owls, screech owls, nesting hawks, woodpeckers, crows, jays, orioles, tanagers, flycatchers, warblers, chickadees, song sparrows, goldfinches

The keys to success: Look sharp and listen

One key to watching birds in vast open, flat areas, such as in the middle of the Great Plains, is to scan for perching birds on any tall, exposed perch, such as a telephone pole or fencepost, a lone tree, or a tall weed stem. In treeless areas, any perch is regarded as valuable real estate to the birds living there. Although some of the grassland species sing while in flight (horned larks, upland sandpipers, bobolinks, pipits, and longspurs), others, such as sparrows and meadowlarks, sing from the best perch. Raptors hunt from the perch. Other birds use perches for resting or preening.

TIP

Two other keys are strategically placed on both sides of your head. (We call them "ears.") Be sure to use them, too. Many grassland species sing from the ground. Rather than diving into the grass to attempt to flush these birds out, wait patiently and advance slowly. They can be much farther away than they sound. Eventually you'll see the birds that you're seeking.

One final key is to look for water. Farm ponds or natural wetlands can be teeming with ducks and shorebirds.

SPECIAL PLACES: PRAIRIE POTHOLES AND BOOMING GROUNDS

In the north-central portions of the Great Plains, you can find thousands of small ponds, pools, marshes, and wetlands called *potholes*. In and around these potholes, the majority of North American ducks and a few species of shorebirds nest and raise young. When birding in the Northern Plains states or in central Canada, be sure to look for waterfowl and shorebirds in these wet areas.

Leks and *booming grounds* are other locations worth seeking out. Early every spring, males of certain grouse species gather to perform their breeding rituals in hopes of attracting a mate. These gathering spots are called leks or booming grounds (for the odd sounds the males make in their displays). Most prairie grouse species choose flat, treeless spots with sparse vegetation for maximum visibility, and so they can watch for predators as they display.

The glamorous males (all of one species) arrange themselves in a given area and begin their individual displays. Females select a male from all the hopefuls, mate, and then leave to begin nesting. By using a concealing observation blind, in some places you can observe this incredible behavior without disturbing the birds. In North America, the species that perform these breeding displays are the greater and lesser prairie-chickens, sage grouse, and sharp-tailed grouse.

Bird-finding guides for Great Plains states, the Rocky Mountain region, and the Southwest can help direct you to some of these special places.

Coastal areas

Humans love going to the ocean and so do birds, but for different reasons. Instead of sun, sand, and surf, birds go for the more mundane: food and flyways! The coasts of the Atlantic and Pacific oceans and the Gulf of Mexico have an enormous variety of habitat types associated with them, and with these habitats come a similar abundance and variety of birdlife. Here are a few of the most common coastal habitats and some of the bird species and families that may be found there:

>> **Beaches:** Shorebirds of all kinds but especially sandpipers and plovers, terns, gulls, black skimmers, pelicans, some herons and egrets, blackbirds, boat-tailed grackles, fish crows, American crows

>> **Rocky shorelines and breakwaters:** Harlequin ducks, eiders, scoters, loons, grebes, turnstones, surfbirds, wandering tattlers, purple sandpipers, oystercatchers, surfbirds, cormorants, pelicans, gulls, terns, osprey, bald eagles

>> **Brackish marsh:** Herons, egrets, terns, black skimmers, swallows, shorebirds (especially whimbrel, plovers, dowitchers, stilts, and avocets), rails, bitterns

>> **Inlets:** Osprey, bald eagles, gulls, terns, belted kingfishers, ducks, grebes, shorebirds, pelicans, herons, egrets

>> **Sea cliffs:** Puffins, guillemots, murres, auks, cormorants, gannets, kittiwakes, gulls, peregrine falcons

The key to success: Scan the horizon

Bird watching along the seacoast is like standing along a very busy street in New York City. Sooner or later, everything passes by you.

A favorite thing to do when birding along the coast is to find a comfortable place to sit and then spend a while just scanning to see what can be seen on the sea. In winter, when lots of ducks, loons, scoters, and gannets are moving offshore, you can sit and watch for hours (provided you're out of the cold wind). In summer, plenty of terns, gulls, and shorebirds are around. During the spring and fall migrations, you can never tell what's going to fly past.

SPECIAL PLACES: WINTER COASTAL BIRDING AND PELAGIC SPECIES

Many bird watchers love visiting the seacoast in the northern parts of North America during winter. There may not be warm water and sunshine, but there are bound to be lots of birds.

Depending on where you go, you can encounter thousands of birds along the coast in winter. As a bonus, you encounter few people on the beach and little or no competition for hotel rooms. Dress warmly in layers topped by a windbreaker, take your bins and a spotting scope, something hot to drink, and you're ready to rumble.

Winter is a good time to see *pelagic species* (birds that spend most of their time far out to sea, perhaps coming ashore only to breed) from shore. Changes in water temperature and currents bring food resources near shore, and the birds follow. Among the species you may glimpse are murres, gannets, shearwaters, kittiwakes, jaegers, murrelets, and auklets. If you're very interested in seabirds, consider taking a pelagic trip on a boat that's specially chartered for birders in quest of pelagic species. For more information on pelagic trips, see Chapter 14.

Deserts and scrublands

If you think that the desert is a barren wasteland, you haven't watched enough nature shows. The desert regions of North America are wonderful places for watching birds. The key is knowing where to look.

Water, being a scarce commodity in the desert, is an obvious attractant for desert birds, but vegetation, especially lush vegetation, is also appealing to birds. Vegetation offers shade, a place to hide from predators, and a place to nest for many species. For example, the saguaro cactus of the Southwest is a source of food, shelter, a place to nest, and a place to perch for a variety of birds. These cacti take the place of trees in spots where no tree can survive.

Here are some of the many desert habitats in North America:

>> **Sagebrush flats** *(areas where sage predominates)*: Sage grouse, sage thrashers, Brewer's sparrows, sage sparrows

>> **Brushy desert with mesquite bushes and cactus:** Roadrunners, Gambel's quail, elf owls, Costa's hummingbirds, phainopepla, cactus wrens, thrashers, black-throated sparrows

>> **Canyons, cliffs, mesas:** Nesting areas for golden eagles, prairie and peregrine falcons, and several hawk species, as well as vultures, canyon and rock wrens, and Say's phoebes

>> **Cultivated/irrigated areas:** Any place with water may have shorebirds, horned larks, ducks, gulls, flycatchers, western cattle egrets

>> **Streams, rivers, water holes:** Kingfishers, flycatchers (including vermilion), gray hawks, Cooper's hawks, migrant shorebirds, yellow warblers, Bell's vireos, yellow-breasted chats, black phoebes

The key to success: Go early or late

TIP

Besides looking for sources of water and cooling shade, you'll further enhance your chances of finding birds if you time your outings for early or late in the day. Getting out to see the sunrise means seeing the most birds, too! Avoid high noon and the hot hours immediately preceding and following noon. Take our advice and find a nice cool café or hotel swimming pool where you can work on your bird list or clean your binocs. Fewer birds are out and about during these times. Take a siesta.

Look along rivers, in shaded canyons, or even in town parks (especially those with ponds or lawn-sprinkler systems).

SPECIAL PLACES: SUN, ROCKS, SAND, AND OASES

Hot sun on rocks and sand make for rising hot thermals upon which raptors soar. Don't forget to look up when birding in the desert. You may see an eagle, falcon, Harris' hawk, zone-tailed hawk, common black hawk, or some other interesting bird of prey.

Gardens and backyards of desert communities are also good spots. In some small towns that draw bird watchers, such as Portal, Arizona, local residents welcome visiting birders to their property to enjoy their backyard feeding stations. They are kind enough to post directions and maps at the visitor's center.

WARNING

Whenever you venture out in the desert, take a few precautions. Wear a hat, cover your exposed skin with sunscreen, carry and drink plenty of water, watch where you step and place your hands (remember that snakes and scorpions live in the desert), and don't venture anywhere remote without letting somebody know where you're going and when you plan to return. Desert dwellers tell visitors to turn back on the trail when you've drunk half your water. Call us overcautious, but you do not want to be bitten by a rattlesnake, run out of water, or fry yourself in the sun — all of which can be easily avoided.

Knowing What to Expect

As noted earlier in this chapter, birding by habitat helps you to know what to expect when you get there. It may seem like a lot of work to study up ahead of time, but after the first few visits to a habitat, you will automatically know what birds are likely to be seen. Soon you begin to feel as though a visit to a familiar habitat is akin to going to a party where you see all your old friends.

TIP

Here's a way to hone your BBH skills. Before visiting a particular habitat, make a list of the species that you think you'll see. Keep a list during your visit to the habitat and compare the two afterward. Believe us, your accuracy improves over time.

IN THIS CHAPTER

» **Hotspots are where the birds are**

» **Finding and hitting the hottest birding hotspots**

» **Seasons come and seasons go**

» **Opting for bird-locating guides and birding trails**

» **Take our advice, please!**

Chapter **16**

Birding Hotspots

For humans, a hotspot is often defined by the fact that others go there. Consider a trendy nightclub: Even if the drinks are expensive and the music is mediocre, people may continue to show up, just because that's "the place to be."

Birds are smarter than that. They may pause to check out a place where they see other birds (that's why ducks, for example, will drop in to a pond with decoys), but if that spot doesn't supply their current needs (food, water, shelter, a place to breed, safe passage), they quickly move on.

Birding Hotspots: What and Where Are They?

Temperature has nothing to do with defining a hotspot. What you're really looking for is a place where the birding is hot. (And that can happen even when the weather is downright cold!) You want a place with a lot of birds, preferably a place with a lot of different *kinds* of birds. Even better is a place that offers not only numbers and variety, but also an element of surprise: the kind of spot where odd birds sometimes show up, far from their normal haunts.

Hotspots for bird watching are scattered all over the world. No matter where you live, there are bound to be some hotspots nearby, others that you can reach with a little effort, and still others that you can dream about visiting someday.

Location, location, location

Typically, what makes a place great for birding is either its location or its habitat. Geography turns some places into big concentration points for migrating birds. A peninsula on the coast or on the shore of a major lake can be a place where birds pause before setting out on the next leg of their journey, especially under certain weather conditions. A wooded park in the middle of a large city may have the same kind of concentrating effect during the migration seasons.

One of the best migration hotspots in the Northeast is Central Park in New York City. It doesn't offer an expanse of wild habitat, but what it does have — green trees and thick underbrush, water, and shelter — is the only choice migrant birds have. The park is surrounded by miles of concrete, skyscrapers, bustling traffic, and people. During spring migration, incredible concentrations of birds can be found on this green island in the center of Manhattan.

Habitat

More reliable for birding in other seasons is a place with really good habitat. Of course, no two kinds of birds will see habitat as "good" in exactly the same way. A horned lark may be happy in a plowed field, while a wood thrush seeks out the forest shadows. Therefore, habitat variety is a key point. It helps to have lots of plant life: A woodland with a brushy understory is likely to hold more birds than a park with nothing but mowed lawns under the trees. Water is almost always an element of good bird habitat. A stream or small pond attracts certain types of birds, while a large marsh or lake attracts many more. (For some additional insight about birds and habitat, see Chapter 15.)

Odd spots

Some kinds of hotspots for bird watching can seem bizarre to normal people. We guarantee that if you pursue birds for long, you'll find yourself comparing notes with other birders about your favorites among the sewage ponds and garbage dumps you've visited. But if you're trying to get a friend interested in birds, it's probably best not to take them to such a place on the first date.

Finding Hotspots

Trial and error is one way to find hotspots. You can pick a random spot and hang around to see if any birds show up. But birds are practically everywhere, so it can take a while to figure out whether a spot is average or great. Some birding hotspots have international renown, but hotspots can be local and known only to birders in the area.

TIP

UNUSUAL USUAL PLACES FOR BIRDS

Birds can commonly be found in spots you wouldn't think to look. Here are some of them:

- **Sewage treatment plants and ponds:** Fertile water means lots of food for birds.

- **Landfills:** Gulls are legendary garbage pickers. Sometimes the regular gull species attract their rarer fellow gulls. Bald eagles, crows, and ravens are also known to find an easy meal at landfills.

- **Urban boating/shipping harbors:** These harbors offer lots of handouts for gulls, ducks, geese, and swans.

- **Urban/suburban lakes, ponds, and reservoirs:** Birds like calm water with little or no disturbance from watercraft.

- **Vacant lots or old industrial sites that are overgrown:** Hawks, owls, killdeer, swallows, sparrows — lots of species move in when humans move out.

- **Arboretums, orchards, and tree farms, even in urban areas:** These make great habitat for attracting all kinds of birds and can be especially good for owls in winter and warblers in spring.

- **Cemeteries:** Quiet places with good habitat allow birds to feed and rest in peace. Historic cemeteries often have big, old trees and shrubs.

- **Roadside rest stops:** Ornamental plantings and the presence of water attract birds. Convenient bathrooms attract bird watchers.

- **Powerline right-of-way cuts:** These often pass right through dense woodland habitats. Poles and lines provide perches for birds, and infrequently mowed vegetation under high-tension lines can provide dense, scrubby, human-deterring habitat.

- **Edge habitats along highways and roadways:** Any edge habitat is good for birds. Notice how many red-tailed hawks you see along the highway. The grassy medians are perfect for mammal-hunting birds of prey.

eBird keeps track of where its users go to enjoy birds, and so can help you find established hotspots, both near your home and around the world. eBird's "Explore" function opens a literal world of possibilities, and we'll explain how to use it below.

In most parts of North America, good birding spots are already known. Nearly all bird watchers are willing to share the good places. It's not like fishing — if too many people go fishing at one spot, they may use up the fish. You're not likely to use up all the birds.

Go clubbing

Unless you live in a really remote region, a bird club is probably located somewhere near you. Bird watchers with local experience can give you a big head start in finding the hotspots. They may be able to recommend a nearby park, lake, refuge, or other location where the birding is great. Most bird clubs arrange birding trips to local (or distant) hotspots, and many offer occasional evening programs — often about where members have traveled to see birds and the birds they have seen there. Newcomers are always welcome to bird club events — even new birders. Birders in general are warm, welcoming folks.

Chapter 19 explains how to go about finding a bird club — local or national — and what they have to offer in addition to insights on hotspots.

eBird knows all

In Chapter 12, we talk about how you can use eBird to report your birding observations. Because countless thousands of bird watchers around the world contribute such data, eBird keeps track of where people go birding, the number of species found at each location, and even the number of birds of each species reported. It is a huge, well-organized database, and it makes all that data available to the public!

Think of a place you'd like to go birding — perhaps your county of residence or a favorite or upcoming vacation destination. Would you like to find out about nearby birding hotspots? Go to https://ebird.org and **click the Explore tab.** (These directions work best on a web browser running on a desktop or laptop computer.) From here, you have two choices:

> » **Under the Explore Regions heading, type in the name of a state, province, or county — or even a country.**
>
> The page that comes up tells you how many species have been reported there, the number of checklists submitted there, and the number of people

who have submitted them. The last two are somewhat of a measure of the popularity of this location. Look for the Map button on the top right of the screen and click on it. A map of that place will show up; red boxes or map pins indicate locations that have the highest species tallies. As you zoom in, boxes turn into colored map pins of all the locations where people have ever reported eBird checklists. Keep zooming in, centering on a location of interest. When you've zoomed in close enough, you can click on one of the pointers to see how many species have been reported at that spot and the number of checklists reported.

TIP

Back to the Explore tab, just for kicks, type in the name of your state or province under the Explore Regions heading. From the navigation menu on the left side of the screen, choose the Hotspots option. The results will show two columns. The Checklist Leaders column on the left indicates the hotspots in your state or province that have the most submitted checklists — an indication of the birding popularity of this spot. The Species Leaders column on the right shows the hotspots that have the largest species tally. If you click on the name of a hotspot, you will find a page that offers directions, a map, a list of species, recent sightings, and even recent photos and checklists. If you click the Bar Charts (in the left column), you will see a chart showing what species have been seen at that location, how commonly, and at what time of year. You can get this information for any region or hotspot in the world!

» **Back at the Explore page, click the Explore Hotspots link.**

A map of the world will appear, with red areas showing the highest species counts. Zoom in to an area of interest or enter the name of a registered eBird hotspot. For example, you could type in "Acadia" and be rewarded with a list of all the registered eBird hotspots in this spectacular national park in Maine.

TIP

We encourage you to play around within "Explore" within eBird. You won't break it, and it's pretty easy to figure out, and it will truly help you find birding hotspots near and far.

How does a place earn an eBird hotspot designation? Birders (just like you) recommend places they bird frequently. The public cemetery where Dawn frequently birds (but few others do) is an eBird hotspot — not because it is the birdiest location in Washington County, Ohio, but because she birds there often, and the area now has 120 species documented there.

REMEMBER

You can investigate birding hotspots using the eBird app on a mobile device, too, but it's not so obvious or intuitive (and there's the fat-finger problem). Launch the eBird app. At the bottom of the screen, tap Explore. (It has a magnifying glass icon.) A map of your current location will appear and may have some pins showing nearby hotspots. Red pins indicate recent checklists submitted from that hotpot. Blue pins indicate hotspots without recent checklists. Zoom in, if you want. Tap pins for more information about various hotspots.

To investigate hotspots that are not near your current location, start at eBird's Start Checklist screen on your mobile device, tap Explore (at the bottom of the screen), then tap the upper corner of the screen. (You might see an icon of slider bars or the word "edit," or maybe something else.) A form comes up, and the top field says, "Radius from" and shows your current location. Tap the icon to the left of your current location, and a form opens that allows you to enter the city, zip code, or place of interest to you; or tap the Region tab and enter the county, state, province, or country of your choice. On this screen you can also tap Choose from Map.

If the instructions above aren't quite accurate, we apologize. Apps are updated frequently, and how-to's change as a result. Just be aware that you can find birding hotspots all over the world using your mobile device (as long as you have Wi-Fi or cell service).

Read up

More traditionally, lots has been published, both in print and on the web, on the best places to watch birds. Countless bird-finding guides are available for North America and beyond. Some cover large areas, such as one or several states or provinces; others detail the birding spots in a small area, such as a single county — and everything in between. Search the internet for "Birding (location name)." Talk to birding pals who have traveled to see birds. If you don't know any bird watchers who can advise you about such guides, your local library will be able to steer you.

Lewis-and-Clark It

You can, of course, discover your own hotspots. If you develop an eye for habitat, you may recognize productive spots at first sight — you may predict, for example, that a marshy pond next to a forest is likely to be good. You may predict that an empty parking lot is likely to be lousy bird habitat — unless it happens to be next to a fast-food restaurant, in which case the gulls and house sparrows are probably going to show up soon.

Timing Your Visit

Some places are great for bird watching at all times of the year. Those are the exceptions. A lot of birds move around with the seasons, so a birding spot that's great in the summer may be Dudsville in the winter, or vice versa. If you don't want to find yourself sitting in a swamp waiting for birds that won't show up for three months, you need some advance information. eBird is a great place to start.

Check the local checklist

A very useful source of such information is a local checklist that tells you the seasonal occurrence of each species. Some such checklists use simple codes: "W-c, S-r" may mean "common in winter, rare in summer." Other checklists use bar charts to show seasons of occurrence, and these can give you a precise idea of when to expect each bird. Your local or state bird club or park system might offer such seasonal checklists in print or online. eBird bar charts (see the "eBird knows all" section, earlier in this chapter) offer seasonal abundance data, too. (*Note:* eBird's Printable Checklists do not offer seasonal abundance information.)

On bar charts, you may see, for example, that many sandpiper species are represented by thick black bars across late July, August, and early September. This would be a sure sign that late summer is the time to go to that hotspot if you wish to see shorebirds. The same bar graph may show you that most of the ducks do not pick up in numbers until October, so if your target is waterfowl, plan to hit that great pond for waterfowl later in the fall.

Using bird-finding guides and birding trails

Bird-finding guides can be a real boon to birders. They may be simple pamphlets published by the local bird club, or they may be professional productions. Many are online, too. Regardless of their format, they can lead you to great birding spots.

Birding trails can be simple marked paths in natural areas, but the term also refers to routes connecting birding hotspots, usually covering a state or region. For example, the Lake Erie Birding Trail spans most of the coastline of northern Ohio and features seven loops. (Search the internet for "Lake Erie Birding Trail.") In this case, what you'll find on the web is expanded in a spiral-bound guidebook.

The Great Florida Birding and Wildlife Trail website (https://floridabirding trail.com/) is quite different, however, and includes a network of more than 500 wildlife-viewing sites across the state. It is intended to be used online and lists hotspots in each county. It offers not only descriptions of birds at each location but also direct links to eBird information on each hotspot.

TIP

To find birding trails or bird-finding guides in a region that interests you, search the internet with phrases like "birding Oklahoma" or "birding Southeast Arizona." Location-specific bird guides vary in format but typically include detailed road directions to a wide variety of birding spots and maps. To make the best use of a bird-finding guide, you should study it before your birding trip and then take it along to check directions as you go.

REMEMBER

Bird-finding guides and birding trails often give specific notes about the best times to look for particular birds at any given place. Don't forget: Some seasons are better for bird watching than others.

In your pre-trip studying, you need to decide which spots to visit. Authors of bird-finding guides usually are not shy about saying which spots they think are best. If your time is limited, you may want to hit only the high points. Check the calendar and try to figure out which spots will be best at that time of year. You may be after a particular bird; if so, check the guide to read up on it and see when and where that bird is likely to be there.

Of course, even the best directions can leave you lost if a certain road is temporarily closed or if a sign has been changed. Also, it's best not to count on cell service when you're way off the beaten path. Load your directions into your phone while you have cell service and take screenshots of the steps if you're headed into the hinterlands! As a backup, you might want to carry an old-fashioned paper road map in your car and check the guide's directions against the map. Also remember that directions do go out of date, especially near cities or other developing areas. Even if a bird-finding guide has been recently published or updated, you should be mentally prepared for the possibility that local conditions might have changed.

Voices of Experience

Jessica, Julie, and Dawn — combined — have not visited all the birding hotspots of North America or even all the hotspots in their home state of Ohio. Few people have because there are so many of them! Even places not (yet) designated as hotspots can offer great bird watching. The back deck of your house could be your own, private birding hotspot.

If you join a local birding club, subscribe to *BWD* magazine (visit `https://bwdmagazine.com/`, please!), or otherwise hang out with birders more experienced than you, you will hear about local, national, and even international birding hotspots. Some of the most famous (and for good reason) include:

>> The Farallon Islands, California

>> Bosque del Apache National Wildlife Refuge, New Mexico

>> Cape May, New Jersey

>> South Padre Island, Texas (and lots of other spots on Texas's Gulf Coast)

>> The Rio Grande Valley, Texas

- » The Massachusetts Coast (all of it)

- » Goose Pond Fish and Wildlife Area, Indiana

- » Big Sur, California

- » Lincoln Park in Chicago, Illinois

- » Magee Marsh, Ohio (and lots of other spots on the southern shore of Lake Erie)

- » Point Pelee National Park, Ontario

- » Florida, Alaska, Hawaii (just about anywhere)

Those are just a handful of the most famous and heavily visited birding hotspots in North America, but there are dozens more that are just as birdy.

REMEMBER

Keep in mind that even these well-known and popular hotspots have off-seasons. Do your homework before you plan your trip but realize that when the bird action is hottest at such places, they are likely to be crowded.

TIP

"The early bird gets the worm," it is said. Bird watchers know that, too, but even so, arriving at a birding hotspot at sunrise might earn you some close-to-alone time with the birds. Many birders like to stop for breakfast or at least a cup of joe before they head out. Crowds seem to peak a little later in the morning at most birding hotspots, and some places at certain times of year can be elbow-to-elbow with avid birders. If you can get there at first light, you'll beat the peak crowds. Don't tell anyone!

The list of famous hotspots found earlier in this section demonstrates that birding hotspots are found all over this continent. Most aren't as famous (or as bird-dense) as those places, but no matter. We can't all move to Cape May. So, find the hotspots near you, enjoy them, but also enjoy birds wherever you go. Not all North American birding hotspots have been discovered yet! If you bird frequently at a little-known but birdy location, or encourage others to do so, consider registering it as an eBird hotspot. When you're traveling, sure, go to the established hotspots, but also check out the retention pond behind your motel. It could be full of interesting birds!

TIP

Follow the crowd for a while — but then go off the beaten track. There's a special pleasure in watching birds at a hotspot that you've discovered for yourself. It's tempting to go for the sure thing rather than explore on your own. The best approach is to do some of both. On her first visit to the Grand Canyon in Arizona, Julie walked up a tiny trail leading to the side of an overlook that was jam-packed with noisy humans. A Steller's jay lured her onward. While watching an entertaining flock of bushtits, a large shadow passed over her. Julie looked up to behold her first-ever California condor circling low overhead and was moved to tears when it was joined by three more: a completely unexpected gift. Take those side trails!

REMEMBER

There is no agreed-upon definition of a birding hotspot. It can be a place with lots of birds, or lots of bird species, or rare birds. Or it can be a place where the birds are easy to watch, so lots of bird watchers visit it regularly. It can be all of the above. A birding hotspot is whatever and wherever you want it to be. Just one thing: If you discover a place that offers amazing bird watching, please share that information!

THE "PATAGONIA PICNIC TABLE EFFECT"

Isn't it amazing how rare birds seem to show up right where the bird watchers are, instead of someplace else? Actually, there's a name for this phenomenon, and the name has a history.

Back in the 1960s, an active birder stopped to look for birds at a roadside rest stop just south of the little town of Patagonia, Arizona. In the trees above the picnic tables, he found a couple of rose-throated becards — a rare species — so he began making regular checks of the area. Soon he found more rare birds there — thick-billed kingbirds, and then the first nesting five-striped sparrows reported in the United States. At that news, other bird watchers started going there as well. They discovered more rare birds, notably the first black-capped gnatcatchers ever found north of the border. More birders started going there, and they turned up even more rare birds, including yellow grosbeak, yellow-green vireo, and others. So then, even more birders started going there.

True, that roadside rest stop was located in good bird habitat, but it continued to produce rare finds partly because all the bird watchers went there and looked for rare things. And every time another rarity was discovered, it made other birders want to go there, so the coverage stayed intense. You can see how this sort of circular cause-and-effect would continue. At least 232 bird species have been reported there. In eBird, the hotspot name is Patagonia Roadside Rest Area, Santa Cruz, US-AZ.

Similar things have happened at other birding hotspots across North America and around the world, but the phenomenon — of rare birds attracting more birders, who then find more rare birds, which then attract more birders, *ad infinitum* — is now known as the "Patagonia Picnic Table Effect."

IN THIS CHAPTER

» Adding up the pluses (and minuses) of formal tours

» Evaluating the different kinds of birding tours

» Choosing a tour and a tour company

» Take me to your leader!

» Asking questions

» Planning ahead

» Following the rules of the road

Chapter **17**

Birding Tours: On Site with a Pro

B ird tours are trips typically designed for fairly small groups, traveling with one or two expert birders who know the area and its birdlife. Such guided tours can offer great opportunities to see new species in new surroundings under the guidance of a real pro.

In this chapter, we take you on a tour of bird tours.

The Good, the Bad, and the Ugly

Even on their trip to Oz, Dorothy and her pals had both dazzling fun and moments of disappointment. Bird tours are no different, except you won't be attacked by flying monkeys and will encounter very few green witches. Green birds, on the other hand. . .

Downside

Let us give you the cons first (because there aren't many). On a tour, you don't have much control over what happens: You have to follow a pre-arranged itinerary and go along with what the leader wants to do. Sometimes you can skip a morning or a side trip, but going off on your own to do something completely different is usually difficult and often impossible.

You also spend a *lot* of time with the group; the days are long on a typical tour. If the group happens to include someone you find annoying, the days can seem even longer.

Birders in general tend to be really nice and fun and easy to get along with. But if you have limited tolerance for others' foibles, you could be doing cuckoo imitations by the end of a two-week tour.

Upside

So, what's good about a tour? Lots of things. You don't waste any time going to unproductive places or getting lost. You save yourself weeks of research about where and when to go, where to stay, and how to travel. You don't have to do any of the driving or worry about finding meals or lodging. It's all part of the tour.

Best of all, you'll always see a lot more birds than you would on your own. The leaders know just where to go, they know the habits and hangouts and calls of each bird, and they can identify those tough little mystery birds that might be nothing but question marks for you otherwise.

Vive la Difference!

Many different kinds of trips are being offered to bird watchers today. They range from casual nature trips that take in a few birds, all the way up to gonzo marathons where sleep and sanity are sacrificed in a mad dash to tick off as many species as possible.

Most professional bird tours are somewhere in between: You see a lot of birds, but you do so at a pace that allows you some time to actually *look* at them. However, the pace won't allow for much else. Days usually start very early; lunch is often a picnic in some birdy spot; time for trinket-shopping is limited or nonexistent; and lodging is usually in a place where there's no nightlife available (except maybe standing around in the dark and listening for owls, which most birders probably prefer to a night out on the town anyway).

YOUR NON-BIRDING COMPANION

The nothing-but-birds aspect of birding tours can be of critical importance if you're thinking of taking along a spouse or friend who is not interested in birds. This can be a *big mistake.* (As the wife of one avid birder said after a particularly intense trip, "I don't know how he's going to pay for the tour and the alimony, too.") If your significant other has not caught the birding bug, you should either consider a solo vacation or look for a tour that will cater to wider interests.

Fortunately, there are a number of possibilities of the latter type. Some companies and organizations offer trips that combine bird watching with other pursuits: history, holidays in exotic spots, local food scenes and wineries, and so on. There are also nature tours on small ships to places like the Galapagos or the Amazon that might appeal to people with more general interests.

REMEMBER

North America has some well-established larger bird tour companies, each running dozens of trips every year. There are also many smaller companies that run fewer trips. If you peruse the pages of any bird magazine, you are likely to see ads for a score of tour companies offering loads of tours. Start searching online, and you will encounter a dizzying array of options. The choices can seem overwhelming.

Going big or small?

Both large companies and smaller ones can offer you a good value for your money.

With a larger, long-established tour company, you may pay a little more, but you can be fairly confident their trips are consistent in quality.

Smaller, newer companies may be able to charge less for a comparable tour, but you have to research these cheaper trips more carefully. Some of these start-up tour companies run outstanding trips so that you're really getting a bargain. Others don't know what they're doing yet, so even a very cheap trip might not be worth what you're paying for it.

Ask around before choosing

One of the best ways to find out about a tour outfit is to talk to someone who has traveled with them. Ask around among members of your local bird club. Chances are good that you'll find someone who has taken guided tours. Personal recommendations are worth more than any amount of advertising.

Choosing a particular trip is a different kind of challenge. After reviewing a tour company brochure or website, you may want to go on all of them! But if you've never gone on a tour before, you might want to start with a relatively short excursion closer to home to see how you like the experience, rather than leap into a three-week marathon trip to some exotic country. You should also consider the pace and intensity of the tour. Some trips are relaxed; others are more gung-ho. The descriptions provided by the tour company should make that clear.

Vetting the leader of the pack

Experienced tour-takers often say that the leader is *the* most important factor in a successful bird tour. (Tour leaders, in rare moments when they aren't being modest, will say the same thing.)

Leaders have to be more than just expert birders: They also must be very good at handling logistics, resourceful in dealing with emergencies, and flexible in interacting with a wide variety of people. In fact, "people skills" are just as important as birding skills for a leader. Individuals who succeed as bird tour leaders are usually friendly, fun, outgoing types who enjoy sharing birds with others.

Ordinarily, a company will proudly advertise its tour leaders. If a company plans and advertises a tour without having chosen the leader first, this may be a warning sign. Although not all tour companies list the leader for a given tour in their information, when you inquire and get additional information about the tour from the company, the leader's name should be included.

Ask the company about the leader. Are they experienced in leading tours, and are they familiar with this tour and area? Finding yourself in the middle of nowhere with an inexperienced leader is little better than being lost in the same place all by yourself.

BIG BUCKS FOR BIRDS

You can spend a lot or a little money when taking a bird tour. The most basic one-day or weekend trips can be as little as $250. A weeks-long safari to Africa may set you back $10,000 or more, not including airfare, tips, and cocktails. We know some birders who like to figure out how much each new species will cost them before they take a big trip. They might consider $200 per species to be a worthwhile endeavor. Before you decide to take a tour, rough out a budget with the planned expenses; then add a few hundred dollars on top for unplanned expenses and emergencies.

As with choosing a tour company, one of the best ways to find out about a particular leader is to talk to someone who has taken a tour with them.

TIP

Another way to get to know a tour company and meet potential guides is to attend a birding festival. (See Chapter 18.) Tour companies often have booths at these events with guides available to answer questions, give presentations, and even lead some of the festival's bird walks. You can learn more about a company and get to know a tour leader's personality and guiding style — a test run of sorts to determine if the company or a particular guide might be the right fit for you.

Questions to Ask the Tour Company

Usually, a bird tour company maintains an office staffed with people who know the tour business. If you can't find out what you need to know by reading the published information, you should call the office and ask questions.

TIP

With an established tour company, these questions usually are answered in a brochure or on their website, so be sure to read the material before calling to ask about these points:

>> **Has the company run this tour before?**

It's usually wise to avoid a company's very first trip to a new region. The tour will probably be held anyway — eager bird-listers will pile on to go check off the specialty birds of that area — and you can go next year, after the bugs are ironed out of the itinerary.

>> **Is the leader familiar with the area?**

The company may have a long history of trips to West Wombat, but that's slim comfort if *this* year's leader has never been there before.

>> **What's the maximum group size?**

Group size can make a big difference in the quality of the experience. If you have 50 bird watchers following one leader, birder number 47 is not going to see anything but dust. But effective group size can vary with the terrain. In very open surroundings, as on a trip to the Antarctic, one leader might be enough for 20 participants. On narrow forest trails, a group of more than eight or nine with one leader is probably too large.

≫ What is included in the tour cost?

What the tour cost covers can vary widely. Some North American trips can look surprisingly cheap until you find out that meals are not included in the price. On foreign tours, airfare from the United States sometimes is included, but usually is not. As a general rule, tour prices don't include laundry costs, alcoholic beverages, or a private secretary to write down all the birds for you.

REMEMBER

A friend once went to lead a weeklong trip visiting a series of small, uninhabited islands. The tour summary had given glowing descriptions of putting ashore on these isolated islands where few other visitors were privileged to tread. At the beginning of the trip, this friend met the group at the airport, and they all were transferred by bus down to the coastal town where the docks were located. As the crew started to carry luggage onto the small ship that the group would be inhabiting for the next week, one of the participants said, wild-eyed, "You mean we're going on a *boat*?! I can't travel by boat!"

Be sure you read the tour information ahead of time.

Be Prepared

We can't say this too often: Before you sign up for any tour, read the published information about it with great care. Most tours are not physically challenging, but there are exceptions. It is supremely disappointing to go on a strenuous trip and discover that you're not up to it. Ask yourself if you're up to the physical challenges of a birding trip to the high altitudes of the Peruvian Andes — and answer honestly.

Note: You don't have to ask these questions to yourself out loud, or even look in the mirror when you ask them, although this technique often helps us.

You might also ask yourself whether you're *mentally* prepared for a particular tour. On a big trip to East Africa or tropical South America, you may feel bombarded with more than 500 species of birds, most of which are unfamiliar to you. This could be either a dream or a nightmare, depending on your outlook.

Suppose you really want to go on a tour, but there's a slight possibility that you may have to cancel for some reason. Should you sign up or not? Most tour companies won't give you a refund, or at least not a full one, if you bail out at the last minute. You can, however, purchase trip cancellation insurance, which will pay back most of your tour cost if you do have to cancel. About the only insurance people *can't* offer is to provide the birds that you miss by not going on the tour.

TIP

PHYSICAL CHALLENGES

Many tour companies specify that tour participants be able to hike, climb hills, and climb in and out of tour vehicles many times per day. If you're someone who has difficulty walking or hiking moderate distances, or if you have trouble breathing at high altitudes, or if you think you may not be up to the physical challenges of a given tour, ask the tour company in advance for their advice. Most tour companies ask participants to complete health questionnaires prior to registration so that health emergencies and accidents can be avoided as much as possible. Rather than assume that you'll be okay on a long, strenuous birding tour, do yourself, your fellow tour participants, and the tour company a favor, and ask for a detailed description about how physically challenging a given tour will be. The tour company may be able to offer suggestions for alternative tours and birding destinations better suited to your abilities.

TIP

Even a tamer trip may expose you to a lot of birding challenges. Before you head out to join the group, make a few preparations. Familiarize yourself with the trip's itinerary. Research the general region you will be visiting so you know what to expect geographically and culturally. Take a look at a field guide to the birds of the area, so that at least you'll be familiar with the names of the birds when the leader calls them off.

Plan Ahead, Reserve Early

Wouldn't it be great if you could call up out of the blue and sign up for a major trip that starts next week? And while we're at it, wouldn't it be great if someone rang your doorbell and gave you a check for $10 million? Meanwhile, back here in the real world, neither of those possibilities is very likely. If you want to go on a bird tour, your mantra should be: Plan ahead, plan ahead, plan ahead.

Birding tours have limits on group sizes, and popular tours may fill up months ahead of time. Even if the trip has not filled to capacity, things like hotel reservations must be established well in advance; last-minute registrants might have the tour office scrambling to find rooms for them.

On the other hand, advertised tours don't always run. They are canceled if no one signs up, of course. But they may have to be called off a couple of months ahead of time, so that the companies can cancel hotel and vehicle reservations without penalties. Operators sometimes receive numerous calls inquiring about a tour, frustratingly just *after* they have officially canceled that trip for lack of participants.

The moral of the story: Register for a tour well ahead of time!

REMEMBER

What if you suddenly are given vacation time, you have money to spend, and you run across a notice of some great tour that's just about to depart? Go ahead and call — it doesn't hurt to ask. Maybe they will have room for some reason, perhaps because some participant has canceled at the last minute.

And for that matter, maybe somebody *will* ring your doorbell with a $10-million check. If that happens, you can hire us to come along on the tour and carry your scope for you!

Rules of the Road

Bird tours tend to be fairly informal. Dress is casual throughout — indeed, a cocktail dress or black-tie-and-tails can be a real handicap on a muddy forest trail — and people usually don't dress up for dinner. Some leaders ask that participants not wear brightly colored clothing in the field (with the idea that such clothing might alarm the birds), but they won't ask you to go naked if bright colors are all you've brought. And they probably won't roll you in mud.

TIP

The rules for taking part in a tour can be summarized in just two points: common sense and courtesy. Practice these, and you'll never go too wrong. It's common sense to keep conversation down while birding because the leaders may find many birds by sound and because noise might scare birds away. It's a matter of courtesy to be considerate of your fellow participants — not blocking their view at critical moments, for example, and not hogging the group's shared spotting scope.

You'll soon find that it comes naturally to be courteous to the other birders: On most tours, within a day or two, you'll have the strong feeling that you're traveling with friends.

You Can't Take It with You: Pack Light

Packing for a birding tour is not that different from packing for a field trip. For more on what gear to take with you, absorb the fascinating information provided in Chapter 14.

KEEP THE TIP

To tip or not to tip? That *is* a question, and the answers vary from one situation to another.

During the tour, if meals and lodging are included in the trip price, the leaders generally take care of tips in restaurants and hotels.

But should *you* tip the leader at the end of the trip? It depends. In some areas of the world, where local driver-guides cater to ecotourists — such as in East Africa or Costa Rica — they expect to be tipped, and your goodbyes at the end of the trip can feel very awkward if you aren't prepared for this moment. It helps if you've checked with the local outfitters or tour operators ahead of time to ask what an appropriate amount would be. You could also talk to other participants during the trip. Seasoned travelers who have gone with this company before can help guide your tipping decision.

As a consumer, though, you should remember that gratuities are just that, and they are *always* optional. If your leader or guide has been a total jerk (it's rare, but it can happen), there's no reason to give them anything. And if some leader has really gone out of their way for you — has gone way beyond the bird call of duty — they will welcome a tip or a small gift.

Whereas on a field trip you can chuck a bunch of stuff in the car, on a bird tour you might be hauling (or watching some poor tour leader haul) your gear through airports, hotel lobbies, and up mountainsides. You want to have enough of the vital things (clean socks, underwear, toothpaste, proper outerwear), but you definitely don't want to take anything unnecessary. For example: If you can't sleep without the whirring sound of a fan, perhaps you can use a relaxation sound app on your phone instead. Don't take the fan on a tour.

Bill Thompson III, author of the first edition of *Bird Watching For Dummies*, recalls a trip to Costa Rica one May:

> I was faced with the age-old question: rain boots or hiking boots? I could not take both. I was told by everyone *but* the tour company that I should plan to get soaked by rain at least twice a day. They said, "It's the rainy season there!" The tour company guy told me, "We call it the *green season.* It doesn't rain that much." I took rain boots. It rained once in about 10 days. We hiked all over the place, me wearing knee-high green waders. Yes, they were hot on my feet. Yes, I got blisters. Yes, Costa Rica was green at that season — almost as green as I was, gazing with envy at my fellow tour-takers who had brought sturdy light, cool, hiking boots.

REMEMBER

Your best bet is to follow the guidance offered by the tour company regarding what to take on a given bird tour. Ask specifically about weather extremes, footwear needed, and luggage allowances. Also ask about any local customs or social taboos. In some countries, you can get looks of horror and disdain (or worse) from the local populace simply for wearing short pants.

Final Stop

Taking a bird-watching tour can do lots of things for you: show you new and wonderful birds, allow you to make new friends, let you test your bird ID skills in a new place, and even lighten your bank account. Some birders are lifelong tour takers. They prefer to visit far-flung hotspots with a guide who helps them maximize their experience. Others like to take the occasional tour to spice up their bird-watching life. No matter which side of the scale you think you'll end up on, plan to take a birding tour at some point. If nothing else, you'll see lots of new birds and lots of other bird watchers.

Chapter **18**

Festivals and Other Events

t has been said that bird watching is the number one spectator sport in North America, which means it's bigger than professional sports such as basketball, baseball, football, hockey, auto racing, and golf.

How does this affect you, the bird watcher? It means that as the interest in birding has grown, so has the number of organized activities for bird watchers. In this chapter, you'll find out about some of the events that are specially designed for bird watchers. This includes everything from birding competitions to festivals to seminars and workshops. As you become more involved as a bird watcher, you'll find out about other events both near to home and far afield.

Let's Party!

It can be fun sitting alone in your backyard or on your deck, watching the birds that pass by. But if you're gregarious by nature, you may find yourself longing for somebody else to share your bird-watching experiences with. Sure, maybe that somebody else is your spouse or best friend. And then there's your local bird club. But maybe you still want more. What to do?

We bird watchers have been referred to as a "clan" many times by fellow birders, and by those outside the loop. "Flock," "family," and lots of less flattering terms have also been used. Like birds, bird watchers do like to flock together from time to time.

To satisfy this flocking urge, gatherings of bird watchers happen, sometimes spontaneously, all over North America, and beyond. Some of them start as informal parties — groups of friends gathering to have a good time and look at birds. Others are started by communities wishing, quite literally, to attract more tourists and their tourist dollars.

No matter what the initial impetus, the good news is that you have lots to choose from among the many festivals, Big Days, and other events for bird watchers.

TIP

Bill Thompson III, author of the first edition of *Bird Watching For Dummies*, recalled the first time he joined a group of birders:

> The first organized gathering of bird watchers I attended was at a hawk-watching and banding site. It wasn't even an open-to-the-public event. These were hardcore bird bums running this deal, and I was just a lowly high school kid interested in birds. I was very nervous. I didn't know the lingo or any of the other people there. And I certainly wasn't up to their speed as a birder. But I found that most of the people there were willing to explain things to an interested beginner. In fact, they were proud to get to show off their hawk know-how. I ended up having a great time.

So don't be shy! Don't assume that a hotshot won't want to share their knowledge with you. Likely the exact opposite is true.

Birding Festivals

Birding festivals come in all shapes and sizes. Some are held near locales where birds naturally have been gathering for eons. Many of the best festivals are organized around a natural phenomenon such as the gathering of sandhill cranes on their wintering grounds or the return of the Kirtland's warbler to its breeding grounds in Michigan. Other festivals are just excuses to get together with a bunch of bird watchers to talk shop and have fun.

New birding festivals are starting up all the time, and as can be expected, a few fold. But most keep steaming on, getting better with each year. The bird watchers in North America have an enormous economic impact. This is why many communities are working so diligently to come up with some "hook" to draw visiting bird watchers. A national survey by the U.S. Fish & Wildlife reports that wildlife watchers, which are dominated by bird watchers, added more than $250.2 billion to the economy in 2022. That's big bucks!

Finding festivals

When the Thompson family began publishing *Bird Watcher's Digest* in 1978, there weren't any well-known festivals for bird watchers. In fact, the only large gatherings of the bird-seeking crowd were when there was an abundance of birds, such as during fall migration at Hawk Mountain, Pennsylvania, or in the spring at High Island, Texas, or in the winter at one of the Florida refuges. Once or twice a year there would be an extremely rare bird found somewhere on the continent, and that would attract the hardcore contingent. But beyond the local bird club, bird watchers had few organized activities that they could attend.

Today, there is a birding festival held every month of the year somewhere in North America. Nearly every state and province has its own "Festival of the Something or Other." There are festivals for cranes, ducks, geese, shorebirds, warblers, vultures, swans, eagles, hawks, hummingbirds, and swallows. You name it, and there's probably a festival for it, or there will be soon.

The best method for finding festivals is to search online or look for ads in bird magazines. (We can think of one bird magazine we'd recommend especially!) Most festival organizers — sooner or later — advertise their event in a publication for bird watchers.

TIP

An excellent source for information is the All About Birds online list of birding festivals and events, hosted by Cornell Lab of Ornithology at `www.allaboutbirds.org/news/birding-festivals/`. This regularly updated list is searchable by date and location and offers event details and contact information.

Attending festivals

Here's some good advice to heed when attending a festival: **Book early.**

Although not all festivals limit the number of attendees, some do. Others may limit the number of attendees in particular seminars, or there may be limited seating in an auditorium where a well-known speaker is appearing. For your own sake, visit the festival's website and review the schedule of events in advance to see what's happening. There might be a can't-miss presentation, seminar, or speaker that you'll want to take in. Alternatively, there may be entire days that have little to interest you. That's the time to spend watching birds away from the hubbub of the festival.

REMEMBER

Many festivals offer numerous guided field trips, which can also fill up quickly. Field trips are usually capped for attendance so as to keep the group size manageable for guides. Plus, a smaller group is less likely to scare off the birds.

In addition to ensuring your place at the festival events, you may also want to make your travel and lodging arrangements in advance. Many long-running festivals have a high number of repeat attendees. These folks book their flights, rooms, and rental cars as much as a year in advance. The local chamber of commerce has a listing of accommodations and eateries, some of which may offer discounts to festival attendees. Because birding festivals tend to be where the birds are (away from major airports and metropolitan areas), your airline and rental car choices may be limited. Book early! Did we say that already?

TIP

While you're preparing to attend a festival in a distant state or province, find out about the weather at festival time. Bill Thompson III learned this the hard way:

> Some years ago, I was to be the featured speaker at a bird festival in a western state. I was so excited about visiting the region in April, thinking about all the life birds I'd see, that I completely forgot to ask about the weather. Somebody from the festival told me in passing that April was when things started warming up, but that was all the info I had. So, I packed for semi-warm spring weather and headed out west. As I got off the plane, my breath was taken away by a blast of freezing air. Before I chipped the ice off my rental car, I was nearly a human Popsicle. As I drove out of the parking lot, the snow started flying thicker than the ice worms on a polar bear. I asked a policeman where I could find a camping outfitter. He said, "Not from around here, are you?" A few hours and $245 later, I was on my way to the festival, looking like some scary vision from the L.L. Bean catalog. What the festival rep meant by "warming up" was that the water wasn't still frozen solid at festival time, and you could actually stay outside for minutes at a time.

Thinking BIG!

For the bird watcher who likes to compete for a personal best or against others, there is another brand of event: the competitive bird count, sometimes called a Big Day.

Bird watchers love to think big, as in Big Day, Big Sit, and Big Year. "What's a Big Day?" we hear you mutter. It's a day during which you try to see or hear as many bird species as possible. Big Days are usually conducted within a set geographical area, such as a state or county, and must be accomplished within a single 24-hour period, often midnight to midnight.

WARNING

On a Big Day bird count, you're supposed to count the number of species, not the number of individual birds you see. One time a guy came to the tally gathering and said he'd seen more than 2,000 birds. He thought he'd surely be the winner. Then someone explained that the competition was to see how many *species* he could see. Oops!

Big Days: What's the big deal?

There are four reasons for doing a Big Day:

>> To get a big list of birds. This allows you to brag to your friends.

>> To record the migratory birds present in your area for scientific purposes

>> To raise money for bird conservation, your local bird club, or another worthwhile cause

>> To have fun! Trying to see 100 species on a May day can be pure fun.

For more on organized bird counts, see Chapter 19.

Organizing your own Big Day

You can create your own Big Day count. You don't need to pay an entry fee or have your veracity checked by a board of governors. Pick a date on which you know lots of bird species will be present in your area and go for it! You don't even need to stay up for 24 hours. You can maximize the number of hours spent in the field and reduce the number of hours spent slumped behind the wheel of your car straining to hear a bird — any bird — and wishing you were home in bed.

A sane Big Day typically starts at or just before dawn with the participants searching for night birds such as owls, rails, and nightjars, and carries on until nightfall. Participants often enjoy meeting someplace for dinner and to tally their species count.

BIRD-WATCHING COMPETITIONS

It was inevitable that, with the (usually) friendly competition that exists among birders, an organized event for teams of birders would be created. The most successful of these competitions is the annual World Series of Birding, which has been run by the New Jersey Audubon Society since 1984. Teams entered in this 24-hour birdathon are racing the clock, the elements, and each other to try to see or hear the maximum number of bird species within the state of New Jersey between midnight and the following midnight on a weekend in early May.

This date coincides with the projected peak in the spring bird migration, which can be an absolutely awesome phenomenon in New Jersey and elsewhere along the East Coast. Northbound migrants flying along the Atlantic Coast are funneled across Delaware Bay to the southern tip of New Jersey. In recent years, the winning teams' totals have surpassed the 200 species mark, and the event has attracted corporate sponsorship. Best of all, many teams raise money for conservation through per-bird pledges. The success of the World Series has prompted spring birdathons in other parts of North America. For more information about the World Series, visit `https://njaudubon.org/world-series-of-birding/`.

Another major player on the scene of competitions is the Great Texas Birding Classic, a month-long, state-wide bird-watching tournament with various participation categories to choose from. In 2024, 212 teams and more than 1,200 birders participated in this tournament! Because Texas boasts one of the highest species tallies among states and provinces in North America, participants in this competition are certain to see lots and lots of birds. Visit `https://tpwd.texas.gov/events/great-texas-birding-classic` for more information.

The Big Sit

For every action, there is an equal and opposite reaction. Isaac Newton's third law of motion applies to bird watching, too. For those who dislike the race-around-ticking-off-birds-on-your-checklist mentality of the Big Day/birdathon set, there is the Big Sit. Not just a birding event for the La-Z-Boy crowd, a Big Sit can be every bit as much fun as a Big Day. What's truly amazing, however, is how many birds you can tally simply by staying put and watching and listening — in some areas, Big Sitters can tally more than 100 species without ever leaving the count circle. The totals of species seen or heard for some of the North American Big Sit counts are quite comparable to many Big Day efforts.

The concept for a Big Sit is to do just that: sit. You're also trying to see or hear as many birds as possible while sitting in a predetermined circle size. Some Big

Sitters have elevated this event to a high art, bringing barbecue grills, entire carloads of provisions, portable heaters, electric generators, and other camping gear. Since 1992, Connecticut's New Haven Bird Club has organized a free international event called "The Big Sit!" held annually on a mid-October weekend. The event has become a beloved tradition for many birders around the world.

The rules for "The Big Sit!" are simple. Choose a good site, one with a variety of habitats. Mark off a circle with a 17-foot diameter. Set up your Big Sit site with all you need, and you're ready to go. You may count the birds you see and hear from the circle, but you may not leave the circle to find new birds. You are permitted to leave the circle to confirm the identification of a bird. Learn more at www.thebigsit.org/.

Going to School

Some events for bird watchers are more educational in nature. A number of online courses, weekend seminars, and skill-building workshops are available for bird watchers. Some are offered as part of annual festivals, while others are from accredited colleges and universities or offered by bird clubs, bird observatories, state and federal refuges, parks, and nature centers.

Among the most popular topics for bird watchers are field identification courses or seminars, particularly those dealing with a (sometimes difficult) group of birds, such as fall warblers, hawks, sparrows, and shorebirds, especially peeps (small sandpipers). Also popular are courses in beginning bird watching, bird song identification, and anything having to do with birds in the backyard (feeding, gardening for, housing for, and so on).

Ask your birding pals about such classes or search the internet for birding courses and seminars on topics of interest to you. We recommend the self-paced online courses offered by Cornell Lab of Ornithology's Bird Academy as an excellent starting point: https://academy.allaboutbirds.org.

Spreading the Word

When traveling in search of birds, you have the opportunity to do your part to promote an awareness of the economic impact of bird watching. Rather than leave your binoculars in your car, wear them into a restaurant, gas station, or shop. Binoculars are the best way to say, "I'm here to see the birds of your region." And implicitly, "So please protect their habitat, and I will be back to visit your establishment again."

If you're asked about them, even better. Explain that you are visiting the area to watch birds. Express your pleasure with the natural areas of the regions and thank the locals for their community's attention to maintaining these spaces. Tell them about the rare bird you hoped to see.

Here's how such a conversation might go:

> **You:** "Hi, I'd like the eggs Benedict and a cup of coffee, please."
>
> **Waiter:** "Are you a bird watcher?" (points to your bins)
>
> **You:** "Yes, I am. You have a lot of wonderful birds in this area!"
>
> **Waiter:** "I see great blue cranes down at the lake all the time."
>
> **You:** "Sounds like you're a bird watcher, too!"

It's important that bird watchers let our economic presence be felt. Some birders even leave small business cards that read, "Your business has been patronized by a bird watcher. Preserve habitat for the birds. Bird watching is big business!"

5
Once
You're Hooked

Chapter **19**

Birding That Makes a Difference

E veryone has their own reasons for watching birds. Perhaps you're captivated by the beauty of birds. Or maybe you're fascinated by the variety of birds and the changing of the guard from season to season. Perhaps you love the rush of chasing a rarity or watching the numbers on your life list grow. Maybe bird watching for you is an excuse to get outdoors or an opportunity for social interaction with other bird watchers. There are nearly as many reasons to watch birds as there are people who participate.

Many bird watchers find satisfaction by participating in data-collecting projects. *Ornithology* (the science of bird study) has been called the last great amateur science. In recent decades, more research has required experts to study the technical aspects of DNA (the genetic fabric that makes each living thing unique), but unlike other sciences, ornithology has been built upon the incredible mass of data collected by amateurs — bird watchers. The opportunity to contribute, even in a small way, appeals to a lot of people, and many opportunities exist for all of us bird watchers to add to the science of the study of birds.

In this chapter, we provide information on many of the most popular bird-watching projects — and ways of finding out about others out there. We also provide information about bird clubs and how to find one that's right for you.

Doing Field Work That Matters

Bird watchers who participate in projects think of them as a way of giving something back for the enjoyment birds afford them. We know, however, that many bird populations are on a steep decline, and we want to help reverse that. Just by reporting our bird observations, we can contribute to avian conservation. Bird watching is a source of great pleasure, and bird watchers are pleased that their recreation can be beneficial to birds and to science. Our individual efforts may not seem to be significant, but as part of a larger effort, we can help scientists understand birds and may help save some species. In fact, birders can become "citizen scientists" when they participate in field research or report their observations.

REMEMBER

Bird watching makes people more aware of the natural world, and bird watchers are among the first to notice when a habitat is destroyed, when bird populations decline, and when the landscape changes. In a small but significant way, the data that bird watchers collect helps scientists and public officials make more intelligent decisions about land use and conservation.

Who, me?

Yes, *you* can make a difference to birds. Absolutely. You don't need to be an expert or a scientist. Everyone can play a part.

As we mention earlier in this chapter, almost everything we know about the real lives of birds — as opposed to, say, the genetic distinctions of related species — comes from information gathered by amateurs. It is the amassed data of amateurs that tells us which bird species are declining and which are increasing, and whether various species' ranges are expanding or shrinking. The great bulk of what we know about the migration of birds has come from the amassed data of amateurs (although geolocators and nanotechnology have added tremendously to that knowledge in recent years).

You don't need to be a hotshot or hair-trigger quick with field identifications. To a scientist, the family of woodpeckers at your feeder may be more interesting than the rarity an expert finds. If you're interested, you can participate in gathering and sharing this information on any level.

eBird is for the birds

By using eBird to record your bird observations (see Chapter 12), you're actually reporting them each time you submit a checklist. Your checklists — and literally millions of others submitted around the world — become part of a database of the geographic distribution of each bird species reported, the timing of their presence at various locations, the growth or decline of populations, the expansion or contraction of ranges, and so much more.

eBird turns recreation into science; eBirders are truly citizen scientists, even when they're just enjoying the birds and keeping lists (as many bird watchers do). If you go to https://ebird.org and click the Science tab, you'll see the data birders just like us have contributed, including population status trends, abundance maps, and ground truthing for long-established range maps. Bird populations are dynamic, and birders' observations continually update our knowledge of range expansions and contractions.

At https://science.ebird.org/en/status-and-trends/abundance-animations, one of the sample animations shows the barn swallow, which has a nearly global range. (See Figure 19-1.) This animation is based entirely on eBird checklists submitted by bird watchers. As the year starts, all the barn swallows on Earth appear to be in the tropics or southern hemisphere, represented by bright colors. The northern latitudes are devoid of this species. But, as the animation progresses through April and May, we can see barn swallows moving to North America and Europe to breed, as South America, Africa, and southern Asia go from vibrant to gray. During September and October, the northern latitudes appear to drain, going from dark purple and red (dense) to orange and yellow (less dense) to gray — empty of barn swallows. Watching this animation takes about 20 seconds, and it's pretty amazing.

Those of us who report our bird observations via eBird — regular people — helped build this map by providing the data of when and where they spotted barn swallows. It's not only cool; it's gratifying to know that our delightful hobby has provided the information required to build these vivid demonstrations of seasonal bird movements.

How to find out what's going on: bird clubs

Projects for interested bird watchers are everywhere. The trick is connecting with them. The place to start is with your local bird club. The local club is nearly always the organizer of field projects in a given area. As soon as you make it clear to others in your bird club that you're interested, you'll be contacted to help, because, as in so many things, there are always more projects than there are volunteers.

FIGURE 19-1:
Juvenile barn
swallows prepare
for migration.

Finding your local bird club shouldn't be hard. We'll get to that later in this chapter. If you don't have a local club, start your own! (We'll get to that soon, too.)

REMEMBER

No matter what your area of interest — tallying species, bird banding, bird feeding, hawk-watching, monitoring nest boxes, observing chimney swifts, managing purple martins, or whatever — a project is going on that you can be part of. All it takes is a bit of enthusiasm and commitment. Since you're reading this chapter, you've demonstrated both.

Tens of thousands of bird watchers in your neighborhood and around the world help with important bird conservation projects. Some you even can help with without leaving the comfort of your own home!

Projects That Count (Birds)

Based on the number of participants worldwide, bird conservation projects that involve finding birds, tallying species, and counting individual birds are the most popular. It's what most birders do for pleasure anyhow, so why not convert those observations to useful, important scientific data? Most of these projects encourage (or require) using eBird to submit your observations, but you'll be adding to your personal lists, as well.

Christmas Bird Count

The Christmas Bird Count (CBC) is the granddaddy of all citizen science projects. Tens of thousands of bird watchers participate every year, and the CBCs have been going on for more than a century. For all of the twentieth century and into the twenty-first, most of what we knew about the winter distribution of birds and about winter bird populations came from CBCs. Today, eBird reveals this information throughout the year, but the CBC is no less important. *Everyone* can participate in a Christmas Bird Count — there's even a category for feeder watchers (folks who count only the birds seen at their feeders). This category is wonderful if you live in the Yukon and don't like being out in the howling wind and snow, or if you live in Hoboken and still hate howling wind and snow.

The Christmas Bird Count is exactly what it sounds like — a count, or census, of birds, and it is held between December 14 and January 5. Sponsored by the National Audubon Society in the U.S. and Birds Canada up north, CBCs are all conducted in designated circles 15 miles in diameter. The purpose is to try to find and count as many individual birds as possible in each given circle on a given day within that timeframe. More than 2,500 counts are held in North, Central, and South America, and on Caribbean and Pacific Islands, so surely there is one near where you live.

Each CBC is organized and run by a local bird club or state bird group. Each group decides the boundaries of the count circle and sets the day of the event. A count compiler works to make certain that all participants are assigned to a territory within that count circle. Crossing into a neighboring territory is considered poaching! Competition among groups within a count circle is all in good fun. The purpose is not to have a winning territory but to get an accurate tally of all the birds and species in the entire circle on that day.

Each count lasts 24 hours, from midnight to midnight, but almost nobody is crazy enough to spend the whole 24 hours in the field. Very few birds can be found in the dark, especially in winter in the colder parts of North America! Some people start shortly before dawn, hoping to hear owls. (See Figure 19-2.) Most people start at sunrise, when birds are just becoming active, and continue counting until late afternoon or dusk, or until they are satisfied that they've covered their territory and have a reasonably accurate count.

Each team can use eBird to enter their observations, creating a new checklist for each spot they visit in their territory. You can create an eBird Trip Report for the date of the CBC, and each checklist you submit will be tallied for the trip. This makes it easy for each group to report their sightings at the end of the day and share with the circle's compiler.

Traditionally, the group assigned to each territory kept a tally sheet on paper, and some still do — not that there's anything wrong with that.

FIGURE 19-2:
Christmas Bird
Counters owling
(Eastern
screech-owl).

A nice part of most CBCs is the *tally-rally*. At the end of the count day — or the following day — the counters gather, usually at a volunteer's house or local eatery. They'll spend a couple of pleasant hours sharing the experiences of the day, warming up with hot soup, and sharing each territory's results. For many CBC participants, the tally-rally is one of the most anticipated social events of the bird-watching year.

At the tally-rally, the count circle's compiler aggregates the day's sightings from each territory so they can send the results to the National Audubon Society or Birds Canada. Groups can share their eBird Trip Report with the compiler with the click of a few buttons (which is convenient), or they can turn in their paper tally sheet.

Now that bird watchers can contribute data throughout the year, at any location, is the Christmas Bird Count still relevant? Yes. The longitudinal data collected by Christmas Bird Counters is invaluable in assessing changing bird populations. (See Figure 19-3.) Many counts have been going on at specific locations for decades. With so many counts scattered across the country, it's possible to see regional differences in which birds are declining and which are increasing. eBird has only been around since the early days of this century. Someday it, too, will be a longitudinal database, but the CBC has a head start of nearly a century.

FIGURE 19-3:
House finch
and loggerhead
shrike population
trends.

The spread of the house finch, a western species introduced to New York by the pet trade, throughout the eastern parts of North America showed up first on Christmas Bird Counts. Similarly, the decline in many bird species, like the loggerhead shrike, was first noted by CBC participants. Whole books have been written analyzing the results of CBCs. Your little corner of the local count circle may not seem important, but when you discover that they've put a shopping center in your favorite field, the lack of birds reported becomes noteworthy. In Christmas Bird Counts, every data point matters, even the absence of birds that were present in previous years!

REMEMBER

The most important thing about participating in a CBC is that you don't have to be an expert. Others on your count can help you with bird identification. All you really need to be able to do is watch for birds — and count. (You do have to be able to count.) To find your local Christmas Bird Count, get in touch with your local bird club, or visit www.audubon.org/community-science/christmas-bird-count/join-christmas-bird-count.

HOW THE CHRISTMAS BIRD COUNT STARTED

The Christmas Bird Count started in 1900 as an alternative to the *sidehunt*, a fairly common custom until the early part of the 20th century. It involved going out for several hours on Christmas morning and shooting every bird and animal that one came across. Frank Chapman, one of the great early ornithologists, started the Christmas Count to counter the hunt. He encouraged a few friends around the country to go afield on Christmas morning and count, rather than kill. For the first two decades, the counts grew slowly, but in the second half of the 20th century, the counts exploded in popularity.

Global Big Days

In North America, spring migration reaches its crescendo in early to mid-May and, for many years, various local bird clubs held "birdathons" or celebrated World Migratory Bird Day (see the aptly named "World Migratory Bird Day" section, later in this chapter) or sponsored competitive Big Days during this exciting period. In 2015, the Cornell Lab of Ornithology planned the first Global Big Day, encouraging individual bird watchers and birding teams around the world to report, via eBird, all the bird species they saw on May 9 of that year. Such an event would provide a one-day snapshot of the world's birds. Organizers hoped 4,000 species would be reported. Well, 6,085 species were reported by 14,060 participants on seven continents! That's some maiden voyage! Since then, this event has grown, both in participation and birds reported.

An autumn Global Big Day is held in October each year to take a similar snapshot of fall bird patterns. Both the May and October Global Big Days occur at the same time as World Migratory Bird Day (more to come on that) and Global Birding Weekend, a project of BirdLife International.

REMEMBER

On Global Big Days, you can either form a team to spend the entire day amassing species and tallies or you can just go walk your dog around the block, keeping your ears and eyes open for birds, keeping track of what you see and hear on eBird. Or bird your backyard for a few minutes — or all day! The only requirement for participating is to submit your observations via eBird.

Too bad all science projects aren't this easy and so much fun!

Project FeederWatch

Like eBird, Project FeederWatch is also run by the Cornell Laboratory of Ornithology, in partnership with Birds Canada. This project attracts tens of thousands of people from across the continent who report how many birds visit their feeders from November through April. If you can identify the birds that visit your feeders, you're qualified to participate, and you can do it from your kitchen (or some other) window. The Lab offers lots of assistance at https://feederwatch.org/.

Project FeederWatch started in the late 1980s, so, like the Christmas Bird Count, it can provide longitudinal data at specific locations. Its data is used to monitor winter bird populations, abundance, and distribution as well as irruptions (sudden invasions of nomadic species) and changes in winter ranges. For example, Project FeederWatch data show that the winter population of painted bunting has steadily declined during the past three decades.

REMEMBER

There is a fee for participation, but it's fun, convenient, easy, and important. For more information or to sign up, visit https://feederwatch.org/.

Great Backyard Bird Count

The Cornell Lab of Ornithology, Birds Canada, and Audubon partner for the Great Backyard Bird Count, a four-day event in February for which "backyard" means virtually any place on Earth. You can submit an eBird checklist from numerous locations during the event as often as you wish, but you must observe and count birds for 15 minutes or more on each checklist. As with Project FeederWatch, you can even observe birds through a window from the comfort of your easy chair, if you like. In this event, however, it's okay to look beyond the feeder after you've finished tallying birds and species enjoying the buffet you provided for them.

TIP

The GBBC is ideal for organizing a community event, and kids are welcome to help find and count birds. For more information on this event, visit https://www.birdcount.org/.

Atlasing

Many states and provinces (sometimes even counties) have conducted Breeding Bird Atlas projects. A Breeding Bird Atlas is just what it sounds like — an effort to determine which species of birds are nesting in a given area and record their distribution within the state/province/county, resulting in maps for each species. In almost all atlases, the focus area is divided into a grid of blocks; volunteers are assigned one or more blocks to survey during the summer to find breeding birds. Atlas fieldwork is conducted entirely by volunteers, and local clubs are always at the center of recruiting for them.

The Breeding Bird Atlas is a project that requires the ability to identify (by sight and/or by sound) all the bird species that possibly nest in your area. Most atlas work is done on the basis of the mere presence of the birds and clues such as seeing birds carrying food or nesting material, not necessarily on finding nests. A persistently singing male, like the Kentucky warbler in Figure 19-4, can indicate breeding activity at a given location.

A lot of bird watchers love atlas work because it's another reason to go afield in the summer, the slowest season for most watchers. Atlas fieldwork also is an opportunity to observe birds in their home life, not as migrants or winter visitors. It is a whole different way of looking at birds, and many people have become nearly addicted to it. Atlasing often takes participants off the beaten path to get to their assigned blocks, rather than to favorite birding patches or hotspots. A feeling of exploration accompanies atlasing fieldwork.

TIP

Most atlas projects take six years, start to finish. After 20 years, the project is often repeated. The way to find out about atlasing is to contact your local or state-wide bird club or ornithological organization. If neither of these sources works, contact the state/provincial Department of Natural Resources. This office may be able to tell you the status of any ongoing atlasing projects. (The U.S. Geological Survey maintains a list of Breeding Bird Atlases in the U.S. and Canada at www.pwrc.usgs.gov/bba/index.cfm?fa=bba.BbaHome&view=list).

FIGURE 19-4:
A singing Kentucky warbler — a bird more often heard than seen.

Atlas projects have turned out to be very useful to state governments as they try to make land-use decisions and plan for long-term development and conservation. The results of atlas projects allow state governments to see at a glance where the greatest numbers of birds are, along with the locations of important habitats.

Breeding Bird Survey

The Breeding Bird Survey, jointly run by the U.S. Geological Survey's Eastern Ecological Science Center and Environment Canada's Canadian Wildlife Service, uses volunteers to monitor breeding bird populations. It requires familiarity with bird songs, and most participants are moderately experienced bird watchers. An online training program is required before routes are assigned.

However, even the newest beginning bird watcher can tag along to help out with keeping records, running the time clock, or driving the vehicle used for the survey — and learning by hanging out with a more experienced bird watcher. Volunteering for this survey is a great way to learn bird songs from experts at birding by ear.

A Breeding Bird Survey (BBS) is a 25-mile route along secondary roads with 50 stops, each stop one half-mile apart. At each stop, the observers count all the birds heard or seen during a three-minute period. More than 4,100 routes across Canada and the U.S. are checked by more than 2,500 volunteers as part of the BBS. This project has been going on since 1966, and its results have been used by more than 450 scientific publications.

These surveys are conducted in late spring and early summer, when migrant species have already passed through the area, and breeding birds have set up territories but haven't entered the less active period during nesting. At this time, which varies with the advent of spring at different latitudes, male birds are most vocally active, singing to advertise themselves and their chosen territories to interested females. BBS runs are begun in the early mornings, just before dawn, when bird song is at its peak. Because it's often not yet light, and because of the short time at each spot, almost all the birds tallied are heard rather than seen. The results of the BBS routes run all over the continent every year provide useful data on changing songbird populations.

To find out more about the BBS, visit https://www.usgs.gov/centers/eesc/science/north-american-breeding-bird-survey.

Hawk watches

Tallying and reporting migrating hawks is a thing — an important thing — conducted at more than 300 designated North American Hawkwatch sites spanning the continent. While hawks are migrating (generally from March through May and September through mid-November), these sites are staffed by volunteer or professional hawk counters who tally raptors as they fly by and then submit a daily report of their observations. Four organizations, the Hawk Migration Association of North America (www.hmana.org/), HawkWatch International (https://hawkwatch.org/), Hawk Mountain (https://www.hawkmountain.org/), and Birds Canada (https://www.birdscanada.org/) collaborate to produce the Raptor Population Index (www.rpi-project.org/).

Visit https://hawkcount.org/ to find a hawk-watching site near you. Follow links as necessary for directions and hours of operation and plan a visit during spring and fall migration. Visitors are welcome and sometimes enlisted to help the official (trained) hawk talliers. While there, don't disturb the official counter on duty. Their attention must be fixed on the skies. An assistant (perhaps a person recording the counter's observations) might have time to answer your questions or chat. At some hawk-watch sites, many visitors are common — some come daily during peak migration, because if your timing is right, hawk-watch sites can be thrilling.

20,145 BROAD-WINGED HAWKS

Several years ago, Dawn happened to be passing by Lake Erie Metropark on the northwestern shore of Lake Erie, about 20 miles south of Detroit, Michigan. From September 1 to November 30 each year, that's the site of the Detroit River Hawk Watch. Since she had enjoyed visiting several other hawk-watch sites, she decided to stop by. The site is on the edge of a waterway with a boat launch. It feels like a metropark, with mowed grass, a playground, and picnic tables scattered around. Kids were playing, dogs were being walked, and dozens of people sat near the raptor counter and his scope and the nearby tallier. The sky was bright blue with puffy clouds, and a slight breeze felt good — a lovely day to be out with the birds. And, oh, the birds! High in the sky, directly above those who were paying attention, were swarms and spirals of broad-winged hawks, soaring on thermals and leisurely making their way south. More and more kettles (flocks) of broadwings appeared at the northern horizon — hundreds of birds in each group, so many that it seemed impossible for anyone to count them. (Official hawk counters are trained on how to do this. Dawn is not.) They kept coming and coming! According to Hawkcount.org, 20,145 broad-winged hawks were tallied at that site on that day, mostly late in the afternoon, when Dawn was there. What amazing luck.

Swift Night Out

Anyone can be a Swiftie, even if you're not a pop music fan. Since you're still new to bird watching, you might not know how cool chimney swifts are, or that their populations are declining. There aren't enough pages in this book to describe all the cool birds in North America, but this one species deserves extra attention:

>> They can't perch on horizontal surfaces or even wires, but instead cling to rough vertical surfaces, like inside chimneys or hollow trees.

>> They winter in northwestern South America but nest across the eastern half of the U.S. and in southern Canada.

>> Their nests, usually inside chimneys, are made of sticks glued together with their spit.

>> There's only one nest per chimney, but they roost communally.

>> When not nesting or roosting, they fly almost constantly. During bad weather, they shelter on vertical surfaces, such as inside chimneys. (Their name is appropriate!)

>> As they prepare to head south in the fall, they mass in spirals at dusk, dropping into chimneys to roost for the night — dozens or hundreds or thousands per chimney. (See Figure 19-5.) They look like a gyre of smoke descending into a chimney. (Their exit at dawn is less dramatic.)

FIGURE 19-5:
Chimney swifts
dive into a stack
in autumn.

And as mentioned previously, the population of chimney swifts is declining. Swift Night Out is a locally organized, continent-wide effort to draw attention and interest in chimney swifts (in the East) and their close cousins, Vaux's swifts (in the West). Bird clubs or nature centers often host these events, usually in late August or early September. It's easy to get the community involved in attempting to count the swirling birds as they dive into a big chimney! Information on chimney swifts and ideas for hosting a Swift Night Out are at chimneyswifts.org. Data from such events are no longer collected at that site since an eBird checklist submission does the job instead.

There's a no-counting-required aspect to swift conservation, too. Since big, old, hollow trees — the natural nesting and roost sites of most North American swifts — are often deemed dangerous and cut, and since so many chimneys are lined or capped, some communities have gone so far as to build thoughtfully designed towers for swifts. There are lots of photos, building plans, and success stories on the internet. Check chimneyswifts.org or search for "swift tower."

No Counting Required (But Important, Anyhow)

The projects above require counting birds, resulting in quantitative data used in scientific research. There are other important ways to help with bird conservation, though.

World Migratory Bird Day

World Migratory Bird Day (previously called International Migratory Bird Day) kicked off in 1993, a creation of the Smithsonian Migratory Bird Center. It began as a celebration of the return of more than 350 migratory birds to North America from their wintering grounds to the south. Since 2007, the event has been coordinated by Environment for the Americas (EFTA), a nonprofit organization with the goal of connecting people to bird conservation.

In 2018, EFTA joined the Convention on Migratory Species and the Agreement on the Conservation of African-Eurasian Migratory Water Birds, and World Migratory Bird Day was born (replacing International Migratory Bird Day). WMBD's goal is to bring attention to the plight of migratory birds (many species of which have been declining in frightening numbers in recent decades) and to encourage birders to get involved in bird conservation. This global alliance spotlights migratory bird conservation around the world through a campaign organized around major flyways. By using one event name and a shared annual conservation theme, World Migratory Bird Day combines many voices into a unified chorus to promote the urgent need for migratory bird conservation around the world.

EFTA continues to focus on the flyways of the western hemisphere, highlighting the American flyways, their habitats, and the birds that use them. Each year, its educational programs are regularly held in parks, wildlife refuges, museums, schools, and at birding club programs.

Just like the spring Global Big Day, World Migratory Bird Day is celebrated on the second Saturday of May in the United States and Canada. In South America, it is often celebrated the second Saturday in October. But the event varies by region, and the organizers of WMBD encourage those who wish to promote migratory bird awareness, appreciation, and conservation to hold WMBD events throughout the year. Educational materials, both free and for purchase, are available at the WMBD website, https://migratorybirdday.org/.

Hands-on experience: banding

Banding birds is another activity in which a beginner can participate. Thousands of people across the continent band birds, many in their backyards. Of course, training is required, as well as a federal license.

**TECHNICAL
STUFF**

Banding birds means capturing the birds and placing a numbered band on one leg. Bird banders usually use fine mist nets designed for the purpose. The process doesn't hurt the birds, and the bands put on the birds' lower legs are lightweight aluminum or plastic. One advantage to banding for the beginner is that having the bird in the hand makes species identification simpler.

What's the point of putting a numbered band on a bird's leg? Banding involves more than installing bling. Each bird captured is weighed, measured, and given a fat check (a health assessment, not a piece of paper with large dollar amount written twice). Its age and sex are also determined and recorded; a uniquely numbered band is loosely closed around the lower leg; and the bird is released. This data is reported to the U.S. Bird Banding Laboratory or the Canadian Wildlife Service Banding Office. When banded birds are recaptured, or when a bird wearing a band is found dead, we can learn about longevity, movements, changes in population, and more. From recapturing banded birds, we have learned that some birds have very different northbound and southbound migration routes. We have also learned that some birds with specific nesting areas they use every year also have specific wintering areas they faithfully use — even when the population of that species has broad nesting and wintering ranges.

TIP

Almost every part of the country has active bird banders who are looking for volunteer help. The easiest way to find them is through a local bird club. To become a bird bander yourself requires working with a licensed bander until you qualify. The bands come from the U.S. Fish and Wildlife Service, which requires that you demonstrate some experience before you can be licensed.

To find out more about bird banding, visit `www.usgs.gov/labs/bird-banding-laboratory`.

Helping Out with Local Projects

Many opportunities exist to volunteer and participate in bird-related projects. Some of them are research-based scientific studies, while other opportunities require only your enthusiasm, willingness to help others, and perhaps a little elbow grease. If there is a national, state, or regional park, nature center, or wildlife refuge near you, odds are high that they would appreciate a reliable volunteer who is interested in wild birds.

Refuge volunteer

Virtually every national wildlife refuge (NWR) is looking for volunteers for a variety of projects, from building and marking trails to counting birds, participating in Christmas Bird Counts, keeping bird feeders clean and full, leading birding hikes, and so on. If you live near a national wildlife refuge, simply drive in and ask the refuge staff about volunteering. Chances are they'll be thrilled by your offer, and you can bet they'll find something for you to do. Some NWRs have a "friends" group that presents programs, helps with work days, organizes events, and otherwise helps out at the refuge. Many NWRs are staffed primarily by seasonal employees with just a few permanent staff, so they are grateful for any help they can get.

State and local parks

The needs and opportunities at wildlife refuges are similar at state, county, and city parks. They are always looking for volunteers to help with bird-oriented projects. Many of the programs at these parks — including bird walks, school outings, bird-watching presentations, and bird censuses — are run by volunteers. You can get information from any local park or by calling your state department of natural resources, department of recreation, or wildlife office.

Bird rehabilitation centers

If you want real hands-on experience, try volunteering at a local wild-bird rehabilitation center. These are the facilities where people bring injured, sick, or orphaned birds. (See Figure 19-6.) Often run entirely by volunteers, usually with donations and a willing veterinarian or licensed rehabilitator, rehab centers are constantly in need of people willing to make the commitment to help individual animals.

FIGURE 19-6:
An orphaned
American robin
fledgling.

Dealing with wildlife is not for everyone. It's time-consuming. (Try feeding baby birds every 30 minutes from dawn to dusk!) Sometimes, no matter how dedicated the rehabilitation effort, the bird doesn't recover, which is disheartening. But for the people who participate in rehabbing birds, the satisfaction of successfully saving a bird outweighs all other considerations.

Bird rehabilitation centers exist across the continent, but not every community has one. Rehabilitation centers must be licensed by state and federal wildlife protection authorities and must meet strict standards for the care of wild animals. That said, they do not receive state or federal funds. Because fundraising for these nonprofits is vital, they tend to be located near larger cities; rural areas, where the need can be greatest, are sadly underrepresented. And nearly all wildlife rehabilitation centers are understaffed.

All birds, except for a few so-called pest species such as European starling, rock pigeon, and house sparrow, are protected by law in North America. You need to have federal and state (or provincial) permits to handle birds, even if you have the best intentions. Believe it or not, you need permits even to pick up feathers! This may sound strange, but it's the only way to protect birds from exploitation or irresponsible handling. It is legal to pick up an ill or injured bird with the intention of transporting it to a rehabber, but it is not legal to attempt rehabilitation without a permit.

TIP

Baby birds hopping around on the ground, even alone, probably don't need your help. Leave them alone — or move them to a higher perch nearby. Odds are very high that their parents are still tending to them. Try to keep predators (dogs and cats) and other dangers (toddlers, lawn mowers) away from such baby birds, but don't take them indoors or move them too far from where you found them. Read more about this in Chapter 22.

The first place to check for a rehab center near you is the internet. Search for "wildlife rehabilitation (your state or province)." If you are lucky, you will find a list of rehabbers that accept birds and aren't too far from you. Or check with the state agency that deals with wildlife because it licenses and oversees the operations of wildlife rehab centers.

One other potential source for information about nearby bird and wildlife rehab centers is your local veterinarian. Vets are faced with many injured and sick birds found and brought to their offices by well-meaning souls, but because it's a slippery slope, almost none will treat them, so it's a good bet that your local vet knows where the nearest licensed rehabilitator is. (Not all vets are trained to treat wild birds or other wild animals.)

Going the Bird Club Route

Along with the well-known national projects, thousands of projects organized and run by local bird clubs exist. The vast majority of bird clubs are local groups of like-minded bird watchers who get together occasionally for field trips and social events. These clubs are, for the most part, entirely run by volunteers, and the dues paid by members cover the club's expenses. These clubs focus on enjoyment, camaraderie, the common appreciation of birds, the desire to draw public attention to wild birds, and to promote their conservation.

Several thousand bird clubs exist in North America, and these clubs come in many sizes, forms, and intensities. Some are well-run, venerable institutions staffed by paid professionals who operate the club, produce the club's publications, maintain their websites, post their social media, hold events, and handle the chores associated with large membership rolls. Perhaps a few dozen clubs operate like this in

North America, but even they rely on volunteers. Most bird clubs are entirely volunteer-powered.

After you get in touch with your local club, you will find no shortage of opportunity and no shortage of work to be done. For example, many parks, refuges, and nature preserves are created because of lobbying by local bird watchers and other nature enthusiasts who have recognized the importance of the site. In addition, many local clubs have bird counts beyond the traditional Christmas Bird Count and spring migration count. Some local clubs sponsor special waterfowl or raptor censuses, some monitor grassland birds, northern saw-whet owls, or chimney swifts, some offer bird-feeder cleaning events as fundraisers or pick up litter in local waterways, some bring bird watching to schools, libraries, or retirement homes, and so on. Most bird clubs arrange birding trips to local (or distant) hotspots, and welcome newcomers, especially those new to bird watching.

REMEMBER

Every bird club, even a small one, has a variety of committees. Someone has to organize the field trips, set up the programs, oversee refreshments, organize letter-writing campaigns, serve as liaison to local government and other groups, and fill the offices of president, treasurer, editor of the newsletter, and on and on. If you really want to feel loved and needed, show up at a bird club meeting and ask: "Is there anything I can do to help?"

You can join a bird club without helping out, but if you volunteer for a project, being a part of it adds something to your experience. Bird watching is a hobby, a pleasurable way of putting the pressures of the world aside, but it can also be a way to contribute to bird conservation. Contributing can be a source of pleasure in itself; it can even be life-affirming!

Finding a bird club

TIP

Finding a bird club in your area can be as easy as asking another bird watcher whom you encounter in the field. Any gathering of more than two bird watchers can be considered a bird club! But it's not always so simple. The American Birding Association maintains a list of birding clubs and organizations organized by state and Canada at www.aba.org/birding-clubs-organizations/.

If you use Facebook, you can search on the name of your city or state and the words "birding" or "birds" or "bird club" to see if there are any Facebook pages or groups in your area. Regional or local Facebook birding groups are a great way to learn the names of serious bird watchers in your area. Such groups can also fill you in on what has shown up recently, indicate some of the local hotspots, and let you know of events coming up.

REMEMBER

Some Facebook birding groups are private to control spam. You might have to contact the group administrator to request membership.

You can also do an internet search of bird clubs in your locale. For example, a search on "Birding club Bloomington Indiana" will inform you that Sassafras Audubon Society exists, as does Bloomington Birders, an Indiana University bird club. It will also point you to the Bloomington Area Birding Facebook page.

The following are some of the most successful and prominent bird organizations in North America. They all do good work.

>> **Cornell Laboratory of Ornithology** (https://www.birds.cornell.edu/home)

>> **American Birding Association** (www.aba.org/)

>> **American Bird Conservancy** https://abcbirds.org/

>> **National Audubon Society** (www.audubon.org/)

>> **Association of Field Ornithologists** (https://afonet.org/)

>> **Birds Canada** (https://www.birdscanada.org/)

Most states and provinces have their own organization, which often hosts the official bird records committee — the group that produces the official state bird checklist. Such groups are the nerdiest of the bird nerds (written here with all due respect and deep appreciation). It is they who make decisions regarding whether an ultra-rare bird species that has been reported is indeed wild, or an escapee, or a mistaken identification. If you search the internet for your state or province name plus "bird records committee," you'll find the birding "authorities" in your area. State and provincial bird clubs also have meetings, outings, and other events that are worth attending if you want to connect with the sharpest birders around.

Starting a bird club

If there is no local bird club in your area, start one! Don't worry, you won't have to memorize *Robert's Rules of Order*. Starting a bird club is easy. All you need to do is locate a few other bird watchers and declare yourselves a club. If you want to be more organized, that's fine. What's important is that you get together with the other members from time to time to watch birds, talk about birds, learn about birds, and so on. If potluck dinners are your jam, go for it.

First, make sure that your town or county has no existing bird club; the members of an existing club (even one that hasn't met since the last passenger pigeon expired) may accuse you of poaching members!

Follow these steps for starting a bird club in a place where no bird club exists (also known as a bird-club-free zone).

1. **Contact other local bird watchers about the club.**

   Set a date for interested bird watchers to meet at a familiar and welcoming site, and publicize the event on social media, and even in traditional media outlets: local radio and TV stations and newspapers — even submit a news release. Hang an invitational poster in the local library and nearby nature centers or ask local commercial establishments if you can post a sign on their public bulletin board or in their window. Get the word out, and ask others to spread the word, too. Some people would be thrilled to be at the inaugural event of a new and promising birding club.

2. **Choose a local site that offers good bird watching and schedule your first club outing.**

   This can be the site of the first meeting, or you can pick this site at the first meeting. The point is: Make plans for a group bird-watching event.

3. **Meet people. Watch birds. Have fun.**

4. **Pick a name for your club. Continue to spread the word.**

TIP

As your club grows, you can decide if you want it to be more formalized (dues, regular meetings, committees, bylaws, and so on) or if you prefer it to be less formal and more social. Both methods (and all variations in between) work.

Teaching the kids

You can have a profound impact on young people if you are willing to spend some time with them and encourage their interest in the natural world. Volunteer to give a short talk about birds or bird feeding at a local school or scout group. Kids are fascinated by birds, so be prepared to answer lots of questions. Invite those who are very interested to attend a bird club outing or lend them your copy of *Bird Watching For Dummies!*

To work with a child individually, wait until they are around age 10 for more than the most casual bird watching. (Younger children might not have a long attention span.) Begin by pointing out easy-to-see birds. Canada geese, great blue herons, and mallards may all be present on a nearby pond or lake. Crows, turkey vultures, and large hawks can be seen along almost any road in North America.

Once you get the youngster to see the bird, you can add a tidbit of information about it. (It's okay to cheat and peek at your field guide for this info.) This tidbit will be a helpful reminder for the child the next time they see that species. Remember to keep things at a pace the child can handle.

Field guides designed for younger users are available from most bookstores, public libraries, or nature centers. Take a few minutes to study the guide with the child and read the introduction together. Show the child the basic technique for identifying a bird and go through the process once or twice.

Spend a few minutes showing the child how to use binoculars. Remember that small hands need small binoculars, so if the child shows a real interest, consider getting an inexpensive child-size one for your outings.

Share the chores: If you feed birds, let the child participate in filling and cleaning the feeder or the bath. Turn a chore into a treat. Create projects, such as building a simple bird feeder or nest box together. Encourage list keeping; each time the child identifies a new bird, have them check it off the list or write it down, adding other information, such as the date, how many birds were seen, and the weather.

Countless other opportunities exist to involve a child in projects, depending on their age and interest. For example, if you have a nest box, let the child determine how many days it takes the eggs to hatch, or how many times an hour the adults bring food to the babies. The range of projects is limited only by the birds' need for privacy and your imagination. As a reward, you may be creating an avid bird-watching companion for life.

Chapter **20**

Bird Photography

Some people carry a camera with a long lens instead of binoculars to watch birds — including some new to bird watching. It's usually more challenging, however, to find a bird through a viewfinder, using only one eye, than it is through a binocular. Cameras are heavy and not designed for quickly tracking moving birds. Most experienced bird photographers carry both binoculars and a camera with a long lens. They use binoculars to find a photo-worthy bird, and then they pick up their camera.

Some folks like to shoot now, identify later. Their goal is simply to get a photo to document the sighting and use it to identify the species. Eventually, they may wish to take better photos that are worthy of publication or printing and framing. There are lots of reasons to photograph birds. Some require practice, better equipment, and patience.

Engaging in bird photography offers a unique blend of technical challenge and artistic expression and can contribute an additional dimension to the joy of bird watching.

Catching the Photography Bug

The reasons people photograph birds (or clouds or mountain ranges or street signs or kittens) are as varied as there are people on this earth. Nevertheless, some reasons tend to dominate. Within the bird-watching community, a photograph usually serves one of the following specific purposes:

» **A proof image** is a photo good enough to prove that you have seen a bird. The photo can be far from perfect, but it captures what you saw, perhaps a new species for your life list. Many proof photos can be obtained using the automatic settings, even from a simple point-and-shoot camera.

» **An identification image,** like a proof image, does not need to be perfect, but good enough to figure out the species. Say you're birding and see an unfamiliar bird. If possible, get pictures of its wings, tail, underside, feet, bill, and even its behavior — images that may help with identifying it. Taking sharp and large images is crucial because a small, blurry image may not accomplish the goal. Be sure to take more than one!

» **A documentary photo** is technically proficient (sharp, well-exposed) but doesn't require creative thought. The main difference between proof, identification, and documentary images is the effort required to create a quality image. The documentary image is good enough to be published or shared online.

» **An artistic image** takes it to the next level. Creative thought is evident in the photo. Color, composition, and lighting are all considered while creating a more aesthetically pleasing image.

» **A storytelling image** is the most demanding to make because it reveals something about how the bird lives. Try to capture the bird's surroundings or some exciting or distinguishing behavior. Interaction between birds creates a visual story. These are the images, like what you see in Figure 20-1, that most commonly win photo contests and get published.

» **Artist reference images** are photographs of birds taken to use as a reference for artwork. High-quality bird photographs offer detailed information for artists who want to create anatomically accurate depictions of birds, their postures, behavior, and natural environments.

FIGURE 20-1: This photo of northern cardinals tells a story. The male is feeding a seed to his mate.

Courtesy of Bruce Wunderlich

Gearing Up: Choosing the Proper Camera Equipment

No matter what camera you are using — good, bad, or in between — the photographer makes the critical decisions that determine the outcome of an image. Sure, we all want top-of-the-line camera gear for our bird photography, but that doesn't ensure that we'll take award-winning photographs. You don't need the most expensive gear to capture great bird images. While the gear is essential, knowing how to use it is even more important.

Seeing which camera is right for you

Choosing the right camera for bird photography depends on your specific needs, preferences, and budget. It pays to invest in good equipment and learn how to use it.

Cell phone

While mobile phones have limitations compared to dedicated cameras, cell phone camera technology has made it possible to capture impressive bird photos — in certain situations. For example, your phone's camera might be all you need at your backyard feeder or any other place where birds have become accustomed to human presence, allowing you to get close enough for a decent shot without disturbing them. But really, cameras are a side hustle of cell phones. Their optical quality is getting better and better, but their zooms don't have much reach, and all settings are on autopilot. The one big advantage of cell phone cameras is that they are usually nearby — in your bag or pocket.

Point-and-shoot/compact camera

Using a point-and-shoot camera for bird photography has limitations similar to those of a cell phone, but many point-and-shoot cameras have more advanced features, better zoom capabilities, and higher optical quality, and those will help you capture good bird photos — but only if you're close enough.

Bridge camera

A *bridge* camera (also called a *megazoom*, *superzoom*, or *ultrazoom*) falls between a point-and-shoot camera and the more advanced interchangeable-lens cameras such as DSLR and mirrorless cameras. It has a built-in long-range zoom lens and offers some degree of manual control. Because the lens is integral to the camera body, a bridge camera is significantly more compact and lighter to carry than mirrorless or DSLR models. Bridge cameras have better zoom capabilities than a point-and-shoot but lack the level of sharpness and clarity that comes with a DSLR or mirrorless camera and a high-quality lens. The advantages of bridge cameras are that they cost significantly less than DSLR or mirrorless cameras, are lighter, and are generally easier to learn to use.

Digital single-lens reflex camera (DSLR)

DSLR cameras offer complete manual control of all settings to give you more control over image quality and allow you a wide range of lens options. While a DSLR camera may be more expensive than the camera types above, the quality of the photos is also higher. If you want to capture high-quality images that you may wish to enlarge, print, and hang on the wall, a DSLR is a good option. Lenses are interchangeable (within brands), and a high-quality lens is as important as the camera.

Mirrorless camera

A mirrorless camera captures high-quality images like a DSLR, but with additional benefits. Those with electronic viewfinders show a live preview of the exposure, allowing you to see precisely how your image will look, which is helpful when light conditions are in flux. The mirrorless camera generally weighs less than a DSLR. Some mirrorless cameras have advanced autofocus systems with eye detection, which can effectively track and focus on birds, keeping the eye in perfect focus. Like the DSLR, lenses are interchangeable and as important as the camera.

DECISIONS, DECISIONS, DECISIONS

If you already own a camera that you are comfortable using and satisfied with, it might meet your needs for photographing birds. Work with it, experiment. But if you're thinking about buying a new camera primarily for bird photography, first consider how seriously you plan to take this hobby. High-quality cameras and a suite of lenses are an investment. Unless you just won the lottery, we recommend against buying a top-of-the-line camera and a bunch of lenses. Consider, perhaps, a bridge camera, or a popular mid-priced DSLR. If or when you decide to upgrade, there is a market for used camera equipment. You won't recoup your full purchase cost, but if you find that bird photography just isn't your thing, you won't have invested the entire lottery winnings.

WARNING

Camera technology is evolving rapidly. Regardless of your final decision, *read your camera's owner's manual* until you are familiar with all its features. You will miss out on many bird photographs if you don't know how to use your camera efficiently.

Focusing on the right lens for you

Selecting the right lens(es) for your DSLR or mirrorless camera for bird photography requires considering factors like focal length, aperture, autofocus performance, build quality, and weight. A top-notch telephoto (zoom) lens with a fast aperture and dependable autofocus will significantly improve your ability to capture clear and detailed bird images in different situations. (If you don't understand all those terms, hang on. We'll get there.)

REMEMBER

As with choosing a camera, when choosing a lens you must consider your needs, shooting preferences, and budget. Bird photography often requires lenses with long focal lengths to get close-up shots without disturbing the birds.

TECHNICAL
STUFF

The focal length is the distance in millimeters between the optical center of the lens (where the light rays converge) and the camera's sensor. It determines the *angle* (also known as *field*) of view. Short lenses have a wide angle of view; long lenses have a narrow angle.

A focal length of 300 millimeters might be fine for bird photography in your backyard, the park, or the zoo. However, lenses in the 400mm to 600mm range are better for capturing birds without disturbing them in their natural environment. Many experienced bird photographers appreciate the flexibility of a long zoom lens, but in general, the optical quality of a fixed focal length lens is superior. Just to be clear: Lenses with a fixed focal length don't zoom. They're also called prime lenses.

Many DSLR cameras come with a fixed 50mm lens, which is too short for bird photography (most of the time). Suppose you decide you need a 400mm lens for more distant birds. Your options are to buy either a 400mm prime lens or a zoom lens — perhaps 100 to 400mm or 150 to 600mm. Zoom lenses are more versatile, but in the same price range, prime lenses generally have better optical quality. Prime lenses tend to be lighter-weight and more weatherproof because they have fewer optical components and moving parts. Only you can decide which type and size of lenses you need.

WARNING

Please be aware that not all lenses work on all cameras. For example, if you have a Canon camera, you'll need to make sure a lens you are considering for purchase has a Canon mount and isn't intended for use on a Nikon camera body. Adapters exist, but you're better off buying a lens designed for your camera.

No matter how large a lens you purchase, from time to time you will find that you need or want more reach, to get you closer to the bird. Teleconverters fit between the camera and the lens and can expand the effective focal length. For example, a 1.4X teleconverter used with a 200mm lens will have the reach of a 280mm lens. A 2.0X teleconverter would have the reach of a 400mm lens. The drawback of tele-converters is that they contain glass, so less light can enter the camera. Just by installing a teleconverter, you will reduce the aperture, so you'll have to slow the shutter speed or increase the ISO to compensate. We'll explain aperture, shutter speed, and the need for compensation in the "Exposure triangle" section omit, later in this chapter.

Looking at tripods and other "necessities"

Do you need a tripod? Perhaps. Occasionally. Long lenses are heavy, which makes them challenging to hold steady, especially if you are pointing them upward. Tri-pods are essential for photographing distant birds for extended periods but expect a learning curve. It takes a lot of practice to get your lens on a moving bird when your camera is mounted on a tripod. Start with a vast expanse of relatively sta-tionary birds, such as waterfowl on water. Then move up to soaring hawks, fol-lowing them with your camera. Don't expect to stay on flitty warblers in foliage while your camera is on a tripod, but with time and experience, you'll get there!

As for the "other necessities," you might consider a camera bag that accommo-dates several long lenses, a harness or other carrier for more comfortably carrying that camera with a heavy lens, a rain shield for your entire rig, photo-editing software, extra file storage devices, a book or two on bird photography, and maybe a better printer and some photo paper.

Tackling Your Camera Settings

Before we dive into the whole settings discussion, we need to define a few terms — the things that your settings will control or affect. Choosing settings for bird photography requires understanding the optimal settings for different situations, such as bright light or shade, a nearby bird or a distant flock, a busy background or a simple one, birds in flight or stationary, and many other variables. The goal is to obtain the best *exposure* — the amount of light used to capture the image — for the subject and its environment.

The exposure triangle

The *exposure triangle* is a fundamental concept in photography that refers to the three main elements that control the exposure of a photograph: aperture, shutter speed, and ISO. Each component affects the image differently and adjusting one will often require compensating with one or both of the others to find the optimal exposure. Each setting of the exposure triangle affects the light available for the image but also has a secondary effect on the image — which can be desirable or undesirable.

Aperture

Aperture is the size of the opening in the lens through which light passes to reach the image sensor. A wider aperture allows more light to enter, resulting in a brighter image. A narrower aperture lets in less light, resulting in a darker image. Aperture is measured in f-stops (f/2.8, f/4, f/5.6, f/8, and f/11, for example). The larger the number, the smaller the aperture. (For example, an f-stop of f/11 is a smaller opening than f/8). An aperture of f/2.8 lets more light into the camera than an aperture of f/11.

The secondary effect of this setting: A wider aperture creates a shallow depth of field, resulting in a blurry background (called *bokeh*) and a sharp subject. This is useful for making the bird stand out from the background. A narrower aperture increases the depth of field, keeping more of the scene in focus. This is useful if you want to show the bird's environment.

Shutter speed

Shutter speed refers to the duration of the exposure and is measured in fractions of a second (1/500s, 1/250s, 1/60s, and 1s, for example). Pressing the shutter button opens a "door" to expose the image sensor to the light of the scene in front of it.

The duration that door is open is the shutter speed. A fast shutter speed (short exposure time) allows less light in, resulting in a darker image. A slow shutter speed (long exposure time) allows more light in, resulting in a brighter image. A faster shutter speed freezes motion, capturing sharp images of fast-moving birds (useful for birds in flight). A slow shutter speed can result in motion blur with fast-moving birds (see Figure 20-2) but is useful in low-light conditions.

FIGURE 20-2: This photo isn't out of focus; rather, the shutter speed setting was too slow to capture this quick-moving pine warbler.

Courtesy of Bruce Wunderlich

ISO

ISO refers to the sensitivity of the camera's sensor to light. (The acronym stands for International Organization for Standardization, which doesn't help in understanding this concept.) ISO numbers don't measure anything, but it allows comparison of light sensitivity. A small ISO, such as 100, indicates low light sensitivity and will require a long exposure (resulting in rich, detailed, high-resolution images). High ISOs, such as 3200, make the image sensor more sensitive to light, but result in images with lower resolution, less detail, and "digital noise" (graininess), reducing image quality.

ISO values are typically 100, 200, 400, 800, 1600, and 3200. Each increase represents twice the sensitivity of the previous number. An ISO of 200 will be twice as sensitive as an ISO of 100. If your aperture is f/5.6, your shutter speed is 1/250, and your ISO is 400 and you snap an image of a bird (or anything else), your photo will be brighter than if your ISO had been 100.

Putting it all together and taking control

Think of it this way: Your camera operates like a window with a curtain that opens and closes. The size of the window represents the aperture. A large window lets in more light than a porthole and makes the room brighter. The amount of time the curtain is open represents the shutter speed. The longer the curtain is open, the brighter the room will be. If you are inside that room and wearing sunglasses, your eyes are not very sensitive to light — like a low ISO setting. If you want a brighter view of what is outside the window, take off your sunglasses (increase the ISO), or keep the curtain open for a long time (decrease the shutter speed), or somehow magically increase the size of the window (increase the aperture).

Bringing the exposure triangle together for bird photography involves under-standing how to balance aperture, shutter speed, and ISO to capture sharp, well-exposed images of birds, often in fluctuating and challenging conditions. Use the camera's light meter histogram to adjust the settings until you achieve proper exposure. (Read your camera's owner's manual on how to get the histogram to appear in your viewfinder or display, and how to use it to guide your settings.) Take a few test shots and review your images to ensure they are correctly exposed. If you photograph a white bird, you may need to underexpose it (make it darker than seems ideal) to avoid blowing out the detail of the white feathers. Likewise, if you shoot a dark-colored bird, you may need to overexpose (increase the light) to bring out the feather detail.

GOING AUTOMATIC: AUTOFOCUS OPTIONS

In the olden days of single-lens reflex cameras, focusing required twisting a ring on the lens until the subject was sharp and clear. With bridge, DSLR, and mirrorless cameras, focusing requires pressing lightly on the shutter button. A little box or icon appears in the viewfinder or LCD representing what your camera thinks is the subject, and when you are satisfied that it has fixed on the subject you intend, you press the button fully. Hold that button down to take rapid-fire shots.

With continuous autofocus enabled, the camera will continuously adjust the focus as the subject (bird) moves — as long as you have the shutter half-pressed. This is called AI Servo or AF-C, depending upon your camera brand. You can also set autofocus points. With single-point autofocus enabled, you can, for example, ensure the camera focuses precisely on the bird's eyes, even if the bird moves. For a bird in flight, you might want to use a larger group (expanded area) of autofocus points, which will make it easier for the camera to keep the bird within the focus area. Some cameras have settings that actually recognize birds. If your camera has bird detection, use it!

Modes give and take control

At this elementary level, let's just say there are three modes you can set on your camera: auto (easiest), manual (hardest), and aperture priority (in between).

Auto mode

In auto mode, the camera makes all the decisions on shutter speed, aperture, and ISO. That makes it easy for you, but the camera has no clue you're photographing a bird — possibly a fast-moving bird. The camera doesn't know whether you want a blurry background or a sharp background. If your goal is to get a proof or identification image just to record that you saw this bird, auto mode will give you that. The exposure the camera selects is usually correct, but the camera is going to pick the aperture, shutter speed, and ISO, and odds are, its balance of that triangle will be less than ideal. If you want a better, sharper image of a bird, *you*, not the camera, need to control the settings. The first step to taking killer bird pics is to make your own decisions about the camera settings.

Manual mode

Here's how each element can be set, and how to balance them for optimal results:

1. **Start with the shutter speed and determine how fast it should be to capture the motion of the bird.**

   For birds in flight, the shutter speed should be 1/1000 to 1/4000, and even faster for fast-flying birds. For perched birds in good light, a shutter speed of 1/500 to 1/1000 makes a good starting point.

2. **Next, adjust your aperture.**

   Since much bird photography occurs in low-light situations, set your f-stop to its widest opening (such as f/2.8) and then adjust as needed for the depth of field you want.

3. **Finally, adjust your ISO while monitoring your camera's light meter for proper exposure.**

   It may be necessary to use very high ISO in low-light conditions to get ideal exposure; just remember that a higher ISO will introduce digital noise to your image, which may be a problem if you need to crop the image or if you wish to print it in a large format.

Aperture priority mode (Av or A)

In this mode, you set the aperture and ISO, and the camera makes the decision on shutter speed. When you set the aperture, you control the depth of field, either isolating the bird from its background to spotlight it or showing both the bird and its environment — which is preferred is your choice.

The camera automatically adjusts the shutter speed for proper exposure. It's good for situations in which light conditions are changing rapidly, like in forests or on partly cloudy days.

TIP

When using aperture priority mode, always pay attention to the shutter speed. If it becomes too slow, you may need to adjust the aperture or ISO so that the camera chooses a faster shutter speed.

For most situations in bird photography, aperture priority mode and manual mode are recommended and commonly used because they give you more control than auto mode. Many bird photographers prefer to keep their camera in AV mode and adjust the ISO as necessary for proper exposure.

Some bird photographers choose to shoot in manual mode, but with auto ISO. In this mode, you choose the shutter speed and aperture, and the camera will set the ISO to get the correct exposure. Shutter speed priority mode is also possible but not recommended for bird photography.

REMEMBER

Regardless of your mode, review your shots on the camera's display to check for focus and exposure issues.

There is no optimal mode or setting configuration for bird photography. Choosing the settings depends upon the specific shooting conditions, your goal for the image, and your level of comfort with your camera settings.

TIP

This is important: Regardless of the type of camera you have, read the manual. As computer geeks say, RTFM (read the frigging manual). That's true for your lenses, too. We can't possibly cover all the various settings available for every brand and model of camera and lens suitable for bird photography. RTFM, track down a book, search YouTube for videos on making the most of your brand and model of camera or lens, or visit the website of the manufacturer. Find a Facebook or web-based user group of owners of your camera model. Sure, you may be able to figure out how to use your rig by trial and error, but watching videos or reading about it is guaranteed to take less time and introduce you to bells and whistles you might never discover on your own.

Lights! Camera! Action!

Settings and modes and aperture and all that technical stuff is half of bird photography. The other half is warmer and fuzzier: taking beautiful, well-planned, satisfying photos.

Light is a crucial element in any form of photography and plays a significant role in determining the quality and impact of the images. In bird photography, proper exposure ensures that the bird's colors and details are accurately captured. Good light helps achieve the right balance between highlights and shadows, revealing fine details in the plumage.

TIP

Face your shadow! The sun shining on your back will provide front lighting on the bird, which is important for several reasons. Front lighting ensures that the bird is evenly illuminated, reducing the chances of harsh shadows and bright areas. Front lighting highlights the intricate details of the bird's feathers, features, and colors, making the subject stand out crisply. Backlighting and side lighting can create stunning, artistic effects, but if you're just starting out, front lighting is a better strategy. So, aim your camera in the direction of your shadow to keep the front lighting on the birds.

Cloudy days can be great for photography. The soft, diffuse light on overcast days reduces harsh shadows and highlights. Even though the light is diffused, positioning yourself with the light source behind you ensures that the subject is evenly lit, making use of the soft, natural light provided by the clouds.

TIP

The best light for bird photography is usually in the early morning and late afternoon, when the sun's light is angled, rather than overhead and harsh. During the "golden hours," the light is softer and warmer, making it ideal for front lighting. The sun's low angle creates a flattering and gentle illumination on the bird. As a bonus, birds are usually more active in the morning and late afternoon than at midday.

REMEMBER

Avoid using flash in bird photography because it can scare or stress the birds, disrupting their natural behavior. Maintaining their comfort and safety should be a top priority; capturing authentic and undisturbed moments is more rewarding, anyway. Furthermore, natural light enhances images, revealing birds' true colors and their surroundings' ambiance.

Framing Feathers: Composition

What makes bird photos pleasing to our viewers? It could be great light, bright colors, color balance, sharpness, or a story. It's often a combination of all of them. To bring those factors together, we need to plan our composition carefully.

Light should catch the eye

Light is all-important in wildlife photography. And having a well-lit eye is a must for almost all bird images. Birds look alive when there is light reflecting from their eyes. This little spot of light in the eye is called catchlight. Without catchlight, the eye will appear black and lifeless (dead-eye). Watch for the bird to turn its head and look for catchlight as you shoot the photo. One reason to keep the light at your back is so that the light can reflect from the bird's eye.

TIP

Place your spot focus point on the eye of the bird to ensure the eye is in focus. Avoid using multiple automatic focus points because you cannot be sure it will choose the eye to be the primary focal point. With most cameras, if you let the camera choose the focus point in the image, it will pick the closest object to the camera, which could result in the bird being completely out of focus! Some cameras have an auto eye-detection focusing mode that does an excellent job of focusing on any eyes — human, pet, or bird. Just beware that all automatic settings have their limitations. For instance, a sparkling dewdrop has been known to fool eye detection.

A shallow depth of field may prevent getting the entire bird in focus, but if the eye is sharp, your image will appear sharp to your viewer, as shown in Figure 20-3.

FIGURE 20-3: Although not all parts of this photo of a red-breasted nuthatch are in focus, it's still a pleasing image because of the sharp focus on the eye and its catchlight.

Courtesy of Bruce Wunderlich

Rules are really guidelines

TIP

A lot of this chapter applies to all photography, but if there is one hard-and-fast rule of bird photography it is this: The bird's eye must be in focus for the photo to be worthy of keeping. If the bird's eye is not sharp and clear, delete the photo. That is true 99.9 percent of the time.

Generally accepted guidelines for photographic composition apply to bird photography, such as the "rule of thirds," in which you imagine a tic-tac-toe grid on your scene, and plan for the focal point to be on one of the grid intersections, not smack in the center. If you place points of interest, such as the bird's eye, on the intersections of the grid, or even along the lines of the grid, your image becomes more pleasing to the human eye. Many cameras will show you a rule-of-thirds grid in the viewfinder or on the LCD screen after you've captured the image.

Shift the camera angle to place the bird on one of these points but aim to suggest that the bird is looking toward the center of the grid. A bird looking off the edge of the image will lead your viewer's eye out of the picture.

Put space in front of the bird, not behind it. With birds in flight, the best compositions will have space in front of the bird in the direction it is flying. Aim for at least two times more space in front of the bird than is behind it. Some of these things can be adjusted through cropping in post-production. We'll get to that soon.

Another guideline worth adopting for bird photography is the rule of simplicity. A plain or blurred background puts the spotlight on the bird. There's more on this in the "Choosing ideal backgrounds" section, later in this chapter.

The "rule of odds" reflects that the human eye is naturally drawn to unusual or uneven composition. So, look for odd numbers; a photo of three ducks on a pond will be more attractive to your viewer than two ducks. This doesn't mean you shouldn't photograph a pair of birds, but look for another object to add balance, if possible. A pair of birds with a nest nearby will be compelling.

There are dozens more "rules" for general photo composition that apply to bird photography. Books have been written on the topic. This is not such a book, but if the idea of capturing frame-worthy images of birds is capturing your fancy, we recommend you find a book specifically on bird photography.

Cropping for composition

In bird photography, it is rare that we are close enough to our subject to fill the frame with it. Most images will require some post-production cropping, which has the effect of zooming in on the subject after the image has been taken. If you've taken a photo with the bird right in the center, cropping can allow you to reposition the subject to achieve the rule of thirds.

TIP

On most cameras, the center focus point is your fastest and most accurate. Most lenses will be sharpest in the center, decreasing toward the edges. Knowing that in most cases bird images will need to be cropped, place the subject near the center while photographing, leaving room to make the final composition decisions — and applying the rules above — through cropping during post-processing.

Cropping is a second chance to improve composition, but be careful not to over-crop, which can cause a loss of image quality, especially when the photo will be printed or displayed in a large format. As you crop and then enlarge an image, resolution will be lost. If the image used a high ISO, you will see noise!

Choosing ideal backgrounds

Make sure the viewer's attention is on the bird and not on a distracting background. Many photographers often overlook or discount the importance of a clean background. As bird photographers, we are sometimes guilty of tunnel vision, only focusing on the bird. If we don't pay attention to the background, the result may be a less-than-great image. The background of the photo should accentuate the bird, not detract from it. A bird can get lost in a busy background. Look for a clean background that will make the bird stand out in your photo. Look for colors in the background that will enhance your image.

MERGANSER IN RED

A few years ago, *BWD*'s wonderful photo editor Bruce Wunderlich was photographing a common merganser at a local lake on an autumn day when he noticed a red truck driving on a road across the lake. As the truck passed by, the water reflected its beautiful red color. Bruce changed his position on the duck so that the water around the merganser reflected the bright red autumnal color. Whether it came from leaves or a passing truck didn't really matter. The best bird photographers make conscious decisions about backgrounds. See the color photos section to view this remarkable photo.

Creating bokeh

An out-of-focus background is called *bokeh* (pronounced *BO-ka*, or *BO-kay*), which is the aesthetic quality of the blur produced in out-of-focus parts of an image. Controlling the depth of field is the key to creating bokeh. There are three ways to control your image's depth of field: camera settings, distance, and lens.

>> **Settings:** The primary setting to control the depth of field is the f-stop, which controls the size of the aperture. A small f-stop number, such as f/2, means a wide aperture, which will give you a minimal depth of field, blurring everything that's not at the center of your focus, and creating a soft background. If you need more depth of field, you can reduce the aperture by a couple of stops. It's a good idea to start shooting with aperture wide open, focusing on the bird's eye.

>> **Distance:** There are two ways the distance affects your background. First, the farther the background is behind the bird, the softer it will be. Second, the farther you are from the bird, the farther objects behind the bird must be to make them blur and become smooth. If the background is too close to the subject, you risk adding too much background detail into the focus area, even if you are shooting at your largest aperture. Moving your camera to the right or left or up or down just a few inches can remove a distracting object from the background.

>> **Lens:** A lens with a long focal length will create a shallow depth of field, which will blur the background. The longer the focal length lens, the shallower the depth of field. (Be aware, however, that long-focal-length lenses will have a narrow field of view.)

Creating pleasing backgrounds

Sometimes you will want to include some of the natural surroundings of the bird. Try to isolate the bird by keeping the area immediately behind it free of distracting objects.

>> Getting on eye level with the bird will help you isolate the bird from the background by making the background farther away. This technique is especially useful with birds on the ground. Photographing a bird from above will make the ground closer to the bird, and the bird will not stand out. With slower-moving birds, rather than looking through the viewfinder, lower your camera to the bird's eye level and use the LCD live view on the back of the camera (rather than the viewfinder), tilting the screen to shoot comfortably.

>> Beware of backgrounds with uneven light. Uneven light in the background, even if it is blurred, can distract from your subject.

>> Watch for hotspots. The human eye will be drawn to the lightest part of an image — the hotspot. If you have a hotspot in the background, your viewer's eye will go there first instead of to the bird.

>> Perform a photography background check before you press the shutter. Look for ways to eliminate distracting objects from your background. (See Figure 20-4 to see what we mean.)

>> Watch out for distracting background objects that intersect with the bird. Change the angle of the camera or take a few steps left or right and try again.

>> The color of the background can enhance your image. Look for colors that will complement the birds.

FIGURE 20-4: Which of these photos of a bald eagle in flight do you think is more aesthetically pleasing? Hint: The busy background in the first photo detracts from the eagle.

Courtesy of Bruce Wunderlich

Miscellaneous Tips That Didn't Fit in Anywhere Else

There's always room for more bird photography tips:

>> **When photographing birds, try to capture head angles that show only one eye.** In other words, avoid having the bird facing full forward with both eyes showing — unless you want an image of an "angry bird." The one exception to this rule is with owls, which have relatively flat faces, and so a full-frontal view showing both eyes is ideal.

>> **Be patient.** Very few people have a natural talent for bird photography. Practice, experiment, and practice some more. Expect frustration and disappointment — at least while you're just starting. Odds are high that at some point you will surprise yourself with a stunning image of a bird you saw and "captured" — a doubly joyful experience.

SETTING UP BACKYARD PERCHES

Your backyard feeders are a great place to capture images of birds that are accustomed to your coming and going — and filling the feeders. Find an attractive tree branch and place a feeder near it, keeping in mind the position of your camera and the direction of sunlight. Birds frequently land on a perch before approaching the feeder, allowing you to capture the bird as it sits attentively on a branch, with the feeder out of view. Alternatively, use a hollow log, stump, or some other natural item as a bird feeder. Carefully select the placement of such objects in front of attractive natural backdrops and remember that these perches or feeders must be far enough from the nearest background object that it will be entirely out of focus. If you look for and consider the ideal locations, and plan and wait for the bird to land right where you want it to, odds are high that you'll be rewarded for your efforts.

>> **Photographing birds from a blind is an effective way of getting close to birds — but only in suitably birdy locations.** Vehicles make excellent bird blinds if the birds you seek to shoot frequently show up near the road or parking area. As long as you stay quietly inside the vehicle, most birds will not be bothered by its presence. Remember, you want the light at your back.

>> **Avoid bright clothing.** Bright-colored clothing will alert the birds to your presence before you get anywhere near close enough for a photo. Instead, wear earth-tone colors that blend into the surroundings. You might also want to put a camo skin on the barrel of your lens, especially if your lens is white.

Editing and Organizing Bird Photos

Bird photography doesn't end with clicking the shutter. Post-processing plays a role in elevating bird images from mere snapshots to stunning works of art. Mastering the art of editing can significantly enhance the impact of your bird photography.

Why do images need editing? Editing bird photography can bring out details and enhance images in a way that reflects the photographer's vision. We bird photographers often find ourselves in challenging shooting conditions, making it unlikely that an image will turn out perfectly without the benefit of some photo editing.

REMEMBER

Almost every published photo has been edited. In fact, an image straight out of the camera has been edited. When an image is saved in JPG format (as is a common practice) the camera automatically adjusts the sharpening, contrast, white balance, vibrancy, and saturation of the photo. The camera presets these adjustments, and the photographer has little control over them. While most cameras today do a great job with these automatic adjustments, many photographers prefer to have more control over the manipulation process.

RAW versus JPG

Your camera's menu allows you to choose the file format of the image: JPG or RAW. JPG uses compression to reduce the image's file size. The process works by changing the color values and grouping pixels with similar colors. Doing this reduces the amount of color information that needs to be stored. This reduction of information results in a loss of image quality and detail and may alter the image. Once this information is lost through JPG compression, it cannot be restored.

The RAW file format contains unprocessed and unaltered pixel information directly from the camera's sensor, similar to a film negative. When shooting in RAW format, more information is saved, providing greater flexibility and more control when editing. Any information saved with a RAW file can be adjusted via RAW photo-editing software such as Lightroom or Photoshop. RAW image files take up a lot more space on your memory card and storage drive than JPG files, however.

Basic adjustments for a bird photo

Post-processing bird photography usually involves using photo-editing software to adjust some or all of the following:

>> **Exposure:** Using exposure adjustments to correct the image's brightness if the original shot was underexposed or overexposed.

>> **Highlight adjustment:** Reduction of highlights can help recover details in overexposed areas, such as bright skies or feathers.

>> **Shadow adjustments:** Adjust shadows to enhance details in darker areas, especially if the bird's plumage lacks detail in shadows.

>> **White and black points:** Adjust the white and black points (making dark areas darker and pale areas lighter) to ensure a full tonal range, adding contrast and depth to the image.

>> **Contrast adjustment:** Increasing the contrast will improve the details of the bird, creating more depth in the photo.

» **White balance:** Adjusting the white balance — the baseline tone or shade of white — can correct any color casts (say, a greenish reflection from surrounding foliage) and ensure that the bird's colors are accurate. It is useful for images of birds in the shade.

Organizing and storing your bird photos

When you start taking bird photos, you'll quickly amass thousands of digital photo files. Your initial impulse may be to store them on your computer's hard drive. However, these files — especially RAW files — can be quite large and will rapidly consume your computer's storage space, possibly slowing down its performance. Instead of burdening your computer's hard drive, it's best to store your images on external hard drives or in the cloud. Every hard drive will eventually fail, so making multiple copies of your best images and storing them in multiple locations is a good idea.

PHOTO EDITING 101

Use a light touch. Avoid excessive use of editing tools. Apply changes judiciously for subtle enhancements. Make changes in small increments.

Be cautious with color adjustments. Try to remember the scene and keep the colors true. While you may want to enhance specific colors, avoid oversaturation that can make the image look artificial. If the edited photo looks like something you could have observed in nature, you're likely on the right track.

The best way to achieve a sharp image in photo editing is to start with a sharp image. It is vital that the bird looks tack-sharp. While every photograph can benefit from some sharpening, an image can be ruined by over-sharpening to the point that it seems crunchy and unnatural. A white halo around the edges of the subject is a telling sign that an image has been over-sharpened.

Don't rely on editing software to fix a bad image. You've probably heard or even said, "Oh, I'll fix that later in Photoshop." While sometimes it is necessary to post-process an image, you never want to rely on software to be the fix-all for every photo you shoot. Get it right in your camera! That is the best practice. Still, almost every image can benefit from a few adjustments.

Now, how do we go about organizing these thousands of photos? It's important to have a logical filing system that is intuitive to you. Place your files into folders that will make it easy to locate later. You might choose to label folders by location and date. For example, if you took photographs of birds in Florida on March 14, 2025, you could label the folder "FL-3-14-25." Alternatively, you might want to organize by bird species using a four-letter code for the birds. For example, a folder for red-tailed hawk images could be named "RTHA." Using subfolders can also make organizing your files easier. For instance, you could have a folder for the year with subfolders for each month in that year or places you visited that year.

REMEMBER

Set up a filing system that works for you and never deviate from it. This is essential for finding your files later. Many editing-software programs offer systems for organizing your files, including the ability to add keywords for easy searching later.

Ethical Bird Photography

Bird photographers are constantly striving for that great shot of our target birds. But we must keep the birds' welfare in mind as we approach our subjects. Keep the following in mind:

» **Don't disturb the birds.** That is the number one rule of bird photography and bird watching in general. Don't chase the bird; let it come to you. Not only is this what is best for the birds but it's also the best approach to getting satisfying shots of birds behaving naturally.

» **Don't intentionally flush a bird for a better photograph.** A bird photographer's goal should be to never cause a bird to fly away. Wait for the bird to decide to fly. During the breeding season, flushing a bird can interfere with courtship and tending the nest. In winter, causing a bird to fly can make them use precious energy needed to survive and hunt for food.

» **Don't frighten nesting birds from their nest.** Approaching active bird nests is best avoided or done with extreme caution. You could flush the parent from the nest, leaving eggs or young unprotected from predators or exposed to deadly heat or cold. You may also lead predators to the nest with your scent or presence. There are ways to photograph active nests without disturbing them, but they are best left to long-experienced professionals. For a novice bird photographer: please steer clear of active nests. Be extra respectful and cautious when around them.

» **Don't play recorded calls of birds during mating or nesting season to try to draw them in, and in general, use recorded calls judiciously and sparingly.** Never use playback during courtship or nesting season or to attract endangered species. This is true for all bird watchers, not just bird photographers. Remember rule #1: Don't disturb the birds.

Check out this book's online cheat sheet at www.dummies.com for the American Birding Association's Code of Birding Ethics. Those apply to bird photography, too.

IN THIS CHAPTER

» **Tackling the finer points of bird identification**

» **Avoiding the more common bird ID pitfalls**

» **Forging ahead (even when you're stumped)**

» **Letting apps do the heavy (ID) lifting**

» **Knowing when to say when**

Chapter **21**

Advanced Bird ID

After you're hooked on bird watching, you want to seek new and different birds in new and different locations. Many of the new species you encounter present challenging identification puzzles. This chapter gives you some shortcuts on the path to becoming an advanced bird watcher.

Going the Extra Mile: Advanced Bird ID

So, do we really need "advanced" bird ID? That's a fair question. Bird ID is not rocket science. Because there are no birds in outer space, rocket scientists rarely even have to think about tough identifications. Any bird can be tough to name if it's a mile away, or hiding in dense shrubbery, or flying away rapidly in the fog.

In this chapter, we'll focus on the kind of bird that is genuinely hard to recognize: One you see perfectly well, that even sits around patiently while you haul out the field guide, but doesn't quite match anything in the book or app.

Getting to know the common birds

The birds probably don't want you to know this, but here's one of their little secrets. When we have big troubles identifying a bird, the problem usually is not caused by some really rare species. No, the majority of the time, it's the common birds that cause all the trouble.

It makes sense if you stop to think about it. Common birds have more chances to trip us up, just because there are more of them. Besides, they need to do something to entertain themselves, and what could be more fun than causing confusion for bird watchers?

TIP

One of the best ways to avoid being confused by strange birds is to get to know those common birds better. After you've identified a bird, don't just walk on immediately in search of something novel; spend some time watching it, committing it to memory. Remember that even among common birds, males and females can look identical or quite different; young birds can have totally different plumage from their parents; some species change color throughout the year; and if you consider all the permutations of all these variables, one common species can have a whole bunch of different looks! Can you recognize them all?

Focusing on more than just one field mark

Beginners often hope to find "the one diagnostic mark" for each species of bird — sort of a "magic bullet" that will nail it every time. Unfortunately, any time you rely on just one field mark, there's a good chance that it will trip you up eventually.

For example, you may latch onto the fact that the snowy egret has yellow feet contrasting with black legs and decide that you don't need to look at anything else about that bird. Doing this sounds fine in theory. In the field, though, exceptions may loom:

» Egrets spend a lot of time wading, so at times you just can't see their feet.

» Snowy egrets that have waded in especially black and sticky mud may appear to have dark feet when they emerge.

» Some young snowy egrets have legs that are mostly greenish-yellow, not black.

» If you're really lucky, you may run into a stray of a European species, the little egret, which also has yellow feet and black legs. Or you may encounter a hybrid snowy egret/little blue heron (which isn't white but does have yellow feet).

A RELEVANT LESSON

Many years ago, Bill Thompson III, author of the previous edition of *Bird Watching For Dummies*, was out with a more experienced older birder, and he spotted a gull that looked suspicious to him. It was one of those motley younger gulls: a medium-sized one, all brown, sitting on a sandbar in the river.

"We ought to take some notes on it," the friend opined. So, Bill whipped out his pocket notebook. "Medium-sized gull," he wrote. "All brown." He didn't realize at the time that most young gulls are brown, and a slew of them are medium-sized. Still, they can be identified if you know what to look for.

As he was putting away the notebook, Bill noticed that his friend was still writing. He continued to write — stopping to look at the bird, then writing some more — for another 20 minutes while Bill stood around, self-consciously shuffling his feet and twiddling his thumbs. Finally, as a last resort, Bill started looking at the bird some more, to see if he could spot something else to write about. But he couldn't see anything else about the gull's appearance that seemed to stand out to his eyes.

His friend's eyesight was no better than Bill's, but he had studied gulls and knew to look for details beyond that first impression of "medium-sized and all brown." The gull turned out to be a first-year California gull, a pretty unusual bird for the area.

In all of these cases, you'll have problems if you haven't paid attention to other field marks besides the supposedly "diagnostic" one.

Getting into shape(s)

TIP

Although most field guides don't mention this, some of the most important field marks involve the shapes of birds.

Sometimes you use shape as a field mark without even thinking about it. Not even a beginning bird watcher is likely to confuse a brown duck for a brown owl: Those birds may be the same size and color, but they are differently shaped.

Shape and posture are useful beyond such general divisions. Pick up any bird guide and look at the sandpipers in winter plumage. Most of them are brownish gray on the back and whitish underneath, but no two species are exactly the same shape. Their legs may be long or short. Their bills may be straight or curved, stubby or elongated. Their heads may be hunched down on their shoulders, or they may have long slender necks. The practiced bird watcher can recognize many of these shorebird species by silhouette alone.

Molt and wear: Good for them, bad for us

Feathers are amazing things, very lightweight and very strong; but they do gradually wear out. And then they have to be replaced, but not all at one time. This orderly replacement of feathers is called *molt*. Each kind of bird goes through its molt at a predictable season.

Molt can be complete, which involves gradually replacing all the feathers, or partial, meaning, say, only the flight feathers (the long feathers of the wings and tail) or body feathers (the small feathers close to the body) are replaced. Some species, including hawks, owls, woodpeckers, hummingbirds, jays, swallows, thrushes, vireos, and chickadees, undergo one complete molt per year. Other species, including buntings, tanagers, and warblers, molt all their feathers after nesting (sometimes changing into their winter plumage during this process) and then undergo a partial molt prior to the breeding season. This is when colorful males grow their bright, breeding finery. Still other birds undergo a complete molt twice a year, including marsh wrens and bobolinks.

To take an example that may be outside your window right now, the house finch goes through its annual complete molt in late summer or early fall, a process that can take two months or more. By mid-autumn, house finches all look crisp and fresh, with neat pale edges on all the wing feathers. Their feathers are then subject again to the very gradual process of wear. Over the next ten months or so, their feathers very gradually become worn and faded, so that by mid-summer the birds can look pretty ratty before they molt again.

Another finch, the American goldfinch, goes through two molts each year. Starting in August, it gradually molts all its feathers, leading to a fresh winter plumage with crisp black wings and tail and pale tan body feathers by mid-November. In the spring it molts again — a partial molt of the head and body feathers, not those of the wings and tail. This spring molt produces the summer plumage, in which the body of the male is bright yellow with a black cap.

REMEMBER

So, the same bird that looks crisp and fresh in one season can look dull and faded in another, and it can look patchy when it is molting in feathers of a different color, or even ratty when it is missing feathers. A bird's tail can look oddly short when its tail feathers are molting, and it may be covered in awkward-looking pinfeathers. There's no need for you to memorize the molts of all these birds. But if you're aware of such things as molt and wear, you won't find their effects so mystifying.

First-year birds molting from juvenal plumage (the feathers that replace the first coat of down) into the plumage of an older bird can be really confusing. For example, there's a short period when young brown-headed cowbirds look like they're wearing camo — a patchwork of browns and blacks in random locations. Images of such birds might not be in your field guide. Even though the plumage is unusual, the size, shape, posture, bill size, and behavior can still distinguish such birds as hatch-year brown-headed cowbirds. (See Figure 21-1.)

Caleb Putnam / Wikimedia Commons / CC BY 2.0.

FIGURE 21-1:
A hatch-year brown-headed cowbird molting from its first real feathers into adult plumage looks like it is wearing camo and can be challenging to identify.

Some bird species, including some gulls and bald eagles, can take several years to attain their full adult plumage. Until then, each cohort has distinctive plumage. A hatch-year bald eagle, for example, has drastically different plumage from a two-year-old eagle: almost all chocolate brown, versus widely mottled with white. One species of bird can have many different outfits!

Steering Clear of Common Pitfalls

If you go out and look for them, you may or may not find *common* loons, *common* grackles, or *common* mergansers. But you don't have to seek the *common* pitfalls: they come looking for you.

The following sections describe ways in which a bird can look unexpectedly odd — problems that are seldom mentioned in field guides.

Illusions of size

Consciously or unconsciously, you often start the process of identifying a bird by considering its size: classifying it as smaller than a sparrow, larger than a crow, and so on. This is great if you have judged its size correctly. If you haven't, you're off on the wrong track immediately, and you may take a long time to figure out what's wrong. Unfortunately, it's easy to be misled by illusions of size, especially when a bird is seen alone with nothing nearby for easy comparison.

It's not *uncommon* to hear people give a perfect, feather-by-feather description of a bird that left them completely puzzled. When someone suggests the obvious, such as a meadowlark, their emphatic answer is something like, "Oh, no, it was definitely too large for a meadowlark." Chances are good that the bird was a meadowlark, and that its larger size was an illusion. There's really no one good way to compensate for this illusion, except to be aware that it is a possibility. If all the field marks except size point to the bird being a particular species, don't rule out the obvious answer.

Tricks of light

As ol' Isaac Newton once pointed out, what we see as color is really an effect of light. Because light can do really strange things, birds often look odd, through no fault of their own. Under the glare of noon, colors can be washed out, and dark blue can look like black. Near sunrise or sunset, the low-angled sun can make birds look redder.

If you see a black hummingbird at your nectar feeder, or even a hummingbird with a black throat, odds are high that your hummingbird feeder is hanging in a shady spot. There are no black hummingbirds, or hummingbirds with a black gorget (the beautiful, iridescent throat patch of some hummingbirds) in North America. It's a trick of light.

Other illusions are possible, too. A bright greenish bird with lots of stripes might reveal itself as a song sparrow — a common bird, brown, with stripes — when it emerges from the greenery in which it is hiding. Light and reflection can be remarkably deceptive.

Stained or discolored birds

Birds get messed up in a variety of ways. Some of them are messy eaters, and it shows — in stains on their plumage.

Perhaps you will see a hummingbird with a big yellow spot on its forehead. You can look for it in your field guide but fail in finding a match. Hummingbirds often pick up pollen from flowers as they forage for nectar. Not just hummingbirds: Lots of birds pick up pollen from blooming plants. Bill Thompson III, author of the previous edition of *Bird Watching For Dummies*, recalled seeing birds that looked just like white-crowned sparrows except that their faces were variably black. Those white-crowned fellas had been feeding on over-ripe olives. If you see a gull with a greenish face — who knows what that scavenger may have been eating.

Odd or aberrant plumages

Question: What bird looks just like an American robin, but has big white patches in its wings? Before you start rummaging through the foreign bird guides, here's the answer: It's an American robin. Colloquially, it's called a partial albino American robin, but albinism is like pregnancy: there is no partial. *Leucism* (*LOO-sizz-m*) is a better term to describe birds (and other animals) with white spots (areas lacking normal pigmentation). Albino birds are exceedingly rare. Not only do they have entirely white feathers, but also pink eyes.

You don't see albino birds every day. But if you do much bird watching, you're going to see leucistic birds eventually. Some leucistic (*loo-SIS-tick*) birds are entirely white — except for their normal eye color. Occasionally a bird is oddly dark in color. Such birds may be *melanistic* — overly pigmented. All these conditions are genetic in origin.

Dawn had a female cardinal whose head was white on one side. It visited her feeders for three winters in a row, disappearing every spring and reappearing every fall. It was fun and cool to figure out that she probably nested farther north somewhere but appreciated the bounty and ample winter cover of Dawn's yard during the colder months.

Every few years there is excitement — sometimes it makes national news — over a bird that looks like a cardinal except that it is entirely bright yellow. Such birds are northern cardinals with a pigmentation anomaly called xanthochromism.

Oddly plumaged birds are not as uncommon as you may think. However, if you happen to spot a gynandromorph, please take as many photos of it as you can. They are extremely rare: male on one side, female on the other, outside and inside. (See Figure 21-2.) Several such gender-bending cardinals have been documented. Feel free to search the internet for "gynandromorph cardinal" images.

FIGURE 21-2:
A gynandromor-
phic northern
cardinal is male
on one side and
female on the
other — both
externally and
internally.

Bill deformities

Very often the shape of a bird's bill is an important field mark. On occasion, you see a bird with a funny bill — twice the usual length, or oddly curved, or deformed in some other way. Really, it's not funny — it's sad, and odds are, that bird doesn't have a long life expectancy. It will have a hard time foraging.

Escaped birds

Visit a zoo with a big aviary, and you may be amazed and impressed by the wide variety of birdlife from other parts of the globe. Then try to imagine what would happen if some of those birds got away and showed up in your local woodlot. Some organizations and individuals keep private aviaries, and sometimes, birds escape.

Some such escapees are obvious. If you see an emu (tall and without visible wings) or a scarlet macaw (three feet long, flaming red) you may immediately suspect that it won't be in your field guide to North America. But a lot of bird fugitives look less exotic than that; they even look superficially like they may belong here. You need to avoid the temptation to "stretch" these birds to fit something in the book. It helps to know where and when you are most likely to encounter such escapees.

Southern Florida, South Texas, and Southern California are three regions where lots of escaped exotic birds are found. Many of the species found in these areas are from the tropics and have done well enough to reproduce successfully in their new homelands. That's true for monk parakeets, which are native to southern South America but are now resident breeders in numerous locations across the U.S., as far north as Oregon and Massachusetts. Some exotic species are accepted as legitimate North American breeding species, and even "countable" by the American Birding Association. Field guides to these regions contain the most often-encountered exotic bird species.

Hybrids

When mating season rolls around, birds don't always behave themselves. Sometimes a bird will pair up with a member of another species. The offspring of these pairings can be very confusing in their appearance.

On one occasion, a bird reported as a black-chinned sparrow in an odd place turned out (after much careful study) to be a hybrid between dark-eyed junco and white-throated sparrow. In another case, a duck that looked a lot like a Baikal teal — a very rare visitor — was actually a hybrid between a northern pintail and a green-winged teal. Your field guide might provide images of Brewster's or Lawrence's warblers — both hybrids of golden-winged and blue-winged warblers. Hybrids happen, but it's not too common.

Planning for Those Tough IDs

What's the best approach to handling a tough bird identification? Sometimes, your approach depends on the type of bird you're dealing with. Here are some suggestions for particular groups of toughies.

>> **Fall warblers:** Fall warblers are really confusing little creatures. The dullest and drabbest are tough to identify even if they pose right in front of you, daring you to guess their identity. But if you focus first on the pattern of the wings and the face, you'll go a long way toward recognizing the birds.

>> **Immature gulls:** Immature gulls are always tough, but they get worse and worse in late spring and through the summer, when their feathers are in worn condition. Gulls can take up to four years to attain adult plumage. The best strategy for a new bird watcher is to ignore the ratty and faded brownish gulls of early summer, and then (if you feel up to it), focus on them again in late fall, when they are in fresh plumage.

>> **Sparrows:** Often called LBJs for "Little Brown Jobs," these are sneaky birds that are hard to see and hard to identify. Often a good approach is to go beyond the illustrations in the field guides — read the text! Read about each sparrow's habitat and habits, which are often more revealing than their markings. For example, Savannah sparrow and Lincoln's sparrow are both little streaky birds, but one lives in open fields (Savannah) while the other hides in thickets (Lincoln's).

>> **Flycatchers:** Some flycatchers are just impossible to recognize when they're not singing — and during migration they can't be counted on to sing (though they give their call notes more often, which can be a help). For beginners, it's best to let flycatcher IDs go if the bird is not calling. You may meet up with them again when they are on their breeding grounds and singing their trademark songs.

Letting Apps Help with Tough IDs

We considered addressing apps that can ID birds for you back in Chapter 3, but if we serve you the dessert first, you might not eat your vegetables. Part of the joy of birding is learning to recognize (or figure out) the ID of a bird all by yourself. The more often you do this all by yourself, the more quickly and confidently you will be able to do it. There is no shame in turning to an app when you are stumped, but if you turn to an app without trying to figure out an ID on your own, you're probably not going to remember that species the next time you encounter it.

Some of the most popular bird ID apps (at the time of this printing) include Merlin, the Audubon Guide, the Warbler Guide, iBird Pro, and Birda. That's not a complete list, and no doubt more are in the works. The first two listed are free; the others must be purchased.

Some of these apps are field guides with superpowers, but ID apps use information you provide to figure out the species of a mystery bird you've seen. If you provide details of the field marks, such as the color of various body parts, bill length, tail length and shape, the overall size, the location and habitat, the time of year, and so on, the app will make a solid guess of one (or more) species that fits the bill (pun intended). They often yield an accurate ID on the first try, with little work (contemplation) required on your part. These apps have come a long, long way since they were introduced early in this millennium.

Merlin, Birda, and others will even accept as input a photo you've taken and use it to identify the species — if the photo is reasonably clear and distinguishing details visible. Such features are super cool and impressive, but if a child only ever uses a calculator, they might not be able to add even simple numbers without one, you know?

Merlin (and several other apps) can also identify birds by sound. We've seen people at birding hotspots with their phones in the air (obviously using Merlin's sound ID app) say excitedly to their partner: "There's a blue-winged warbler singing nearby!" That is very cool, but will the person ever learn the *bee-buzz* song of a bluewing without Merlin?

Dawn, who birds primarily by ear and then by sight (when she is in her home region), readily admits to using Merlin often for sound ID whenever she hears an unfamiliar bird sound — especially chip notes and contact calls. She aims to remember those sounds, but most chip notes and contact calls are hard to distinguish and remember.

The Warbler Guide app is the companion to a book of the same name by Tom Stephenson and Scott Whittle. The book is an encyclopedic guide to warblers, and the app allows you to, for example, narrow down warblers by comparing undertail color patterns, side by side. It also has an amazing feature that allows you to see every warbler species in full 3D by "spinning" the image on your phone! We often observe warblers from odd angles — especially straight up from below, and the Warbler Guide app allows us to view every North American warbler's underparts to find a match. It is extremely cool.

We can't go into more detail than this on the various ID apps and how to use them, but you'd be wise to download those that are free, figure them out, and then upgrade to something with even more species and bells and whistles — if you like. Figuring out birding apps is really kind of fun.

Throwing in the Towel

You'll never be a real bird expert until you can be comfortable saying three little words: "I don't know."

Not even the top experts in the world can name every bird they see. If you feel as though you have to put a definitive label on every single bird, you're likely to wind up frustrated — or, worse yet, trying to fool yourself. It's better to admit that you just don't know.

It's *always* okay to walk away from a confusing bird and go looking for something else. No one can fault you for saying, "It's an unidentified flycatcher." (Even if it's really an unidentified vireo, you're still half right.) Bird watching is supposed to be enjoyable. If you make yourself unhappy by struggling too long with impossible birds, you're missing the whole point.

6

The Part of Tens

Chapter **22**

Ten Ways to Help Save Birds

n 2019, the renowned journal *Science* released the startling results of a study of bird populations, declaring that *three billion* birds have been lost in the U.S. and Canada over the past 50 years. That's one in four birds since 1970! (Visit www.3billionbirds.org/ to access the full study.)

Such a statistic can make a bird watcher feel helpless and wonder where to even begin to reverse this trend. Well, birders and non-birders alike can take action in simple ways to improve the situation for birds.

Are you ready to do your part? Read on!

Drinking Bird-Friendly Coffee

Let's start with an easy one. If you drink coffee, which the vast majority of bird watchers do (especially on those days when birding excursions start while it's still dark out), consider switching out your morning brew with one that is certified Bird Friendly® by the Smithsonian Migratory Bird Center.

Aggressive deforestation to accelerate and expand coffee production over the past few decades has resulted in extensive habitat loss, whereas Bird Friendly coffee is shade-grown. This is good for the birds *and* the beans, because this coffee is grown under a forest canopy that's great bird habitat. And the coffee beans mature to their full flavor potential in shade. Learn more about Bird Friendly certification and where to buy certified brands at https://nationalzoo.si.edu/migratory-birds/bird-friendly.

Keeping Cats Indoors

Many bird watchers are also cat lovers, but there are no two ways about it: Outdoor cats are responsible for an estimated 2.5 *billion bird deaths each year* in the U.S. and Canada. Not only is keeping cats indoors better for birds, it's also better for cats, which live shorter, harsher lives outdoors. Building an enclosed outdoor "catio" for your pets can be a great compromise.

Gardening with Native Plants and Reducing Your Lawn

The U.S. has 40 million acres of lawn, which offer little food or shelter for wildlife. Replacing open lawn with a variety of native plants benefits birds *and* bird watchers, as it will attract more birds to your property for you to enjoy. Conservation begins at home and works on any size property — even converting a corner of your yard can make a real difference.

Avoiding Herbicides and Pesticides

Common weed killers around the home can be toxic to the birds that eat the contaminated seeds or prey on the insects that feed on the plants (not to mention that some are probable human carcinogens as well). Simply put, insects are vital to birds' survival. Reduce pesticide use around your home, consider purchasing organic produce, and also avoid rat poison, the new stronger forms of which bioaccumulate in predators all the way up the food chain and are killing raptors that don't even eat small rodents, like bald eagles.

Making Windows Safer

Too many of us have heard the sickening *thump* of a bird hitting a window. To minimize these collisions, apply bird-friendly adhesive film or tape to make a window visible to birds while still allowing the homeowner to enjoy the view. At night, turn out lights or draw curtains to avoid attracting migrating birds to your windows.

For more information on these and other cost-effective methods for deterring birds from windows, visit `https://abcbirds.org/glass-collisions/`.

Using Less Plastic

Plastic is everywhere and impossible to avoid, but even a small reduction in single-use plastic can help keep it out of oceans and other habitats — and ultimately out of birds' bellies. Reduce, reuse, recycle . . . there's always room for improvement in allowing less plastic into our lives. And picking up any trash you encounter while birding is an excellent habit to develop, too.

Watching Birds and Sharing What You See

If you are going to watch birds, why not take it a step further and share what you observe? Anyone can be a citizen scientist, whether you've been watching birds your whole life or just identified your first bird yesterday. (See Chapter 19 to learn of a whole host of ways your bird observations can benefit science and conservation.)

Buying a Duck Stamp

While hunters are required to purchase a Federal Duck Stamp each year, many birders and other nature enthusiasts also purchase the stamp to support wildlife habitat conservation. Since 1934, more than $1 billion has been raised by Duck Stamp sales — funds that have been efficiently used to acquire and protect six million acres of wetlands habitat for national wildlife refuges. The stamp, which also serves as a pass for free admission to any national wildlife refuge, is available at a variety of outdoor retailers, wildlife refuges, and some post offices. Learn more about the stamp and where to purchase it at www.fws.gov/service/buy-duck-stamp-or-e-stamp.

Joining a Conservation Organization

Countless nonprofit organizations focused on helping birds and saving bird habitat are seeking like-minded members — this could be your local bird club, your state ornithological society, national organizations such as Cornell Lab of Ornithology and American Bird Conservancy, or even a global organization like BirdLife International. Modest membership fees support their conservation efforts and provide opportunities to make the world a better place for birds and the people who love to watch them.

Helping Others Discover Birds

Now that you've started noticing and appreciating birds, help others do the same — birds need all the advocates they can get! If you notice an interesting bird (we would argue all birds are interesting . . .), point it out to the person next to you. As you likely know by now, once you start noticing birds, it's hard to stop.

Chapter **23**

Ten Frequently Asked Questions About Birds

Over more than four decades of fielding phone calls and e-mails at *BWD* magazine, ten questions have fluttered to the top of our Most Frequently Asked list. We do our best to answer them all.

Not surprisingly, the most frequently asked questions originate in the backyard, which is where we forge bonds with birds by offering them food, water, and shelter. That's where most of us get to know birds as individuals, and get involved in their family lives, too.

Here goes!

Why Is That Bird Pecking on My Window?

Oddly, most people who find a bird flinging itself against a window assume the bird wants to come inside the house. No, it's very much still wild, just obsessed and reacting to its reflection on the glass. It's fighting to defend its territory against an illusion. This is bad for the bird, which wastes time it could be devoting to feeding its young, and also bad for people trying to sleep after 5:30 a.m.!

Defusing the behavior involves removing the stimulus. Try neutralizing the reflectivity of the glass by pressing plastic food wrap on the outside. Artificial snow-in-a-can, sprayed on the outside surface, will do the same thing. If the bird simply switches to another window, take your strategy to the next level by tacking shiny Mylar balloons with big, googly eyes (Elmo works well) to the window frames, so they bob in the breeze.

There's a Woodpecker Excavating My House Siding! Help!

In early fall, you may find a woodpecker pecking away, apparently with dastardly intent, at your house siding. Unless your wooden siding is rotten and infested with termites, it isn't looking for food; it's trying to excavate a roost site for the winter. The first thing to try is putting a nestbox with an appropriately sized hole (1.5 inches for a downy woodpecker; 2.5 for larger species like northern flicker) over the spot it is excavating. Fill the nestbox with wood chips so it can "excavate" the box, and hope it settles down within. If that doesn't work, see the Mylar balloon hack above. Crop netting or hardware cloth stretched over the area and 3 inches off the wood surface works, too.

A Bird Just Hit My Window! What Should I Do?

No one likes to hear that sickening *thunk* that means a bird has mistaken reflective window glass for trees and sky. Grab a brown paper grocery bag and a clothespin or clip. Pick up the bird and put it in the bag, then fold over and clip the top closed. Bring it inside, putting it near where you're working. When you hear strong flutter/scrabbles, take the bag outside and release the bird.

Much as we'd love to tell you that's the easy fix, know that not all such window-struck birds recover. Some may need veterinary care, and many simply won't make it, even if they fly off seemingly fine. But the paper bag solution is better for the bird than being grabbed by a hawk, cat, or chipmunk while it's lying stunned.

The ultimate solution is to permanently treat your windows to prevent birds from colliding with them. A stunningly effective, cheap yet unobtrusive hack is using a white, oil-based Sharpie paint marker to draw vertical lines on the outside of the glass, no more than 4 inches apart down the length of the windowpane. Julie used a yardstick to keep the lines straight. She's got ABC Bird-safe tape on the high clerestories (windows just below the roof line), and three large expanses of fine crop netting stretched over PVC frames, protecting birds from hitting the bigger picture windows of her house. It's like a showplace for window treatments! A wealth of effective solutions is at the American Bird Conservancy website at `https://abcbirds.org/`.

There's a Nest on My Front Porch. Can I Move It?

No, you can't move a bird's nest and expect the bird to come to a location you selected. In most cases, moving a nest will cause the parents to abandon it. Though it's counter-intuitive, a bird nesting right above your door on a porch light, or even in a wreath on the door itself, knows what it's doing! Birds come into our living spaces to avoid predators, trying to get as close as they can to us big scary humans, and betting that a raccoon, snake, or crow won't want to follow. In most cases, you won't have to alter your behavior much to accommodate the nesting birds, since they knew what they were getting into when they chose this location.

If the nest is in a hanging basket, don't stop watering the plants! Just slow-water a bit more frequently and avoid getting water directly in the nest. The birds need the cover and shade afforded by the plants. Keep them alive!

Most birds will sit tight through your comings and goings (more so as the season progresses) and they get used to your activity. One caveat: If the nest is in a wreath on your door, you may need to use the back door at night. Frightening a bird off the nest in the dark is bad, and it can result in chilling and death of eggs and young. House finches are notorious both for nesting in door wreaths and being flighty, too — a bad combination.

When you see bright, alert eyes and feathers covering the young birds, fledging is near. Be extra quiet and careful, avoiding loud noises or sudden movements, to avoid frightening them off the nest before they're ready. Needless to say, stop peeking!

I Found a Baby Bird! What Should I Do?

The first thing to do if you find a baby bird on the ground is to take any dogs and (heaven forbid) cats indoors and leave it where it is. If it is feathered and mobile, chances are a parent is taking care of it. Watch from a distance, preferably from inside the house, to see if the parents are in attendance. Even if you don't see an adult bird nearby, chances are that the parents are near and the nestling will be fine. Most baby birds leave the nest before they're able to fly very well, so the occasional landing on the ground is perfectly normal. If the bird isn't covered with feathers, is not mobile, and you're certain it has fallen from the nest, but you cannot locate the nest or can't return the bird to it, remember, it is illegal to possess native wild birds. You'll need to call a licensed wild bird rehabilitator for help. To find one, type the nearest city, state, and "wildlife rehabilitator" into your favorite search engine, such as Google.

TIP

You'll sometimes see rehabilitators advise not to feed baby birds anything. But if you're more than an hour's drive from help, and/or no one answers your call, which is common during peak "baby season" of May through August, scrambled egg or soft, soaked kitten chow are good emergency foods for baby birds. Live mealworms are great, too. NEVER feed preserved meats, dried fruit, bread, or milk to a baby bird. If the bird is opening its mouth, begging, push chunks of food well down into the gape to stimulate swallowing. Tweezers help. If the bird won't open its mouth, very gently use your thumbnail to pry the corner of the bill open, and hold it open with thumb and forefinger while inserting some food. Don't worry about overfeeding it; underfeeding is far more common.

Baby birds need to be fed every half-hour dawn to dusk, during all daylight hours, so keep it fed, warm, and swaddled in clean tissues in a small cup or box and try to get it to an expert rehabilitator as soon as possible. Should you make contact with a rehabilitator, send a sharp, well-lit cellphone photo of the bird to aid in its identification, and be sure to specify your exact location and the circumstances under which you found it. Wildlife rehabilitators have more than they can do to care for all their charges, so don't expect them to pick it up for you. You'll have to deliver it. And donations to support its weeks of care are always appreciated.

There's a Completely Bald Cardinal at My Feeder. What's Wrong with It?

For many years, it was opined, without evidence, that feather mites caused baldness, and the reason the bird's head is bald is because it can't preen the mites out of its head feathers. However, skin scrapings of bald bird scalps have never turned up mites. It is now known that "catastrophic head molt" is a normal part of the molting process for some individual birds. It is most frequently seen in cardinals and blue jays, usually in late summer when the birds are molting anyway. The feathers eventually grow back, but until then they look pretty vulturine!

There's a Sick Bird under My Feeder. What Should I Do?

If you see a bird all puffed up and sleeping on the ground or on your feeder, you can assume it's ill. Feeders, unfortunately, can become hotspots for diseases such as salmonellosis, botulism, house finch disease (*Mycoplasma*), avian pox, and others. And though good feeder hygiene is vital, it can't prevent disease transmission. It's best to discontinue feeding and allow the birds to disperse, rather than continue attracting them to concentrate. Keep the feeders down for a few weeks. Always wash your hands after filling or cleaning feeders, and take off your shoes at the door after servicing feeders. If you can capture the bird, you'll need to call a licensed wild bird rehabilitator for help. To find one, type the nearest city, state, and "wildlife rehabilitator" into your favorite search engine, such as Google.

Where Have All My Hummingbirds/ Goldfinches Gone?

Each spring, we take calls and messages from people wondering where all "their" hummingbirds have gone. Hummingbirds respond to bloom flushes in their favorite flowers, and they forsake feeders when, for example, Japanese honeysuckle is in bloom in the eastern U.S. Generally, you won't see a buildup of birds at your feeders until the honeysuckle or other local wildflowers have done their thing. By July and August, with new fledglings and dispersing migrants adding to the population, more hummingbirds will appear.

Likewise, goldfinches are nomadic and have their ebbs and flows at feeders. When weed and tree seeds are peaking, goldfinches don't need feeders. Julie stops feeding birds in early May, and the goldfinches in her yard raise their young mostly on zinnia, coreopsis, coneflower, native sunflower, and birch seeds, as they should!

If I Stop Feeding My Birds, Will They Starve?

Birds survived for millions of years before bird feeding became popular in the 1960s, and they will certainly survive without subsidy. Will they do better in hard, snowy winters when fed? Yes. But if you go on vacation, they will resort to natural food sources or seek out other feeders. Julie takes her feeders down as soon as the weather warms reliably in May and doesn't start feeding birds again until it gets cold, around Halloween in Ohio.

Take your hummingbird feeders down when the last birds have left (generally about the third week of September in Ohio, but your results will vary). Leaving a feeder up won't keep them from migrating; they are answering the strong call of instinct and will leave when they need to.

There's a Hawk at My Feeders! What Do I Do?

Watch it! Feeder birds outnumber most hawk species at least 200 to one. How many of us get the chance to observe any hawk at close range? The bird-eating specialists include Cooper's and sharp-shinned hawks — those long-tailed, slender streaks of mayhem that occasionally bomb through the yard in pursuit of a panicked bird. The sharp-shinned hawk, once a common winter visitor, has declined greatly in recent decades. Treasure your backyard predator; it's a gorgeous natural force, keeping the flock healthy by picking off the slower ones. You might become a raptor fanatic. We all have our specialties!

Index

bayberry shrub, 166
beaches, species found on, 272
bear-proof birding stations, 128
bee balm, 160, 167
behavior, 67–86
  bathing/preening, 72–74
  courtship, 75–77
  foraging, 70–71
  identifying birds by, 43–44, 85–86
  intelligence, assessing, 68–70
  nest building, 78–80
  reasons for, 68
  singing and sound-making, 71–72
  territoriality, 80–81
  watching, tips for, 81–85
belly
  in bird identification, 28
  field marks, 39
belted kingfishers, 79
berries
  Allegheny serviceberry, 162
  blackberries, 157
  common winterberry, 162
  red mulberry trees, 163
Big Days, 300–303
  Big Sit, 302–303
  organizing own, 301–302
  purpose of, 301
bill, 38–39
  in bird identification, 28
  deformities of, 358
binding, field guide, 198
binoculars, 171–187
  to avoid, 181
  carrying, 186
  choosing, 175–181
  cleaning and caring for, 187
  comfort of, 179
  comparing, 173–175
  cost of, 177–178
  diopter, 21–22
  eye space, 20–21
  eyecups, 21
  focusing, 22–24, 183–185
  lifting and holding, 182
  obtaining, 18–19

porro-prism, 173–174
power and size of, 178–179
reverse porro, 175
role in bird watching, 11
roof-prism, 174–175
teaching children to use, 328
using, 181–183
Bird Academy courses, 303
bird banding, 236, 321–322
bird baths. *See* bathing
bird calls, categorizing, 91
bird feeders. *See* feeders; feeding
Bird Friendly coffee, 365–366
bird watcher, defined, 14
Bird Watcher's Digest (*BWD*), 14, 84, 137–138, 284
bird watching
  becoming good at, 16
  birding vs., 14–15
  history of, 11
  location for, 16
  popularity of, 13
  reasons for, 14
birdathons, 314
birdbath list, 213
BirdCast, 244, 261
birder, defined, 14
birdhouses, 113
birding clubs. *See* clubs
birding groups on social media, 251
birding hotspots. *See* hotspots
birding vs. bird watching, 14–15
birds. *See also* bird watching; identifying birds
  defining characteristics of, 9–10, 53–54
  history of, 8–10
  parts of, 28–31
  taxonomy, 49–65
  terminology, 10–11
bitterns, 57
bittersweet vine, 167
black bears, 128
blackberries, 157
blackberry shrub, 166
blackbirds, 59, 135
Blackburnian warbler, 98–99
black-capped chickadees, 61
black-eyed Susan, 167

F

official common names of birds, 59

olive-sided flycatcher, 96

online courses, 303

open water, species found in, 267

open-cup nesters, 78

optics, defined, 172. *See also* binoculars

orders, by number, 63

organizing photos, 348–349

orioles, 59, 62, 135, 148–149

ornithologists, 15, 192. *See also* taxonomy

ornithology, 307. *See also* projects

oscines, 64

ovenbirds, 79, 80

owling, 311, 312

owls, 55, 96, 266, 312

P

Pacific coast, pelagic trips on, 263

Pacific Flyway, 243

Pacific region, as flightpath, 243

packs, eBird, 216

palm warbler, 85

paper, taking on field trips, 249

paper field guides, 25, 50, 189, 198

parakeet, monk, 379

Paridae family, 58

parks, projects at, 322

partial migration, 231

parts of birds, 28–31

Parulidae family, 59, 60

Passeriformes. *See* perching birds (Passeriformes)

passerines, taxonomy of, 64–65

passive anting, 74

Patagonia Picnic Table Effect, 286

patterns, in bird song, 97

peanuts, 138, 139

pelagic species, 273

pelicans, 71

pendulum display, hummingbirds, 75

pens/pencils, taking on field trips, 249

perches

    enhancing bird feeders with, 121–122

    looking for in grasslands and prairies, 271

    putting next to bird bath, 109

    song, 90

perching birds (Passeriformes)

    families within, 56, 58–59, 64–65

    in field guides, 12

    general discussion, 55

peregrine falcon, 84

pest species, 323

pesticides, 115–116, 366

Peterson, Roger Tory, 11

pheasants, 135

photography, 329–350

    backgrounds, 343–345

    cameras, 331–333

    composition, 341–345

    cropping, 343

    editing, 346–349

    ethical, 349–350

    in field guides, 197–198

    gear for, 331–334

    lens, 333–334

    lighting, 340–341

    organizing and storing, 348–349

    purposes of, 330–331

    rules as guidelines, 342

    tripods, 334

pigeons, 55, 135

pishing, 253

plants, 152–155. *See also* flowers

    bird-friendly, 114–115

    flowers, 167

    hanging gardens, 161

    for hummingbirds, 160–161

    inventory of, 156–157

    native, 154–156, 366

    quantity of, 153–154

    shrubbery, 162, 166–167

    trees, 163–166

    vines, 161

plastic, 367

platform nesters, 78

plumage. *See* feathers

pocket knives, 250

pockets, 249

point-and-shoot/compact camera, 332

poison ivy, 157

poison-free yard, 115–116

X

Y

Z

About the Authors

Jessica Vaughan is the editor of *BWD* magazine, her career having come full circle from when she was a college intern at *Bird Watcher's Digest*. It was during this time that her spark bird, a pileated woodpecker, sent her running for a field guide for the first time. She didn't become a serious bird watcher until she was in her thirties, a new mother who realized birding was something she could do anytime, anywhere, even with small children in tow. She lives in Columbus, Ohio, with her flock of four children, who keep her quite busy when she is not reading, thinking, or writing about birds or traveling the world adding to her life list.

A college course in lab ornithology hooked **Dawn Hewitt** on birds — not the class itself, but the field trips she took with the local bird club for extra credit. Her spark bird was the common grackle, a flock of which she noticed in her neighborhood while she was taking that class and just beginning to understand the excitement birds could bring. The first species on her life list, spotted in 1979, was a red-bellied woodpecker. That list is now above 1,300. She was the editor of *Bird Watcher's Digest* and is now the managing editor for *BWD* magazine. She lives in Marietta, Ohio.

Julie Zickefoose has been hooked on birds since finding a bathing blue-winged warbler at age eight. She is a natural history author and artist who illustrated this book and wrote part of it as well. Her books include *Natural Gardening for Birds* (Rodale, 2001/Skyhorse 2016), *The Bluebird Effect: Uncommon Bonds with Common Birds* (2012), *Baby Birds: An Artist Looks into the Nest* (2016), and *Saving Jemima: Life and Love with a Hard-luck Jay* (2019, all from Houghton Mifflin Harcourt). Julie contributed to *Bird Watcher's Digest* from 1986 until its close in 2021 and is now advising editor and contributor to *BWD* magazine. She lives with a good dog on her 80-acre private sanctuary in the Appalachian foothills of Ohio, which she manages for wildlife. Her yard list stands at 198 bird species.

Authors' Acknowledgments

The three authors would like to acknowledge invaluable help from several quarters as they worked to update and rewrite this book. *BWD* magazine's photo editor Bruce Wunderlich wrote the chapter on bird photography (practically a book in itself) and provided the cover photo and most of the gorgeous photos in the color section. Ryan Tomazin lovingly scanned Julie's original art with lightning speed and great care. Lisa White provided expert technical editing. Rob Ripma lent his expertise in ecotourism, group travel, and birding festivals. Scott Weidensaul, a beloved *BWD* magazine contributor from the very start, graciously wrote our Foreword. We thank our agent, Russell Galen, for his advocacy and advice. Thanks to Wiley editors Jennifer Yee and Paul Levesque for the chance to make a great old book brand new and relevant. Most of all, we thank Michael Sacopulos and

Rich Luhr, without whose miraculous support *BWD* would have ceased to exist. We are all grateful for the chance to present the Beauty, Wonder, and Delight of birds to anyone who will stop long enough to watch them.

Dedication

Twenty-eight years. That's how long it's been since Bill Thompson III, editor and publisher of *Bird Watcher's Digest*, finished writing *Bird Watching For Dummies.* He and his wife, Julie Zickefoose, had just welcomed their daughter, Phoebe, into the world. As this revised and extensively updated edition sees publication, Phoebe is married, living and working on her own. Bill passed away in 2019. *Bird Watcher's Digest* ceased publication in 2021, and *BWD* magazine sprang from its ashes in 2022.

The changes in all our lives have been profound, and the world of bird watching has seen profound change as well. In 1997, rare bird alerts were transmitted by (landline) telephone trees. Online birding resources consisted of America Online chat rooms. Social media didn't yet exist; there were no birding apps, no digital field guides, and smartphones and digital cameras wouldn't become popular for another few years.

In the 1997 edition, Bill's prescience, legendary among his friends and co-workers, was in full play. In Chapter 22, he predicted the coming change:

> *Computers and satellites now have as much business being part of bird watching as bird feeders and binoculars. And I have a feeling that we are just at the start of birding's technological revolution. Just think about when all the little kids who have been using computers from age two start becoming avid bird watchers. Look out!*

It's clear that he inherited this prescience, as he quotes his father, Bill Thompson Jr., who, with Bill's mother, Elsa, founded *Bird Watcher's Digest:*

> *My dad used to say he wanted to develop a magic, gun-like device you could point at a distant bird. The device would have sensors to analyze the bird's size, shape, color, and song. After obtaining this info, the device's internal computer would tell you what species the bird was. I tried to explain to Dad that this would take all the fun out of watching birds. He said, "But we'd be millionaires!"*

"Smart" binoculars that can identify the birds you spot now exist, as do bird photo and song identification apps. Far from taking all the fun out of birding, they've served to welcome more people to the fold, and for that we are grateful.

The authors of this revised edition wish to dedicate it to Bill Thompson III, for his energy, vision, enthusiasm, and lifelong work to bring the joy of bird watching to more people. As he always used to say, "See more birds, have more fun!"

Publisher's Acknowledgments

Acquisitions Editor: Jennifer Yee

Senior Project Editor: Paul Levesque

Copy Editor: Jennifer Connolly

Tech Reviewer: Lisa White

Senior Managing Editor: Kristie Pyles

Cover Image: Hooded Warbler, Courtesy of Bruce Wunderlich

Scissor-tailed
Flycatcher
by Jim Burns

Look at birds in a new light

BWD brings you birds in a way you've never seen before. Beautiful photography and fascinating articles by renowned experts will deepen your knowledge, expand your appreciation, and inspire you to look up.

Readers of *Bird Watching for Dummies* can receive a special offer: Start a new subscription (6 issues per year) for just $19. That's a discount of $7 from the regular subscription rate. Use discount code **DMX2025** when subscribing online. Offer expires December 31, 2025.

Subscribe today to North America's premier bird-watching magazine at **bwdmagazine.com** or by calling **(812) 645-4646.**

BIRD WATCHER'S DIGEST

bwd

www. bwdmagazine.com